D0540773

The Cause of Humanity
and Other Stories

Rudyard Kipling's (1865-1936) work is known and loved the world over by children and adults alike, it has been translated into many languages, and onto the cinema screen. This volume brings together for the first time some 86 uncollected short fictions. Almost all of them will be unfamiliar to readers; some are unrecorded in any bibliography; some are here published for the first time. Most of them come from Kipling's Indian years and show him experimenting with a great variety of forms and tones. We see the young Kipling enjoying the exercise of his craft; yet the voice that emerges throughout is always unmistakably his own, changing the scene every time the curtain is raised.

Thomas Pinney is professor of English, emeritus, at Pomona College, Claremont, California. He has edited for the Cambridge University Press Kipling's Something of Myself and the Cambridge Edition of the Poems of Rudyard Kipling as well as the Letters of Thomas Babington Macaulay. His History of Wine in America, 2 volumes, appeared in 1989 and 2005.

RUDYARD KIPLING

THE CAUSE OF HUMANITY
AND OTHER STORIES

Uncollected Prose Fictions

EDITED BY
THOMAS PINNEY

CAMBRIDGE
UNIVERSITY PRESS

University Printing House, Cambridge CB2 8BS, United Kingdom

One Liberty Plaza, 20th Floor, New York, NY 10006, USA

477 Williamstown Road, Port Melbourne, VIC 3207, Australia

314–321, 3rd Floor, Plot 3, Splendor Forum, Jasola District Centre, New Delhi – 110025, India

79 Anson Road, #06–04/06, Singapore 079906

Cambridge University Press is part of the University of Cambridge.

It furthers the University's mission by disseminating knowledge in the pursuit of education, learning, and research at the highest international levels of excellence.

www.cambridge.org
Information on this title: www.cambridge.org/9781108476423
DOI: 10.1017/9781108568296

First published 2019

Printed in the United Kingdom by TJ International Ltd. Padstow Cornwall

A catalogue record for this publication is available from the British Library.

ISBN 978-1-108-47642-3 Hardback

Contents

꙰

CONTENTS

CONTENTS

Editorial Practice

The note at the head of each story gives the date and place of publication, if any, the evidence for attributing the story to Kipling, the source of the text presented, and any notes that seem useful, including the record of reprinting, if any.

In the stories themselves I have aimed to use a light hand in annotating. I try to identify the following things: explicit quotations; individuals whose identity I assume is not common knowledge; allusions to unfamiliar events and things, especially in the stories about Indian affairs. More than that I have not attempted.

A glossary of Indian words appears at the end of the book.

Abbreviations

The following abbreviations and titles are used in the headnotes, footnotes and endnotes.

Chandler	Lloyd H. Chandler, *A Summary of the Work of Rudyard Kipling* (New York: Grolier Club, 1930)
CK Diary	Excerpts and summaries made by C. E. Carrington from the diaries kept by Mrs Kipling, 1892–1936; the diaries themselves are understood to have been destroyed. Copy, Special Collections, University of Sussex Library (see also Rees Extracts below)
CMG	*Civil and Military Gazette*
Diary, 1885	Rudyard Kipling's diary, 1885, Harvard University. Printed in Thomas Pinney, *Something of Myself and Other Autobiographical Writings* (Cambridge University Press, 1990)
Harbord	Reginald Harbord, ed., *The Readers' Guide to Rudyard Kipling's Work*, 8 vols. (Canterbury and Bournemouth, 1961–71; privately printed edition of 100)
Hobson-Jobson	Henry Yule and A. C. Burnell, *Hobson-Jobson: The Anglo-Indian Dictionary* (1886; reprinted Ware, 1996)
JLK	John Lockwood Kipling, Rudyard Kipling's father
Kipling Papers	Personal papers of Rudyard Kipling, now the property of the National Trust and held on deposit in the Special Collections archive, University of Sussex
Kipling's India	*Kipling's India: Uncollected Sketches, 1884–88* (Basingstoke: Macmillan, 1986)
Letters	*The Letters of Rudyard Kipling*, ed. Thomas Pinney, 6 vols. (Basingstoke: Macmillan, 1990–2004)

Livingston	Flora V. Livingston, *Bibliography of the Works of Rudyard Kipling* (New York: Edgar H. Wells & Company, 1927; with a *Supplement*, 1938)
Martindell–Ballard pamphlets	Unauthorised reprints in pamphlet form of uncollected items attributed to Kipling, privately printed by the collectors E. W. Martindell and Ellis Ames Ballard between 1923 and 1937, without place and date of publication
Poems	*The Cambridge Edition of the Poems of Rudyard Kipling*, ed. Thomas Pinney, 3 vols. (Cambridge University Press, 2013)
Rees extracts	Excerpts from and summaries of passages in Caroline Kipling's diaries, 1892–1936, made by Douglas Rees for Lord Birkenhead when the latter was at work on his life of Kipling. Copy, Special Collections, University of Sussex
Richards, *Bibliography*	David Alan Richards, *Rudyard Kipling: A Bibliography* (New Castle, DE, and London: Oak Knoll Press and the British Library, 2010)
RK	Rudyard Kipling
Rosenbaum, *Index*	Barbara Rosenbaum, *Index of English Literary Manuscripts*, volume IV, *1800–1900* (London and New York: Mansell, 1990)
Scrapbooks	Scrapbooks of cuttings of his work kept by Kipling, now in the Kipling Papers
Something of Myself	Rudyard Kipling, *Something of Myself, for My Friends Known and Unknown* (Kipling's unfinished memoir) (London: Macmillan, 1937)
Something of Myself, 1990	RK's memoir, edited by Thomas Pinney (Cambridge University Press, 1990) as *Something of Myself and Other Autobiographical Writings*
Stewart–Yeats, *Kipling*	James McG. Stewart and A. W. Yeats, *Rudyard Kipling: A Bibliographical Catalogue* (Toronto: Dalhousie University Press and University of Toronto Press, 1959)
Watt, UNC	A. P. Watt Papers, Wilson Library, University of North Carolina

Introduction

This edition gathers together for the first time some eighty-six uncollected[1] prose fictions by Rudyard Kipling, including four unpublished items, two of them only fragments; sixteen unreprinted items; twelve of them previously unrecorded in the bibliographies, and three items doubtfully attributed. The remaining items have all been reprinted at one time or another, some in accessible form, but even more in publications so obscure or inaccessible that they hardly provide publication: the *United Services College Chronicle*, for example, or *The Victorian* – the journal of Victoria College, St Helier, Jersey – or Reginald Harbord's *Readers' Guide to the Work of Rudyard Kipling* (8 volumes, privately printed in an edition of 100 copies, 1961–72). The stories are now all made available in accessible form.

By far the greater number of items – fifty-one out of the total of eighty-six – appeared in the *Civil and Military Gazette* of Lahore, the paper with which Kipling was most closely associated in his Indian years. Another seventeen were published in the *Pioneer*, the paper that Kipling joined in late 1887. Since most of the stories have an Indian origin, a brief account of Kipling's career as a journalist in India may be useful to the reader.

Kipling was not yet 17 years old when, on leaving school, he went to Lahore, the capital of the Punjab, to join the staff of the *Civil and Military Gazette*. The title of the paper refers to the two official communities of British India: one was either in the Army or in the Civil Service. A journalist was not part of the system, and that fact gave the young Kipling a special freedom of movement and understanding that certainly helped his creative work. The *CMG*, as it may be called, was issued from a large printing establishment that held government contracts and also did extensive job printing. But the entire editorial staff of the paper consisted only of Stephen Wheeler, the editor, and of the

---

[1] By 'uncollected' is meant a story that Kipling himself, for various reasons, never reprinted in any one of his authorised volumes. It does not mean 'unknown' or 'unreprinted' although there are a number of stories in this collection that are unknown (unrecorded in any bibliography) and unreprinted, as well as uncollected.

teenage Rudyard Kipling, the assistant editor. When one of them was ill or absent, then the other did all the editorial work, often, of course, in blazing hot weather, and always with a staff of compositors and proof-readers, most of whom knew no English.

The offices of the *CMG*, the one daily newspaper in the Punjab, saw a stream of visitors of all kinds; they provided Kipling with a striking education in the diversity of God's creatures. As he wrote in 'The Man Who Would Be King', 'a newspaper office seems to attract every conceivable sort of person', and the long list of examples following that statement no doubt reflected Kipling's own experience. The journals that it was his duty to scan for stories were also of 'every conceivable sort':

> Some thirty papers go through my hands daily – Hindu papers, scurrilous and abusive beyond everything, local scandal weeklies, philosophical and literary journals written by Babus in the style of Addison. Native Mahommedan, sleepy little publications, all extracts, Indigo papers, tea and coffee journals and official Gazettes all have to be disemboweled if they are worth it.[2]

In Lahore, where his father was head of the local school of art and curator of the museum, Kipling lived with his parents; they were joined late in 1883 by his sister Alice, always called 'Trix', and the four of them formed a family square, as they called it, of bright individuals – all of them writers – devoted to books and to lively discussion of things in general. The arrangement lasted from Kipling's arrival in Lahore at the end of 1882 until his departure for Allahabad at the end of 1887.

Kipling was at first confined to routine labours on the *CMG* but gradually began to be trusted for more various work – a weekly column of local news, reports of official events in cities around the Punjab, and, sparingly at first but growing more frequent, special reports, poems, and stories. As the capital of the Punjab, Lahore society was thick with official dignitaries, starting with the lieutenant governor and his council. The lesser administrators and officials Kipling knew both through his work and through his membership of the Punjab Club, where, he wrote, 'I met none except picked men at their definite work – Civilians, Army, Education, Canals, Forestry, Engineering, Irrigation, Railways,

---

[2] To the Reverend George Willes, 17–[18] November 1882 (*Letters*, 1, 24–5).

Doctors and Lawyers – samples of each branch and each talking his own shop.'³ The Army was also represented by the garrison at Fort Lahore and by the cantonment at Mian Mir, a few miles outside the city. These civil and military folk provided much of the substance of Kipling's daily reporting, and he got to know them as well, intimately enough to supply the stuff of his poems and stories of the English in India.

Then there was Simla. The supreme government, at that time resident in Calcutta, had adopted the practice of abandoning the city in the hot weather – effectively half the year – for the village of Simla, 7,000 feet up in the foothills of the Himalayas. Kipling was not allowed such generous time in Simla as the civil and military people enjoyed, but he was given a month or more there – the ' hills' of *Plain Tales from the Hills* – every year from 1883 to 1888, except for one leave spent at Dalhousie in 1884 – five visits in all. He already knew the Punjab set from his life in Lahore: now the superior people of the Calcutta establishment, including the viceroy himself, and others of high political or military rank, were added to that knowledge: Lord Roberts, Sir Auckland Colvin, Sir William Hunter, Sir James Lyall, Sir David Wallace, and many others great and small.

> Simla was another new world. There the Hierarchy lived, and one saw and heard the machinery of administration stripped bare. There were the heads of the Viceregal and Military staffs and their Aides-de-Camp, and playing whist with Great Ones, who gave him special news, was the Correspondent of our big Sister Paper the *Pioneer*, then a power in the land.⁴

Simla is the setting for several stories in this collection (e.g., 'The Hill of Illusion', 'An Unequal Match') or it appears as a foil to other places (e.g., 'From Olympus to Hades'). Many of the high officials visible to Kipling at Simla figure in the stories, very thinly disguised if at all. Their policies, their conflicts, their foibles all were fare for Kipling's newspaper treatments, most of them satires directed by the politics of the paper.

³ *Something of Myself*, p. 43.
⁴ *Something of Myself*, p. 57.

In his years at the *CMG*_Kipling found Stephen Wheeler difficult to work for. Wheeler mistrusted 'creative' work, preferring that Kipling keep 'to the sober paths of précis and abstract writing wherein his [Wheeler's] soul delights'.[5] Wheeler resigned in March 1887, to be replaced by E. K. Robinson, who already knew Kipling's stories and poems, greatly admired them, and freely admitted them to the paper. The tally of Kipling's publication of original work zooms under Robinson's editorship.

In November 1887, Kipling was summoned away from the *CMG* to the *Pioneer* of Allahabad, a paper under the same ownership as the *CMG* but regarded as more powerful and influential. The move, in recognition of Kipling's growing reputation among the readers of English papers in India, had been long in prospect. The managers of the *Pioneer* made Kipling in effect a special correspondent, regularly assigned to travel and report on whatever he might find to write about in India, old and new. He was, as well, made editor of a new publication, a supplement to the *Pioneer* called the *Week's News*. This, Kipling said, was 'but a re-hash of news and views'. It was also the medium for an unlimited quantity of the fiction in Kipling's head, and this material, Kipling wrote, was 'infinitely more important' than a rehash of the week's news.[6]

Kipling never, at any time in his career, lacked for ideas to write about, but he was now prolific to an astonishing degree: ''Twas ask and have, Choose for more's ready,' as he said of this period in the language of his favourite Fra Lippo Lippi.[7] By my count he published 144 stories, articles, and poems in 1888 in the *Week's News*, the *Pioneer*, and the *CMG*, to which he continued to contribute. That is a rate of almost three items a week, some of them substantial and all of them showing some originality. This was in addition to his regular miscellaneous, anonymous journalism (though he did less of this while at the *Pioneer*) and a long series of 'Letters from Simla'.

Because they are fiction, the stories about Indian occasions in this collection can hardly be said to exhibit Kipling's settled ideas about India. Certain things recur, however. Lord Dufferin, the viceroy from

---

[5] To Edith Macdonald, 4–5 December 1886 (*Letters*, 1, 141).
[6] *Something of Myself*, p. 71.
[7] *Something of Myself*, p. 71.

1884 to 1888, and personally known to Kipling and his family, was a
favourite character in the stories here collected, appearing in at least ten
of them, in which he is lovingly satirised for his elaborate courtesy and
florid speech. Another repeated interest is in the language and style of
the educated *babu*. In a politically correct age, Kipling's comic versions
of this style will be disapproved, to put it mildly. So it is worth noting
that the real object of his treatment is not the *babu* himself (though
he is the immediate object) but the authorities who have grafted an
alien system of education on to an utterly unrelated tradition with pre-
dictably incongruous results. The figure of The East in 'The Burden of
Nineveh', dressed in foolish western externals to which she is quietly
superior, enforces the idea even more strongly. As the Englishman says
of 'Chuckerbutti' at the end of 'A Free Gift', 'What a product!' But the
defects of the product are the fault of its designers.[8]

A more pressing subject is the organised political movement behind the
then recent creation of the Indian National Congress (see 'In Wonderland').
It was too new for its critics to be sure of themselves, but it challenged
most of the ideas that Kipling had formed about India. Those ideas were,
in a word, conservative, and in no way differed from the received opinions among the generality of the British in India. Kipling and his father
were at one in this matter. The British, they believed, brought peace and
justice and prosperity to India; the Indians themselves were not yet ready
to maintain these things, and so the official *raison d'être* of the British
presence remained unaltered. Increased self-government – leading finally
to independence – could only have destructive results. Such beliefs are not
explicitly argued in these uncollected stories, but their latent presence may
be frequently detected. At the same time, the more imaginative side of
Kipling clearly understood that the British rule in India was an anomaly
and could not endure (e.g., 'The Burden of Nineveh').

Other topics inevitably associated with stories of India are frequent
among these stories: the hot weather and the boredom of the plains
('From Olympus to Hades'); fever ('De Profundis'); the behaviour
of native servants ('The Tragedy of Crusoe'). But what must strike a

---

[8] RK explicitly recognised this: 'Babu English,' he wrote, was the product of 'a ludicrously
inappropriate education'; Young India may write 'ill-assorted prose', but 'the fault lies
with his teachers, and not with him' (untitled item, *CMG*, 29 January 1886).

reader going through the sequence is the unpredictable variety of subject and form: every time the curtain goes up the scene is different. It is as though the apprentice Kipling were testing his skill by trying every possible form and mode – narrative, anecdotal, farcical, tragic, historical, fantastic, confessional, parodic, dramatic. Some were dead ends, others full of possibility. What may especially surprise a reader is the prominence of the fantastic and the absurd: the Frenchified monologues of 'The History of a Crime' and its fellow pieces, for example, or the grotesque melodrama of 'An Official Secret', or the wild nonsense of 'Susannah and the Elder', a model, as well, of Kipling's highly developed skill in parodic imitation. Lewis Carroll's nonsense inventions are a strong influence in a number of the stories.

Only two of the stories in this collection are identified as juvenilia (a third, 'Ibbetson Dun', is placed among the incomplete stories). 'The Tragedy of Crusoe', the first item in this collection, was written when Kipling was only 18, but it is a perfectly assured performance, just the sort of literary mimicry that he loved to practice for the rest of his writing life.

After Kipling's return to England at the end of 1889 the number of uncollected stories drops dramatically: only twelve of the eighty-six, including some unpublished manuscript fragments, come from the post-Indian years. The occasions of the later stories are various, and only one of them ('The Cause of Humanity') appears to have been seriously intended for publication.

Why did Kipling leave all of these stories uncollected? Many reasons can be guessed at. Perhaps most of the stories about Indian affairs – the decline of the rupee, the maintenance of the railways, the arguments about financial policies, and so on – are highly topical and remote from the general understanding and interest. Others, such as 'The Inauthorated Corpses', derive from situations long since settled and forgotten, or they may reflect anxieties that Kipling felt only briefly ('The Comet of a Season'). Some of the stories are, it must be admitted, very slight and unimpressive, and so were not, in the writer's judgement, good enough to preserve. But they can be interesting to us, who see them in the light of later achievement.

Kipling's uncollected work has long attracted interest, an interest that has led to many hopeful attributions, many of them, in the absence of any evidence, wrong. The result has been much confusion and uncertainty until rather recently, when new and reliable information has become available.

To take the confusion and uncertainty first. The problem arises from the fact that much of Kipling's early work, including what he wrote in seven years of journalism in India, is either anonymous or pseudonymous. During his lifetime Kipling himself could have helped the searchers, but this he steadfastly refused to do, holding, as he did, that it lay with the author to choose what he would acknowledge and what should remain unknown. He knew perfectly well that the work of other people was being ascribed to him, but he grimly accepted that annoyance as a condition of giving no help at all. As he wrote, 'I do not think it part of my work to correct or limit the fancies of bibliographers.'[9]

Since the author would not help, the collectors and bibliographers were forced to rely on a number of imperfect aids of various origin: the Crofts Collection (from a list supplied by the young Kipling), the Garth Album, the Denham Letter. Some of the pseudonyms that Kipling used were known, others were guessed at. And if an item exhibited anything Kiplingesque in subject or style, that might be added to the list of attributions.

Kipling himself provided, indirectly, a considerable list of previously unknown work at a time when he was still young and had not yet determined to reveal nothing of his early work. His sister-in-law, Josephine Balestier (afterwards Mrs Theodore Dunham), who had literary ambitions, undertook to compile a *Kipling Birthday Book* in the early 1890s. This was a then popular form, consisting of quotations from an author's work for every day in the year on pages provided with space for notes and comments on each day, including a record of birthdays. To help supply her with material, Kipling had evidently shown her much of his early work, some of which he never otherwise acknowledged.[10] So far as is known, this is the only time that he did such a thing.

[9] To A. S. Watt, 25 June 1928 (*Letters*, v, 439). I have a list of more than 300 items attributed to Kipling wrongly or without evidence. It is certainly not complete.

[10] A full list of the new attributions in the *Birthday Book* is in Richards, *Bibliography*, pp. 95–6.

Most of the guesses about Kipling's authorship, right and wrong, have been preserved in such lists as that in Rear Admiral Lloyd H. Chandler's *Summary of the Works of Rudyard Kipling* (New York, 1930) or by being reprinted in the long series of limited edition pamphlets privately printed by E. W. Martindell and Ellis Ames Ballard between 1923 and 1937, or by reprinting in R. H. Harbord's privately printed *Reader's Guide to Rudyard Kipling's Work* (8 volumes, 1961–72). Each of these sources is unreliable, mixing as it does authentic with inauthentic attributions. The comprehensive bibliographies, those of Florence Livingston, J. M. Stewart and A. W. Yeats, and, most recently, David Alan Richards, are far more cautious about guessed-at attributions and deliberately err rather on the side of incompleteness. The Richards bibliography, by far the fullest record of Kipling's work, scrupulously avoids conjectural attributions.

In 1976, on the death of Mrs George Bambridge, Kipling's daughter Elsie, the collection of family papers and books in her possession passed to the National Trust and was deposited in the Department of Special Collections in the library at the University of Sussex. This collection, or archive, includes a number of items that have allowed the identification of Kipling's uncollected writings with a confidence not previously possible. They may be briefly enumerated:

1. Three verse notebooks containing ninety-two holograph poems, many uncollected.
2. Separate MS drafts and fair copies of about fifty-eight poems, some uncollected.
3. Eight scrapbooks kept by Kipling containing cuttings of his writings, mostly from newspapers. The first four volumes contain the work from Kipling's years as a journalist in India and are the main source for identifying his anonymous and pseudonymous work. They contain many hundreds of new attributions, from brief notes to long reports.
4. A copy of Rear Admiral Lloyd H. Chandler's *Summary of the Work of Rudyard Kipling* annotated by Kipling himself. Against many entries he has written such responses as 'not mine' or 'none of my work'. In a few cases he has denied authorship of items that are certainly his, but unless there is indisputable evidence for his authorship his denials in this list must be accepted.

5. A copy of an MS 'Index of 1st Lines of Kipling's Verse and Verses Quoted or Used by Him', by Admiral Chandler, including unsupported or mistaken attributions. This too has been annotated by Kipling.

Other sources of authentic information about uncollected work include a copy annotated by Kipling of Flora Livingston's *Bibliography*, now at Wimpole Hall in Cambridgeshire; a bound volume of the *United Services College Chronicle* with his contributions identified by Kipling, presented to Haileybury College by Mrs Kipling; the diary that Kipling kept in 1885, now at Harvard and reprinted in my edition of *Something of Myself*; and the six volumes of *The Letters of Rudyard Kipling*. The collection at Sussex has attracted other family papers containing authentic information, among them the Baldwin papers and the Macdonald papers. The record of Kipling's uncollected work is now on reasonably solid ground. No doubt it remains incomplete, but it no longer need be contaminated by mistaken attributions.

In this collection I have included three doubtfully attributed items: 'Verbatim et Literatim', 'The Minstrel', and 'A Parable'. They have been set apart in an appendix and their status clearly indicated.

The Tragedy of Crusoe, C.S.[1]
(From a Correspondent.)

Published: *Civil and Military Gazette*, 13 September 1884.

Attribution: The article called 'Music for the Middle-Aged', *CMG*, 21 June 1884, included in the Sussex Scrapbooks (28/1, p. 1), is signed 'Jacob Cavendish', as is 'The Tragedy of Crusoe'. RK later maintained that more than one writer used the same pseudonym on the *CMG*,[2] but since the only other Englishman on the editorial staff of the *CMG* was the editor, Stephen Wheeler, and since Wheeler is not known ever to have written anything in the way of fiction or verse, it seems safe to assume that a pseudonym known to have been used by RK was exclusively his, unless there is clear evidence to the contrary.

'Crusoe' is probably the item RK refers to in a letter of 17 September 1884 as a 'specimen' of 'a set of weekly articles' that he intends to begin in the *CMG* in order to liven up the paper (to Edith Macdonald: *Letters*, 1, 76).

Text: *Civil and Military Gazette.*

Notes: This is, so far as is known, the first piece of prose fiction that RK contributed to the *CMG*, which he had joined at the end of October or in early November, 1882. He had had opportunities to indulge his inventiveness in a few poems and in a handful of humorous articles (e.g., 'Music for the Middle-Aged' in June 1884), but the paper under Stephen Wheeler was not yet open to RK's 'creative' work. In September 1884, however, Wheeler had gone off to the Hills on vacation and the *CMG* was for the time entirely in RK's hands, which may explain the appearance of 'The Tragedy of Crusoe, C.S.' RK himself had been at Dalhousie, in the Hills, while Wheeler remained in Lahore. They had now switched places, and RK, like Crusoe, had just returned to 'the island'. RK also thought at this time that his transfer from the *CMG* to its bigger, sister paper, the *Pioneer* of Allahabad, was imminent, so that any move of his that might offend Wheeler would not matter: he would, he supposed, soon be out of Wheeler's reach.

Reprinted in *Kipling's India: Uncollected Sketches*, 1986.

Monday.—Reacht the Island – I would say the station – this morn,
Mrs. Crusoe being, at my own desire, left, it may be for a month or
twain in the cooler air of the hills. Now, since we were first wed (and I
shall not, even in my own diary, write down how long ago that was) I
have never been a day parted from Mrs. Crusoe; which I take it is not
altogether becoming to a man of my spirit. Howbeit, yesterday, when
I hinted, very gently, at this much to Mrs. Crusoe – for though she is
mine own dear wife, yet I dare not speak *all* of my mind to her – she
seemed in no way offended, but only laughed a good deal; saying that
"men's insides were made so comical, God help them",[3] and if I had *that*
fancy in my brain I had best go to the island and there live as I might
for two months, till she saw fit to join me. Though I was a little taken
aback, and, to tell the truth not over well pleased, at her ready agree-
ment in my plan, yet I made shift to look vastly content, and left the
mountains in so great a haste, that both sherry flask and sandwiches
were left behind. This, I hold, was the fault of my wife, who should have
given them both to me.

When I reacht the ship – I should say of course my house – I found
that it had leakt greatly fore and aft, through the late heavy rains, spoil-
ing my wife's new spinet, and, what is of far greater importance, many
of my newly bound volumes that had but lately come out from England.
I spent a dreary day soothing their swelled and blistered backs as well
as might be, and thus forgot my tiffin. At dusk I went forth to explore
the island, on mine old horse, whom I dare swear that the *sais* hath not
exercised any time these two months. By him (the horse, not the *sais*) I
was fought with for two miles, and runned away with for another two;
the beast only stopping for want of breath. I find the island, as far as I
can see, to be wholly uninhabited except by the natives. Nor am I altogether sorry for this, since I cut but an indifferent good figure, this even,
laid, for the most part, astride of my horse's head, and swearing, Lord
help me, in a manner that I hoped I had long ago forgotten. Home,
exceeding sore and disposed to be very wrath with all about me. I was
made none the sweeter when my man Friday told me that there was
no whisky in the house. Says I, "How then did Friday manage to get
so beastly drunk?" Friday takes me up short at this, and says he is not
more drunk than I, but he has been rejoicing at once more meeting his
old friend At this he sits down very quick, and says that I am his Father

2

and Mother and goes fast asleep. I cannot find it in my heart to be very angry with Friday, but rather envy one who can be so merry – though it is true he has no library to be ruined by roof leakage. For form's sake I have admonished him with a new leathern punkah rope, its end; and so grimly to dinner at the Club.

Here I fell in with Jones (Cadwallader – He that I quarrelled with last July, because of a horse he sold me) and we dined together alone. He is the only inhabitant of the island; Mrs. Jones, like Mrs. Crusoe, being in the cooler hills. I see that I was a fool ever to fall out with thus pleasant a fellow, and withal one that can talk so well. Moreover, I will at once write to Mrs. Crusoe and tell her that she must call on Mrs. Jones. We two then smoked each other's cheroots in great friendship till close upon midnight, when I returned home; and finding no lights in my house but all in Friday's, I did again fall to with a punkah rope for five good minutes. To bed shortly after, where I lay awake till Friday had howled himself asleep.

Tuesday.—A woful day. This morning came Friday to me, smiling for all the world as though no words had passed between us over-night – whereat I suspected mischief but said nothing. Presently, while I was taking stock of my sodden library, he says:– "*Kerritch hogya*" but I made shift to escape into the garden and there examine the roses. Yet no man can avoid his fate, or, for the matter of that, Friday, when he is bent on being heard. So, at breakfast, I, being in a white-hot heat to get away betimes to work, my man bows himself double and says several times very loud:– "*Kerritch hogya*". Then I thought how Mrs. Crusoe, she that is now at the Hills, would have dealt with him at once, and that with no inconvenience to myself. For, though I can speak Thibetan, Nagri, Malay, and the Lord knows how many other tongues, the barbarous and hybrid speech wherein the affairs of a household are wont to be ordered is a great stumbling-block to me. Friday, methinks knows this, for which I hate him the more. I clutch my hair (what is left of it that is) three several times, and prayed inwardly that Friday might not see the great depths of my ignorance. Then says I, with my finest air:– "*Kitna che?*" "*Sahib*," says he, "*Sarce che* worshter, *tael che, nia kunker estubble kiwasti, rye che, marubber che*"⁴ – and if I had not taken him up short there, I believe he would have continued till now. As soon as I had stoppt him he goes off again, like a crazy clock, telling me that Mrs.

3

Crusoe had dismist her dhobie ere she went hillward, and askt me to get another; that there were three kinds of meat, all good, in the bazar, and I was to chuse what I liked best – that I was to say what I would have to eat not only for this week, day by day, but the next and the next. Also he askt whether I should retain the old cook, whose face I had never seen, or whether I should be fed by contract; and a thousand other things that till now I had fancied came in the course of nature – as do *tiffin* and dinner. I have sent him away for a while to fill me a pipe while I try to make ready against his return. Oh that my wife were here!

11 of the clock.— Even though I know that none will read this foolish diary save I, yet I dare not, for very shame, write down all that I have done and suffered within the two hours past. How Friday saw that I, Civil and Sessions Judge and a ruler among men, was helpless as a little babe when there was any talk of *degchies*, storerooms, and the like; how I floundered from one blunder to another (for I hold that housekeeping is in no way man's work) trying all the while to keep up my sorely shrunken dignity; how Friday led me on, little by little, as men coax an unwilling dog into the sea, until he had gauged the sum total of my ignorance; how I sweated and turned hot and cold under his words, as I have often seen prisoners sweat and change colour under mine. All this, I say, I dare not set down. Let it suffice for my humiliation that, at the end of my torment, Friday had roughly, and after his own fashion (which I take it was not of the best), shewn how I was to manage my own house in the matter of jam, clean sheets, and two daily meals, and in the doing of it had so trampled on and crushed my spirit, that I could but sign all he wished (and the papers were not few) in hope of being released from his tyranny. But Lord! Lord! how many things be necessary to a man's sustenance whereof I have scarcely even heard the names till today – much less smelt and handled of them. Moreover, I see now what a strange and terrible car of Juggernaut it is that Mrs. Crusoe, my never enough to be valued spouse, controls. I, who have rashly taken its guidance into my hands, and laid spent and prostrate among the wheels whereon I have ridden so smoothly before. All day I have done nothing at all save wonder how Mrs. Crusoe can receive me with so smiling a face each evening, when she is on the island, if this be the kind of torture that falls to her lot. But it may be that she has some management to overcome it, for I have never, now I think, seen signs of

4

it in her face, and this day has gone far to age and sour me, who am still, thank Heaven, a young man for my years.

To the Club again in the evening where I met Cadwallader Jones, but for shame, lest he should laugh at me, durst not enquire how he fared when his wife was away. To bed at midnight, wondering which of all the dainties I had so plenteously provided in the morning would be given me for my next day's meal. Surely it is not too warm for Mrs. Crusoe to visit the island now.

Wednesday.—I am sorry that I ever smote Friday with a punkah rope, for I see that he is minded to poison me. This morn, in my big silver dish, set forth with many flowers and on a fair white cloth, came three sodden fragments of flesh which seemed as though they had been but newly torn from the inside of some dead beast. There was rice also, but I have never eaten small shot, so I put it all aside, and for two rupees of my own money Friday got me certain sardines in a tin, and a very little oil. With these I must stay my stomach as best I can. They taste wondrous fishy, and the tea is smokt and of a new flavour. Mrs. Crusoe never gave me anything like it.

I had naught in the middle of the day at my office – neither meat nor drink – and returned home through the mire in a conveyance hired from a native. (*Nota Bene.*– It was girded about with ropes, like Paul's ship,[5] and I held both doors shut with my own hands till I was mired to the elbow.) When I askt Friday what he means by sending neither tiffin nor carriage, he says that I gave no order, which was true enough, but I fancied that tiffin was eaten at least once every day by most men. I am very sick and tired and dare not abuse Friday as he deserves, or he will leave me altogether and I shall starve. Was too ill to go to the Club, so gave Friday two annas to get me a cup of tea. It tastes sadly of Friday his hookah. To bed wondering whether starving outright is better than being slowly poisoned, and also what became of the stores I had ordered yesterday. Dreamt that Friday had boiled sardines in tea for my breakfast, and that Mrs. Crusoe stood by with a basket of tripe and laught. A very terrible dream.

Thursday.—Friday hath a new turban with two broad gold stripes and a pink one in the middle, and walks not over steadily. He asks me at nine in the morning what I would eat. Said that I was too sick to attend to work, and desired a savoury omelette. At ten 'twas ready, but there was neither tea, milk, bread, or anything else, saving two forks that were not of the same set, and a plate. Friday says I made no *bundobust*, and my head aches too sorely to reply. Made shift to eat the omelette which, methinks, was of bad eggs mainly; and lay down for the rest of the day, never a soul coming nigh me. In truth I am wrong here. Friday's children did harry an old turkey-cock in the verandah, which was close to my head, for two hours; and I thank Providence that made me a Civil and Sessions Judge and gave me Mrs. Crusoe, for the fever that rackt me till I could stir neither hand nor foot – else I should have assuredly killed them all. In the evening my distemper went from me a little, but am still too weak to eat. Friday hath gone to the bazar and hath forgotten to bring me iced water. To bed, where I dreamt that I smothered Friday and all his children under an omelette of turkey cock's eggs. I have never been wont to dream in this fashion before.

Friday.—The fever left me in the night. Found this morning that I had but one clean shirt, and that frayed and chafed at the wristbands. Now I know I had twelve when I left my wife, so askt of Friday – who walks as though ground was air under him – what had become of all my gear. At this he wept for ten minutes (over mine only towel) and prayed me to send him to prison since I had blackt his face thus far. At this I was very wrath and said that no one had called him thief, but that I wanted my shirts again. Thereat he wept more than before, till I kickt him out of the room and shut the door. When next I opened it after smoking a pipe to consider how I should do, I found seven of my shirts – three that had been worn and four that were new – lying in a heap on the threshold. They smelt terribly of cocoanut oil and bad tobacco, and were marked and stained with all manner of stuffs. But Friday knew nothing of them at all, save that I was his father and mother and had suspected him of robbery. He wept all day by fits and starts, and I gave him four annas to quiet him. But this did not amend the quality of my meals. Dined again at the Club where Cadwallader Jones (who, methinks still, cheated me in the matter of that horse) called me a "sick dove" and clapt me on the back with his hand. Mrs. Jones returns to the island shortly, I would I were Jones, or at least that Mrs. Crusoe was here. To bed thinking sorrowfully how I have done no work at all this week by reason of the pestilent Friday, who was more in my mind than anything else. Lord! Lord! and I had a thousand and one matters to finish and furbish up ere the Courts opened! Yet I will give him one day more of grace, and

6

then – it is surely cool enough for Mrs. Crusoe. Stoppt the punkah to see if this were so, and went off in a strong sweating till dawn.

Saturday.—Friday is again drunk nor was there any sign at all of breakfast. I eat sparingly of my sardines, with a cheese scoop, the rest of the table gear being all filthy with the remains of some feast. I found them in the pantry and judge that Friday hath been entertaining his friends. I have telegrapht for Mrs. Crusoe, and till she come must make shift to live on sardines.

Jacob Cavendish, M.A.

---

[1] 'Covenanted Servant', i.e., a holder of one of the higher posts in the Indian Civil Service. The rank was then exclusively British.

[2] His statement is reported in a letter from RK's bibliographer, Flora Livingston, to Mrs Kipling, 1 October 1936 (Kipling Papers, University of Sussex, KP 25/53). Since RK resented the intrusions of bibliographers and other searchers after his early work, it is more than likely that he meant his statement to create uncertainty.

[3] Mrs Poyser's remark, in George Eliot, *Adam Bede.*

[4] 'What?' 'Sahib,' says he, 'Worcestershire sauce, cooking oil, new gravel for the stable, mustard seeds, fruit preserves.'

[5] Acts 27:17: 'they used helps, undergirding the ship'.

Twenty Years After,
(Or What It May Come To.)

⁂

Published: *Civil and Military Gazette*, 9 January 1885.

Attribution: In Scrapbook 1 (28/1, p. 39).

Text: *Civil and Military Gazette.*

Notes: RK records this item in his diary for 1885, under date of 6 January 1885: 'Skit about Punjab police'. He also includes it in the summary list of his year's work at the end of the diary.

Reprinted in the Martindell–Ballard pamphlets and in Harbord, 1, 566–8.

⁂

At present it seems to be the popular idea that no one but the police is responsible for the protection of property, but this impression, I submit, is erroneous. If the European community would only secure their houses and property, or keep chowkidars, there would be much less rascality and robbery abroad than at present exists. As the country becomes more and more civilized, and natives cease to fear the conquering race, as they have hitherto done, we Europeans will find, to our sad experience, that we cannot live in the open, unprotected, with twenty or thirty open doors for robbers to enter and help themselves. Hence, in one way these Anarkali thefts are doing good: they are educating the Englishman in India, awakening him to the fact that, in this, as well as in all civilized countries, a robber is not a respecter of persons.

—*vide* Punjab Police Report, 1883–84.

From Mr. Orion Golightly – to the Deputy Commissioner, Chorpur

Chorpur, April 1st, 1906.

Dear Sir,

Last night a gang of dacoits, armed with repeating rifles and several pounds of dynamite, attacked my house and blew up the fourteen

armed chowkidars stationed in the front verandah. They then proceeded to loot the premises, and eventually decamped, after lashing the
various members of the family to trees in the compound, and removing
four valuable horses. My wife has succumbed to the shock; and I fear
that there is but small hope of my eldest child's recovery from three
bullet-wounds in the head and neck. My guard were only armed with
Sniders, and the bomb-proof roofing of the house had been a good deal
damaged by a previous attack from the same gang. Nevertheless, I submit, that this is a case for police interference.– I am, &c.

From the Deputy Commissioner, Chorpur, – to Mr. Orion Golightly.

Simla, August 8th, 1906.

Dear Sir,

In reply to your exceedingly temperate communication of the 1st
April, I have the honour to refer you to my last Monthly Report (in four
vols. octavo) on the "Incentives to Local Crime." At present it seems
to be the popular idea that the police is responsible for the protection
of property; but this impression, I may say, is utterly erroneous. If the
European community would only employ Gatling guns, or keep a small
park of Artillery in their compounds, there would be much less rascality and robbery than at present exists. Hence, in one way, I trust that
the sudden death of Mrs. Golightly, and the moribund condition of
your eldest child, will do you good. These incidents are educating the
Englishman in India, and awakening him to the fact that, in this as well
as in all civilized countries, a robber is not a respecter of persons.

I have, etc.,

Clive Hastings Macaulay Bulstrode[1]
D.C. Chorpur

From Mr. Heastey Dryver, – to the Deputy Commissioner, Chorpur.

December 15th, 1906.

Dear Sir,

A fortnight ago, while driving through the Badzat Bazar, my horse
was tripped up by a string which had been stretched from side to side

of the road by some young gentlemen anxious to ascertain the effects of suddenly retarded motion on a moving body. My horse has chipped both his knees, I myself have sustained a compound fracture of the clavicle, and the dog-cart had to be sold on the spot for firewood. My bullet-proof driving hood was up at the time, and I was, according to your last issued municipal regulations, not going more than seven miles an hour, for fear of wounding the feelings of those on foot. Could not the police be induced to take some notice of the matter? – I am, etc.

From the Deputy Commissioner, Chorpur – to Mr. H. Dryver.

Simla, May 28th, 1907.

Dear Sir,

It is astonishing, that in these days of general advancement and enlightenment, an idea should still exist that the police of this country need take notice of any thing at all. This impression is, I need scarcely say, utterly wrong.

As the country becomes more civilized, Young India ceases to despise the conquering race, and condescends as you yourself have very ably set forth, to make experiments on them. Europeans will find nowadays that they cannot expect to drive down an open street without exposing themselves to the enquiring mind of youth, as fit subjects for the illustrations of those great forces of gravity whereby the world is governed. If the European community would only affix a cowcatcher to their horses' collars, or send on their saices at a footpace to report upon the state of the road as they went along, such accidents as you have described would become comparatively rare. I have no doubt that your mishap will educate you, as an Englishman in India, to recognize that, in this as in other civilized countries, the indigenous *gamin* is no respecter of persons.– I have, etc.,

C. H. M. Bulstrode.
D.C. Chorpur.

Form B. 101-1553 *for general use. To Mr. Brown, Jones, or Robinson.*

190–D.C.'s Office, Chorpur

Dear Sir,

It seems to be the popular idea, that the police are responsible for the performance of their duties. This impression, I am directed to inform you, is erroneous. If the European community would only look after their house and property themselves, and catch any thieves that might intrude into the one, or remove the other, there would be no robbery or rascality at all. In the meantime, I trust that the case of * * * * * just reported, will awaken you to the fact

*Here insert murder, robbery with violence, dacoity &c.as reported

that, in this as in all other civilized countries, the robber is no respecter of persons. – I have, etc.

C. H. M. Bulstrode

¹ For the identification of Clive, Hastings, and Macaulay, see the headnote to 'Dis Aliter Visum', below.

Dis Aliter Visum
(Being the lamentable and veracious history of Job Charnock's *exeat*).

ᛞᛟᛞ

Published: *Pioneer*, 4 July 1885.

Attribution: In 'Summary of the Years Odd Work' at end of Diary, 1885. In Scrapbook 2 (28/2, p. 64).

Text: *Pioneer*.

Notes: This is the first item in this edition from the *Pioneer* of Allahabad, a paper owned by the proprietors of the *Civil and Military Gazette*.

The actors in this scene are leading figures from the past of British India. Job Charnock (1630?–93) was head of the East India Company's affairs in India. In 1691 he founded what became Calcutta, from 'three small villages on an inhospitable tract of riverbank' (*ODNB*). Robert, Lord Clive (1725–74) was the military commander in the service of the East India Company whose victories over French and native forces established the civil authority of the Company in India; he was afterwards Governor of Bengal. Warren Hastings (1732–1818), Governor-General of India (1773–85), preserved and extended Clive's conquests in India. Both Clive and Hastings are subjects of celebrated essays by Thomas Babington Macaulay (1800–59), the historian, who served as the Legal Member of the Supreme Council of India (1834–8); in that office he wrote the Indian Penal Code and helped to establish Western learning in English as the basis for government-supported education in India.

The unstated subject of this fantasy is the annual migration of the Supreme Government from the damp heat of Calcutta (Kolkata) to the mountain air of Simla, high in the foothills of the Himalayas and far removed from Calcutta, the regular capital. The government of the Punjab also made Simla its hot-weather base. Those left behind in Calcutta or on the plains of the Punjab of course resented 'The Exodus', as it was called, and others thought it an indefensible indulgence on the part of the administrators. Simla was imagined as 'Capua', all luxury and no work.

'Dis Aliter Visum' was reprinted in the *United Services College Chronicle*, 15 December 1887, and in Harbord, 1, 568–75. The title, which may be translated 'The Gods will otherwise', is from the *Aeneid*, 11, 428.

ᛞᛟᛞ

> ..... *"such stuff*
> *As dreams are made of."*[1]

It was a cosy nook in Purgatory – a ground-floor suite in one of the eligible mansions there, and handsomely furnished. To be sure, none of the doors would shut; and there was no good hookah tobacco. Clive, enervated by long residence in Madras, felt the draughts more than Hastings; but, on the other hand, Hastings resented the loss of his own particular conserved *guldari* very bitterly, If they had taken the trouble to inquire they would have found that old Job Charnock in the attics felt the deprivation most keenly of any. But the two ex-Governor-Generals did not inquire; they were very comfortable. Macaulay, whose doom it was to read his own remarks on Warren Hastings[2] into that somewhat short-tempered statesman's ear, had gone to *table d'hôte*. Hence the relief of the two worthies. Of course, they were quarrelling in a perfunctory sort of manner. Hastings, for the eleven hundred and nineteenth time, was vindicating his execution of Nuncomar.[3] This was part of Clive's punishment. Clive was interpolating contradictions and anecdotes regarding the Nawab of Murshidibad,[4] also for the eleven hundred and nineteenth time. This was part of Hastings' weird.[5] Matters had reached their usual five o'clock in the afternoon stage. That is to say Clive was wearily preparing to do duel with his inane pistol which never went off, and made Hastings protest that Clive had arranged it beforehand, when the door of the sitting-room was violently dashed open and old Job Charnock, his venerable pig-tail as stiff as the palm trees of his beloved Kalighat,[6] sank exhausted on a divan in the centre of the room. "Humph!" grunted Hastings. "Macaulay been at *you*, has he? Damme, Sir, if I've pistolled that insolent commentator once I've pistolled him two thousand times." "Not Macaulay," gasped Job, "something much worse my friends." "Haven't seen Job so excited," mused Clive, "since he heard John Company was dead, and that's a matter of thirty years ago."[7] (It may be mentioned *en parenthesis* that one of the irksome regulations of the Intermediate Institute (as its *habitués* styled it) was that every member must be, outwardly at least, the equal of every other member. Job Charnock was deferential in manner to a degree, but he was forced to use the word "friends" where he would of his own mention said "honourable gentlemen" at least. This, however, is a digression.)

There was a silence of some minutes, during which time Job had managed to hopelessly entangle himself in Clive's hookah-stem, and to swallow a gallon or two of such beverage as the Intermediate Institute provided for the delectation of its members. (It tasted like tepid port-wine negus would taste at eight o'clock on the morning after a dissipated night.) Finally he gurgled, "I've taken my *exeat*; and I assure you, gentlemen, I'm thankful, positively thankful, to be back in my present quarters." Now the roster in the Intermediate Institute for *exeats*, which varied between four and twenty hours and a week in duration, was a long one, and the turns came round about once in fifty-four years if a member behaved himself. Clive and Hastings declined theirs on principle, as being beneath the dignity of English gentlemen to shirk punishment. They gained little, however, for it was the custom, whether a gentleman took his *exeat* or not, for certain members of the Inferior Institute to come up and hold a house-warming in his rooms. This singed the chairs and sofas a good deal and left behind an intolerable odour of something like gunpowder. Clive, however, protested that he rather liked it; said it reminded him of old times on the bastions of Fort William. Both men, however, were pathetically anxious to hear whatever Job had to tell. Hastings slid the emerald-studded mouthpiece of his pet hookah into Job's hand, while Clive lit and blew a perfumed ball atop of the tobacco. "Sit down and tell us all about it, Job. Found everything a good deal changed, eh, since last time," said the former. "By the way when was your last *exeat*?" "1820. Me and the widow together.[8] We spent four days' honeymoon in the old cemetery. It was delightful. But now. Oh!" Job pulled at the hookah for consolation. Then, after a long pause, "But you won't believe me, I know?" Clive smiled grimly. "Well, Charney, you know they *say* you founded my Calcutta, and stocked it with enough lies to last all the inhabitants for all time. But I think we can credit you here." This was perfectly correct. The members of the Intermediate Institute could only lie within certain well-defined limits when their inventions would most ruffle and irritate their neighbours. The truth, and the whole truth was quite sufficient on this occasion. "Well, gentlemen, I went first of all to Calcutta." "Of course, you did," interpolated Hastings gruffly," who wouldn't? Go on." "And the Supreme Government, the Governor-General and Councillors were not there." *Click, click, click,* went an arrangement something like a nickel-plated billiard marker, by the side of the mantelpiece, and there slid into the polished frame a plain card marked "Extras;" underneath this heading appeared bracketed together the simple titles:– "Clive, Hastings, two days – profane oath." It is needless to repeat here what Charnock's listeners had uttered – the form was identical, but recondite and unfit for ears polite. "Where are they, then," chorussed the two together. "Twelve hundred miles away at a place in the mountains that I've never heard of, called Simla. They won't be back for another four months." "Twelve hundred miles away! Yes, it will take 'em fully that time to come back if they move with anything like my escort," said Hastings. Charnock was warming to his work. "They go backwards and forwards in three days, or four at the most." "Job, *dear* Job, (the late Governor-Generals were almost in tears), for pity's sake don't go on like that, Job. You'll make us say something in a minute and that infernal (*click, click*) 'ticker' will begin again." Job was nearly as much moved as his friends. "I protest, gentlemen, that I am, as I hope some day to escape from the Institute, only speaking the solemn sober truth as I have seen and heard it." "Very well, then. They are twelve hundred miles from Calcutta and they take four days to cover it. How is it done?" Hastings was evidently speaking under strong restraint. "They go by train." "By *train*! That must be some new breed of Madrassee cattle. I always said we never knew what those long legged Bellary⁹ trotters could do if they were put to it. Where do they breed 'em, what are they like?" asked Clive. "They aren't cattle at all. They're a kind of palanquin on wheels; only the wheels run on strips of iron and the palanquins are pulled by a big brass and iron sort of cooking pot with a jury mast rigged where the handle ought to be." At this particularly lucid definition of the modern locomotive and its funnel, Clive and Hastings marvelled. "All right, Job, I dare say you are quite correct. We must certainly take our *exeats* next time, if only to see the cooking pots on iron strips. Go on." Charnock continued: "The strips run from Calcutta to a place called Umballa, somewhere beyond the Emperor of Delhi's territory, which they've annexed." "*They've* annexed! Egad!" Hastings interrupted. "Call 'em we, Sir, call 'em we. They are our descendants, I hope, and do us credit." Charnock shifted uneasily in his chair, and replied: "I don't think they are 'we' gentlemen." Clive leapt as if he had been shot. "Do you mean to say that those accursed French have come back then, after all I did too. Oh, Job! Job! You're trying me too hardly." The nickel-plated ticker was silent, and the hasty expression passed unrecorded in the Intermediate Institute. "No it's not the Frogs, thank heaven!" said Charnock, "for these men speak English; but it does not seem to me that they in any way belong to us, for we weren't one little bit like them when we were we." "Humph, that's particularly easy to understand" said Hastings. "I suppose we're changed a good deal, but we'll understand you presently. Why aren't they doing their work in Calcutta like men, instead of leaving the whole boiling of writers to come to loggerheads in the buildings?" Charnock drew a preliminary pull at the hookah and nerved himself for his answer: – "Because there are no writers; because there aren't any writers' buildings; because they say Calcutta is too hot for 'em; and – oh Lord, Lord! – they are a hundred *koss* from anywhere, along a most unchristian *dâk* road, through a lot of hills, and there's an unbridged river behind 'em that can cut 'em off at any minute." The grizzled head was bowed with emotion, and the billiard marker clicked out a remission of four days for J. Charnock on account of "violent mental anguish not included in the rules of the Institute." But Charnock was far too overwhelmed with grief to take heed. "Say it again slowly, Job," cried Clive, "and give us time to think over it." Charnock did so, and silence reigned in the drawing-room for the space of five minutes. Hastings was the first to break it. "Charnock's right, Clive. It's they and not we." Clive was considering the situation from a military point of view. "One hundred *koss* of *dâk* road before they can get to the cooking pots on iron strips. That's five days' steady marching if they go quickly. I don't suppose they've altered the rains in these days. Rivers can fill up then in twenty-four hours. Supreme Government on one side, and the whole country ablaze on the other. Certainly Charnock *was* right." Hastings took up the tale:– "Calcutta too hot for 'em. Bless my soul, it was never more than pleasantly warm there" (the late Governor-General's mind was warped by his present situation). "Why, I remember we used to hold the big Company dinners at three o'clock on a July afternoon, and drink the King's health in hot punch afterwards. I should like to look at 'em. Do they die as much as we used to do?" "Not one-third," said Charnock; "but then they don't live as we did, or drink or gamble or enj –" (*click* went the warning "ticker" and Charnock recovered himself just in time) "– are themselves as much as we used to do. And they are going to live in this place Simla for always. Leastways they have built two sets of Writers' Buildings, all of plaster and iron ramrods on the side of a hill." "Plaster and iron ramrods" What on earth are you driving at, Job?" asked Clive. "Well, I can't put it any clearer than I have. 'Tisn't my fault if I can't understand their new-fangled ways. *You* couldn't either." This was carrying the war into the enemy's country, and Clive – in his fear lest Charnock should take offence and stop his story – collapsed. The worthy founder of Calcutta then plunged into an animated account of social life in Simla from his own point of view, and at this juncture it would not be well to follow him too closely. It must be remembered that Job's language was that of a bygone century and his expressions coarse. "Hundreds and thousands of 'em," he concluded rapturously, "all white, and more of 'em than the men." "Clive, my boy!" "Hastings, oh!" The incessant rattle of the ticker here brought both offenders to their senses, but not before all three men had run up an appalling total of "extras" for improper aspirations. "Not so bad as I thought then," said Hastings, "but it would be lively there at times. Who's the best shot in this – this Simla?" Charnocks's face grew sorrowful at once. "There's none of the old business now. They go to law instead, and it isn't often they do that!" An expression of unutterable scorn flitted across the listeners' faces. "Have they forgotten Francis and Me?"[10] "All but a very few. No one knows where you winged him, and no one cares." The voice of the ticker recalled Clive and Hastings as they murmured simultaneously:– "Such is fame! Go on, Charnock, you can't hurt us much more than you have."

Charnock began afresh on another tack – a safe and general one enough. "Kalighat's grown out of all knowledge, and they call it the City of Palaces!" "Could have told you that," said Hastings savagely. "And you can buy port for twenty rupees a dozen." "That might suit your stomach, Job, but it wouldn't suit ours." Charnock had succeeded in ruffling both his hearers' tempers finely, and was being suppressed at every turn. He was a tactful man in spite of his many failings, and proceeded to throw oil on the troubled waters. "I went to a meeting of the Council." "You did, did you? What was it like?" Peace was restored once more. "What did they do?" asked Hastings. "Well, they couldn't do much, you know. Everything is done by orders from England." "Hum. They used to try that in my time," murmured Hastings with a smile of blissful retrospection. "It did not come to much, though. Go on. How many guns did they fire, and where do they get their elephants from?" "There's only one carronade in the whole place, and the roads would not bear an elephant. It was very wet when I went there." "Where?" "To the place where the Governor-General lives." "Call it Government House, then," rapped out Hastings: "and be careful how you speak of your betters." "I shall call it no such thing," retorted Charnock, thoroughly aroused. "It's a beggarly little wood-and-plaster hovel cut into the side of a hill." Then he resumed hastily, as if to prevent the others edging in a word:– "It was very wet and there were five or six little ponies standing in the porch, and five or six old men in black clothes with cloaks on, walking up and down a little verandah. Then they went into a dark dining-room and sat around a table and smiled. Then a little man in a velvet coat"[11] ("Ah,! That's something better," ejaculated Clive. "What were his ruffles and sword like? I used to – but never mind.") "You wouldn't have thought so if you'd seen him. 'Twasn't the sort of velvet coat you mean. He came in with a slip of blue paper and sat down. Then he mumbled something under his breath and the old men nodded. Then one of the old men read something under his breath from another blue slip, and they all nodded again. That was one law passed, or something of the sort. Then another old man read something else, and the little man in the velvet coat read something more. Then they played with a lot of papers and clean pens on the table, and this mumbling and paper shifting went on for ten minutes. Then they all got up and went out to their ponies in the wet and rode away. There were no *chobdars*, no palanquins, no *massalchies*, and no wines." Hastings contemplated the phenomenon in all its vastness for half a minute, then murmured with the intensest conviction: "They were all drunk beforehand. We used to do queer things at the Council now and then I remember when the new Madeira came in: but we never forgot what was due to our dignity. Say they were drunk, Job." Alas! Job could not say this. "They were all as sober as I am; and you know how *that* liquor – he pointed ruefully to the port-wine negus which never grew cold – "doesn't lead one to tell lies." "Then they must be mad. Did you catch what passed at that sitting?" "No; but I learnt what they have passed some months ago, and I think you must be right." Charnock summarised the leading features of a recent memorable bill[12] and returned to his hookah with the pride of a pyrotechnist in his latest display. But Job had not lit a squib merely.

It was a hand-grenade that he threw into the midst of his hearers. For a few minutes the "ticker" kept up its work gallantly, then fell hopelessly behind, and finally ceased altogether. When the outburst had subsided, Hastings was nervously fingering his bladeless sword-hilt, and Clive with his head on the table was weeping bitterly. "After all I did, too!" he sobbed. "After all I did for them. Good Heavens, Job, I built them the foundations of an empire that has no equal in all time; and they are throwing it away with both hands – with both hands, do you hear?" His voice rose almost to a scream, and his eyes wandered in deadly earnest this time, to the pistol that would never go off. But the futility of it all struck him in a moment, and with bowed head he sobbed more bitterly than before. Hastings, silent and chalk-white, was glaring at the door, when Macaulay entered book in hand. "What was it you said the other day, Mac," he asked, "the last time but one I put a bullet through you?" The great historian replied in a monotonous undertone, as of a wearied man reading from a book he knows all too well. "What the horn is to the buffalo."[13] "No! No" No! Not that, you idiot! The other thing! Something original I fancy. About monkeys!" "Visionaries from their closets and children with the mother's milk hardly dry upon their lips, ruling tigers and monkeys with the undigested theories of madmen and the wisdom of the nursery."[14] The sentence rolled *ore rotundo* from Macaulay's lips, and Clive, with his face hid in his hands, shuddered. Charnock could scarcely understand his emotion, for long residence in the Intermediate Institute had converted the living world, in Job's eyes, to an assemblage of unsubstantial shadows. Be it remembered that Clive and Hastings had never taken their *exeats*, and the world they had left was still strong in its influence upon them. Job was rather pleased than otherwise with the effect he had produced, for in his attic he met with slight consideration, as a rule, from the gentlemen on the ground floor. Macaulay repeated his sentence with the precision of a calculating machine, and would have recommended a third time had not Hastings fiercely motioned him to be silent.

"Clive, my friend," whispered Hastings, laying a hand tenderly on the bowed figure. "It can't last long. Indeed it can't. Remember, they don't see as clearly as we do what it all means. There'll be time enough to put it all right some day; but it is hard, bitterly hard." The great Governor-General struggled with his emotions for a few seconds and broke down as hopelessly as his comrade. Charnock turned his head from the one to the other in blind wonder and proceeded to pile on the agony. "There are plenty of people in England, and some in India, who say that my Khalighat and all the country that it stands in, from the big mountains in the north to Ceylon, is nothing but a burden and an expense, and the sooner it's got rid of the better. They are called the 'Perish India Party,' I think, and they speak and write a good deal." Charnock had accumulated a vast deal of knowledge in his week's *exeat*: but we must take into consideration the fact that he was a spirit and that his knowledge had been arranged for him like the lies he occasionally told within well-defined limits. For the next hour the founder of Calcutta, seeing that there was no one to interrupt him, poured out the wisdom he had gained in terse and not always grammatical sentences. Much may be said in an hour including a brief resumé of fifty years' political incident in India and in England as affecting India. Charnock, despite his dull, drawling undertone, spoke as neither man nor spirit has ever spoken before. He was free from party bias and forced in a great measure to speak the truth. And the bowed heads of two of the greatest men that the world has ever known bowed lower as they listened. From time to time Macaulay on the divan would get as far as "Visionaries from" – but Job went on ruthlessly. Evening was falling over the Intermediate Institute when he concluded with these words:– "And so they are educating them as fast as they can. Twenty years to a month. And they are swallowing it all like over-ripe bananas. But it can't last long, gentlemen. It can't last long."

Hastings sprang to his feet as the speaker ceased. "No, Job, it can't last long. Listen, Clive! Stand up and listen, man! What's that?"

Loud and clear above the innumerable murmurs of the imprisoned spirits of the Intermediate Institute reverberated the clang of a bell huger than any human foundries have ever cast. "*One.*"

Then, after an interval, another thunderous stroke drowned the rising confusion. Every soul in the Institute was alert and expectant, each hoping that the summons was for him. The Governor-General clasped hands. "It is for us, and the hour *has* come."

Then for the first time since the spirit of Machiavelli, shorn and clipped indeed of many of its splendid powers, passed away to become the abiding scourge of England for half a century and to rule her for her ruin – the "ticker" ran back on itself with the whirr of released clockwork;

and the room was empty of its occupants. Charnock removed the emerald studded hookahs to his own attic with a grunt of satisfaction, and Macaulay finished his often interrupted sentence alone.

Transmigration may or may not be a fiction.

At half-past seven that evening the wife of a struggling doctor in sleepy Arundel, infinite millions of leagues away, was cooing in her new found happiness over her first babe; and there was joy in far off Denver when it was made public that the "Jedge's" wife had presented him with as "fine a boy, Sir, as ever gummed a *coral*."

Yet the world spun no wit the less steadily on its axis because five decades hence the two great Anglo-Saxon nations should be welded together by the genius and statesmanship of Clive and Hastings into one vast empire, and that the united flag should wave from the Azores to the Golden Horn, and from Behring's Straits to Tasmania.

---

[1]   *The Tempest*, iv.i.

[2]   'Warren Hastings', *Edinburgh Review*, October 1841.

[3]   Nuncomar, a high Indian official and an enemy of Hastings, was hanged in 1775; Hastings was accused of having rigged the case against him but the accusation is no longer accepted.

[4]   Moorshedebad was the capital of Surajah Dowlah, Nawab of Bengal; he was defeated by Clive at the battle of Plassey. Before that, as part of a conspiracy against Surajah Dowlah, Clive had duped one of his untrustworthy agents, who threatened to betray the conspiracy. Clive deceived the agent by two treaties, one genuine, one false, including a forged signature.

[5]   Weird: in the old sense of 'fate', 'destiny'.

[6]   One of the villages from which Kolkata (Calcutta) grew.

[7]   The rule of the East India Company came to an end in 1858 following the Mutiny of 1857.

[8]   Charnock married a Hindu widow in 1664.

[9]   A town in southern India.

[10]   Hastings fought a duel in India with Sir Philip Francis, his opponent on the Supreme Council of India.

[11]   Lord Dufferin, the Viceroy.

[12]   Identified as the Ilbert Bill by RK in a cutting of the article that he lightly annotated and sent to W. C. Crofts, his classics master; the cutting is now at Syracuse University. The Ilbert Bill was a measure proposed in Lord Ripon's time as Viceroy allowing native judges to try British subjects. It provoked a fierce opposition and was passed only in a much diluted form.

[13]   From Macaulay's essay on Hastings: 'What the horns are to the buffalo ... deceit is to the Bengalee'.

[14]   I do not find this sentence in Macaulay, whose style is not so extravagant: RK's invention?

De Profundis
(A Study in a Sick Room.)

Published: *Civil and Military Gazette*, 7 August 1885.

Attribution: In Scrapbook 2 (28/2, p. 21).

Text: *Civil and Military Gazette.*

Notes: Written in Simla, where RK spent three months in 1885, in good health. But he was soon to return to Lahore and to renewed bouts of fever.

Reprinted in *Kipling's India: Uncollected Sketches.*

A brisk canter in May on a pulling horse; violent perspiration, followed by twenty minutes' lounge at the public gardens, where the flooded tennis courts reek like so many witches' cauldrons and the Enemy is upon you. Neither Mrs. Lollipop's *banalities*, the maturer charms of the Colonel's wife, nor the fascinations of a gin and tonic at the peg table will keep him at bay. With the dreary foreknowledge, born of many previous experiences, you shall recognize that for the next twelve hours at least, you are "in for it;" and shall communicate the fact with a sickly smile to your friends. The instinct of the stricken wild beast for rest and retirement drives you to your bachelor quarters. Man's wisdom recommends quinine and an early retreat bedward. Your pony, finding that you sit much after the fashion of a sack of flour, and are to be dislodged at any moment, mercifully forbears putting his knowledge to practical use, and walks home in the twilight soberly. He is stepping, you can swear, on wool; the reins thickening and lengthening in the most marvellous manner throughout the journey. Finally four ponderous hawsers control a huge head twenty feet away, and there is no end to the white line of the mall. It runs straight as an arrow into the sunset, whence hot breezes, bearing on their wings the choking savour of a hundred brick kilns, fly out to meet and buffet you in the saddle. A grey backed, red bellied cloud closes the vista; and as you gaze, you are conscious of a feeling of irritation. Somehow or other it has got into your head and lies like a red-hot bar just below your hat-brim. Decidedly tonight's experiences will be lively.

The stifling breezes have turned to marrow-freezing as the pony stops at your door. One last test remains – though you yourself know that it will only render your certainty more assured. If the gorge rises at a tea-ripened, vanilla-scented "super," if the mind turn with loathing from a well-loved consolation, then indeed lie down and wait with what patience you may for the morning. Alas! nerveless fingers drop the match ere it is well alight. One half – nay one quarter puff, is sufficient to convert you, for the time being, to the views of King James of blessed memory.[1] "*Bearer, Sherry sharab quinine ke botal lao! Khana ne chahseay.*"[2] Kurim Buksh guessed as much from your face when you half tumbled, half slid off the pony three minutes ago, and has already communicated the joyful news to his familiars. The Sahib is *bokhar*, and there will be an evening party in the servants' quarters to-night. Meantime his countenance expresses nothing save dumb grief. He pours out the wineglassful of sherry, and departs with the decanter – to be seen no more. As you have not ordered the lamps, or given any express instructions about iced water being placed by your bedside, he has not thought fit to perform either of these offices himself. The fever has you bound hand and foot for the night; and your voice, even at its most powerful pitch, will be far too weak an hour hence to disturb the revellers in the *serai*. It's an ill wind that blows nobody any good!

The great red cloud has faded out behind the *ferashes*, the moon looks down through the dusty heat haze, and the cicalas are hard at work outside. *Crick! crick! crick! crick!* in the silence of the evening; and some miserable ragamuffin returning from the bazaar joins his notes to theirs. Every howl, chuckle and quaver echoes and re-echoes in your head like whispers in the gallery of St. Paul's. Have patience, for, as you yourself well know, your torments are but beginning. When those thirty grains of quinine shall have effected a lodgment in the sick brain, and wrestle with the phantoms there, the play will be at its height. At present you are merely hot and cold by turns; the moods varying so rapidly that you dare not regulate the punkah by them. Scarcely has the *zor se kencho*[3] left your lips, than the burning wave has rolled by, and your teeth are chattering like castanets. If you told the coolie to *chor do* now, he would probably curl up to slumber, and be beyond your reach before the cold

23

fit had passed. By knocking the books off the table and appropriating the tablecloth for a wrapper, something may be done; but above all things it is advisable not to look at the *punkah*. It has an unpleasant knack of growing big and little with exasperating rapidity; of retiring anon to the beams on which it is slung, and thereafter descending till it sweeps the floor. Moreover, it is iridescent at the edges, as long as the half light lasts. When that has gone, you had best follow the sun's example, and sink to rest – though this is a brutal sarcasm – at once. Wait, if possible, till the cold fit has overtaken you, or the sheets will strike icily chill on first getting into bed. Thus you may snatch a little comfort out of the jaws of pain.

You were to have dined out to-night, and by this time should have been in your trap on the way to Mrs. Lollipop's. But man proposes and the fever disposes. You have sailed far out of the reach of such mundane matters as dinners and flirtations, and are alone in that strange phantasmal world that lies open to us all in time of sickness – on the first stage of your journey towards the Purgatory of sizes and distances. Of this you are dimly conscious, for the racking pains in legs and trunk have given place to pains in the eyes and head only. The cold fits have passed away, and you have been burning steadily for the last ten minutes, preparatory to a final glissade down a rolling bank of black cloud and thick darkness, and out into the regions beyond. Here you are alone, utterly alone, on the verge of a waste of moonlit sand, stretching away to the horizon. Hundreds and thousands of miles away lies a small silver pool, no bigger than a splash of rain water. A stone is dropped into its bosom, and, as the circles spread, the puddle widens into a devouring, placid sea, advancing in mathematically straight ridges across the sand. The silver lines broaden from east to west and rush up with inconceivable rapidity to the level of your eyes. You shudder and attempt to fly. The innumerable lines retreat with a long-drawn "*hesh*-sh" across the levels, and the terrible sea is contracted to the dimensions of a little puddle once more. A moment's breathing space, and the hideous advance and retreat recommences. The unstricken observer would tell you, if you cared to listen (which you do not, for you are deep in a struggle for life), that this phenomenon is simply the result of the quinine taken a few hours ago. But it is a very real Hell to you, for the advancing and receding tide gives place to all manner of strange dreams, wherein you are eternally progressing between infinite parallel straight lines, as eternally being driven back in terror by a something that advances and retreats at the further end of the passage, or overwhelmed by immense agitations of the solid earth, all directed against your poor Personality. Mountains are riven from top to bottom, that their fall may block up the ravine in which you are trapped. Rivers are diverted from their beds to pursue you across doabs of never-ending quicksands; and when you have shaken yourself free from these horrors, the round globe herself opens to let you down into the darkness of her central depths, or it may be to lap you in her central fires. You are alone on some way-side railway station, planted amid burning sands. A tropical sun is searing your brain as you pace up and down the platform waiting for the train that is to bear you away from your pain. At length it comes. Showing first as a tiny speck on the polished burning metals, nearer, nearer, nearer, in a reverberating *crescendo*, till it halts hotter even than the mid-day sun, a monster of winking brasswork and roaring fires. From the foot-plate, where he had hidden himself till now, leaps off a royal Bengal tiger with yellow eye balls and opened jaws, and as he springs at your throat, the masterless train flies away out of your reach, and disappears as rapidly as it came. The sands bubble and heave with underpressure of some volcanic power and – you have a brief respite before entering on the second stage of your journey – the Purgatory of Faces. Your cheeks are deep purple, your eyes blood-shot, and your lips cracked and dry. Kurim Buksh has forgotten the iced-water, for the table by your bedside is empty; and if your life depended upon it, you could never raise your voice above a whisper. Nevertheless, you imagine that your shouts for *peene ka paney* [4] would raise the dead. As a matter of fact, they have not even reached the punkah coolie outside. The thirst will pass off in a little – or at least you will have other things to do than to cry, as Dives did, for a little cold water to moisten your tongue.[5] So far quinine has bred the visions you have seen. From midnight till about two o'clock you must deal with the delirium of fever by itself, and the second circle of your torment will be followed, as you well know, by a third and a worse.

Even now, the space of unadorned white-washed wall between the almirah and the gun cases at the end of the room is filling up with your visitors. Ladies and gentlemen, who call at unseasonable hours, and are not to be hastened but by the law of nature, which jealously watches the tension on the silver cord,[6] and relaxes it when the strain becomes too severe. If your mind is an active one, and your habit of life – I will be considerate – tumultuous, I scarcely envy you what you will see. At the best, the Purgatory of Faces is a weary and profitless experience. At the worst, only those who have been driven through its lowest circles can testify what it is. The six square feet of whitewash at which you are staring so piteously frames, it may be, a truthful but none the less unpleasant epitome of your past life. Phantasmagoria of the mind's magic lantern – each slide projecting its image clearly, thanks to the lime light of a brain that just now cannot lie even to itself. What they represent to you, it would surely be bitterly unfair of me to say – and would, moreover, impel you to denials unbefitting the character of an English gentleman. Your voice has recovered its volume, and your language, forgive me for saying so, is unparliamentary and even profane. As that queer frieze on the wall slides by, thickens, dissolves and re-forms, you are giving away with both hands much that it would have been well to keep to yourself – if you could. But the delirium has opened your lips, so that you cannot close them, or even cloak your thoughts with the decent conventionalities that our respectable life here below demands. The recurrence of that one face, in spite of the jostling crowd behind it, is exceedingly annoying, but capable of explanation on the simplest psychological grounds. The punkah coolie, whom your ravings have attracted to the chick, argues that the sahib has, for the time being, gone pagal, and will consequently not notice whether the punkah is pulled or not. Once more, it is an ill-wind .that blows nobody any good. Peroo, Dalloo, or whatever his name is, has disposed himself for a nap, while you fight your way out of the purgatory, or lose consciousness of its horrors through sheer exhaustion. The time is not far off, and, if you only knew, your skin is beginning to show signs of moisture. Violent declamation, accompanied with fantastic gestures, leads, by a natural law, to violent perspiration – and it is now close upon two o'clock. That uncanny picture frame fills less quickly than it did, and it is dawning upon you that your visitants were nothing more than idle shadows and not, as you first held, an avenging army of avenging sins. You have dropped your voice to something a little above a sigh, and are slowly coming to. The last face dies out on the wall, raging thirst has returned, and but one more purgatory remains, wherein the half awakened mind shall scourge you with irrational terrors, and you shall be broken in spirit as children are broken at the prospect of impending and inevitable punishment.

The Purgatory of Vain Imaginings has opened to receive you, and already you are deep in its labyrinths. You are working against time at some hopeless task, which, in spite of your exertions, unfolds itself before your wearied eyes like the endless paper reel of a telephone.[7] Official displeasure, the contempt of your juniors, degradation, forfeiture of your pension, and beggary are staring you in the face; and the burden of your daily work rides you like the nightmare. In a glimmering sort of way you can reason and elaborate consequences. You have embezzled money, taken bribes, sold appointments, betrayed your friend, and the judgment for these acts is even now at hand. The past six hours have broken your self-control, and ludicrous and pitiable delusions force you to sob like a child whose sum "*won't* come right." For a married man, terrors are reserved far more formidable than any that can assail the bachelor. His wife and children are starving, have disgraced themselves forever; he is repudiated by those he held dearest, and so on till the inevitable climax is reached – hopeless despair, and (the woman's refuge) tears. With these last, and the protracted mental strain, comes the end of the penance – in the prosaic form of a violent sweat till dawn, and the night's experiences are drowned in that first deep draft of iced water that Kurim Buksh – taught by experience – brings with *chota hazree*. What was it Byron said about hock and seltzer after a night's debauch?[8] You will answer that the crisp tinkle of the ice against the glass, those three or four deep delicious gulps of cold water, when the sparrows in the rose bushes are beginning their day's quarrels and intrigues, are worth a thousand times all the liquors that ever human ingenuity brewed or compounded. Have you not just explored the three circles of your fiery inferno, and returned unscathed; or at the most, if your journey has been a long one, only so weak as a little child? Entitled by right of past sufferings to the delights of an unmitigated Europe morning and the protracted pleasures of an after breakfast cheroot – those six inch incense sticks which you may burn this morning with a clear conscience in honour of the Joss of Idleness, wondering how it was that they tasted so villainously last evening. By the time that the first honey coloured darling has bunt to the stump, you will be prepared to swear that I, your faithful historian, have, to put it gently, wilfully and falsely exaggerated. "Of course I was a bit light in my head and all that. Every fellow with fever is. But all that stuff about infernos and pictures is awful bosh. Man's a l— " and Mrs. Lollipop, on whom fever once laid no gentle hand, will lispingly back you up in the assertion: for out of her mind too, as out of yours, has passed all recollection of the time when an evening's chill "drove the delighted spirit"⁹ a wanderer through the caverns of that very inferno whose existence is so impiously denied, and that with lips still blue and parched from the vehemence of the fires.

¹ James I, who abominated tobacco, wrote 'A Counterblast to Tobacco', 1604.
² 'Bearer, a bottle of sherry and quinine. I don't want dinner.'
³ 'Pull hard.'
⁴ 'A drink of water.'
⁵ Luke 16:24.
⁶ See Ecclesiastes 12:6.
⁷ Perhaps 'telegraph' is meant?
⁸ Byron, *Don Juan*, an unincorporated stanza appearing at the head of Canto I.
⁹ Perhaps an echo of *Measure for Measure*, III.i.121–2: 'and the delighted spirit / to bathe in fiery floods'.

The Unlimited "Draw" of "Tick" Boileau

Published: *Quartette: The Christmas Annual of the Civil and Military Gazette,* Lahore [19 December] 1885.

Attribution: Diary, 1885: 'Evolved my idea for the unlimited Draw of Tick Boileau, and did some of it' (24 September 1885); 'Went ahead on the Tick Boileau biz' (3 October 1885).

Text: *Quartette.*

Note: Reprinted in the Martindell–Ballard pamphlets and in Harbord, 1, 626–33.

He came to us from Naogong, somewhere in Central India; and as soon as we saw him we all voted him a Beast. That was in the Mess of the 45th Bengal Cavalry, stationed at Pindi; and everything I'm going to write about happened this season. I've told you he was an awful Beast – old even for a subaltern; but then he'd joined the Army late, and had knocked about the world a good deal. We didn't know that at first. I wish we had. It would have saved the honour of the Mess. He was called "Tick" in Naogong, because he was never out of debt; but that didn't make us think him a Beast. Quite the other way, for most of us were pretty well dipped ourselves. No; what we hated about the fellow was his "dark horsiness." I can't express it any better than that; and, besides, it's an awful nuisance having to write at all. But all the other fellows in the Mess say I'm the only man who can handle a pen decently; and that I must, for their credit, tell the world exactly how it came about. Everyone is chaffing us so beastily now.

Well, I was saying that we didn't like Tick Boileau's "dark horsiness." I mean by that, you never knew what the fellow could do and what he could not; and he was always coming out, with that beastly conceited grin on his face, in a new line – 'specially before women – and making the other man, who had tried to do the same thing feel awfully small and humble. That was his strong point – simpering and cutting a fellow out when he was doing his hardest at something or other. Same with billiards; same with riding; same with the banjo; he could really make the banjo *talk* – better even than Banjo Browne at Kasauli you know; same with tennis. And to make everything more beastly, he used to pretend at first he couldn't do anything. We found him out in the end; but we'd have found him out sooner if we'd listened to what old Harkness the Riding Master said the day after Tick had been handed over to him to make him into a decent "Hornet." That's what the bye-name of our regiment is. Harkness told me when I came into Riding School, and laughed at Tick clinging to the neck of his old crock as if he had never seen a horse before. Harkness was cursing like – a riding master. He said:– "You mark my words, Mister Mactavish; he's been kidding me, and he'd kid you. He *can* ride. 'Wish some of you other gentlemen could ride as well. He is playing the dark horse – that's what he's doing, and be d—d to him!" Well, Tick was as innocent as a baby when he rolled off on to the tan. I noticed that he fell somehow as if he knew the hang of the trick; and Harkness passed him out of Riding School on the strength of that fall. He sat square enough on parade, and pretended to be awfully astonished. Well, we didn't think anything of that till he came out one night in the billiard line at Black Pool, and scooped the whole Mess. Then we began to mistrust him, but he swore it was all by a fluke. We used to chaff him fearfully; and draw him about four nights out of the seven. Once we drugged his chargers with opium overnight; and Tick found 'em asleep and snoring when he wanted to go on parade.

He was a trifle wrathy over this; and the Colonel didn't soothe him by giving him the rough edge of his tongue for allowing his horses to go to sleep at unauthorized hours. We didn't mean to do more than make the chargers a bit bobbery next morning; but something must have gone wrong with the opium. To give the Beast his due, he took everything very well indeed; and never minded how often we pulled his leg and made things lively for him. We never liked him, though. "*Can't* like a man who always does everything with a little bit up his sleeve. It's not fair."

Well one day in July Tick took three months' leave and cleared out somewhere or other – to Cashmere I think. He didn't tell us where, and we weren't very keen on knowing.

We missed him at first, for there was no one to draw. Our regiment don't take kindly to that sort of thing. We are most of us hard as nails; and we respect each other's little weaknesses.

About October Tick turned up with a whole lot of heads and horns and skins – for it seemed that the beggar could shoot as well as he did most other things – and the Mess began to sit up at the prospect of having some more fun out of him. But Tick was an altered man. 'Never saw any man so changed. 'Hadn't an ounce of *bukh* or bounce left about him; never betted; knocked off what little liquor he used to take; got rid of his ponies, and went mooning about like an old ghost. Stranger still, he seemed to lay himself out in a quiet sort of way to be a popular man; and, in about three weeks' time we began to think we had misjudged him; and that he wasn't half such a bad fellow after all. The Colonel began the movement in his favour. 'Said that Tick was awfully cut up about something or other, and that we really ought to make his life more pleasant for him. He didn't say all that much at once. 'Don't believe he could if he tried for a week, but he made us understand it. And in a quiet sort of way – Tick was very quiet in everything he did just then – he tumbled to the new *bandobast* more than ever, and we nearly all took to him. I say nearly all, because I was an exception. He had a little bit up his sleeve in this matter too.

You see he had given all his skins and his heads to the Mess, and they were hung up in trophies all round the wall. I was seeing them being put up, and I saw in one corner the Cabul Customs mark, in a sort of aniline ink mark, that all the skins that come from Peshawar must have. Now I knew Cashmere wasn't Peshawur [*sic*], and that bears didn't grow with Customs marks inside the hide. But I sat tight and said nothing. I want you to remember that I suspected Tick Boileau from the first. The fellows in the Mess say I was just as much taken in as the rest of 'em; but in our Mess they'd say *anything*. One of Tick's new peculiarities just at this time was a funk of being let alone. He never said anything about it. He used to be always coming over to fellows' quarters in the afternoon though, just when they were trying to put in a little snooze and he'd sit still or *bukh* about nothing. He was very queer altogether in that way; and some of us thought he'd had D.T.; others that he was engaged, and wanted to get out of it; and one youngster, just joined, vowed that Tick had committed a murder and was haunted by the ghost of his victim.

One night we were sitting round the table smoking after dinner, and this same youngster began *bukhing* about a Station dance of some kind that was coming off. 'Asked old Tick if he wasn't coming, and made some feeble joke about "ticks" and *Kala Juggas*. Anyhow it fetched Tick awfully.

He was lifting a glass of sherry up to his mouth, and his hand shook so that he spilt it all down the front of his mess-jacket. He seemed awfully white, but perhaps that was fancy; and said as if there was something in his throat choking him:– "Go to a ball. *No!* I'd sooner rot as I stand." Well, it isn't usual for a fellow to cut up like that when he's asked if he's going to a hop. I was sitting next to him and said quietly: "Hullo! what's the matter, old man?" Tick was by way of being no end of a dawg before he took leave, and that made his answer all the queerer. "Matter!" said Tick, and he almost screamed. "You'd ask what was the matter if you'd seen what I have!" Then he turned on the youngster. "What the this and the that do you mean, you young this and t'other thing" – [It's no good putting down the words he used. They weren't pretty.] – "by asking me a question like that?" There would have been decanters flying about on the wings of love if we hadn't stopped the shindy at once; and when Tick came to himself again he began apologising all he knew, and calling himself all sorts of hard names for raising the row. And that astonished us more than anything else. Tick wasn't given that way as a rule. 'Said the Colonel from his side of the table:– "What in the name of everything lunatic, is the matter? Have you gone mad, Boileau?" Then Tick chucked up his head like a horse when it's going to bolt, and began to speak. Goodness knows what he said exactly; but he gave us to understand that, if he wasn't off his head, he was next thing to it ; and that any man would have been the same in his place; and, if we cared to listen, he'd tell us all about it. You bet we *did* care, for we were on needles to know the reason of the sudden change in the fellow. Tick half filled his peg-tumbler with port – it was the nearest decanter, – and told us this story. I can put it down word for word as he said it, not because I've got a good memory, but because – well, I'll tell you later. This is what Tick said in a shaky, quivery voice, while we smoked and listened:–

"You know I took three months' leave the other day, don't you? And that I went into Kashmir? You mayn't know" – [we didn't] – "that I put in the first month of my time at Mussoorie. I kept very quiet while I was up there, for I had gone up on purpose to follow a girl that you men don't know. She came from Pachmarri; and she was the daughter of a doctor there. I used to know her very well when I was stationed out Naogong way, and from knowing her well I got to falling in love with her."

He pulled up half a minute at that, and glared all round the table to see how we took it. We aren't whales exactly on falling in love with unmarried girls in our Mess. The Colonel doesn't hold with it, and he's quite right. But none of us moved a finger, and Tick went on.

"She was absolutely the most perfect girl on the face of this earth; and I'd knock any beggar's brains out who denies it." [None of us wanted to, I give you my word.] – "Upon my soul, I meant marrying her if she would only ha' taken me. And she did. O Heaven, she did! She has accepted me!" Tick covered his face with his hands and went on like a lunatic. I fancied he'd got a touch of the sun, or that the peg-tumbler of port was beginning to work. Then he started off on a fresh track, while we were staring at one another and wondering what on earth was coming next.

"Do any of you fellows recollect the Club Ball at Mussoorie this year?" Curiously enough not one of us had been up of the Mess; but you may be certain that we knew all about the ball – [By the way, take us all round and we're the best dancers in India; but that's neither here nor there.] – Someone said "Yes;" and Tick went on again:– "It happened there! It happened there! I had arranged beforehand that she was to give me four or five dances and all the extras. She knew long before that, I think, that I loved her; and I as good as told her before the dance began that I intended proposing. It was the first extra – there were going to be three that evening – that I had arranged to sit out with her and tell her how I loved her. We had been dancing together a good deal that evening, until she began to complain of a pain in her side, and then we sat out in the verandah."

Tick shovelled his hand through his hair and rolled his eyes about, more like a maniac than ever, and we sat tight and filled up our glasses quietly without saying anything.

"At the end of the last *pukka* waltz she went into the cloak-room, because her slipper-elastic had become slack – I heard her explain that to the man she was dancing with – and I went out into the verandah to think over what I had got to say. When I turned round I saw her standing at my side; and before I had time to say anything she just slipped her arm through mine and was looking up in my face. 'Well, what is it that you're going to say to me?' said she. And then I spoke – though honestly I was a little bit startled at the way she herself led up to the point, as it were. Lord only knows what I said or what she said. I told her I loved her, and she told me she loved me. Look here! If a man among you laughs, by Jove, I'll brain him with the decanter!"

Tick's face was something awful to look at just then – a dead white, with blue dimples under the nostrils and the corners of the mouth. He looked like a corpse that had been freshly dug up – not too freshly, though. I never saw anything more beastly in my life – except once at the front. Then he brought his hand down on the table in a way that made the dessert plates jump, and almost howled: – "I tell you I proposed to her, and she accepted me. Do you hear? She accepted me!"

Well, that didn't strike me as anything particularly awful. I've been accepted once or twice myself; but it didn't turn me into more than an average lunatic for the time being.

Tick dropped his voice somewhere into his boots – at least it sounded awfully hollow and unearthly:– "Then as the extra stopped she got up to go away from the sofa we'd been sitting on, and I asked her to stay. She told me that she was going to her next partner. I said: 'Look here, darling, who *is* your next partner if it isn't me, for ever and ever? Sit down and let us wait till your chaperone is ready. 'My chaperone is ready, dear,' said she, 'and I must go to her. But remember that you are my next partner for ever and ever. Amen. Good-bye.'

"Before I could say anything she had run out of the verandah and into the ball-room. I stopped to look at the moon and to thank my stars I was so lucky as to win her. Presently a man I knew hurried by me with a rug out of one of the dandies. My heart was so full I just pulled him up where he stood and said: 'Congratulate me, old boy! She's accepted me. I'm the happiest fellow on earth!' Now everyone in Mussoorie knew pretty well that I meant business with that girl; but instead of congratulating me the man just let the rug drop and said: 'O my God!'

"'What's the matter?' said I. 'Were you sweet on her yourself, then? All right, I'll forgive you. But you'll congratulate me, won't you?'

"He caught me by the arm, and led me quietly into the ball-room and then left me. Everybody was clustered in a mob round the cloak-room door; and some of the women folk were crying. A couple of 'em had fainted. There was a sort of subdued hum going out, and everyone was saying: 'How ghastly! How terrible!' I leant up against a door-post and felt sick and faint, though I didn't know why. Then the fellow who had taken the dandy rug came out of the cloak-room and spoke to one of the women."

Tick had nearly emptied the decanter by this time; and as I looked up and down the Mess I could see two or three of the men looking awfully white and uncomfortable. My hair began to feel cold, as if draughts were blowing through it. I don't mind owning to that. Tick went ahead:–

"The woman – she was an utter stranger – came up to speak to me, and she told me that my little girl had gone into the cloak-room at the end of the last dance before the extras came on, complaining of a pain in her side. She had sat down and died of heart disease as she sat! *This was at the end of the last pukka waltz. Do you hear me? I tell you it was at the end of the last pukkla waltz!*"

[I don't know much about printing presses; but if you printer fellows have got any type big enough and awful enough to give any idea of the way in which Tick said that you are seven pounds better than I thought.]

I felt as if all the winds in the Hills were crawling round my hair You know that cold, creepy feeling at the top of the scalp, just when the first dropping shots begin, and before the real shindy starts. Well, that was how I felt – how we all felt, in fact – when Tick had finished and brought down his hand again on the table.

We shifted about as if our chairs were all red-hot, trying to think of something pleasant to say. Tick kept on repeating – "*It was at the end of the last pukka waltz!*" Then he'd stop for a bit and rock to and fro; and ask us what he was to do. Whether "a betrothal to a dead woman was binding in law," and so on – sometimes laughing and sometimes chucking his head about like my second charger when the curb-chain's tighter than it should be.

It may sound awfully funny to read now; but I assure you sitting round the Mess table with Tick's white and blue face in front of one and Tick's awful way of laughing and talking in one's ears, the fun did not dawn on us till a long time after. And even then we weren't grateful.

Our Colonel was the first to move. The old man got up and put his hand on Tick's shoulder, and begged him, for his own sake, not to take it to heart so much. Said that he was unwell, and had better go to his own quarters. Tick chucked up his head again and regularly yelled:– "I tell you I have seen it with my own eyes. I wish to Heaven it had been a delusion." All this time the Colonel was soothing him down, just as you or I would gentle a horse; and the other Johnnies stood round and mumbled something about being awfully sorry for his trouble, and that, if they'd known it, they would have dropped pulling his leg like a shot. Whether it was too much liquor, or whether Tick really had seen a ghost, we didn't stop to think. He was so awfully cut up no one could have helped being sorry for him.

Well, I and another Johnnie went with him over to his quarters, and Tick chucked himself down on the charpoy and buried his face in the pillow; and his shoulders shook as if he were sobbing like a woman. The other Johnnie turned the lamp down, and we left him and went back to Mess. There we sat up the rest of the night pretty nearly, the lot of us; *bukhing* about ghosts and delusions, and so on. We were all pretty certain that Tick hadn't got the "jumps" or anything foolish of that kind, because he was steady as a die in those things – 'couldn't have played to win unless his head had been fairly cool you know. Finally we decided that there was no need to tell anyone outside the Mess about the night's business, and that we were all awfully sorry for Tick. I want to remind you that *I* was sitting tight all this time. I thought of the Customs' mark on the bear skins, and browsed quietly over a peg. About parade time we went to bed. Tick turned up awfully haggard and white on parade.

He took the noon down-train to Lahore that day and cleared out, he didn't tell us where to, on a few days' leave. We did not look at his quarters. Three of us went over to the Club that afternoon, and the first thing a man asked us was "what we thought of it?" Then all the Johnnies in the smoking-room began to laugh, and then they began to roar. It seems that that blackguard Tick had been over to the Club directly after parade and told all the men there about his yarn over-night, and the way we'd sucked it in from the Colonel downwards. It was all over Pindi before nightfall; and you may guess how they chaffed us about "pukka waltzes" and men with "dandy rugs" and whether a "betrothal to a dead woman was binding in law." Just you ask one of the 45th that question, and see what happens! When we three rode back to Mess I can tell you

that we didn't feel proud of ourselves. There was a regular indignation
meeting on, and everyone was talking at the top of his voice. Fellows
who had just come in from polo, or from making calls, had all been told
of it; and they wanted Tick's blood.

The whole blessed business was a *benow* from beginning to end,
and we had believed it! We moved over to Tick's quarters to begin by
making hay there. Nothing except the chairs and charpoy (and those
belonged to Government) had been left behind. Over the mantelpiece
a double sheet of note-paper had been pinned, and above this, in letters about two-foot high, was written in charcoal on the wall:– "The
Unlimited Draw of Tick Boileau." The Beast had carefully written out
the whole yarn from beginning to end, with stage directions for himself
about yelling and looking half mad, in red ink at the sides. And he had
left that behind for our benefit.

It was a magnificent "sell;" but nothing except Tick's acting would
have pulled it off in the perfect way it went. We stopped dead, and just
pondered over the length and the breadth and the thickness of it. If we'd
only thought for a minute about the improbability of a woman dying
at a Mussoorie ball without the whole of Upper India knowing it we
might have saved ourselves. But that's just what we didn't do. And if
you'd listened to Tick you'd have followed our lead.

Tick never came back. I fancy he had a sort of notion it wouldn't
have been healthy for him if he had. But we've started a sort of Land
League – what do you call it? Vehmgericht? – in our Mess; and if we
come across him anywhere we're going to make things lively for him.
He sent in his papers and went down to Pachmarri, where it seems he
really *was* engaged to a girl with money – something like two thousand a year, I've heard, – married her, and went home. Of course he
had spent his three months' leave at Pachmarri too. We found that out
afterwards.

I don't think I should have taken all that trouble and expense (for
the Mess room is full of those horns and heads) to work out a sell like
that, even if it had been as grand a one as "The Unlimited Draw of Tick
Boileau."

P.S. – Just you ask any one of us if "a betrothal to a dead woman is
binding in law," and see what happens. I think you'll find that I've written the truth pretty much.

My Christmas Caller

or

The Prescription of Sieur Asmodeus

Published: *Civil and Military Gazette*, 25 December 1885.

Attribution: In Scrapbook 1 (28/1, p. 41).

Text: *Civil and Military Gazette*.

Notes: Asmodeus, or the Limping Devil, comes from *Le Diable Boiteux* (1707) by Alain René Lesage. In Lesage's book Asmodeus provides the same sort of service that he does in Kipling's story. 'The Land of Regrets' is the title and refrain of a poem by Sir Alfred Lyall, prominent Indian civil servant; at the time of this story he was Lieutenant Governor of the North-West Provinces and Oudh. RK alludes to the poem in a letter of 10 June 1884 (*Letters*, 1, 68).

The narrator's name in full – Hastings Macaulay Elphinstone Smallbones – alludes to three important figures in British Indian history. For Hastings and Macaulay, see the headnote to 'Dis Aliter Visum'. Mountstuart Elphinstone (1779–1859) was Governor of Bombay, 1819–27, and the author of a *History of India*.

'My Christmas Caller' has been reprinted in *Kipling's India; Uncollected Sketches*, and in the *Kipling Journal*, December 2015.

"I am strictly proper now" said a voice from behind the big almirah which forms the principal ornament of my bachelor dining-room.

Now it couldn't have been the Bearer, because in the first place he doesn't speak English and in the second, if he did, even he dare not utter so huge a fib. This was on Christmas Eve, yesterday – a day of all days in the year I detest because it makes me homesick, and morose and irritable. That's why I always keep within doors and reflect on all the unpleasant things I know – the disgusting ingratitude of the Punjab Government to an able and efficient officer among others.

"Strictly proper, and immensely improved since Le Sage's time" repeated the voice from behind the almirah. "May I come in?"

"Come in" said I shortly, for my thoughts were not pleasant ones. As a rule, I dislike men dropping in uncalled for.

"Thanks many. Will you make room for me at the fire? – your almirah's rather drafty."

It was the Le Diable Boiteux. I recognised him even before I read the card which he presented. As he said, he was wonderfully improved frm Le Sage's inimitable but somewhat coarse original. A neat dress suit, studs, a rose in his button-hole, and a pair of immaculate pumps had converted him into a very pleasant gentleman of the nineteenth century, with a slight – a very slight – limp. He pulled an arm-chair up to the fire, and stretched out his feet to the blaze.

"Hope I haven't inconvenienced you in any way, Smallbones?" he said.

"Not in the least I assure you *mon ami*. I've had the pleasure of knowing you so long by name, that it's almost like meeting an old acquaintance."

Le Diable Boiteux did not seem pleased:– "You knew me at once then" he said. "On my honour I shouldn't have thought it. I've changed so – improved I may fairly say – of late years."

He adjusted the rose in his buttonhole with a look of ineffable complacency. "Le Sage – old Alain René you know – evolved me in the first instance; and since then I've been marching in the van of progress. I *hope* you understand that my moral improvement is on a par with my physical. I'm a reformed character. One of these days I may even lose my tail!"

He must have tucked it into his inexpressibles, for never a sign of a tail could I see.

"You were much nicer as you were, I think" said I judicially. "Reforms are bad things."

"Don't generalize. In your department perhaps. In mine, never. Just conceive me if you can, knocking about the back streets of Madrid with a vagabond student! I wonder how I could ever have been so low. But I've used my opportunities well, haven't I?"

"I don't know. It seems to me you've spoilt, if you'll pardon my saying so, a really superior – ahem – Devil to make a very every-day English gentleman."

"Spoilt!" retorted Le Diable Boiteux. "I'll show you whether reform has curtailed my executive powers. By the head of the great God Mammon, I can strip off a roof as neatly as ever! Would you like to see me do it?"

"I beg your pardon a thousand times" I said "but I really thought from your appearance you had taken your place permanently with us."

"Say no more about it" returned my guest courteously. "I'm of an excitable nature – easily roused, but over in a flash, you know. And it *was* hard to call my powers in question, just when I'm going to give you a sample of them – a first class *séance* in fact. I've toured all over India to see if there was a more discontented man than yourself in the country, and there isn't. Consequently – *me voici*. Can I take a cigarette?"

"By all means. But my dear Devil, it is hardly necessary to remind a man of the world – I may say of *both* worlds – like yourself, that to call your host discontented, after hiding in his almirah and toasting your shins over his fire is not good form."

"True" said Le Diable Boiteux – "but I've been attending a meeting of a Bombay Cotton Mills Company, and there's nothing so democratic as shareholders in bulk. Still the fact remains that you *are* the most discontented man in India, and I'm going to spend an evening with you for your benefit and my amusement."

"One moment though, my dear Sir! If I'm to go careering about on your back through this frosty night all over the station, I must really put on my ulster."

My guest sprang to his feet, and addressed me oratorically:– "Hastings Macaulay Elphinstone Smallbones! I ask you as a sane and sober man, *do* you think that I, a self-respecting gentleman, so advanced that I've almost forgotten the use of my wings, shall deliberately expose myself to rheumatism and bronchitis by flapping from roof to roof of this particularly chilly station with you on my back? Why you must ride nearly fourteen stone!"

"Thirteen seven to be strictly accurate, Devil. How *am* I to guess how you are going to manage your *séance*, except after the approved fashion of Le Sage? You really ought to stick to it, you know."

"What a fine old crusted Conservative it is! Besides I'm not a devil any longer. I've been promoted to the place of a benevolent imp, first class, third grade, *sub. pro tem.* In time I shall be a graded Goblin, entitled to draw the pay and allowances of a Robin Goodfellow. Ha! Ha! Le Sage never contemplated *that*! Conduct my *séances* after his bungling manner – not I! Science has done wonders since his death, and I avail myself gratefully of her aid. Come my friend let us begin!"

"I don't quite know what you're going to do; but give me your word there's nothing wrong with the business – no writing in blood or any lunacy of that kind."

Le Diable Boieaux laughed merrily:– "Blood and parchments and sulphur are relics of an effete and outworn generation. They served their purpose in life; and in death you use 'em for the Christmas magazines. I dropped them – let me see – a hundred and forty years ago or there-abouts. No, my methods would make old Le Sage stand aghast with horror. Look here." He lifted delicately between his finger and thumb a pair of *pince nez*, that till then had been reposing unobserved on the ample contours of his waistcoat, slung from his neck by a cord.

"Ever used a telephone?" said Le Diable Boiteux airily. "Sometimes" I answered; the telephone in my office being the bane of my daily life. "That's all right" said Le Diable Boiteux. "You will see when you put them on, that this pair of glasses is to the eye exactly what the telephone is to the ear. One hundred and fourteen years hence similar instruments will be invented by your kind, when you shall have brought electro-magnetism to a higher pitch of perfection. Let me slip the cord over your head and adjust the nippers on your nose. It's an improvement on roof-lifting. What do you want to see?"

I reflected for an instant. Le Diable Boiteaux nudged me in the ribs.

"I know what you are thinking of *mon ami*. What you are pleased to call Home. Be it so. You shall see it."

Even as he spoke, I found myself staring at the hustle and bustle out-side the Criterion. The fog hung heavy over Piccadilly, and there came to my nose, or seemed to come, that delightful composite odour of gas, orange peel and hot asphalte so characteristic of Babylon the mighty. I am a Cockney by birth and education, and both sight and smell were inexpressibly delightful to me.

"Oh for a glimpse of my own people!" I sighed aloud.

The scene shifted in a flash, and I was staring at my two brothers, my sisters and a host of relations gathered round a mid-day dinner in the old brown house in West Brompton.

"Hideous notion, eating a heavy meal in the middle of the day'" mur-mured the Le Diable Boiteux in my ear. "It would kill me in a week. Your people seem to be enjoying themselves though: listen a bit and see how much you are in their thoughts."

I listened attentively for about ten minutes, before it dawned upon me that Le Diable Boiteux was speaking sarcastically. I heard much – the babble of fifteen tongues over turkey and beef and ham and all manner of dainties; but for any reference to myself I might have been dead and buried a century back. Stay, though, when the dinner was at an end, and everyone was toasting every one else, a small curly-locked boy brought down his pudgy fist on the table with a bang, and gravely swallowing a wine glass full of water cried:– "Uncle Djimmy! He gived me my bwicks." So my health was drunk in water by a baby unnoticed in the general uproar.

"What *can* you expect?" said Le Diable Boiteux soothingly. "You never 'gived' the others 'bwicks' my dear fellow. Just face the fact that the best and kindest of one's own people drop you out of their lives as much as you drop out of theirs. Unpleasant notion I admit; but it is so. You haven't been home for eight years, and that youngster's 'bwicks' only came a month ago. However, try some more, and see if any one remembers. The nippers will work as fast as you can think."

I tested their powers exhaustively, and found that Le Diable Boiteux had spoken the truth in both instances. They enabled me to see and hear as quickly as I could think, and also to understand that Hastings Macaulay Elphinstone Smallbones had disappeared from the thoughts of all the great family of Smallbones as well as from the minds of his friends. Eight years' absence is a long time, I am willing to allow; but still I expected that I should have heard my name mentioned at the Christmas gatherings of our clan.

"Human nature all the world over" murmured Le Diable Boiteux once more. "Didn't old Alan René make me show Don Cleofas something of the same kind? You know his works better than I."

Le Sage was the last person in my mind as the visions flashed past. I was penetrated with a deep sense of my personal insignificance – a wholesome but unpleasant experience which some men go through life and miss. I made no answer, but continued to gaze steadfastly through the magic *pince-nez*. Sisters, cousins, aunts – I have two – old and once dear friends at home, had all alike forgotten me in their Christmas feastings. And here had I been nursing my *heimweh* over my solitary fire, and hungering for the sight of their faces – aye even for a glimpse of the surliest and least loveable among them!

Le Diable Boiteux broke in once more upon the current of my thoughts and his pictures.

"Haven't you seen enough yet?" he enquired. 'Take my word for it – in the multitude of their occupations and interests and desires they have naturally enough forgotten you. What else would you have? See! Your elder sister has six, and your younger four children – ten good and substantial reasons for forgetfulness. Blisworth is gone to Australia; Billiter is engaged; Von Downiski gone to the dogs, Pawson of your college going, if my old insight is what it used to be; and Teague so superbly successful in the things of your penny-farthing world, that he'd cut you if you spoke to him."

"But – but – these were all my oldest friends!" stammered I, still glaring at the pictures as they fled past.

"I know it –" returned Le Diable Boiteux composedly. "(Can I have another cigarette. Thanks.) That's why it does you good to look at 'em. Old Alan René himself couldn't have improved on the notion!"

(Le Diable Boiteux seemed to relish referring to his creator in this flippant way – just as a shopboy might snatch a fearful joy from calling his employer by his surname unadorned.) He gently tweaked the *pince-nez* off my nose, and patted me familiarly on the shoulder.

"It's unpleasant, but it is also necessary. The memory of you isn't so indispensably necessary to the comfort of your extensive family circle as you would like to believe. You have all gone your own ways in the world, and you naturally lose touch. Do you mean to say that you've been eating your heart out all these eight years through sheer home-sickness and dislike of your surroundings?"

"I'm afraid so," I murmured.

"Skittles!" retorted Le Diable Boiteux scornfully, flicking the ash off his cigarette. "It's your morbid vanity. You don't see a maravedi's worth of good – I mean a *pice* worth of good in the whole country, do you?"

"I'm—blessed, if I do" I responded fervently. "Don't swear" said Le Diable Boiteux. "It's not good form. Only Doré's[1] imps do it with us, and they are reckoned very low in the social scale. His anatomy always *was* most queer you know. Well as I was saying, it's your morbid vanity that makes you a dull, discontented, commonplace, unsocial man. Why *can't* you accept the conditions of your life?"

"You are rude Asmodeus," I retorted, calling him by his (un)Christian name.

"How often am I to tell you that I'm no more related to the genuine Asmodeus[2] than you are? Old Alain René gave me that name, but I'm only one of his creations all the same – just like Guzman D'Alfarasche and the rest. Homilies aren't much in my line, or I'd read you one as long as my ta – hum, as long as my arm. There's a deal of good in this 'Land of Regrets' as one o' your fools of songsters called it. An enormous amount of good. Just look here'" He slipped the *pince-nez* on my nose, and stood behind me like a lecturer before a magic lantern.

"Here's old Battlesby of the Commission. You know him and hate him, don't you? Screw, cold blooded old reptile and all the rest of it? He's in his *duftar* now, spending Christmas eve in a way that would startle you. Look over his shoulder!"

I peeped, and saw, to my unutterable surprise, that old Battlesby was writing cheques, and no meagre ones either, in favour of five or six charities I'd never heard of. I hate charities – specially for whitey-brown little boys who snivel and wear magenta comforters and sing hymns on state occasions in tuneless falsetto. Battlesby, however, seemed to appreciate them as much as he did soldiers' children, drunken mariners, widows, or hospitals. The way that grey headed old skinflint squandered his cash in the ten minutes that I looked over his shoulder was sinful!

"Bad going over the Chedputter race course, Smallbones, when you were stationed there I fancy?" said the Devil. "But there's a first class thing in the way of Christmas dinners for loafers to come out of it. Pity Battlesby didn't subscribe, isn't it?"

"Go on to the next picture Devil" I said sharply. "Ha! Ha!" chuckled Le Diable Boiteux. "You didn't know him, wouldn't come out of your shell to know him; believed the worst you heard – and lost a good friend. Bravo Smallbones! Let me introduce Mrs. McStinger – another person you don't love."

"Tongue set on edge by the fires of" – "Hush!" interrupted Le Diable Boiteux. "Not in *my* presence. She's a tongue of her own I admit, but here she is in camp."

Mrs. McStinger was seated in a double-poled tent with McStinger by her side, addressing Christmas cards – some fifty at least. "What a wicked waste of time and money" I growled.

"Not in the least" said Le Diable Boiteux. "She uses the ones she receives to send on, being a thrifty soul, but there isn't a man in the

Commission who knows her, who doesn't worship her. Look at young Sapless, he's sent her a ten-rupee card fit for a girl of eighteen. Who pulled Sapless through his go of typhoid by sheer nursing? Who lent Crane her own shawl-wrap when the boy was coughing himself dead on a frosty night after a Cinderella? Who looked in on the quiverful of kids when their governess was down with diptheria? I've the whole world to see after, and you've only got about three hundred people to know and like; and *yet* I know more about the McStinger than you do. That's another case where you wouldn't take the trouble to know; *would* take the trouble to dislike – with the usual result. Come, I haven't half done yet. Shut your eyes a minute, while I see if I can work a panorama of the province on this size of lens. The instrument's as good as they make 'em; but it mayn't stand the strain."

I closed my eyes obediently, while he whipped off the *pince-nez*, did something to them, and resettled them upon my nose. There then appeared a perfect miniature picture of the province in which I have the honour to serve, from Peshawur to Delhi – all as clear and as finished as if I had been merely looking down from the top of the Ghor Kathri[3] on to the city below. It was a most curious sensation to watch this tiny struggling world, and to catch the clamour that came up from it.

As I looked, I saw that my brothers were filled – for a time at least – with that peace and good will which for my part I do not pretend to understand. I gazed and gazed and gazed again, and saw and heard English men and women exchanging good wishes and congratulations; saw the letters that bore these flying north and south and east and west in the trains; heard the arrangements for dinners, "weeks", picnics, dances and the amusements that bring together our scattered bands from Khaibar to the sea being canvassed and discussed; saw old estrangements and misunderstandings, petty spites, small envies and jealousies die away under my feet as the hoarfrost dies when the sun shines; saw hand meet hand in friendly grasp, and in one station – wild horses shall not induce me to say where – lip meet lip behind the sheltering shade of a clump of bougainvillea.

I chuckled audibly at this last. "Never mind" said Le Diable Boiteux cheerily, "I've got my eye on 'em, and I think I shall personally interest myself in seeing that that little business runs smoothly. Now just take a look at yourself. Morbid vanity is of use at times."

I looked, and wherever I looked I saw myself a figure of enormous proportions "out of it." There is no other way to describe the manner in which it was brought home to me that I had neither part nor lot in the general mirth around. No letters save of the most business-like nature were borne to me by the flying mail trains; for me no telegraph clerk clicked out a message of good cheer from some far off friend; in arrangements of balls and "weeks" I stood outside all the arrangements, alone and unconsulted. The very subscription papers for these merry makings flew every way but mine; and gigantic and grotesque in the foreground loomed my dinner table laid with dinner *for one*, and decorated by my Khitmagar with a few frost-nipped roses.

"Cheerful sight isn't it?" said Le Diable Boiteux. "By the way, you're the only man in the province who dines alone to-night from choice and not necessity. *One* bottle Bass, *one* tumbler, *one* chair and *one* lamp. Very pretty arrangement indeed!"

Le Diable Boiteux fell back a step, and contemplated the panorama in the *pince-nez* with an air of critical satisfaction. While I gazed on the huge presentment of myself, that stopped now like a cloud on the hills of Peshawur; anon stepped over the Indus at Attock; rested on the Dharmsala peaks and blocked out the view of the Simla range, I began to grow uneasy. *I was utterly alone in the province.*

"Devil" said I shuddering, "I am frightened."

"Oh it's all right. You're not so big in everybody's eyes you know."

"It isn't that, Devil,'" I replied. "Can't you see that I am alone in the whole panorama? It's awful – Here roll it up or take the jugglery away."

"Can't I see? Of course I can. But you might ha' seen it any time this eight years if you'd cared to look. Magnificently your chin comes out against the sunset by Mooltan, doesn't it? Yes, you are completely alone on this Christmas Eve in the year of grace 1885 – after eight years passed in the country. What do you think of it?"

"Devil, I don't like it at all. It's very horrible! Can you get it altered?"

"It rests with Monsieur alone as old Alain René would have said. Which life would you prefer? Eating out your heart after a life you can't get and which wouldn't be the faintest pleasure to you when you'd got it; let alone the fact that it doesn't want you in the least; or coming out of your shell, taking some trouble to know the people you've cast in your lot with, and finding the 'Land of Regrets' (I should really like to pay the man who wrote that nonsense a visit), a country of charity, and kind offices, and good will, and broad thought and honest human helpfulness and – Well, homilies aren't in my line, but you can fill in the rest from what you've seen."

"There's no choice about the matter, Devil. My mind's made up. But how am I to set about it?"

"So bad as that, is it? Go round and mix with your fellows to begin with; though it's too late for any one to ask you their Christmas dinner now. Where was I? Yes, mix with your fellows and – by the great Alain René himself – I had nearly forgotten the most important part of the prescription! Bend low and Il whisper."

⁂

"But that's nonsense Devil!" I said. "She'll never accept me!"

"Try and see! I can't say *I'm* fond of grumpy recluses of your kidney. But there's no accounting for tastes."

He fell to reckoning up my table gear as before while I laughed aloud out of sheer comfort of heart at the prospect he had opened to me.

"Well, I'm off. Goodnight, Smallbones" said Le Diable Boiteux settling himself into his ulster.

"Oh Devil, Devil!" I cried. "I'm afraid you're an awful imposter. Is *this* the end of your homily?"

"I wish you wouldn't call me 'Devil'" said Le Diable Boiteux, as he pushed the *chick* aside preparatory to stepping into the verandah. "Don't you know my other name?"

"No, indeed!"

"'Le Dieu Cupidon: car les poetes m'ont donné ce joli nom et ces messieurs me peignent fort avantageusement' – Queer French perhaps, but old Alain René never wrote a truer word."[4]

He dropped the *chick* with a bang, and I woke up.

⁂

My Le Sage and Dickens had tumbled on to the floor from the reading table.

47

"Bearer!" quoth I, "*Mi aj rat nautch kojaiga Larens Hall men. Khana ki kupra thaiyar karo*"[5]

There's nothing like taking a prescription on the spot.

H. M. E. Smallbones.

[1] Gustave Doré (1832–83) French artist, who illustrated *The Divine Comedy* and *Paradise Lost* among many other titles.
[2] The 'genuine' Asmodeus is a devil who figures in the apocryphal Book of Tobit.
[3] The ancient city of Peshawar.
[4] 'The God Cupid, for the poets have given me that pretty name, and they present me very favourably.'
[5] 'Tonight I will go to the dance at the Lawrence Hall. Get my dinner clothes ready' (Harbord).

The History of a Crime
(After V-CT-R H-G-O)

Published: *The Englishman*, 3 February 1886.

Attribution: In Scrapbook 1 (28/1, p. 57).

Text: *The Englishman*.

Notes: This is the first of four comic articles in Frenchified English that RK published in India (see 'Les Miserables', *CMG*, 28 August 1886; 'Le Roi en Exil', *CMG*, 15 November 1888; and 'An Interesting Condition', *Pioneer*, 20 December 1888). RK explained their genesis in 'Souvenirs of France': 'At that time –'83 to '88 – the French Press was not nationally enamoured of England. I answered some of their criticisms by what I conceived to be parodies of Victor Hugo's more extravagant prose. The peace of Europe, however, was not seriously endangered by these exercises.' They do not, in fact, have anything to do with 'French criticisms' but have a local reference.

The topic here is the financial measures of the Indian government, measures that RK also satirised at this time in 'The Rupaiyat of Omar Kal'vin', *CMG*, 30 January 1886, when, as the heading to that poem puts it, 'Government struck from our incomes two per cent' (*Departmental Ditties*).

Sir Auckland Colvin, the finance minister responsible for the new measures, sent a note to RK complimenting him on the 'wit and delicate humour' of 'The Rupaiyat of Omar Kal'vin', but included a reply to the criticisms expressed in RK's poem with a poem of his own called 'Proverbs of Sillyman' (*Pioneer*, 5 February 1886) in the form of 'a parody of Solomon's proverbs'. RK then 'rushed a Victor Hugo skit into a Calcutta paper in revenge' – that is, 'The History of a Crime' (*Letters*, 1, 120). The epithets for the three 'Sirs' – 'huge', 'ascetic' and 'taciturn' – are meant to be wildly inappropriate.

The Englishman was a Calcutta paper to which RK contributed a few poems as well as this skit. 'The History of a Crime' has been reprinted in the Martindell–Ballard pamphlets, in *The Victorian*, July 1939,[1] and in Harbord, 11, 1054–6.

"*Et la dèche eternelle regne de nouveau!*" It was Sir Colvin who spoke. He who reads the classics of *la belle France* and above all *Sara Barnum*.[2]

49

He is a great man. *Oui*. Can he understand Finance? No – a thousand times.

He has drawn pictures of ballet girls. No man who draws pictures of ballet girls understands Finance. One does not reconcile the Incompatibles.

They had dined then, these English Sirs – Sir Dufferin, Sir Colvin, and Sir Hunter.[3] They would now talk business. The Englishman talks while he digests. He is of the beef, beefy. Of the rum, rummy. He is very strange. Sometimes he plays the Devil at four. As these Sirs played it. – the huge Sir Dufferin – he who is Lord Maire of *les Indes Orientales* – the ascetic Sir Colvin – the taciturn Sir Hunter. I was there in the spirits. I write all. On the side board. It is my custom. It is my mission. I write all. It is my mission. I speak truth. It is my infirmity.

"They are patriots," said Sir Dufferin. "English colonists. Or it may be *les indigenes*. *N'import*. They are patriots."

"They are our servants," said Sir Colvin. "Enfin they are our slaves. What more would you?"

The amiable Sir Hunter wept. He sobbed. "I mourn. I am desolated. Alas my poor compatriots! Yet if so, why not more?"

He is a strange *mélange* this Taciturnity. He dissolves himself into tears and yet – But he is not an Englishman. He is a Scot, magnificent. He can explain anything. He can also write anything. It is said that he believes in what he writes. "*Que voulez-vous?*" A man must believe in something.

Sir Colvin did not weep. Have I said that he is an ascetic? It is true. He denies himself the luxury of tears.

"They will protest," said Sir Dufferin. "A people who protest are dangerous."

"They are our own countrymen," said Sir Colvin. "They will protest. It is their habit. They are a people of full habit. They must be bled."

Sir Colvin laughed. It was an epigram. It was also a Financial Exigency. She is the stepmother of Necessity, and has no bowels. But it must not be forgotten that she is the daughter of Sir Colvin who drew the pictures of the ballet girls.

She is the offspring of the union of the Two Incompatibilities.

They protested – after the manner of their country. That is to say, they growled. You British are the only nation that growl when you are disturbed. We – *nous Français* – shriek. It is *spirituel*. But it is not so impressive!

The British Growl is pyramidal. Immense.

Also it is a great Sham.

What say then your grocermen of their drugs?

"Innocuous to the weakest constitution."

Perceive there the British growl epitomized in an advertisement. You English are all advertisement.

Sir Hunter sympathized. *Pourquoi non?* He sympathizes with all things. This Scot who is an Aryan.

Sir Colvin did not sympathize. He is without tact. *Mon Dieu*, how terrible!

He made *calembours*?[4] He laughed at the journals. He laughed also at the Madras journalist! Can you wonder that Madras did not love Sir Colvin?

After all, he was the father of the Financial Exigency.

Let us respect the claims of paternity. Even though Sir Colvin denies them. In the case of the Financial Exigency only. That is understood.

Then the tide rose. It was the *révanche* of that Lever without a Fulcrum, which men call the press of India. Sir Colvin had made *calembours*.

He was encountered by statements. Worse still, by letters which were brutal. They were more than brutal. They were *exposés*. They demonstrated the Crudity. They mangled the Necessity. They annihilated the Logic . They made clear the Unwisdom. They made Hay.

It is a free country. Therefore they must be silenced. A free country has its privileges. Also its financiers. It is a privilege to have a financier. How were they silenced? Can you ask?

Those three Sirs wrote together in the night through a Medium. What is a Medium? That is a mystery. But they wrote nevertheless.

There was an argument, an appeal, several appeals, also a threat, a hint, a suggestion. *Encore* an appeal. Bah! It makes evil to my stomach.

It was Brutality made printable. It was Insolence incarnate. It was Expediency exquise.[5] It was the apotheosis of the Financial Exigency.

You have not seen it?

How strange!

It is true that only an Englishman could have written it.

It is also true that only an Englishman could have read it without laughter – this *effronté* and cynical manifesto.

It threatens. It appeals. It menaces. It supplicates. Lastly, it is cursed with the curse of your land. It is without tact.

You, who are a nation of shopkeepers, do not know this. Perhaps it is as well. Can you laugh at it? No. Unfortunates that you are! To pay and yet not to laugh at the colossal Impudence. I have discharged my function. Are you still grave? Yes, *Mon Dieu! How* you English are fools!

[1] *The Victorian* was published by Victoria College, St Helier, Jersey. Several uncollected Kipling items appeared in it between 1935 and 1939, contributed by the noted Kipling collector Captain E. W. Martindell, an alumnus of the college.

[2] Marie Colombier, *Mémoires de Sarah Bernhardt*, 1884, a satiric treatment of Sarah Bernhardt's career.

[3] Sir William Wilson Hunter (1840–1900), member of the Supreme Council, 1881–7, and a frequent writer on all Indian subjects. RK was evidently much impressed by Hunter, though he treated him satirically here and in other stories in this collection as well as in the uncollected poem 'To the Address of W.W.H.', *Pioneer*, 1 June 1887 (*Poems*, III, 1885).

[4] Puns.

[5] The *ui* text reads 'exquied'.

Prisoners and Captives
(By One of Them.)

Published: *Civil and Military Gazette*, 4 March 1886.

Attribution: In Scrapbook 3 (28/3, p. 4).

Text: *Civil and Military Gazette*.

Notes: A lightly corrected galley proof of this article was sent by RK to W. C. Crofts and is now in the Rare Book Division of the Library of Congress (Carpenter Collection). The heading, ostensibly from the medieval legend of Prester John, is RK's imitation, suited to the story he tells.

'Prisoners and Captives' was reprinted in the Martindell–Ballard pamphlets and in Harbord, II, 1098–101.

> "Now in Prester John's country there be certain sillie Fowls which having wandered within the boundaries of this Sandie Sea, can in no wise escape, but flie miserable thereabove till they die."

"I can't get out" quoth the Starling, and Sterne, maudlin sentimentalist that he was, wept.[1]

Fellow Starlings, neither you nor I nor our mates nor our nestlings can get out; and Sterne, who would have immortalized us – had he no *liaison* on hand – is dead. The bars of our captivity are hard to endure, and the Black Water which divides us from the pleasant hedgerows, whence we came, broad and impassable. We are the "sillie fowle" of Prester John's country, who have flown eastward with a light heart, and find, all too late, that there is no return.

How does it come about? Who knows? or knowing, who would care to say? It may be we were froward Starlings in our youth – bold bad birds shipped eastward by wearied relatives in the fervent hope that we might never come back. It may be that we are weighed down by the claims of our own kind – that callow nestlings or old birds, flit merrily

53

over the home pastures at our expense; and that we must catch the early worm for several beaks beside our own. It may be that you or I are tied and bound by the chain of our own sins to these shores in a hundred thousand different ways. What is the good of curiosity? It is enough that we came here many, many years since; that we are always "going home" and we never go.

You know, my brothers and sisters, how this little peculiarity makes us a race of birds special and apart – a tribe whose members are bound together by a common bond of "tarrididdles;" (Our miserable pretences are too shallow to attain the dignity of "lies.") You know the tender regard we show for one another on such an occasion as this, for instance:– "I'm going home this spring" says a Starling predestinate to his friend. "Ah! 'was thinking that myself, if I can get leave" is the shameless response; and the two imposters fall a chirruping over plans for their holiday diversion.

But the one bird knows that the other has exactly as much chance of escape as he himself, and the other knows that *he* knows this; and so on and so on. Get leave indeed, my brother in bondage! You have the better part of a year's leave owing to you, and you know it! You will spend three months of that time flitting up and down Kashmir, and you know this also. "Go home!" The ship's keel is not yet laid that shall carry you westward; and to you is denied even the consolation of the pious and expatriated Chinaman – a pleasant southerly slope above the Pei-ho river, and a little gilt paper morn and evening. You and I and our mates and our nestlings are of the company of the Starlings who "can't get out."

Do we admit it? Not we. The Spartan boy with the stolen fox was a Sybarite to us. What did he know of *Heimweh* – that fiend persistent as Conscience – inevitable as Remorse? Liver, jaundice and fever are the lot of all birds, but we Starlings have the *Heimweh* Devil to ourselves. In the hot June mornings, when the white-heat sickens prostrate nature, he is with us, whispering cruellest suggestions of the glories of English fields or of rain-sodden English skies. In the Spring, when each day carries with it a suspicion of increasing heat, and the *Kōil*[2] rings the passing-bell of the cold weather, he is more impudent and clamourous than ever.

"What would you give for Home, Starling?" he asks. "What have you got to give? Your morning ride, which you loathe; your evening drive which you detest; the *kutcha-pukka* cage that gives you fever; the evening gossip, the small, small talk and the penny farthing scandal of the Assembly Rooms; your shadow of a ghost of a flirtation with Mrs. Such-an-One; your not too pleasant reminiscences of Mrs. Such-Another; your little ambitions and a dirty brown-backed cheque-book; your flickering spites, mean jealousies, small strifes and passing friend-ships. Give them away. Cast them behind you and go home – home where the lights shine and the great city smokes and roars and rattles under a chilly sky – where your own kith and kin are, and wherein lies the better part of your heart. Go home Starling! In dignity and decency, as befits a first class passenger by a first class line if possible; but, how-ever it is done, go home!"

I proved to this fellow only yesterday, by all the logic at my command, that he was a pestilent visionary and he was still for a while. This morn-ing the peach has blossomed in my garden, and I found him abroad and awake as soon as I had risen. He is *very* hard to kill. Day and night, night and day, for five weary years, has this frightful Imp clung to me till I begin to despair of shaking him off.

Fellow Starlings, he is bad enough in all conscience, when you are a young and (what mockery the word is?) gay bachelor bird. How does it fare with the mated Starlings? Surely ten thousand times more hardly.

(There was once a bird of passage called Trevelyan,[3] who wrote a book, and Time, the oldest and most ravenous of all birds, has turned into lies many of its statements. But Trevelyan twittered the truth in one particular; though I doubt if he knew the full bitterness of what he wrote. It is when the little Starlings should be returned to the nests of their fore-birds or when the mother bird sickens and droops, that the Devil of *Heimweh* falls upon us; bringing with him other devils.)[4]

The hopeless longing; the bitter remorse at opportunities missed, and silver squandered; the unavailing repentance and sickness of soul; all these we have. The burden is as heavy as we can bear. Think of it multi-plied by two – the impossible rendered more impossible, and the desire doubled! Let us live and die alone, Starlings, if we can.

But the advice is not likely to be accepted. Our ranks are ever increas-ing, and we form to-day no inconsiderable army in the land – we of the Lost Estate; ever amiable, spend-thrift babblers; infirm of purpose; incapable of self-denial; cursed with the curse of Reuben;[5] crushed with invisible burdens; pressed back, crippled, restrained, hampered, shack-led, bound and caged – we the Starlings who "can't get out." We exist from Peshawur to the sea, striving to be of good heart, and twittering our cheap jests and lying little hopes into one another's ears.

Look you fellow prisoners! I have been "going home" any time these five years. So have you. We have told each other about it many, many times, and we have pretended to believe what we said and heard.

The pitiless Indian spring us upon us now, and I assure you, on the word of a Starling, that "I'm thinking of going home you know." I shall tell you this at dinner parties, at afternoon tennis and at gatherings of all kinds. You will make answer with the same old, old lie:– "Ah! 'was thinking of that myself. May to August you know. Would P. and O. or Rubattino be better?"[6]

No! The keel is not yet laid that shall carry us home, and to us is debarred the consolation of the pious and repatriated Chinaman – a grave in his own land, among his own people.

---

[1] Laurence Sterne, 'The Hotel at Paris', in *A Sentimental Journey through France and Italy* (1768). Sterne encounters a caged starling that repeats this complaint. He tries to free it, but he does not say that he wept.

[2] A singing bird of the cuckoo family, named for its call during the mating season.

[3] (Sir) George Otto Trevelyan (1838–1928), Macaulay's nephew and the father of G. M. Trevelyan. When his father, Sir Charles Trevelyan, was appointed financial member of the Governor-General's Council in 1863, Trevelyan accompanied him to India as his private secretary. His observations about India were published in 1864 as *The Competition Wallah*, a copy of which was given to RK when he won the prize poem competition at school (*S. of M.*, p. 24).

[4] 'The drawbacks of Indian life begin to be severely felt when it becomes necessary to send the first-born home ... After two or three years have gone by, and two or three children have been sent home, your wife's spirits are longer what they were' (*The Competition Wallah*, 2nd edn, 1866, p. 127).

[5] 'Unstable as water, thou shalt not excel' (Genesis 49:4).

[6] The English Peninsular and Oriental Steam Navigation Co. and the Italian Rubattino Shipping Co., both serving India. The P & O is the subject of RK's poem 'The Exile's Line' (*Verse, Inclusive Edition*, II, 1322) and of the uncollected poem 'It was a ship of the P & O' (*Poems*, III, 1998).

"From Olympus to Hades"

Published: *Civil and Military Gazette*, 12 August 1886.

Attribution: In Scrapbook 3 (28/3, p. 40).

Text: *Civil and Military Gazette.*

Notes: RK himself had returned from a month in Simla in early August, no doubt with those feelings of hopeless dreariness assigned here to Ixion. The route from Simla to Lahore runs downhill to the river Gugger ('the Styx'), crossing at Kalka, and thence to the railway at Umballa. The mountain road was travelled by the two-wheeled *tonga*; the plains route by *dak gharry*.

RK sent a copy of the article to his old teacher, W. C. Crofts, with the comment that 'the Mythology of "Ixion" is a trifle mixed but one can't combine Olympus and the East without some sort of sacrifice' (14 September 1886: *Letters*, I, 138). The title is treated as a quotation; I know no source for it.

Reprinted in the Martindell–Ballard pamphlets and in Harbord, II, 1078–80.

Facilis descensus Averni[1]
It is easy to go downhill in a tonga

Whether Ixion had kissed a married goddess, and so drawn on his presumptuous head the wrath of the Insulted Gods, does not in the least concern us. It is enough to know that they returned him to his Wheel; despatching him downhill at the heels of the terrible horses of Dis, who are changed every five miles and live upon human flesh – when they can get it.

The sun was high in the heavens above the silver-roofed palaces of the gods[2] when Phaeton yoked the chargers to the instrument of torture arranged for the conveyance of Ixion –the Car of the Two Square Wheels, to be succeeded later on by the Bed of Procrustes.[3] And Ixion, watching drearily the tortuous downhill path which led from the gates of Olympus to the Abode of the Damned below, wept on the hillside; while Phaeton swore at the horses of Dis.

Far overhead among the asphodels passed Venus, in her chariot drawn by four dusky Cupids; and she looked down at Ixion and smiled. But the smile brought him no comfort, for he knew that as soon as he had passed beyond her sight, she would turn to Mars – offensive Mars, who dwelt in a suburb of Olympus – and bestow no further thought upon him. Hereat Phaeton bade him mount the Car of the Two Square Wheels, and the mist rolling up from the Plains of the Damned, hid alike Venus, and Olympus, and all the world, even to the very ears of the mettlesome horses of Dis, who chewed each other's manes in alternate bites, and wrangled as they went along.

So he fled – downward ever downward – through chill mists to warmer ones into the heated heavy air, of the Plains of the Damned, which closed above the head of Ixion like hot oil. And he gasped as they brought out the Bed of Procrustes and laid it on wheels and Ixion atop; and yoking fresh horses, set off to the borders of the Styx which is the uttermost boundary between the lowlands of Olympus and the Plains of the Damned. Now the nature of the Styx is this. When a soul is released from torment and would escape speedily to the Gods, that river is always in flume[4] or spate; but when a soul returns again to its troubles and would fain linger on the road, the river may be overpast dry-foot at the tails of the Oxen of Hercules whom Phaeton drives. And it was while he lay on the Bed of Procrustes, which fits no man but racks everyone, that Ixion met a host of released spirits flying upward to Olympus, and they gibed at him and laughed and made merry as they went along; assured in the knowledge that their troubles for a time were ended. So Ixion cursed and went down; wondering whether Venus had already forgotten him, and thinking with no pleasure of the Wheel to which he returned. Since the Wheel of Ixion may never stop, it had been arranged by the Gods that a substitute should spin thereon, while Ixion gathered breath in Olympus; and this substitute went Ixion to relieve.

Worn and ill-tempered, dusty and hungry, Ixion returned to the all-too-familiar Abode of the Damned, where his attendant spirits received him with a strained affectation of overpowering joy. From these creatures Ixion turned away, and sought the principal gathering place of the Damned, where thrice weekly the limp and flaccid spirits listen to the music of infernal choirs. The place was empty save for Sisyphus who was drinking deeply after the labours of the day. "Glad to see you, Ixion. There's your Wheel waiting for you." Ixion shuddered slightly and turned the conversation by inquiring after his friends. "Where's Radamanthus?" "Gone, a week ago; the Infernal Courts are up; didn't you know that?" "And Procrustes?" "On his bed as usual;-- with fever this time. He can't come out." "And Tantalus – surely Tantalus is here?" "No! It's a burning shame. He has managed to get a month's leave to which he's no more entitled than you are." (Ixion winced again.) "His substitute has got rheumatism from standing in that pond; besides nearly killing himself over the idiotic game of cherry-bob. No one can do Tantalus's work but Tantalus. He ought never to have been allowed to go up."

Sisyphus drank deeply and sighed. "And how does it go with you?" asked the new arrival. "In arrears as usual. Never saw such a stone. I fancied when all you fellows were gone, I'd have time to overtake the top of the hill; but it's as bad as ever it was. Nothing but arrears of work and no chance of clearing it off." "You should get an assistant" said Ixion dreamily. He was thinking of his own Wheel, and wondered in what condition he would find it. "Assistant," snorted Sisyphus. "Do you suppose Pluto gives assistants to a man who *wants* 'em?" Here the indignant stone-hoister launched into ten minutes' abuse of the administration of Hades, which, as he had heard it all before at least five hundred times, did not interest Ixion. He was thinking of Venus – and Mars – which accounts for his next question. "Sisyphus, you're uninteresting. By the way, any of the Danaids⁵ down still?"

"Danaids! What in Hades do you want with Danaids? I think there are two left, but Æsculapius has ordered one off to Olympus this evening, and the other leaves at mid-day." So saying, Sisyphus dragged himself lazily out of his chair and lounged back to his stone which he had managed to "skid" with rolls of paper pending his interval for rest and refreshment.

"Heighho!" yawned Ixion. "I'd better get over to my Wheel. The other fellow will be wanting to go." Ixion was right. The substitute received him with every demonstration of delight, for spinning didn't agree with him. "You'll find the Wheel in fair working order," said the substitute, stepping off and straightening himself. Never had the worn and polished wood-work, the faded and blistered paint, the well-thumbed straps, and sun-warped spokes looked less inviting. The axle wanted oiling, and creaked dolefully, as Ixion gave the tire a preliminary spin with his hand. "H–m," quoth Ixion; "it's not nice to look at. But I s'pose I must."

"Good-bye," said the substitute; "see you again some day I suppose. I'm off to Olympus to-night" . . . . and he disappeared. Ixion took off his coat, hitched his arms through the straps, settled his feet on the rests, and with a dry, austere grunt the great Wheel began its monotonous course afresh.

It is spinning still.

---

1 'The descent to Avernus is easy' (Virgil, *Aeneid*, VI, 126).
2 Many Simla buildings were tin-roofed.
3 The *tonga* and the *dak gharry* (see Glossary).
4 'flame' in *CMG*; 'flume' in Martindell–Ballard and Harbord.
5 The fifty daughters of Danaus, condemned to carry water in a sieve. I do not find any special relation to Mars in the story.

"Les Miserables."
A Tale of 1998

Published: *Civil and Military Gazette*, 28 August 1886.

Attribution: In Scrapbook 3 (28/3, pp. 43–4).

Text: *Civil and Military Gazette.*

Notes: For RK's several exercises in Frenchified English, see the headnote to 'The History of a Crime'. The decline in the exchange value of the rupee was a standard topic for most of RK's years in India.

Reprinted in the Martindell–Ballard pamphlets and in Harbord, II, 1081–3.

> "The rupee grows each week more worthless for any purpose
> but that of immediate spending. Under these circumstances,
> who could wonder if a spirit of recklessness should have taken
> possession of the Anglo-India community; if the text of
> to-day should be 'let us eat and drink, for to-morrow we fast.'"
> —*See yesterday's Simla letter.*

To be virtuous one must be happy.

This is a fact. More. It is a fact which can be proved.

And to be happy, it is necessary to be rich. How rich, do you ask? Enormously – Vanderbiltonically! As were once Messieurs les Anglais in the land of Dupleix and Plassey.[1]

Ces Anglais who have now disappeared.

You smile? It is not so then?

I have with my proper eyes seen them abolished – assimilated – blotted out – these Consuls and Pro-Consuls so arrogant. Listen to my tale.

The Roupé was a coin abnormal – monstrous.

It wavered.

Have you ever seen a franc waver? A Napoleon? No, ten thousand times.

The English are a nation of drunkards. All drunkards waver. The Roupé caught the contagion. *Voila* the explication. Let us return to our sheep.

I abhor the involutions of Finance. They are to me detestable. And why? Alas, I am poor always.!

But this Roupé.

It wavered. It flickered. It sank. It descended.

It contracted itself as a lady in her corsage.

Have you, my pupil so virtuous, ever seen a lady in her corsage?

She contracts marvellously.

She is also lovely.

The Roupé contracted. But it was not lovely.

It was one schelling and eight pence.

It was one schelling and five pence.

It was one schelliing and two pence.

These English, once so arrogant, had been despondent.

They now laughed. It was the laughter of the Pit.

They grew reckless. It was the ferocious *abandon* of the unpitied.

The Englishman reckless, is the brute bestial.

He boxes. He drinks. He wallows. He runs about. He even rides a horse at full speed.

No logical man rides a horse at full speed.

The French are a nation of logical men.

⁂

The Roupé was one schelling.

For the Market useful? Perhaps. For the Bourse – for little economies? No.

It was not worth – said these English – a Dam.

What is the English Dam? Who knows? The National Deity it may be. These English rate their Gods cheaply.

They rated the Roupé still more cheaply.

They spent it. Mon Dieu, how they spent it! They scattered it. They disbursed it! They shed it. They spread it abroad like mud.

It was superb. It was also wise. The Roupé had no value outside that Empire of Pro-Consuls.

They could not return Home. To their fogs.

They could not despatch Home their progeny so numerous.

The English are a prolific race. They bear children, as they eat *biftecks*. Several at a time and often.

This is a weakness of the Englishman. Also of the Englishwoman.

Why should they then not dissipate their rentes?

They eat. They drank. Twice as much as usual. They died. Riotously. In scores.

It was a magnificent spectacle.

All nations are going to the Devil. They move, however, like glaciers.

The English are an avalanche of a nation.

The Roupé fell lower.

The English did their best. But they could not fall lower.

Then a strange thing happened.

The English Mees disappeared.

You do not know her. She is a thing marvellous. With Feet and Teeth. A creature *furibonde* who deals the blows of men, and plays savage games till she is warm to execration.

From the English Mees is evolved the English Matron.

She is large. She eats well. She snores in her sleep. Money – much money – is necessary to her sustenance.

There was no money in the country. Nothing but this revelry atrocious and diabolical.

The English Mees is a prude.

She withdrew. With her the English Matron.

They withdrew because there was no money. They were "schocked."

The woman of England is always "schocked" when there is no money.

It is to her a blasphemy.

Only the men remained. With their Roupé.

Which was now ninepence.

The Saturnalia was terrible!

Imagine, then, a nation of Englishmen, alone, at all hours drunk, rabid, raving, under the sun so enervating of the tropics.

Can you ask what followed?

The English Mees had withdrawn. Let us spare her blushes.

The Englishman turned cream colour, café-au-lait, brown, ochre, bistre.

You say it was the sun?

In a measure – yes.

He grew darker with succeeding generations.

The Roupé was now fourpence. With some British fractions.

It was then hard to find an Englishman of the type Saxon.

His hair was black.

His eye-ball was opal.

His calf thin.

His hand attenuated.

His mind . . .

Let us draw a veil over his mind.

It is enough to know that he sat on his heels in the fashion oriental.

A nation that sits upon its heels is lost.

Literally and metaphorically.

The English race in India was lost.

At the same time the Roupé disappeared.

A coincidence merely?

Mille tonneres, No!

You have underestimated the vengeance of the Gaul, and the power of the Parisian Bourse.

It was the *revanche* of Plassey, of Blenheim, of Crecy, of Agincourt: Of Waterloo!

---

[1] Joseph François Dupleix (1696–1763), Clive's French opponent in the struggle for mastery in India. The battle of Plassey, 1757, established British control of Bengal.

A Nightmare of Rule

Published: *Civil and Military Gazette*, 3 September 1886.

Attribution: In Scrapbook 3 (28/3, pp. 44–5).

Text: *Civil and Military Gazette.*

Notes: The sketch is no doubt prompted by the government's financial policy – 'a thief which took and restored not again' – and by the difficulty of fixing blame for that policy. The imagery and action satirise the Theosophy movement, then attracting much attention in India, where Helena Petrovna Blavatsky, the founder of the movement in 1875, had taken up residence in 1878. RK recalled her vogue thus: 'At one time our little world was full of the aftermaths of Theosophy as taught by Madame Blavatsky to her devotees. My Father knew the lady and, with her, would discuss wholly secular subjects; she being, he told me, one of the most interesting and unscrupulous imposters he had ever met' (*Something of Myself*, p. 35).

RK also satirises the movement in 'The Sending of Dana Da' (*Soldiers Three*), which opens thus: 'Once upon a time, some people in India made a new Heaven and a new Earth out of broken tea-cups, a missing brooch or two, and a hair-brush. These were hidden under bushes, or stuffed into holes in the hillside, and an entire Civil Service of subordinate Gods used to find or mend them again.'

Reprinted in the Martindell–Ballard pamphlets and in Harbord, ii, 1088–90.

Now, because IT was a thief which took and restored not again – not once but twelve times yearly – and wrote vain tales, and wrought confusion in places and brewed anger among men, I said:– "I will go forth and will not rest until I find the Government of India; and I will straightway disembowel IT and force IT to disgorge. Needs must that IT is somewhere to be found concrete, and therefore vulnerable." With me came the Greybeard of the Himalayas – even the great Mahatma Koot Humi Lal Singh – the Wizard of the Broken Tea Cup. We sware by the Public Works Department and the heads of all the Members of Council, from the young man who sits on the left of the Viceroy to the old men who nod and wink at either end of the long polished table, that we would find the Government of India.

So we went first to the Responsibilities and Co-responsibilities; the Accessories before and after the Act; the men who present their Bills to each other at the polished table; and we asked: – "Are ye the Government of India – the IT that we have set forth to unmask and utterly abash?" And they answered with the collective voice of disclaimer: – "Alas, no! We are the Hands.!" Then we saw that they all – even the most untruthful among them, and he is *very* untruthful – said the thing which was. So we left the Responsibilities after their kind and the Accessories in their degree and went our way.

"It may be" cried the Greybeard of the Himalayas "it may be that IT has fled to other and narrower paths – to the Milky Way of the Lesser Lights." So we haled these into our presence – all the Lesser Lights, from Mars whose house is in the North, to Sirius, who rails among the palm-trees in the South – from the star who sheds his rays in the West, to him who burns hard by the Newer East.

But they answered with one accord:– "Go to! We are the Heads." And they smiled after the manner of men who know more than it is expedient to say. So we departed, seeing that our search was vain: while Sirius went out with an evil smell.

"It may be" cried the Greybeard of the Himalayas "it may be that IT has gone up into a Department, as the anchorite crab into the shell of the 'winkle." Then we dried our tears, and departmented through every Department, dead, living, still-born, bastard, legitimate, bond and free, subordinate, insubordinate, extortionate, adulterated – the lean kine with the fat and the gravid with the barren – till we left not a single Babu unturned. There was no Department where men are gathered together to weave ropes of the purest sand or to cut blocks with the finest razors that we let pass. For we said always:– "IT has escaped in a lunch basket! IT is hid among the waste paper! IT has departed in an office-box!" But we got neither profit nor honour in our searching; and again were our faces blackened.

"It may be" cried the Greybeard of the Himalayas "it may be that IT has taken refuge in an Anjuman, been secreted in a Sabha, or disguised in an Association!" And we summoned the Anjumans with the Antivaccinationists and the Sabhas, and the Associations and the

Gatherings, and all manner of unclean fowl. And to our question they said, in the collective voice of appropriation:– "We are IT! We are! We are! We are!" But or ever we came against them to slay them, we saw that they said the thing which was not. So we bade them depart with their Besoms against the Atlantic and their Jackdaws and the Peacock Feathers that were in their tails.

"It may be" cried the Greybeard of the Himalayas, "it may be that IT is where men say IT has always been, in the Street of the Daily Sheet, where wheels and black slime are ground together for the world's good; and where the air is heavy with the savour of ink and hot coolie." So we went there, and the Great We arose at our entry with its Undeniable Sources and Reasons to Believe and Regrets to Announce; answering after the manner of the Anjumans and the Sabhas:– "Verily We are IT. We are! We are! We are!" But we saw that they spoke leasing. and we left them to labour on the Lever that has no Fulcrum, and to deliver the Mountain of the Rat after their fashion. And again were our faces blackened.

"It may be," cried the Greybeard of the Himalayas "it may be that IT dwells among the Kine, that ITS feet are set upon the Share and ITS hands upon the tail of the Plough. Surely this time IT shall not escape!" So we went to the Great Plains where the Rice and the Ryot and the Bajra and the Bunnia[1] dwell together and perish. We made inquisition hurriedly, for the dawn was upon us, of the Plough, and of Him that drave it – of the Galled Neck and the Staring Ribs saying:– "Are ye the Government of India – the IT that we are minded to destroy?" And He that drave the Plough, laid both hands prayerfully to his nose and said:– "Alas, no! I am but the foundation – I and the Galled Neck and the Staring Ribs."

Then cried the Mahatma:– "IT is an abstraction which abstracteth and no more. IT is an Eidolon neither upright nor visible. Let us go." But I prevailed upon the Mahatma, by the memory of the Cracked Tea Cup and the Missing Brooch, that he should perform the last Incantation of Materialization. And the manner of the incantation was on this wise. With the light of the Lurid Side Light, he traced upon the ground the dread circle of the Wheel within the Wheel, and the crooked Line of the Inexplicable Course of Action, and in the centre laid he the sealed Book of the Unholy Job, which smelt noisomely. And when all was ablaze, he adjured IT by the Spell of the Greater Wire, and the Lesser Wire, and the first and last chapter of the Book of the Unholy Job, to reveal ITSELF in whatsoever might be ITS real form. And we were afraid, for we knew not what we had evoked. And there rose smoke, and lightning and flame, and faces that were not the faces of men, and the sounds of laughter; and the Lurid Side Light burned blue. Thereat the Mahatma hollowed his hand to his ear and said:– "IT is a Woman" and abased himself in the ashes of the Book of the Unholy Job. And we saw Hands that were not the hands of men, which turned the Wheel within the Wheel and drew straight the Crooked Line of the Inexplicable Course of Action, and pulled the Great Wire and the Lesser, and made plain the Book of the Unholy Job.

Lastly there fell from the Clouds a Powder-puff and a Fan, and a left-hand Shoe in white satin whereof the number was Two, and the heel two and a half inches. And the Mahatma, trembling, laid aside these things reverently, for he said:– "We have seen a visible God."

Thus was it that we found the Government of India – the IT we set forth to destroy. But we let IT go.

---

[1] In this sequence 'Rice' balances 'bajra' (millet) as 'ryot' (farmer) balances 'bunnia' (merchant).

What Came of It

Published: *Civil and Military Gazette*, 17 September 1886.

Attribution: In Scrapbook 3 (28/3, p. 49).

Text: *Civil and Military Gazette*.

Notes: An Indian Finance Commission was at work on the matter of 'retrench-ment'. RK had made fun of it earlier in the uncollected poem 'Parturiunt Montes' in the *CMG*, 26 April 1886: 'Let the fat Departments blench, / We are yearning to retrench / In a clip-and-cut and skin-removing style!' (*Poems*, III, 1705). 'What Came of It' is another burlesque of the Commission's efforts.

Reprinted in the Martindell–Ballard pamphlets and in Harbord, II, 1093–5.

ꛥ

Being extracts from the diary of Orion Golightly, formerly of the Bengal Civil Service, now:– Employé No. 1159 in the service of the Government of India, Limited.

April 14ᵗʰ, 1902—The recommendations of our thirty-fourth Retrenchment Committee have been published, and come in force next month. They seem rather drastic. I didn't mind the regulation about washing nibs to prevent expense, because my mehter helped me; but I do *not* like the order enforcing the use of one's shirt front as a blotting pad and pen-wiper. Besides writing resolutions on the back of used D.O.¹ covers is smudgy work. I recollect the time when we used to do our work on white paper with a Government stamp. Heighho! They are going to appoint a permanent Retrenchment Committee with absolute powers. Don't quite see where they can retrench further. I've put in twenty-three years' service, and I'm drawing Rs. 210 a month. Have to do my own *bazaar* before office, and stuffed bullock's heart is cheap but indigestible.

April 24ᵗʰ.—Government of India let out by contract to the lowest tenderer. Economical, but doesn't strike me as likely to be pleasant. Hear that a man of the name of Dowler has arrived from England offering to "run the blooming show" for five hundred a month and vittles. Don't quite like the allusion to blooming show. It seems disrespectful. However, the Retrenchment Committee say it's all right, and I'm a "haristocrat" for objecting. I'm supposed to be Finance Minister, I believe; but I look after the Burdwan, Delhi, and Orissa Sections as well, when I can get travelling allowance to go there. Retrenchment Committee say an honest working man could do my work cheaper. I wish he'd come. My Under-Secretary wears a red shirt, and braces, and spells Finance with two nn's. His father was a plate-layer.

May 14th.—Saw the new Viceroy, His Excellency Dowler, in a *tikka gharri* to-day, going down Chowringhi. He has taken over the other man's Khaki kit, and it doesn't fit. But he's an improvement on Blawkins. He doesn't stick his feet out of the *gharri* windows. Got an invitation, on the back of an ace of spades, asking me to dine with him to-night. Thank heaven my old dress-suit holds out still.

May 15th.—A lovely dinner. Quite a treat after bullock's heart. Roast duck, tinned peas, boiled beef with turnips and carrots and suet pudding. The Viceroy drank rum and water – much, too much of it. So did the Commander-in-Chief. His Excellency said he didn't see any blasted use in the red-coats any'ow, and His Excellency the Commander-in-Chief said "if Dowler would stand up, and 'ave it hout like a man, he'd jolly quick show 'un the use of a British sodger." Then they cried into the Viceregal spittoon, and fell down into the saw dust. I helped to take Dowler to bed. Wonder if this means any increase in salary for me? Fifty rupees would be a god-send just now.

May 22nd.—Learn that His Excellency was very angry with me for coming to dinner in a dress coat. He sent me a D.O. to-day, saying if a bloke was too proud for his company, he'd better cut his stick. He'd never had a dress coat in his life, and wasn't going to let his underlings put on frills.

July 5th.—Fainted today. I'm getting old and the bullock's heart is too much for me, otherwise I might have borne the shock when I heard a big Bengal Zemindar call Dowler *tum*. To be sure Dowler banged him on the back and asked after the Missus; but the dignity of the empire should be preserved. Spoke to the Zemindar afterwards, and he laughed. Said that the Sirkar had gone *pagal* and was sending out low caste *sahibs* to govern men with pedigrees five hundred years old. He told me some awful stories about the Commissioner. I mean No. 723

employé at Rajshahye. Says he goes to Kutcherry drunk, and tries to kiss all the female witnesses.

The Zemindar was very kind when he saw me cry (I am old and weak, very weak I fear). He said that I was one of the few *sahibs* with any *izzat*, and when the smash came he'd make me Dewan of his *zemandari*.

August 19th.—New batch of Employés reported arrived at Calcutta. I was introduced to them when the *ticca-gharries* came in from the river. They are rather boisterous, and when you try to tell them anything about their duties as administrators, they all say "cheese it" together. They walk arm in arm down Meadows Street singing a new popular Music Hall Song.

September 23rd.—His Excellency the Commander-in-Chief and Dowler had a stand up fight today in Council about the Army estimates. By virtue of my official position I had to hold the sponge for Dowler. He got a black eye and a cut lip, but the Commander-in-Chief's face is mashed into a pulp. The Commander-in-Chief wanted some more regiments I think, and Dowler said he was going to rule by the voice of the people. The Legal Member was the Commander-in-Chief's second, and wanted to fight me. I said I was too old and too sick of life for such things. The Legal Member was Secretary of the Clapham Clerks' Athletic Club before he came out.

November 19th.—On tour with His Excellency the Viceroy. His Excellency has won the hearts of the soldiers by drinking at all the regimental canteens and singing songs afterwards. The men say he's a proper spicey Viceroy – and no error. They tell him this to his face and he likes it. Commander-in-Chief at loggerheads with His Excellency. Says he is sucking up to the army. Don't quite know what "sucking" up means, but am quite certain that another week of this canteen life will kill me. Have discovered that the employés in the districts – or what used to be districts, wear corduroys mainly, and smoke claypipes on the platform when they receive Dowler. Some of them call him "matey." Met an old Bengal Civilian at Kalka. He says he daren't go up to Simla, his heart would break, but stays as near it as he can.

Decr, 2nd.—Got nearly Rs. 100 T.A.[2] and travelled third class to the sections I am supposed to look after. Saved Rs. 7–8 from T.A., and spent it on a good meal. Saw enough when I was on tour to persuade me I had better close with the zemindar's offer about the Dewanship.

January 20th.—Dowler quite happy. It has been discovered that he let out his contract at enormous profit to a wealthy bunnia who is now Raja of all India, subject more or less, to the Secretary of State. Home Government quite contented, and have knighted Dowler for his laudable economy. I have resigned, and am now with the zemindar.

[1] Demi-Official (Harbord).
[2] Travel allowance.

An Official Secret

Published: *Civil and Military Gazette*, 12 October 1886.

Attribution: In Scrapbook 3 (28/3, p. 5)

Text: *Civil and Military Gazette.*

Note: The occasion of this fantasy is obviously some official demand for secrecy, but what in particular is meant I do not know. Perhaps it *was* about 'the flashing point of kerosine'.

'An Official Secret' has been reprinted in the Martindell–Ballard pamphlets and in Harbord, II, 1107–10.

It was night – thick night on the Capuan Hills. In a secluded cave known only to the leopard, the bear and the members of the Legislative Council, were gathered the eight leading men of the Indian Empire, and by the unsteady torch light they discussed and attempted to read their notes on a Measure. The V—y, jauntily seated on a powder barrel, with a lighted cigarette between his lips, took no part in the debate, but watched the mouth of the cave, and from time to time shifted the butt of his army revolver within easy reach of his hand. Press Correspondents were bold and daring, and under cover of the darkness might trifle with the Secrets of the Empire.

The debate was a short one, for the cave was cold, and each member, himself armed to the teeth, laboured under the fear that his own or his neighbour's weapons might "go off." In a quarter of an hour all was over, and His Excellency got off the powder barrel. "We are agreed then" said he "that the flashing point of—," but here his voice died away in a sepulchral murmur, and the rest of the sentence was inaudible save to the knot of men clustered round the Viceregal lips. The Bill was passed into law with the usual oaths of secrecy, and the members separated after giving the grip and the password, which was:– "A little before the light." The Viceroy looked relieved, and, disguised in the blanket and felt headpiece of a *pahari*, made his way home by devious *pugdandies*.

The Bill would be published a week hence; till then all was veiled in impenetrable mystery, and death was the portion of the indiscreet tale teller and the eaves-dropper alike.

The Special Correspondents of the *Backwoodsman* and the *Abusive and Martial Journal* were bold men, who held their lives cheaply, and were resolved to perish in their attempts to secure early information. They wore shirts of chain mail next their skin, and carried double-barrel, Snider-bore, breech-loading, patent hammerless, X.Y.Z. action pistols, gracefully about their persons. As a rule both defences were needed; it having been enacted that, to shoot, maim or cripple any person or persons who bore the appearance of looking for State Secrets, was a public service, rewardable with a C.S.I.;[2] or, in the case of a native, with a Rai Bahadurship. Consequently, the Correspondents appeared in public rarely, and were constrained and distant in their manners. But they worked in the dark stealthily and without cessation.

Their chances of success were scanty. His Honour the Lieutenant-Governor of the Punjab went abroad under a military escort, who had instructions to shoot him if they saw him conversing with anyone unconnected with the Government. A Gatling gun, with a complement of six blue jackets, defended Gorton Castle,[3] where Sir Theodore Hope[4] lay drugged and in chains. The road to Eric's Own was mined, and Colonel W. G. Davies,[5] barred into his bathroom and fed through a hole in the wall; Sir Auckland Colvin was apparently free, but he knew that all his servants, from the Jemmadar of *Chaprassis*, to the *Mehter*, were Foreign Office attachés in disguise, and that the ivory-hilted knives in their belts were *not for show*. Mr. C. P. Ilbert[6] was perched on an inaccessible crag of Mashobra, and half a Goorkha regiment were encamped around about him. General Chesney[7] was locked into one of his own trunks, and fed through the key-hole by means of a baby's feeding-bottle. Absolutely the only men at liberty were the Viceroy and his Private Secretary[8] – a gentleman dumb as the Pyramids and inscrutable as the Sphinx. There were seven days wherein to gain possession of the priceless secret – what was the Bill passed by Government of India at that midnight sitting?

Correspondents are not easily daunted. These two men – having first made their wills – matured a bold scheme – nothing less than the capture of the Private Secretary. The Viceroy was sure to be missed, and all attempts to bribe the guards of the Members of Council had proved futile. Their reputation depended on the *coup* which they were about to undertake, and life-long glory or certain death was their reward.

Disguising themselves in the classic raiment of a *dhobi* and a barber, respectively, and with their pistols under their *cummerbunds* they crept stealthily along, on the night of the second day, in the direction of the Viceregal Lodge. The guards and the gunners of the three batteries posted just above the Foreign Office allowed them to pass without comment, and they found themselves by two o'clock in the morning at the door of the Private Secretary's elegant, detached villa. The Private Secretary was asleep – his hand still clasped upon a Derringer. Quick as thought, a bolster was thrust on to his head, and one Correspondent sat upon it, while the other bound the struggling victim in the sheets. The pseudo-*dhobi's* bullock was waiting in the verandah, and across its back was laid the helpless form of the Private Secretary, while his week's wash was heaped upon his head. The two conspirators passed out unnoticed as they had come, and reached their hotel with their prize.

Short and decisive was their interview with the Private Secretary, two icy-cold pistol barrels stirred the hair on his right temple, and two more his left – "what did last week's Council decide?" said the Correspondents together, stifling an attempt at a scream on the part of the captive with a pen-wiper.

"I will die before I reveal the secret," gasped he between mouthfuls of inky flannel. The hammers of one pistol went back with a cold, crisp "*snick*," and the Private Secretary shuddered.

"The flashing point of kerosine," he began and stopped; two more hammers went back as he went on "has been raised to one hundred and thirty-six degrees for American, and one hundred and forty-one for all other brands imported into the country from the 1st of November."

The Private Secretary fainted, for the tension had been beyond endurance of mortal man. The Correspondents bound and gagged him afresh, propped him in one corner of the room, and fled into the night towards the tonga office. There was half an hour's delay in stealing tonga horses and a driver, and they had, strictly in self-defence, to heave a babu – filled with the dreams of a Rai Bahadurship – down the khud. Meantime the Private Secretary had spat out the pen-wiper and alarmed the hotel. Also he had taken horse, and in the scantiest of night gear was thundering along the Mall to alarm the Viceroy.

They heard the clatter of hoofs overhead – a wild cry of:–"They know, they know; kill, kill!" and almost immediately after the boom of the mid-day gun, telling Simla that a correspondent had escaped without a permit. The whole town in two minutes was buzzing like a hive. The tonga-driver, stimulated by an offer of five hundred rupees, lashed the ponies to full gallop, and the perilous downward descent began. But the half-hour's delay had proved fatal; and the Private Secretary, mad with fear and rage, had roused Viceregal Lodge. Could they pass under it in time?

The roar of a hand-thrown bomb on the cart-road was their answer. The ponies reared at the light and galloped forward more furiously than ever. A heavy beam fell just behind the Tonga, and there was a pause. But the men knew their troubles were not over. At the bend in the road, where the Municipal conservancy carts are stacked for the night, stood three figures in great-coats. They were the Viceroy, the Military Secretary, and a member of the Commander-in-Chief's Staff – a noted and deadly shot.

All three fired together, and one of the Correspondents rolled out of the back seat, shot through the lungs. He had only time to hand to his companion the leaf of the note-book containing the *verbatim* account of the Private Secretary's revelation before he fell. The ponies flew forward, and a safe bend in the road had been nearly reached, when one of the three men fired again – a random shot in the darkness, and a Reade's explosive shell fractured the thigh of the remaining correspondent. One last hope remained. The agony of the wound was fearful, but, sustained by the thought of the deathless glory even now within his grasp, the correspondent fired both barrels of his pistol at the telegraph wires and heard them part with a terse twang. The road to the plains lay open. Handing the now bloodstained leaf of the note-book to the driver, with a sheaf of banknotes, he bade him drive to Umballa without stopping, and thence go south by train to the office of the *Backwoodsman* and give the precious slip to the Editor. Then he, too, sank down helpless as a log into [*sic*] the foot board, and was jolted out on to the road a few corners further on.

Fifty-six hours later there stumbled into the office of the *Backwoodsman* a worn and tattered tonga-driver who clasped in his hand a dirty blood-stained piece of paper with the legend:– "The flashing point of kerosine has been raised to one hundred and thirty-six degrees for American and one hundred and forty-one for all other brands imported into the country from the first of November."

The paper told its own tale. The Editor, a man of few words, turned it over and said laconically "*Sahib murgya?*"[9]

"*Jee han. Gureeb purwar, dono murgya,*" was the reply.[10] "I must tell the printers," said the Editor to himself, "that to-day's front page comes out in gold, and the rest of the paper with a three inch black border."

Then he went on with his work, and sang as he toiled.

The price had been a heavy one, but the news was worth it.

---

[1] RK's names for the *Pioneer* and the *Civil and Military Gazette*. The narrator of 'The Man Who Would Be King' is a journalist with the *Backwoodsman*.

[2] Companion of the Order of the Star of India.

[3] A government office building in Simla.

[4] Hope (1831–1915) was the Public Works Member of the Supreme Council, 1882–7. He also figures in 'New Year's Gifts' and 'Deputating a Viceroy', below.

[5] Colonel, later Major-General, W. G. Davies (1828–98), Indian Staff Corps; a member of the Vicreroy's Legislative Council from 1880.

[6] C. P. Ilbert (1841–1924), he of the Ilbert Bill (see 'Dis Aliter Visum'), was Legal Member of the Supreme Council, 1882–6.

[7] General Sir George Chesney (1830–95), Military Member of the Supreme Council, 1886–91.

[8] Sir Donald Mackenzie Wallace (1841–1919): correspondent for *The Times*, now serving as Dufferin's private secretary. A man of great scholarly attainments. RK describes him as 'a good watch dog is the faithful Donald, and when he is on duty he refuses to unbend' (17 June 1888: *Letters*, 1, 217).

[9] 'The Sahib has died?'

[10] 'Yes sir, poor family, both have died.'

Le Roi en Exil

Published: *Civil and Military Gazette*, 15 November 1886.

Atrribution: In Scrapook 3 (28/3, pp. 50–1).

Text: *Civil and Military Gazette*.

Notes: This imaginary episode, RK's burlesque imitation of Victor Hugo's 'extravagant prose' (see headnote to 'The History of a Crime'), brings together Thibaw (1869–1916), the exiled King of Burma, and his consort Supayalat, with Lord Dufferin, the Viceroy under whom Thibaw had been deposed at the end of 1885 by the so-called Third Anglo-Burmese War. Upper Burma, its capital at Rangoon, was officially annexed by the British at the beginning of 1886; Lower Burma had been annexed long before. But, though the country had been annexed, it had not been pacified, a fact exploited by RK in several stories and poems. Rutnagiri, the place of Thibaw's exile, is a port on the western coast of India.

Reprinted in the Martindell–Ballard pamphlets; in *The Victorian*, April, 1937; and in Harbord, III, 1541–4.

Between the Conqueror and the Conquered exists of necessity a gêne – a *mauvais_honte*.

Only the French can surmount that gêne.

But the French were not conquered. *Jamais!* Nevaire! They suffered certain reverses, with the inimitable *politesse* of their nation, at the hands of a race who eat raw sausage and bacilliferous pork.

How can one fight with a people who assimilate bacilli undisturbed?

But I become patriotic.

Sir Dufferin had conquered the amiable Thebau.

He now visited him at Rutnagiri.

Amicably; as certain soldiers once visited Paris.

But he was not impressed, as were those Teutons. On the contrary. He was hot and tired. His boots were filled with sand.

The ascent from the beach to the house of the amiable Thebau lay through deep sand.

The amiable Thebau and the lovely Supialé received His Excellence with sherbet of the most possible cold and a Burmese cheroot.

The Burmese cheroot is like the British Policy. It is not strong enough and takes long to finish.

Also it makes men sick.

The silence was profound. His Excellence looked dutifully at the cheroot.

The lovely Supialé, with grace inexpressible, lit it.

Before women and tobacco all men are equal.

When both are good.

Or bad.

Thebau smiled.

His Excellence smiled.

The lovely Supialé blushed.

The *gêne* disappeared. When a lady blushes there is no *mauvais honte* possible.

"My country?" said Thebau.

It was at once a protest and an interrogation.

"It is there," said His Excellence.

He pointed to the East.

"It is mine" said his Excellence. "With Reservations."

"And a Reservation is?" –

His Excellence hesitated.

A man who is burdened with secrets of *la haute politique* always hesitates.

It is to him a disease.

"A Reservation is an Unforeseen Contingency."

The lovely Supialé blushed. Her knowledge of the English tongue was limited. But she was a woman.

Remember what says the adorable Michelet.[1] "A woman understands all, knows all, suspects all."

The amiable Thebau was puzzled.

He was also persistent.

"And an Unforeseen Contingency is?"

His Excellence hesitated no longer. He would spare the blushes of Supialé.

"A dacoit – or dacoits. *Voila tout!*"

The amiable Thebau smiled.

The lovely Supialé smiled.

His Excellence blushed.

You will perceive, then, that the situation was reversed.

His Excellence made a plunge.

Metaphorically.

When he was young he had read books. The *Delectus*.[2]

Not from choice, but from necessity

In the *Delectus* is a phrase.

We French know it. You English do not.

"*Fas est ab hoste doceri.*"[3]

It is the keynote of all policy. Even Burmese policy.

"Your country," said His Excellence, "is a country abominable. It is expensive."

The first consideration of the Englishman is his money.

"It is unwholesome."

The second consideration of the Englishman is his health.

"It is disturbed."

The third consideration of the Englishman is his comfort.

The amiable Thebau laid a jewelled hand on the pages of that journal so illustrious, the *Espioneer Officiel*.

He received it regularly.

It was the homage of literature to fallen royalty.

"I have heard these things before" said the amiable Thebau.

His Excellence blushed a second time. He sat in the presence of superior wisdom.

Even a Viceroy must bow to a journal quotidien.

"You know then" –

"That they are dacoits by night and villagers by day. That they shoot and run into elephant-grass. That they cannot be caught, and when caught are released, because they have not actually been seen killing men. That your soldiers are your police. That your Civil Courts frustrate the work of your soldiery. That you try to govern with slow law, when a quick bullet is needed. Yes. It is written here. It is the custom of your race."

His Excellence wept like a child.

But he thought of the *Delectus*.

And of the Empire.

"You would, then, do – what?"

This time it was the lovely Supialé who made answer. Not verbally but by signs.

She drew her right hand across her throat so delicate.

She wound her necklace round her neck, and protruded her tongue. In a manner suggestive.

She placed one hand on her heart, staggered, and sank into a golden chair – smiling.

The answer was complete.

The amiable Thebau nodded.

"When an elephant is mad, the mahout does not tie its legs with jasmine-wreaths."

The wisdom of the West pales before the wisdom of the East. As the coarse Teuton intellect pales before the vivacity of the Gaul.

"I would do all these things" said the amiable Thebau.

"But it is barbarous," said His Excellence "and the Penal Code provides –"

"When there is a fire in the land the leaves of law-books make it burn more fiercely."

His Excellence was dumb. One cannot argue with the *Vedas*, the *Upanishads*, the *Bodhisats* and the *Aryavartas*.[4]

They are old – but practical.

The amiable Thebau was young, but practical.

He spoke, under the influence of the tobacco – as a man to a man.

The lovely Supialé spoke also.

As a woman speaks to a man.

That is to say persuasively.

***

"But there are telegraph wires" said His Excellence.

"Cut them off."

"But there are correspondents."

"Cut them down."

"And the thousands of your late subjects?" . . . .

"Cut them up. I, who have done all I recommend say so."

"But they are innocent agriculturists."

"It is possible. You can enquire afterwards."

"But that would be a massacre."

The amiable Thebau smiled contemptuously.

"Your Excellency, listen to me – I who have no cause to affect for your admiration. There will be no massacre. You will kill two, five, possibly fifteen hundred – but no more. The land will be still."

"It is a paradox," murmured His Excellency, pouring the sand from his boots.

"You will kill on suspicion. Severely. Without enquiry."

His Excellency put on his boots.

"That is, as says our great Buddha, the Perfect Way. By the Perfect Way each one attains his own Nirvana."

"And the Nirvana of Burma is?" –

"The Pacification."

---

[1] Jules Michelet (1798–1874), French historian, with perhaps a glance at his *La Femme*, 1860.

[2] A book of extracts from Greek or Latin authors for use as an elementary text.

[3] 'It is right to be taught by the enemy': Ovid, *Metamorphoses*, IV, 428.

[4] The terms are not parallel, presumably by design: *Vedas* and *Upanishads* are sacred texts of the Hindus; a *bodhisat* has reached the stage of holiness below Buddha; *aryavarta* is the abode of the Aryans.

A Scrap of Paper

ꝏ

Published: *Civil and Military Gazette*, 13 December 1886.

Attribution: In Scrapbook 3 (28/3, pp. 60–1).

Text: *Civil and Military Gazette*.

Notes: The story is no. 14 of the newspaper series called 'Plain Tales from the Hills', but was omitted when most of the series was collected in book form under the same title in 1888. RK perhaps omitted it on account of its double structure – two stories rather than one. It is otherwise very much in keeping with many of the collected *Plain Tales*.

In 'Quo Fata Vocant', the reminiscence that RK wrote for the *St George's Gazette*, 31 December 1902, the magazine of the Royal Northumberland Fusiliers, he recalls the elements of the first part of 'A Scrap of Paper' as though they had actually happened: 'Do they [any regiment that succeeded the Fusiliers at Lahore] know a "writer" when they see him, and can they make that "writer" happy and contented down by the elephant lines?'

Reprinted in the Martindell–Ballard pamphlets and in Harbord, III, 1558–62.

ꝏ

Some men ought to be hanged – especially London Tradesmen. They never seem to understand when to leave you alone; and they never realize that, in this country, you have quite enough expenses of your own, without attending to their claims.

Every one who has dealt with them knows what an unpleasant firm Rentoul and Brannigan are. They have no sense of common decency, and if you lie on their books for more than eighteen months at a stretch, they send you first a letter on thin white paper, then another letter on thick blue paper; and lastly they send a writ. Writs are unpleasant things; even in so quiet a part of the world as Assam. They begin with lions and unicorns, like the first stage of *delirium tremens*, and then go on to "all whom it may concern;" and finish up with "wherefores" and "therebys." The general effect is depressing – distinctly so. But, as I may have said elsewhere, it takes a good deal to depress a Subaltern of the

Line, and when Chubbuck got first the white paper, and next the blue, like a seidlitz powder,[1] he knew what was in store for him, and told the rest of the "Inextinguishables" that a writ was in the air. There's a deal of brotherly love in a Mess. The "Inextinguishables" took that writ under their wing, so to speak, and made a personal matter of it, and offered to dig rifle-pits for Chubbuck to hide in when the writter appeared. They were unanimous on the indecency of Rentoul and Brannigan's conduct, and their language was powerful, and to the point. Chubbuck said he would never give Rentoul and Brannigan his patronage any more – not though he lived to retire on his off-reckonings[2] as a Commander-in-Chief. The rest of the "Inextinguishables" agreed with Chubbuck. Then they went about on horse and foot, and whenever one of them had nothing to do, he raised a false alarm that the writter was coming – just to keep Chubbuck in training, and prevent him brooding over his woes. Chubbuck didn't brood *much*; but they fancied he might. Goodness knows what value a Queen's writ has in this country; I fancy it merely serves to amuse the tradesmen at home.

In the same cantonment as the "Inextinguishables" was quartered a native regiment, and the cantonment being a happy family, the news of Chubbuck's little misfortune spread naturally into that Mess too; and they were all very sorry and a good deal amused. The Junior Subaltern of the native regiment offered to do sword excrcise on the person of the writter, or lead his regiment to walk over him once or twice; but, as events proved, he was of much greater use than if he had done all those things.

One day Chubbuck and the Junior Subaltern were riding together and talking horse, when a dogcart appeared on the horizon. Anybody with a little experience would recognize a writter a quarter of a mile off, even though the writter were disguised as a Lord Mayor with his corporation on. This particular writter was a public man, though not known by sight to most of the subalterns. The dogcart pulled up, and Chubbuck shifted his reins ready to wheel round and bolt, when the writter said to the Junior Subaltern:– "Would you be good enough, Sir, to tell me where Lieutenant Chubbuck lives." "Certainly" said the Junior Subaltern "his house is over there" pointing to the nearest barrack; "but at the present moment he is down in the Commissariat lines." Now the Commissariat lines were only four and a half miles away, and to get at them you had to – but that comes afterwards. The writter whipped up his horse, and thanked the Junior Subaltern and pounded away over the desert.

The Junior Subaltern turned in his saddle. "I was made for a great general," said he. "Presently our friend will get into the elephant lines, and he will be unhappy. The *Soldiers' Pocketbook* says that an enemy should be harassed whenever possible." "Come to the Mess and let us drink" said Chubbuck. So they went, and the Mess being full at the time, the Junior Subaltern was made much of by the "Inextinguishables," and the mellow "Macdonald"³ went round as they drank prosperity to the Junior Subaltern.

When a horse, however old he may be, gets among elephants – many of them – he does not feel happy. The writter swung round the corner of the Commissariat lines, and found himself, so to speak, in the bosom of the family of the Transport elephants as they rocked to and fro in their stalls. There were six on one side of the road and six on the other; and it being near feeding time they trumpeted. The old horse stood on one leg, and tried to stand on his head and beat holes in the splash-board and settled down to a fifteen-anna gallop over Assam generally. At the end of a few miles he was pulled up, and the writter, very hot and angry, turned towards the "Inextinguishables" Mess to lay hold of the man who had misled him. He argued that he must have been Lieutenant Chubbuck. So he drove into the Mess compound, and an intelligent "Inextinguishable" lifted his voice and said to the Junior Subaltern, "Chubbuck have a drink." As the Junior Subaltern turned, the writter jumped out of the dog-cart and went for the Junior Subaltern. "Lieutenant Chubbuck I believe," – the Junior Subaltern smiled in a saintly and polite sort of way, but said nothing. – "I serve this writ on you," and he tapped the Junior Subaltern on the shoulder. "I'm awf'ly obliged," said the Junior Subaltern. "It's very pretty; but what am I to do with it? You see, I'm not Chubbuck, and I'm in a native regiment, and I have no truck with Rentoul and Brannigan, so it's of no use to me. But I'll keep it as a memento of your visit all the same." Then the writter wanted the writ back, but the Junior Subaltern said he valued it as a work of art and a touching proof of confidence; and all the "Inextinguishables" came up to point out to the writter that these accidents *would* happen now and then, and he had better get a new writ from England. Now this writter was the best in Assam as all who have had dealings with him know, and he had no wish to make things generally unpleasant, so he went away, and the "Inextinguishables" said that the Junior Subaltern deserved a statue in the middle of the parade-ground. Chubbuck said the little mistake gave him three months' law, and in that time he could settle Rentoul and Brannigan, and give them his mind in a letter.

That is the first part of the story. The second shows the ingratitude of men, where amusement is possible. The writter made no sign. He had sent Home for a new writ, I fancy, and it was none of his business adding to his work by beginning legal proceedings against the Junior Subaltern. Even if they could have held good. But other men thought that if the writter did nothing, they might run an amateur legal performance of their own. To the honour of the "Inextinguishables" it must be written that they refused to assist in any "draw," saying that the Junior Subaltern had helped one of their own fellows. *But* they said they would not stop any "draw" that was going forward. So the business had to be managed by two men in the Civil Station. They spent a week or so dropping it into the Junior Subaltern, that he had laid himself open to the most awful penalties by "personating" Chubbuck and misdirecting the writter. The more he vowed he never personated, the more they quoted the Penal Code – with alterations – and they proved satisfactorily that about three years' hard labour was the most he could expect. The Junior Subaltern didn't know much about law, and he felt a little uneasy. The "Inextinguishables" lay low; and only hinted that he had better take six months' leave to do his sentences of imprisonment, and mean time they would look after his polo ponies. In the course of that week men discovered that the Junior Subaltern's views on the subject of law were much the same as an infant's ideas of a policeman. That gave the opening they wanted. The two men caused to be prepared on Government of India paper a lawyer's letter. It was long but comprehensive. It showed that the Junior Subaltern came under three or four sections of the Penal Code, for deluding the writter, and it threw in a few other charges of "intimidation by means of elephants" and putting in extreme and bodily fear. Reading it over with no knowledge of the law, it was perfect; and being touched in with red ink, and written in a clerk's hand, and signed in a crabbed hand and crammed full of "whereases" and "to wits," its mere appearance was striking. There was a dinner that night, it doesn't much matter where, and seven-and-twenty men sat down to it, including the Junior Subaltern. About coffee-and-cigar time a servant brought in the huge envelope with the letter, and the Junior Subaltern turned green. He read three lines and said something impressive; and the balance of the table gave their undivided attention to the letter. Then some one read it aloud, and the Junior Subaltern groaned. Then everyone offered advice, and the uproar was fine. There were two men of the "Inextinguishables" dining, and they swore, if the worst came to the worst, to help the Junior Subaltern through thick and thin. And the man who was reading the letter went on shooting out the "wherefores" and "to wits" like an owl. Then men said:– "Fetch the Penal Code," and bad luck prompted an Assistant Commissioner to get his copy, and the book fell into the hands of a ringleader, and he read the sections – with alterations – quickly, and shut the book up with a bang, and said the case was very bad. Now remember, only the Junior Subaltern knows how the Junior Subaltern felt, but ordinary men declared he was filled with one of the best and most solid panics that ever grew in the heart of man. The advice and comfort from the "Inextinguishables" only made things worse; and the Assistant Commissioner sailed into the trouble with the cheerful remark that, "if the facts were as stated, the Junior Subaltern was lost." It was an impressive scene. In the centre stood the Junior Subaltern, pale but calm, holding the letter in the tips of his fingers; on the left was the Assistant Commissioner anxious to help and believing in the genuineness of the letter; on the right was a man of the "Inextinguishables" swearing he would commit perjury for the sake of the Junior Subaltern; behind was another man of the same regiment advocating a sea-trip down the coast; and all round were twenty men going out into verandahs to lie down and roll with laughter, and coming back to suggest various ways of squaring the writter. Some men offered to go out and beat him with clubs. Others said he should have been dropped down a well in the first instance. But all agreed that the Junior Subaltern was done for. They would never forget the way he saved Chubbuck, and the thought of this might cheer him grinding corn in Gowhatti gaol; whither he would soon go. Little by little the men settled into their parts, and the last agony of the Junior Subaltern was worse than the first. They kept the right side of absurdity and – well, it was meant for a long and elaborate draw, but the visible misery of the Junior Subaltern was too touching, and the men of the "Inextinguishables" said he could not be allowed to sleep with the prospect of a felon's cell hanging over him.

He was told tenderly of the fraud and the blessed relief at first blunted a natural indignation against the men who had prepared the letter. Then some one suggested that the fact of the Assistant Commissioner going so readily for the Penal Code was suspicious. That was quite enough. The Junior Subaltern started off for the Assistant Commissioner, and the rest of the gathering laughed themselves speechless on different parts of the floor. It took some time for the Assistant Commissioner to explain he was innocent as the babe unborn, and he leapt several fences or a ditch or two before the Junior Subaltern understood he was *shikarring* the wrong man. After a bit the beauty of the "draw" began to strike the Junior Subaltern, and he settled down to explaining how he had never really cared at all. Everybody – even the Assistant Commissioner – said he had taken things beautifully, which was strictly true; and so he was formally christened "The Felon" before the evening broke up.

If this should meet the eye of the writter, he will understand that the Junior Subaltern has tasted all the bitterness of arrest, trial and imprisonment in the terrible two and a half hours that his friends prepared for him.

If this should meet the eye of Messrs. Rentoul and Brannigan, they will understand, as Chubbuck says, that "we owe more to them than we shall ever be able to repay."

---

[1] Harbord explains: 'As now sold in chemist shops each dose [of Seidlitz powder] is in two papers –first into the water goes the powder from the white paper – stir a little, then put the powder from the blue paper' (Harbord, iii, 1562).

[2] Funds provided to the commanding officer with which to buy clothing for his men; now in the form of a reduction in pay.

[3] Presumably Scotch whisky is meant.

The Mystification of Santa Claus

Published: *Civil and Military Gazette*, 25 December 1886.

Attribution: In Scrapbook 3 (28/3, pp. 62–3).

Text: *Civil and Military Gazette.*

Notes: Reprinted in the Martindell–Ballard pamphlets, in the *Civil and Military Gazette Annual*, Lahore, 1936, and in Harbord, III, 1565–71.

When reindeer get their heads free and bolt, there is no controlling them; because, you see, they pull from their horns. Santa Claus' team had, through sheer freshness – for they had been in stable for twelve months past – shied at the Northern Lights behind Copenhagen, wheeled round through Finland, and so bolted straight across European Russia before Santa Claus could get a pull on them.

Now Hans Anderson,[1] and one or two other writers in America and the north of Europe, had made Santa Claus the great power he was. So he kept, as a rule, to the place where he had been created and where every one knew and loved him. But those reckless reindeer had dragged him hundreds and hundreds of miles out of his course; and he puffed and blew in the sleigh all alone under the stars somewhere on the wrong side of the Ural Mountains with the noses of his team – the eight big white reindeer – pointing full across the Kirghiz Steppes.

"This is a bad business" said Santa Claus, looking at the jumbled pile of presents in the sleigh. "I must steer back to the Northern Lights." Just then a wolf howled, and this set the deer off faster than ever, southward and eastward across the Kirghiz Steppes. "There ought to be Christmas twice a week" thought Santa Claus, "to keep these brutes in order." The parcels were flying about like hot peas, and Santa Claus had only one hand free for the reins; so the deer did pretty much what they liked. They had eaten the green moss at the foot of the Rjica Vom[2] and drunk the glacier water that comes from the crest of the Rjica Vom for a twelve month; and every body knows how that puts strength into cattle.

Once the sleigh bumped horribly on the Altai Mountains; once it cracked a runner on the snow-glazed rocks of the Hindu Kush, and once it nearly bounded on to the near wheeler's back coming down the Takht-i-Suleiman.³ "The roads are infamous hereabout" said Santa Claus breathlessly, as the Golden Sleigh whizzed over the sands of the Indus. "I should really like to know where I am." Santa Claus' knowledge of geography was limited, but presently, as the reindeer trotted on through the heart of a big cantonment, Santa Claus saw by the light of the headlamps, a broken toy-cart of German manufacture lying near a masonry gatepost.

"If there are little children here," said Santa Claus cheerily, "all is well. I had better distribute the presents, and hold over my northern circuit till another day; or get St. Christopher to take over my duties." He jumped out and began, as was his regular custom, to make his way down the chimney of a big white four square-house – it was the Commissioner's as a matter of fact – landing feet first in a huge, white-washed room with a small cot in the centre. In the cot was a pale little boy about seven years old, with a fretful expression on his face, and big dark rings round his eyes. Santa Claus felt sorry for him, because he looked so lonely, and moved, therefore, to the foot of the bed to fill the boy's stocking. Only – the stocking was nowhere to be found – and as he had forgotten to blow on the child's eyes, the little one awoke. He stared at Santa Claus, and then said imperiously:–

"*Tum kon ho?*"⁴

Santa Claus nodded and smiled, not knowing the language, but afraid the child might be frightened. But he was not. He sat bolt upright in his bed, eyeing Santa Claus with great disfavour and said:–

"*Jawab do? Kon ho tum?*"⁵

"For an English child who ought to have read Hans Andersen, he speaks a singularly queer tongue" thought Santa Claus. But he smiled still more, and showing the pile of presents in his arms, said as gently as he knew how:– "Don't be afraid, *bubchen*. I'm Santa Claus. Don't you know me?" To this the child, seeing that his visitor had no vernacular, made answer slowly and in English:– "I is not afraid. My papa are a Commissioner. If you is a *Boxwalla*, this house is shut. We do not want things. My mamma is asleep. If you do not go *jut-put*, I will call my servants and they will *puckerao* you. Now go!"

You might have knocked Santa Claus down with a feather. "Good gracious, Baby!" he gasped. "Is it possible that you do not know Santa Claus – Saint Nicholas? I carry presents for children – good children – and a birch for bad boys." Here he shook a big birch he always carried in a threatening way. The child was not impressed. He returned to his pillow and his vernacular, speaking with his eyes shut:– "*Bahut accha! Shayad khalassi, ho, shayad mehter ho; lekin abi karma mut saf haro. Sat bajai no. Mi seijaiga iswaqt.*"[6] Then he turned away on his side. Santa Claus sat down on the floor in a heap with his parcels. Words could not express what was in his mind just then. Presently he got up very slowly and sorrowfully, and began to climb up the chimney. But his heart was heavy, and the soot got into his eyes, and a survivor of the summer wasps, who had crept into the chimney for the sake of warmth, stung him badly. He sat upon the roof shaking his head. "Good heavens! What fearful depravity!" he muttered. "I wonder who the abandoned little wretch took me for?" He was thinking of the boy, not the wasp.

Then he got into his sledge and trotted drearily up and down the roads looking for someone he could visit; for he had arrived at the conclusion that the little boy was mad. He was not altogether successful in his work. The Assistant Commissioner's little daughter, aged five, set up a most lamentable howl as he came down the chimney, and cried "*Chor! Chor!*" So Santa had to retire with undignified haste. The D[istrict].S[uperintendent of].P[olice].'s son, aged four, received him with a yell of delight and asked him to fetch in the *baloo* and "*nautch karo ek dum.*"[7] Santa Claus didn't know what *balooing* or *nautch karoing* was, but he fancied it was something derogatory to his dignity, and retired in a huff.

Then he made an awful discovery, which inclined him to believe that the reindeer had somehow or other run him right off the surface of the globe into another and much worse place. *There were only three English children in that station!* He went everywhere, but the Commissioner's son, and the Assistant Commissioner's daughter, and the D.S.P.'s son were all he could find. Then he lashed the reindeer into a gallop, and visited scores of other stations. Sometimes he found four, or five or eight children, but more usually none at all – except little bits of babies under three years old, and they didn't count.

"This is no fit place for the likes of me" said Santa Claus ruefully. "I've been treated with scorn and disrespect in my old age. Told to *jao* and *nautch* and *boxwalla* myself, whatever that means! I believe there are only changelings in this part of the world. If it *is* a part of the world."

After a time the night air sobered him down and he remembered how all old people, the grandfathers and grandmothers of the children, took an interest in him for the sake of the little folk. "I must stretch a point in their favour" said Santa Claus, and look them up. "May be some of my presents will fall into proper hands that way; for these unearthly children refuse to accept me."

So he scoured over the plains in search of the old people – the white haired men and women who sit in a corner by the fire, and tell the babies stories of Santa Claus and Kris Kringle – and make Christmas a great and memorable day to their children's children. The deer galloped till the sledge hummed and boomed with pure speed as it went through the air; but the second part of Santa Claus' search was a bigger failure than the first. Every one knows that looking for old folk in India is as wise as looking for young ones in an almshouse; because we all lie within the compass of a generation and a half and the children and the old folks go away, leaving only those who are working for their bread.

Santa Claus, however, did not know this; and after much driving, his original suspicion about the mistake of the reindeer returned in full force.

"By the Great Log of Yule, and the Christmas Tree of the Ten Thousand Lights" said Santa Claus, "I have surely dropped into the infernal regions – a land without the beauty of childhood or the reverence of old age. And Christmas all the whole world over going to ruin, because those pig-headed reindeer have dragged me off creation." Then he buried his head in his beard, and gave himself and Christmas up for lost. But the rattle of the toys in the sleigh roused him; and he remembered how all these things must be got rid of before day dawned, or they would spoil in another year.

"Perhaps" said Santa Claus to himself very humbly, "perhaps these terrible middle-aged creatures, who keep no grandmothers and no children of a companionable age, and who don't seem to know what a holly-bush or a miseltoe [*sic*] bough means, might like some of my presents. At all events I'll try." So Santa turned to the first house he found and walked in very shamefacedly with the children's toys in a basket on his arm.

There was a man in the house working very hard among papers and pieces of tape. "I beg your pardon" said Santa Claus, "but I've come this way by mistake, and there doesn't seem to be any room for me among the few children you own. But may be you would like some of my toys." Santa Claus, very red in the face and in a great hurry lest he should be rebuffed, held out the first thing in the basket his hand fell on. It was a big trumpet painted blue and white. The man looked up and said:– "Thanks for the hint Santa Claus. I shouldn't wonder if it attracted the attention of the Government. I'll begin blowing it for myself to-morrow."

Then Santa Claus left very pleased that one at least of his presents had been accepted; and passed on to distribute the rest of his toys elsewhere. There were many people whom he called upon, for the basket was a big one.

There was a lady who over estimated Santa Claus' power entirely, and as soon as she heard he arrived with gifts with him asked for the last twenty years of her life over again and three-fourths of her back-hair with them. All that Santa Claus could give her was a nice violet and magenta and black comforter for her dear old neck. But she grew angry, and Santa Claus left in haste.

There was a young man who told Santa Claus to his face that Santa Claus was a myth, and then asked for all manner of unreasonable things in the way of Love and Honour. Santa Claus said he kept only things for children, and, very apologetically, gave the young man a secondhand mechanical doll that could talk. He was glad to see how many grown-up people received his poor little gifts willingly and seemed to set great store by them.

There was a young lady who misunderstood Santa Claus and demanded to be taken back to England and the shops and the gas-lights at once. Santa Claus did all he could to console her, and finished by giving her a hurdy-gurdy to dance to, and a regiment of little tin soldiers. She was quite happy with them for a long time, till the music stopped with a click, and the men melted away one by one.

There was an elderly man who took, under protest, a box of toy bricks from Santa Claus. He said that the gift was kindly meant, but it was of no use to him, because he understood that with bricks it was necessary to build from the foundation upwards; whereas he all his life had been building from the roof downwards.

Indeed, he was at that very time occupied with the help of a few distinguished friends in putting the finishing touches on to a roof that under no circumstances would be fitted on to any foundation. Santa Claus couldn't understand what all this meant, but he smiled very politely, and gave the elderly gentleman very nearly two hundred toy balloons – the remnants of an old stock – to play with if he liked.

What struck Santa Claus most, was the kindness of the grown-up people in taking so much interest in toys meant only for children. For instance, there was a man with a Grievance who was most grateful for a toy rattle; and a man with a Future took as many comic and serious masks as Santa Claus would give him; while a woman with a Past thanked Santa Claus effusively for a little slide-lid paint-box with twelve colours and two brushes – such as they sell at home for 10½ d.

There was a man – a little, quiet, inoffensive man – who begged Santa Claus for a pair of child's stilts, and Santa Claus gave him them, and was delighted to see how they were appreciated. Every one was most kind to Santa Claus, except the lady aforesaid; and *she* threw the black and violet and magenta comforter away, and called Santa Claus "a goblin."

"Depend upon it" said Santa Claus as he gave away the last parcel. "Depend upon it, I ought to establish an agency for the yearly distribution of presents among the meritorious middle-aged in this part of the world. I never knew children in Germany or Sweden one half so enthusiastic as these are over my little trumperies."

Then he whipped up the reindeer, and guided by the very pale light in the East, headed northward for the Khyber and so back to his own place again. But as he whirled through the stations, a little child, who knew all about him, caught a glimpse of the Golden Sleigh and the white reindeer in the early morning.

"Santa Claus. Have you anything for me, Santa Claus?" Santa Claus pulled the reindeer on to their haunches till their horns cracked, and swung round. "Here" said he "is a properly educated child." Then he felt sorry because the sleigh was empty of gifts, and the child was holding up the skirt of its little nightgown expecting a present. Santa Claus thought of the box of bricks which the elderly gentleman had exchanged for the balloons. They were in the bearskin wrap. He handed them over the side of the sleigh.

"Bwicks!" said the child, and its eyes sparkled.

"Begin building from the foundation – then the walls – and lastly the red and gold windows" said Santa Claus.

The child hugged the box to its breast and replied scornfully – "Corse I will. I know how to play wif bwicks!"

"I beg your pardon" said Santa Claus gravely "but that's more than most people seem to know in this country. Good bye yunker!"

Next morning, when Santa Claus loosed the eight white reindeer under the Rjica Vom, where the Trolls and the Christmas Fairies live, he told his friends all about his extraordinary journey.

"You've been dreaming" said Atta Troll.[8] "There's no place in the world where there is no childhood and no old age, and where people have to be taught to build with bricks."

"Then the reindeer must have carried me into another world" said Santa Claus mournfully; for his night's experience had made him mistrustful of himself.

"That is much more probable" said Atta Troll.

R. K.

---

[1] Hans Christian Andersen, *A Christmas Greeting to My English Friends*, London, 1847.
[2] Not identified.
[3] An ancient site on the rim of a crater in Iran.
[4] 'Who are you?' (Harbord).
[5] 'Answer. Who are you?' (Harbord).
[6] 'All right! Probably it's a bearer or perhaps the sweeper; but don't clean my room now. Come at 7 o'clock. I am going to sleep now' (Harbord).
[7] 'Fetch in the bear and dance at once' (Harbord).
[8] The dancing bear in Heinrich Heine's poem 'Atta Troll' (1841).

"Love in Old Cloathes"

꙳

Published: *Civil and Military Gazette*, 4 July 1887.

Attribution: In Scrapbook 3 (28/3, p. 6).

Text: *Civil and Military Gazette*.

Notes: Unrecorded and unreprinted. RK has altered the title to 'An Old Story' on the cutting in Scrapbook 3. The story is one of the items that RK chose for the unpublished *Book of the Forty-Five Mornings*.[1] That would be one reason for changing the title. Another is the fact that the story is closely modelled on a story of the same title by the American H. C. Bunner that appeared in *Stories by American Authors*, vol. IV, New York, 1884. That story begins thus: 'Newe York, yᵉ 1ˢᵗ Aprille, 1883. / Yᵉ worste of my ailment is this, yᵗ groweth not Less with much nursing …' and so on. Like RK's, Bunner's story concerns a jealous lover.

꙳

Being extracts from the Diary of C. Heymann Esq.

Monday.—It came to me this Morn on my Awakening yt I was a Beaste; my evil Conscience helping my more evill Heade to this sad End. Six of ye Queen's Officers – most ungodly Men and never slaked no more than ye Dust – had me to Mess overnighte; I foolishly consenting and taking, Lord knows, thrice as much of thrice as many Mixings of their Drinkes as was right for me: my Stomach being always tender and ye Heate extreme. A half of a Sheep's Tongue to Breakfaste and a Gallon of Soda Water wh. I make no sort of doubt, was devised for sinful Soules. *Videlicet* Christopher Heymann.

Sware a great Oathe to go to Messes no more till ye Heate be abated, or ye Queen's Captains have browst more gentle Drinkes.

In ye Verandah after Breakfaste, awaiting a Letter wh. never came, and laughed at myself for a Foole, who am so put in such an Extremity of Trouble and Unreste because She will not write dailie from ye Hills to a poore, sweltering, swilling Wretche – to wit Christopher Heymann yt loved Her since She first came to this accursed Land.

To Office, and on ye Way beat my Horse – a better than I – because of ye Letter, he running as fast as mighte be in ye Sun. Being angry with Myselfe for being vext, did beat him afresh and he kickt out ye Splashe-Board. A new one. This lies to my Charge.

An evil Day for my Baboo, his Devill making him rude, and of high and proud Conduct. He is now gone in Tears, saying he will swear an Information for Assault and loss of Character. But this hath wrought greate Peace in ye Office, and I can now thinke of ye Letter wh. never came.

Sweare a bigg Oathe to put ye Matter from my Minde, and so hugged it to me till Tiffin time and after, till ye Office closed: I having done no Work save to settle ye Hashe of ye Baboo. Poore Beaste! Bethought me yt ye Baboo in his Youthe wooed a Maide of ye Moores, and so gave him a Rupee for his broken Head. But ye Black Bullock mistook my Tendernesse, and said ye Gifte was through Feare of ye Information. I have resumed ye Rupee, and told him to go to ye Divel and swear Informations till ye Cracke of Doom.

To Dinner alone in my House and in ye Middle of Eating was stung by ye Knowledge that Jobbson – him with ye large Eyes and pink Choppes – hath To-daye been ye better Part of two Months at Simla where She lives; She having met Jobbson before yt I was betrothed to Her.

Swore a big Oathe to wringe Jobbson his Necke for going thither, and upset ye Potatoes which I said was ye Fault of my *Consumah*. Ye *Consumah* said it was so, and I did most foully berate him for yt he was a lying Hounde who sought to currie Favour with me. Ye evening Dawke hath brought no Letter.

Went to my Bed vext and dreamed that I slew Jobbson with a Potato, he being black all over like ye Baboo.

Tuesday.—To-daye no Letter. Have writ a long one before Breakfaste to Her, asking what I have done, and so heated my Fancy with conceiving a thousand horrible Things of Her – who is a Sainte – and Jobbson – who is a Whelpe – that had no Hearte to my Food. Hereat blamed ye *Consumah* and in pullinge ye Punkah-rope, ye Coolie sleepinge, broke it in twaine. Sent my Letter to ye Dawke and began to wait for ye Answer. Ye Babu has sworn his Information, but he cannot abide within ye Boundes of Truth. Hath sworn yt I beate him senseless with ye Office Ruler and stampt on him. This can be disproven, and after he shall be stampt on.

No Letter to-day. To Whiste at ye Clubb where I did grievouosly insult Porkiss for yt he said he had News of Jobbson and yt he – Jobbson of ye pink Choppes, – was very happie in ye Hills. Thereon, later, calling to Minde yt there were ninety-six other Maidens in Simla for Jobbson his Liking, did make amendes to Porkiss and aske him to Drinkes. Porkiss says yt my Wits are gone wool-gathering. They have butt followed my Hearte wh. is far enough from this desolate Place. Heaven send yt they soon return, for I have no Stomach to my Worke.

Wednesday.—As I lay a thinking in ye Morninge under ye Punkah, found yt I had made a Plann of Sick Leave to avoide my Worke and hie to Her in ye Hills, and so blusht under ye Sheets being mightilley ashamed of myselfe. Did also remember ye Time when I was proude of my Worke and beate no Baboos. Swore a big Oathe yt Love was Poison and lookt at her Picture till it was time to Tubbe.

To-day no Letter, and I am in no sort fit to be trusted with an Office. Ye Chaprassi askt leave to go and be wed; and I foolishly gave it without Question. There was no Wedding but a Law-suit only and all ye Cobbe-Webs I wove on ye Loves of my Chaprassi is come to nothing. I writ her Name seven and thirty Times large upon my Blottinge-Pad and then did tear up all ye Sheetes for fear yt ye Inke had soaked through and so bewrayed my Shame. Have written off ye Blotting-Padd to State Charges; but cannot so write away my Unreste.

Ye Baboo is afresh contumelious, having suborned Punkah-Coolies to bear witness yt he lay senseless on ye Floore while I stamped upon his Stomach. I have no Hearte to treat him as he deserves and I cannot eate. Have made review of my Actions of ye laste few Days and see yt there is a bigger Foole on ye Earthe than was ever before borne – to wit, Christopher Heymann, my most distraught Self.

Thursday.—This Day is Pain to me, and I would I were dead! This Morn came ye Dawke with one Letter that methought was from Her but it was Jobbson – a Hounde and a Pig and all evil Things – writing of a Love yt he hath found in ye Hills. She is, he saith, fair (She) and tall (She), with great grey Eyes (She), and a most marvellous Knowledge of Horsewomanship (She), and a little Dowrie (She), and, above all, she hath given him her Hearte into his keeping, and they are to be wedded in the end of next Month. Nay, but I cannot write to this Laste "She," for I will not so wrong Her to believe that She hath forgotten me, and in so little space for yt Barber's Block Jobbson.

Have read ye Letter fortie times, and my Throate is drie with abusing of Jobbson, his Eyes and Soule. I have nineteen Times believed that he hath taken Her from me, and one and twentie Times I have said that it was another Maide, there being ninety-seven (or six, if She be still my own) for him to picke and chuse among, nor ever come nigh my Love at all.

Now I know not what I believe, and I will not go to Office for fear yt I should slaye ye Baboo, and so ende my most miserable Life and Love on ye Gibbett. Which were far ye better Way. I have lockt all my Doores, and am alone with Jobbson his wicked, wicked Letter.

He saith that he loved her, this new Love of his, when yt he first saw her in this Place, wh. is She, if His evil wriggle-tailed Scrawle hath either Sense or Meaninge. I make no doubt now that He hath taken Her from Me; She being fickle after the rest of Her Kinde, and he hath not set down the name out of Evil-Kindness. Did, on the Belief, drinke much at my lonelie Dinner and smoked seven Cigars, thinking of Jobbson and She that were then riding, (so my Fancy made it) round Jakko Hill; both ye Horses very neare together.

To my Shame found that I wisht She, and Jobbson might both be heaved over ye Khud at Sanjaoli where it is steepest, and so thinking could not sleepe at all.

Friday.—A blacke Friday for me. I lookt at my Heade in ye Glass this Morn; my Eyes being puffed and my Haire in great Disorder, and I saw yt no Maid could love a Beaste (*exempli gratia*, Christopher Heymann,) and yt Jobbson was ye better Mann with his pinke Jowle and big Eye-browse, as long as Leeches but more nastie. Hereon, I went to Breakfaste and made Pretence to myself to eate heavily yt I might show ye *Consumah* and ye little black Lizard on ye Mantelpiece yt I cared for no Man nor Woman neither. But ye Heate and my Trouble sickened me, and I pusht away my Plate and fell a-smoking.

There was To-daye no Letter, and I am now assured yt She means to caste me off by Her Silence wh. Tricke She hath doubtless learnt from one of those ninety-six Wenches that were not sweete enough for ye Thing called Jobbson. But She hath made Her Choice well, and he is a

Prettie Fellow, fit to be beaten into a Jellie by Me. I will take my Farewell of Her as a Gentleman should, courteously and with Laughter; saying yt since She hath seen Her Error of chusing I will e'en keep my Wordes between my Teethe, and send 'em a pair of Silver Sugar-Tonges.

Then I saw in my Minde's Eye, She and Jobbson akissing at ye Backe of Summer Hill, where a Spit runs out from ye Mountaine, where I kist Her once, when our Love was new, and She said yt it would not die. Wh. Vision threw me into such a Posture of Grief and Indignation yt I kickt my Dog round ye Room for yt he laid his Paws on my Knee and whined for ye Sake of my Grief wh. he saw in my Eyes.

In ye Evening, after great Torments, I made shifte to write yt Letter and Another to Jobbson both merrie Ones and my Hearte cut in two in ye writing, promising ye Sugar-Tongs and a concerne in ye Welfare of him and his . . . When that She should be wed to him; this Latter making me nigh sick. Sente both ye Letters to ye Box, and so bade adieu to Love; thanking I would live and die a Bachelor.

Saturday.—I have no power to put my Wordes on Paper aright! I have robbed ye Queen's Mail on ye Queen's Highway, from ye Pillar Box over against ye Mall, wh. is seven Yeares in Prison and was Twenty Rupees into ye Hand of ye Poste Man! But I will essay to begin in order. It was ye Fever and no Jobbson at all, who is ye best of Good Fellowes and is contract to Her Sister who is Her Double had I but thought in my Selfishness, and They woulde not let Her tell me of ye Fever – (this her Mother's Worke, who will be my Mother-in-Lawe and I dare not even in these my private Papers call her a sillie Woman) – and so no Letters came to me.

Thus far I had reade in Her most blessed Letter yt came this Morn, running straightway to ye Pillar Boxe wherein my two Follies lay, and was for drawing them up and out with a crooked Sticke till ye Poste Man came, and was first beaten and then bribed by me who have broken the Lawe, and am full to my Hearte's Brimm of Thankfulness and Delight. Ye two letters are burned and I have kissed the new One yt came from Her but half an Hour since a thousand Times; vowing yt I will buy Jobbson a Thousand Sugar-Tongs against his Wedding.

This is no common Affair, yt hath been so marvellously set right by Providence; and We Two are now many Lakhs of Kisses in mutuall Debt yt nothing save a Journey to Simla will pay. I will take ten Days for my Sickness' sake (having loste all Shame in Desire to be neare Her again) and ye Babu may swear Informations till I return, for, by all ye Horrors of this last Weeke, Love is ye only serious Matter in this fair Earthe of ours, and ye Reste is Bubbles and Froth.

---

[1] The book, advertised for publication in 1891, was to consist of uncollected items from RK's Indian journalism. The list of titles to be included is in RK's letter to A. P. Watt of [27 January 1890] in *Rudyard Kipling's Letters to his Agents*, 2016, pp. 7–8.

The Case of Adamah

Published: *Civil and Military Gazette*, 6 July 1887.

Attribution: In Scrapbook 3 (28/3, p. 131) and Scrapbook 4 (28/4, p. 192).

Text: *Civil and Military Gazette.*

Notes: This is one of the series of articles attributed to one 'Smith', a civil servant who writes of his domestic affairs and whose voice we hear in this piece (see also 'A Rather More Fishy Case'). The series gently mocks the Public Services Commission, then at work. The Smith articles were first collected in an unauthorised edition, called *The Smith Administration*, published in 1891 in Allahabad and then suppressed at RK's demand. In 1899 RK published a slightly different selection of the stories as *The Smith Administration* in *From Sea to Sea*. Neither selection includes 'The Case of Adamah'.

Reprinted in the Martindell–Ballard pamphlets and in Harbord, III, 1609–10.

"If any fault be found with the packing or contents of this box, the undersigned will feel obliged if this paper is be returned to them with remarks.

R———& Co.
Cheroot Manufacturers"

The name of the packer, as "this paper" sets forth, is Adamah; and there is no fault to be found with the cheroots. My friends deny this; vowing that, though excellent to me, the smoker, the smell of the black, rank, little twists is poisonous and annoying to all within nose-range. But this is a frivolous objection, and my mind is full of larger issues.

I see reflected on the two square inches of "this paper" the whole of the mighty administration of India whereof I am a small part – a cog in a wheel or, having regard to weather at present, a heated bearing. "If any fault be found with the packing or contents of this box." Why should R——— and Co. be so anxious for me to find fault, and why do they

thrust the name of the packer, Adamah, under my nose? Even sup-
posing that he had filled the box, for his own profit, with half-smoked
stubs, do R——— and Co. suppose that I, seventeen hundred miles
away, shall strike at Adamah, demanding his head per V.P.P.[1] in the
next consignment of coconadas? What concern have I with that distant
Tamil? I would fain answer "none whatever," but that my conscience
tells me Adamah and I are in the same boat – or box, if you please.

Nay, my case is even harder than Adamah's. He is responsible only to
R——— and Co, Cigar Manufacturers, when "this paper" is returned
to them "with remarks;" which return may take place once in five years,
perhaps.

And I? I am responsible to a far more exacting firm – a thing without
bowels that insists on my filling a greater number of boxes than the day
and a fair portion of the night permits. Once despatched, the whole
wide Indian Empire is at perfect liberty to find fault with the "packing
and contents." My employers ask it to do so. They are unhappy if it
declines the invitation, and forthwith examine the boxes themselves;
counting each blur and blotch in the stencil, and pointing out each place
where the red tape that keeps down the cover has been hastily or imper-
fectly knotted. On these faults they write remarks of a haughty and
contemptuous nature. But the Indian Empire in its hours of idleness is
worse than my employers. The insignificance of my work, the certainty
that to-morrow it will all be reduced to smoke, gives me no protection. Men rise up from obscure corners of the Empire, from Burmah
or Biluchistan to write "remarks" on the "packing and contents." I read
these remarks, and the years do not make them less bitter. They irritate me needlessly, and I would give much to take each caviller aside,
and explain to him over one of Adamah's cheroots, that I really did
my best and there were reasons – hundreds of reasons – why this or
that little slip should have occurred. My employers are right when they
say administration is not conducted so pleasantly and personally; and I
must bear with misunderstandings both from the Firm and the Public.
None the less, the "remarks" are galling.

I wonder if Adamah has ever been brought to book for bad packing – whether he waits in fear and trembling for the returns of "this
paper" which is to betray his shiftlessness. Does each day's *dak* fill him,
as it fills me, with anxiety that strips the scalp, and a sense of injustice

done that frets and wears the temper? I think not. Adamah is a native, but he might be made to feel. "This paper" lies temptingly to my hand. Shall I cover it with remarks on the vileness of Adamah's packing? The percentage of broken and unsmokeable cheroots, and the disgraceful state of the red paper lining? Adamah would never know that I had lied away his fair fame as a packer; and R——— and Co. would talk to him and, possibly, cut his pay.

How does the old puzzle run? If you in England could, by raising your little finger, save the life of a peasant in Central China, would you do so? Adamah is, for me, that peasant, and, the question is, shall I fill up "this paper" or shall I throw it away? It is true that Adamah has never written "remarks" on my boxes; but it is equally true that he has been at perfect liberty to do so if he liked. Why has he held his hand? From generosity and innate courtesy, knowing that I was already sufficiently harassed, or simply through deep ignorance of me or my works? Shall I give him the benefit of the doubt, or shall I deliver him into the hands of R——— and Co. because he does not take an interest in one of his rulers? Let me be just and turn over the cheroots with an Imperial and administrative eye. One, two, three, – five are slightly cracked, not sufficiently to spoil the "draw," but quite enough to excuse damning Resolu— remarks. Theoretically, there should not have been one flaw in the hundred. I must vindicate the principles of cheroot-packing quite apart from any personal feeling. Men – English and native – have casti-gated me for lesser *lâches*, and I will, for principle's sake and the dignity of the Empire I serve. . . . . pass on punishment, which I am unable to resent, to Adamah in Coconada.

Never! Adamah, my fellow-sufferer, my yoke-bullock, my Brother, continue to pack thy cheroots in peace. Are we not linked by the same chain of Destiny, I the puffer, thou the packer, and over the lives of each does there not hang the shadow of "this paper" which says:– "If any fault be found with the packing or contents of this box, the undersigned will feel obliged if this paper be returned to them with remarks"?

Shall we increase each other's burdens? A thousand times, no.

Smith.

---

[1] Value Payable Post.

A Tale of '98

※

Published: *Civil and Military Gazette*, 18 July 1887.

Attribution: In Scrapbook 3 (28/3, p. 133).

Text: *Civil and Military Gazette*.

Notes: Unrecorded and unreprinted. Complaints about the Indian rail system were endemic. From Bombay, Lahore was served by the Rajputana Line, about which RK wrote a few days after this item:

> We are told that the damage [to the line at Ajmere] consisted only of the 'washing away in two places of a few yards of ballast'. Nevertheless, we in Lahore know that the delivery of last week's Home mail was delayed for fourteen hours on account of a few yards … What would the Rajputana line do if it were breached in earnest?
>
> (*CMG*, 21 July 1887).

※

It was growing monotonous, and His Excellency began to complain. The Easily Interfered-with, the Gone Immediately Phut, and the Burat Bund and Cracked Irrigation-cut Railways, had split themselves into half-mile lengths, and were swimming about their respective provinces like dominoes in a puddle. The Not Worth Running Railway shut up all its bridges with a click, and retired from business after the first five inches were recorded.[1] As long as the papers could struggle on without any Home news or exchanges, they said that the interruption to traffic was very serious, but they had no doubt that the zeal and energy of the nearest C.I.E.[2] would mend matters shortly.

Then the telegraph-posts began to fall out of the hill-sides like old teeth; all the Simla communications were interrupted. No one knew what His Excellency was saying or thinking, for there was a mile and a half of raving, roaring Gugger between the nearest Telegraph-Engineer and the first broken telegraph-post. The Council were shut up with His Excellency, and Naini Tal was cut off from Allahabad.

The newspapers led a hand-to-mouth existence for another fort-night, on fragments of old reports, and then they went out – reluc-tantly and apologetically – one by one. *The True Briton, Last Week's Information* and the *Politician*³ vowed that, if the Government had stayed in Calcutta, this abnormal monsoon would never have occurred; and the "fatuous folly of a crassly unsympathetic administration was absolutely and solely responsible." They subsisted on Police Reports and Municipal Meetings for a few days after the others had ceased from troubling. The *Backwoodsman* said that "the display of tact and firmness was highly creditable to all concerned," and finished its life with a Latin quotation and a front page full of advertisements. The *Abusive and Martial Journal* hinted that the monsoon was the work of Russia or the Kukas, printed an epic in blank verse to prove this, and went to bed.

The *Trombay Bassinette* and the *Chimes of India* laughed.⁴ They had all the Home news to themselves, and filled in the spaces with articles on the depreciation of the rupee, and the "shameful want of enterprize of our up-country contemporaries."

The *Madras Female*⁵ fell back on the files of the *Tit-Bits* and old Jubilees, which it used economically in leaded type. The others were mortified, through being cut off. They waited till the country dried up again.

It was a most peculiar monsoon. It rained for five weeks without stop-ping. And, at the end of that time, there was not enough railway-line in Upper India to make a crowbar out of.

Then the "second-leave" men began to enquire how they were to go to the Hills. They asked each other first, and, later on, the Engineers. Any Engineer, but Superintending ones for choice. The Engineers said they really did not know. They expected that through communi-cation from Calcutta to Peshawar might perhaps be restored in three years.

At this time, His Excellency and the Council were cut off from everything, and no one could get a message into or out of Simla. Some of the husbands in the Plains cried. Others were very happy, because they had no household expense.

The "second-leave" men were covered with prickly heat, and this spoilt their tempers. When they met an Engineer they used to throw pieces of *kunkar* and soda-water bottles at him, to express their disapproval of the Indian Railway system.

They used to get up in the morning and hunt Engineers over the *maidan*, in the water, with stirrup-leathers and polo-sticks.

The "second-leave" men got no leave, and there were few Engineers left alive in the larger stations. The *True Briton* published a spasmodic issue, condemning the slaughter as "injudicious," but the *dâk* was washed away at Mogul Serai and its words were cast on the waters.

Then the floods began to subside, and as soon as there was not more than two feet of water on the Kalka road, all Umballa waded upstream to see what would come over the Gugger.

The first thing they saw was a cock-nosed Indus stone-boat full of the Viceroy's Council. The mariners were pale and thin, and gesticulated wildly. They asked for food and Engineers, Royal for choice. The Umballa people thought their minds had gone.

Later on, another stone-boat, trimmed with red *saloo*, was poled across the Gugger. In it sat His Excellency. He looked worn but determined. He made no speeches fit for publication, but explained that he was waiting for the Commander-in-Chief and the Jutogh Mule-Battery. Next day all three punted down to Umballa, where there was a special parade of troops. Next week nearly eighty Engineers of various grades were sent in from out-stations where they had taken refuge, and the seniors were executed in front of the garrison, near the muddy smudge that marked where the Dâk Gharri Office had once stood. The Sappers were in full-dress uniform. Gentlemen not entitled to uniform wore morning dress. But there was no difference in the charges of powder.

It took His Excellency and the Commander-in-Chief three months to reach Calcutta; and they executed three Engineers every ten days between Delhi and Bankipore. The promotion in the Department was satisfactory even to the most down-trodden juniors.

In one year, all the bridges and railways were in working order, and the curious thing is that, though we have had many severe monsoons since, they have never given way. The feed-pipes at the watering-stations are convertible into a gallows at five minutes' notice, which may be given by the Senior Military or Civil Officer in the station, when he considers that an embankment shows signs of unsteadiness.

[1] RK's comic names for the following railways: Easily Interfered With > East Indian Railway; Gone Immediately Phut > Great Indian Peninsula Railway; Burat, Bund and Cracked Irrigation-Cut Railway > Bombay, Baroda and Central India Railway; Not Worth Running Railway > Northwestern State Railway.

[2] Companion of the Indian Empire, a decoration awarded for service in India.

[3] That is, *The Englishman*, the *Weekly News* and *The Statesman*.

[4] *Bombay Gazette* and *Times of India*. As Bombay (Mumbai) papers they had no need of the railway, the mails coming to the port of Bombay.

[5] *Madras Mail*.

A Rather More Fishy Case

Published: *Civil and Military Gazette*, 26 July 1887.

Attribution: In Scrapbook 3 (28/3, p. 5).

Text: *Civil and Military Gazette.*

Note: Unrecorded and unreprinted. For the series of 'Smith' stories, see the headnote to 'The Case of Adamah'.

The following is the letter of the Chief Secretary of the *** Government to the Commissioner of the _____ Division; conveying the orders of the Government upon the action of Mr. Skrewson:–

(1). It appears from the reports and records now submitted, that there is a large loose-box (or enclosure, surrounded on three sides with mud walls, and on the fourth with *bails* or wooden bars) in the Chorpur Sub-Division, the property of one Smith, a European. In the enclosure (or loose box) was occasionally to be found a *ghoont* (or horse of Himalayan extraction) assessed by the Municipality under the by-laws which provided for the taxation of horses and vehicles. It is noteworthy, as showing the extreme perversity of the Sub-Divisional Magistrate of Chorpur, in the prejudiced view of that animal taken from the outset, that Smith, owner of the enclosure or loose-box, had frequently, in the hearing of witnesses whose evidence has been commented on by Sir Homer Botheram, declared the *ghoont* or Himalayan horse to be a "wild beast." J. Tompkins, C.E., also a European, whose evidence would naturally lean to the defence of his fellow-countryman, stated before the magistrate on oath that Smith had, on several occasions, asserted openly that the *ghoont* was "the wildest beast he knew."

(2). The night of February 11th, 1887, Smith received information from Balloo, *sais*, that in the course of the past ten days, four horses had been taken out of their enclosures on the grounds of two English persons by some native gentlemen in pursuance of the immemorial custom set forth in the ancient Sanskrit proverb which says:– "Finding's keeping, losing's seeking." The records of the Chorpur Sub-Division show that horses, which include *ghoonts*, were annually removed from their enclosures by native gentlemen in the months of February and March.

On the night of 18th February four native gentlemen entered the enclosure, and proceeded to take out the *ghoont* which, it must be remembered, has been ruled a wild animal; this act of taking constituting possession. The horse, at that time, was in a state of nature and, from evidence recorded at the first trial even more wild than is necessary for the purpose of Sir Homer Botheram's decision. It is described by three of the four native gentlemen as a *"pukka shaitan*," which, the learned judge lays down, is the exact equivalent of *fera naturæ*. On seeing these four gentleman, Dulloo, sais, told them of his employer's objection to the removal of any thing from the enclosure, and at the same time despatched his son, Mugha, to inform the man Smith, who ran towards the enclosure which three of the men had entered. These three men were than lying in various portions of the enclosure suffering from abdominal and facial injuries caused by the feet and teeth of the wild horse. The fourth gentleman was overpowered by the man Smith, Peruu, coachman, Dulloo, *sais*, and it is believed, from the marks of diminutive teeth in the calf of his leg, by the boy. Mughin, still at large. The man Smith had stated before the Magistrate that he had whipped with the butt of a hogspear the fourth gentleman; and thereafter subjecting all four to an unlawful restraint composed of heel-ropes, despatched Dulloo, *sais*, for a policeman.

(3). The evidence at the trial before the Magistrate showed that the animal or *ghoont* was required by the defendants for the Ashwamédra or horse-sacrifice, a revival of one of the most remarkable and instructive of the ceremonies of the later Vedantic period and especially cherished by all Hindus of the advanced and enlightened school. It is actually on record, in the files of the *Suchi Durpan*, Brahmo Sumaj Journal of Chorpur,[1] that the Magistrate observed that "where property was concerned, he did not care in the least for the Ashwamédra." The four native gentlemen were, after a trial of less than two hours, sentenced to two years' rigorous imprisonment each.

(4). The two errors of which the sub-divisional Magistrate appears, from his judgment, to have been guilty are (1) that he found the accused guilty of theft and (2) that he sentenced them to imprisonment. As regards the first point, it seems to the Lieutenant Governor that the Magistrate, never from the beginning entertained any doubt that the removal of the *ghoont* from the enclosure against the will of the man Smith amounted to theft. It was an undoubted fact that catching *ghoonts* in enclosures against the will of the owner or lessee had heretofore (as shown by the cases of the Queen Emperor v. Shere Singh, Afalla Khan and others, Queen Empress v. Mangal Khan and others) been regarded as theft; though, even on this view of the general law, the Magistrate should have had regard to the fact that the existence of a curious and interesting custom had been pleaded.

(5). It remains, then, to deal with the Magistrate's action in rejecting the plea of custom, and in sentencing the accused to rigorous imprisonment; and on these points His Honour is compelled to observe that the Magistrate showed a want of appreciation of the proper way of dealing with the case and that the punishment was unreasonably severe. It seems, therefore, to His Honour that the Magistrate should have referred the lessee of the enclosure to the Civil Court. A slight fine would have sufficiently marked the illegality of the act which has been demonstrated by Sir Homer Botheram to be perfectly legal.

(6). In deciding how he should deal with the magistrate His Honour is somewhat confused. He considers that by the judgment of Sir Homer Botheram the position of *ghoont*-holders has become slightly anomalous; but he feels also the necessity of bearing in mind, on the other hand, that it is impossible to overlook the insensitivity to the customs of the people and the excessive deference paid to the man Smith's claim to the right of property in the *ghoont*, which has been abundantly shown to be a "wild beast." Under pressure of circumstances and out of a not unnatural reluctance to stigmatise Sir Homer Botheram as incorrect in law, His Honour has determined to remove the Magistrate from the sub-division of Chorpur and to remove him to a sultry station. He further directs that he be deprived of his magisterial power for six months and of his pay for four and devoutly wishes that Sir Homer Botheram could be treated in the same way.

(7). In the course of your letter, you raise the question as to the position in which persons possessing *ghoonts* or horses would be placed if it be found that, following the decision in the present case, they are unable to invoke the aid of the criminal law in defence of their rights, even when such rights are finally established by Civil Courts. His Honour prefers to state the question in its naked absurdity and to leave its decision to time and the Legislative Council. It would certainly appear that a *ghoont* for which Rs. 500 have been paid, should not be taken away, even for an Ashwanédra sacrifice. But circumstances alter cases and His Honour must have better information than is furnished by the very grotesque judgment of Sir Homer Botheram and his learned brother on the Bench.

[1] The Brahmo Somaj was a reform movement within Hinduism; the name 'Suchi Durpan' ('Mirror') was also used by RK as that of a newspaper publishing 'cheap sedition' in 'The Finest Story in the World' (*Many Inventions*).

The House of Shadows
By Its Occupant

Published: *Civil and Military Gazette*, 4 August 1887.

Attribution: In Scrapbooks 3 (28/3, p. 138) and 4 (28/4, p. 142).

Text: *Civil and Military Gazette.*

Notes: This is the first of RK's stories to appear as a 'turnover', beginning on the just remodelled front page of the *CMG* and 'turning over' to the second page. The cutting in Scrapbook 4 has been lightly corrected by RK.

Reprinted in *Kipling's India: Uncollected Sketches.*

A woman had died and a child had been born in it, but these are accidents which may overtake the most respectable establishments. No sensible man would think of regarding them. Indeed, so sound is my common sense, that I sleep in the room of the death and do my work in the room of the birth; and have no fault to find with either apartment. My complaint is against the whole house; and my grievance, so far as I can explain it in writing, is that there are far too many tenants in the eight, lime-washed rooms for which I pay seventy-five rupees a month.

They trooped in after the great heats of May as snakes seek bathrooms through drought. Personally I should prefer the snakes, the visible, smashable snakes, to the persons who have quartered themselves upon me for the past ten weeks. They take up no space and are almost noiseless, like the Otto Gas Engines[1] – but they are there and they trouble me. In the very early morning when I climb on to the roof to catch what less heated breeze may be abroad, I am conscious that some one has preceded me up the narrow steps, and that there is some one at my heels. You will concede, will you not, that this is annoying, particularly when I know that I am officially the sole tenant. No man, visible or invisible, has a right to spy on my outgoings or incomings. At breakfast, in the full fresh daylight, I am conscious that some one who is not the *khitmutgar* is watching the back of my head from the door that leads into my bedroom; when I turn sharply, the *purdah* is dropped and I only see it waving gently as though shaken by the wind. Quitting the house to go to office, I am sure – sure as I am of my own existence – that it is at once taken possession of by the people who follow me about, and that they hold who knows what mad noiseless revels in the room when the bearer has done his duster-flapping and the servants have withdrawn to their own quarters.

Indeed, once returning from office at an unexpected hour, I surprised the house, rushed in and found . . . . nothing. My footfall rang through the barn-like rooms, and as the noise ceased, I felt that the people who had been crowding the floor were rushing away – pouring out into the garden and the verandahs, and I could not see them. But I knew they had been there. The air was full of the rustle of their garments.

Still an assembly is preferable to the one man – he must be a man; he is so restless – who comes in to spend the evening and roams through the house. His feet make no noise, but I can hear in the hot, still night the jar of the *chik* as he comes into the verandah, and the lifting of the *purdah* over the drawing-room door. Then he touches a book in the drawing-room, for I hear it fall, or he thrums the Burmese gong ever so lightly, for I catch the faint ring of the smitten metal, and passes on, shifting things, scratching things, tapping things, till I could shriek aloud with irritation. When he comes to the room I am in he stops, puts the *purdah* aside and looks at me. I am sure of it, for when I turn the *purdah* has always just fallen. He must be the man who takes so impertinent an interest in my breakfast. But he will never face me and tell me what he wants. He is always in the next room. Though I have hunted him through the house again and again, he is always in the next room.

When I enter, I know that he has just gone out. The *purdah* betrays him. And when I go out I know that he is waiting, always waiting, to slip into the room I have vacated, and begin his aimless stroll among the knickknacks. If I go into the verandah, I know that he is watching me from the drawing-room. I can hear him sitting down on one of the wicker-work chairs that creaks under his weight.

The Sundays, the long, hot pitiless Sundays, when the consciousness of arrears of work prevents their clearance, he comes to spend the day in my house from ten in the morning till the hour of the evening drive. I can offer him no amusement. He cannot find me cheering company.

Why does he hang about the house? He should have learnt by this time not to touch a *punkha* fringe with his head or to leave the door on the swing, I can track him then and prevent him sitting down on the chairs in the next room.

I would endure the people who hide in the corners of the lamproom and rush out when my back is turned, the persons who get between the almirah and the wall when I come into my dressing-room hastily at dusk, or even the person in the garden who slides in and out of the *ferash* trees when I walk there, if I could only get rid of the Man in the Next room. There is no sense in him, and he interferes sadly with one's work. I believe now that if he dared he would come out from the other side of the *purdah* and peep over my shoulder to see what I am writing. But he is afraid and is now twitching the cord that works the ventilating window. I can hear it beating against the wall. What pleasure can he find in prowling thus about another man's premises? I asked him that question last Sunday, but my voice came back to me from the high ceiling of the empty room next my bedroom, and that was all my answer.

One of these days, perhaps, if I enter my own house very, very silently, with bare feet, crawling through a window, I may be able to catch him and wring from him some sort of explanation; for it is manifestly absurd that a man paying seventy-five rupees a month should be compelled to live with so unsatisfactory a chum as the man in the next room.

On second thoughts, and after a plain statement of facts to the doctor, I think it would be better to go to the Hills for a while and leave him to maunder about the empty house till he is tired. The doctor says he will be gone when I return; taking all the other persons with him.

---

[1] A stationary, one-cylinder internal combustion engine developed by Nicolaus Otto, introduced in 1864.

The Confession of an Impostor
(By the Man Himself)

Published: *Civil and Military Gazette*, 11 August 1887.
Attribution: In Scrapbook 3 (28/3, pp. 141–2).
Text: *Civil and Military Gazette.*
Note: Unrecorded and unreprinted.

I make no complaint. I do not even blame Fate – that last scape-goat of the luckless. Indeed, to-day I have nothing to complain of; for I am accounted a rising man. There are those who consider me successful.

It was ordained that I should fight the battle of life early. A gap in the ranks offered itself; and I was thrust into it almost before I knew what had happened. The last words of counsel from those who had ordered my days were: "Pick up as you go along!"

On my conscience, worn and frayed as a bullock-trunk, I declare to you that sentence is the only education I have thoroughly taken into my system. My *métier* was "to pick up as I went along" and a vast lumberage of scrap-ends of knowledge, disconnected facts – all useless, unpacked and unavailable – are witnesses to the zeal with which I followed the advice of my elders. There was the line of battle – in front lay the smoke of the great Action of Life and – could I do anything else? – I went in. That year's draft of recruits moved forward. Had I desired it I could not have stepped back. I was a man fighting with and against men. I was "picking up as I went along." Among the many dreams that vex a man in the night is one wherein he finds himself, clad in the scantiest of night-gear, thrust into a brawling street full of friends all decently dressed. You know the agony and shame of that dream? Imagine it translated into life – drawn out through year after year – and you may conceive the distress I have suffered and do still endure. My curtailed shift of knowledge, piece it out as I will, is for ever threatening to disclose the abject nakedness of my ignorance. I have patched it in a hundred places, but the patches show, the patches show, and my abiding fear is lest my well-clad comrades should notice the deficiency.

I am picking up as I go along, you know. I have to be very careful, very alert, and painfully active, at a time when men are decently forgetting the less valuable portions of their teaching. I do not know what to collect and what to cast aside any more than the caddis-worm that weights its shell with the indiscriminate small-drift of the stream's bed. "It may come in useful one of these days," and therefore "I must pick up as I go along." Does a soldier lace his boots, or begin to get into his knapsack when the first dropping shots from the front open? The text is a stale one, but I could preach such a sermon from it as the wisest divines could not hope to equal. The horror of my life is that men have been known to envy me – that I have been forced to pass over the bodies of men to attain to my goal. And those who envy and those whom I have defeated by trickery and foul thrusts are better men than I. They know at least some one thing accurately; while I must "pick up as I go along." I cannot even lie thoroughly, for much of this is true; and I cannot wholly speak the truth, for much of this is a lie. If I would do *one* single thing with the certainty of assured knowledge I should be happy and, perhaps, permanently successful. But all my imperfect knowledge, and all my fragmentary accomplishments have been "picked up as I went along" and, since I was lightly weighed at the beginning, I stand a little way – not far it is true, but still a little way – beyond the regular ranks – the solid files of the men who know, the men who have been taught, grounded and educated.

If this unlucky prominence brings me preferment, what can I do? Take the proffered post, and trust the luck that has hitherto enabled me to "pick up as I go along," or disclaim the responsibility and shirk the test that it carries? I cannot tell. I could not be altogether honest if I tried – the strain of pretence of equality has destroyed honesty in me. It is probable that I should arrive at a compromise. And then, the descent will begin. A man who "picks up" must be always "going along." If he halts, some one may see and understand what a pitiful thing he is. If he go forward he may die before the crisis comes, and be only unmasked on the other side of the grave.

In my own case, the end – which is Discovery – is not far off. I cannot "pick up" and "go along" at the same time. The pace is too good, and there are better men behind – calm-eyed, confident men, who have not daily and hourly to hide their ignorance from their equals. Presently they will close up on me, open to let me through, and then go forward, while I toil behind defeated and discredited.

Later on it is possible that some one of the host, looking back will say, "By Jove! there was nothing in the fellow after all." He would be wrong – quite wrong. I maintain that I could have fought a good fight had I been properly equipped with weapons of tried steel instead of silvered paste-board "picked up as I went along." Had they given me time I should have done well, but there was no time allowed, and the fight, sooner or later, came to be with men who knew and could not be imposed upon.

But I have gone too fast. The end is not to-day, nor to-morrow, and to all appearance I stand now a just and upright worker. The event of my fall will not shake empires or reach your ears. I will only be sent to the rear as useless.

And after? What can I do to earn my bread? Happy thought! "Pick up as I go along."

The Judgment of Paris
(By a Witness)

Published: *Civil and Military Gazette*, 12 August 1887.

Attribution: Included in the suppressed *City of Dreadful Night*, 1890, but not included in any Scrapbook. The attribution is not supported by clear external evidence, but 'Tods' is RK's creation, and all of the other stories in the suppressed *City of Dreadful Night* are correctly assigned to RK. 'The Judgment of Paris' deliberately echoes the earlier 'Tods' Amendment' in details; e.g., Tods' mother is described in both stories as 'a singularly charming woman'.

Text: *Civil and Military Gazette*.

Notes: This is the second appearance of the child named 'Tods', who is first encountered in 'Tods' Amendment' *CMG*, 16 April 1887 (*Plain Tales from the Hills*). Roger Lancelyn Green identifies the stylised childish speech in 'Tods' Amendment' and 'The Judgment of Paris' as another exercise in dialect, like the Yorkshire, Cockney and Irish dialects that RK would soon present in *Soldiers Three*. The model for the children's speech is the American John Habberton's *Helen's Babies* (1876), a book that set a fashion that 'was to run riot for twenty years' (Green, *Kipling and the Children*, 1965, p. 83). It contains a character named 'Toddie'. RK's story is set in Simla.

'The Judgment of Paris' has been reprinted in the Martindell–Ballard pamphlets and in Harbord, III, 1611–13, as well as in the suppressed edition of *The City of Dreadful Night*.

There had been a children's party near the top of Jakko, and the small guests, weary with frolicking, were going away. Some, however, were absent; and among these was my estimable friend and ally the blue-eyed, fearless Tods. There were many reasons for his flight. In the first place, his Bearer, a gaunt *Poohbeah* was awaiting him. In the second he had, half an hour before, sat down upon the tea-things generally; insomuch that his brown Holland blouse was one messy defilement of jam, treacle, butter, milk and rich black forest-earth. His Mamma, a singularly charming lady, asked me to find Tods; and I sought till I found him, my self unseen, just over the road that leads to the Convent. There was a murmur of children's voices in grave debate. Tods had wriggled himself along the trunk of a moss-grown leaning tree that overhung a tiny path on the hill-side. Below him, eyes turned upward, mouths open, with eager catching hands beating the air stood three small ladies. *Videlicet* Nora, aged eight, flaxen-haired, white-eyebrowed, the model of propriety who owned a real English Governess, and a pony; Kitty, sallow, bead-eyed and desperately inquisitive, aged seven; and a certain small, fat, pink, flossy five-year old who had, long ago, christened herself "Chikky" and refused to answer to any other name. She was ignorant of the knowledge of the schools and could hardly speak plainly; but she had a marvellous faculty for miring her raiment in scrambles on the *khuds*.

Tods worked his way along the tree, with all the wood-lore of seven uncramped years, till he came to the clump of the main branches; the children prancing with impatience meanwhile.

"What is it Tods?" shrilled Nora, who led the little party. Tods was too busy with the ragged trunk to reply. "Is it a bear?" said Kitty. "They climb trees sometimes. Oh Tods come down!"

"Hi-yi-yi!" shouted Tods, astride of the trunk. "It's a monkey. A little, dead baby monkey. All dried and nasty."

"*Very* nasty?" said Nora.

Tod investigated for a moment. "*Pilpy* nasty" said Tods. "You'd cry if you saw it – all little white teeth, and hands black and crinkly." "How horrid!" said Kitty, rapturously. "Oh! do bring it down Tods! We'll take it home and play military funerals with it. Poor little monkey!" "And we'll k'y over it with hannashifs," piped Chikky.

Tods lay full length along the trunk, and the male Imp of Perversity took hold of him. He drew the shrivelled little corpse from the rift in the tree that the children might see it, afar and unattainable, and said:– "No I shan't!" Nora, the impetuous, stamped her foot – "Tods you're a – you're a – little beast!" "I don't care," said Tods; "Besides Miss Ogilvie said you weren't to say 'Beast,' and I don't think I will bring it down." "Oh Tods! I didn't mean it and I *do* want to see it so. *Please* let me look at it." "Why?" asked Tods, chewing a leaf of the tree. "Because it's so nasty, and I've never seen a little dead monkey. It will make me scream." "Cweam like evvyfing," said Chikky, who had found standing wearisome and had sat down to play with the pine-cones.

"Nonie," said Tods, judicially, "you pinched me at joggerfy to-day, when Miss Ogilvie wasn't looking. You are nasty, too; but what will you give me if I bring it down. It's all like leather and rattles." Nora danced with irritation in the path below: – "I won't give you anything. You didn't ought to be up that tree, and you are all green in front. I'll tell. It's con-con-confounding a defence – I heard Papa say so, – not to tell when Kitty does bad things; and *you* are worse. But, if you give it me for my own, own, own, I won't tell. And I'll help you in jogerraphy to-morrow. There!" "Huh," grunted Tods, "Miss Ogilvie daren't climb trees, and the puppy has tored my joggerfy book this afternoon. So I won't be able to know anything never till I get a new one. – Kitty, what will you give me if I bring it down?" He shook the corpse seductively. "I don't know any jog'fy" said Kitty mournfully "but I know where Miss Ogilvie keeps the week reports about us that only Mamma sees and never tells us about; and I know when we can look at them too, and *then* you'll know just what Miss Ogilvie writes about you, and all that my Mamma knows about me. I found out yesterday. If you bring it down I'll show where the cupboard is."

Tods deliberated for half a minute, and then, holding the corpse by the tail in one hand, scrambled down. "The cupboard under the staircase –" began Kitty, when Chikky who had been playing with the pinecones woke to the affairs of this world as Tods touched the hill-side.

"Is that the little dead monkey?" said Chikky. She rose and barred Tods' progress towards Kitty. "Tods," she said, putting up her little arms "show me, and I'll give you a tiss."

Tods hesitated. "Two!" said Chikky; reaching up and paying the first instalment on Tods sun-tanned chin.

"You've been eating marmalade," said Tods severely, "and you haven't wiped your mouf. But you can have the monkey. A girl who looks into Miss Ogilvie's cupboard to see reports that only my Mamma sees, shan't have any dead monkeys. If you have wiped your mouf, Chikky, you can give me the other kiss."

The kiss was given and taken, but Kitty's dark head was down on the pine-needles in a passion of weeping, and Nora was telling to heedless ears the awful penalties that would follow unauthorized researches into Miss Ogilvie's private papers.

Chikky and Tods, swinging the dead monkey between them, marched up the hill-side.

Five Days After Date

Published: *Civil and Military Gazette*, 24 September 1887.
Attribution: In Scrapbook 3 (28/3, p. 144).
Text: *Civil and Military Gazette*.
Notes: Unrecorded and unreprinted. RK was in Simla in August and September, 1887, when no doubt he saw much rain.

A Letter from "Nessus"[1]

Sir, stronger than my sense of helpless baffled rage is my sense of the absurdity of the situation. I, "the heir of all the ages in the foremost files of time and, what is more, a house-holder and one that hath had losses,"[2] am positively unable to dine, dance or mix with my neighbours. Had I, in an access of frankness, beaten my best friend and kissed my best friend's wife on the open Mall, I could not be more utterly ostracised, abject, or alone. The desolate freedom of an old flannel shirt and unlimited tobacco is to me poor consolation for social pleasures foregone and – but my more tender emotions concern myself only.

On Thursday last the rain began to fall; on Friday it really made up its mind to continue falling; on Saturday it discovered that it had forgotten something and went back to the beginning to find it; on Sunday it settled down to business; on Monday it rained heavily; to-day is Tuesday, and it is still raining. I am – how shall I put the fact most delicately? House-keeping matrons, all India over, listen to me. Since Thursday last the *dhobi* – may he perish miserably of pneumonia at his own *ghat* – has ceased to take any interest in my movements, has vanished, fled with the whirling, ragged brown clouds, gone, Heaven knows whither, with the valleyward-falling waste-water of the roads.

He has informed me, by the mouth of a perfectly nude and drippingly wet child, that so long as the rain falls he, though always my servant and revering me as his father and his mother, is wholly unable to return me my raiment. The small child, with a piety I considered hypocritical, added of his own notion that the rain was the will of God; and, on the strength of this, demanded *bakshish*. The situation stands thus. As a man of means and many engagements I can purchase in the shops of Trouville-sur-Khud, duplicates of every garment now soaking twelve hundred feet below in the *dhobi's* hut, with one single exception. Mine is, and time was when I was proud of the fact, an eighteen-inch neck. In all Trouville-sur-Khud shirts stop at seventeen inches. I harried the whole station before I accepted the bitter truth. To-day I stand before creation shirtless, excepting only for six flannel things in which I need hardly say it is impossible to go abroad. With due economy one flannel shirt can be made to last for seven days, at the end of which time I presume, from the present aspect of the heavens, the rain will have thoroughly settled down to its work. Then I shall be – ahem – but at least I can cut up my travelling rug; and after – a coolie's sack and a leaf umbrella yawn for me; and this is the boasted British jurisprudence of your so-called nineteenth century! Trouville-sur-Khud has been the capital of the Indian Empire for half a century. Trouville-sur-Khud supports a Viceroy, a Commander-in-Chief and a Lieutenant-Governor, not to mention galaxies of smaller stars, a municipality, a telegraph office, and three photographers, instead of which I have to swathe my eighteen-inch neck in checked flannel for the most part, and write my friends that an attack of fever "renders it impossible for me to accept," &c. &c. Ages since, a week ago, I dined down my patrimony of white shirts, such shirts! Heedless as the May fly in the sunshine, and yet I might have. . . . Great society! To what depths will shirtlessness not drive a decent man! I was gravely contemplating the expediency of wearing a dress-shirt *twice*, and wishing I had done so. Another black mark against the *dhobi* to be wiped off when we next meet.

After all, the usages of society are barbarous. Why should a man case his bosom in starched linen of evenings ere he can mangle food with a chosen band of rivals and enemies. A blood-red sailor's knot against a cool grey background of unshrinkable flannel would be infinitely more effective than the magpie monotony of black and white. I would attempt it if I dared; but a thought of two merrily critical grey eyes, whose devoted slave am I, forbids the trial. And she will be at dinner to-night, and there is a dance to-morrow and . . . . an empty shelf of the almirah recalls me to myself.

May all the gods of his pantheon protect my *dhobi* when he returns from his wallowing in the valley. I am compelled to think of him, to turn the whole weight of my eighteen-inch – massive, I mean – intellect on him, and, as a rule, I never take an interest in less than half a million Aryans at a time. I catch myself alternately hoping that he is not dead, and wishing that a landslip would slay him, and the naked child who attempted to make capital out of the decrees of Providence. The best, and most fascinating diner-out, and most irreproachable dancer in Trouville-sur-Khud is incarcerated in a flannel-shirt without hope of escape for the next week. If this should meet the eye of any gentleman with an eighteen-inch neck – but of what use is my appeal. My throat-girth and my misery are alike unique.

The dâk has just arrived bringing your paper and two invitations to dinner. At one of these detestable entertainments I believe she will be present. "Mr.——— regrets that an attack of fever," &c. &c.; and now I will go out and drown myself on the public road, after glancing at your esteemed journal.

The infamous print is bristling, absolutely bristling, with advertisements of shirts – white, single-stud dress shirts.

Be so good as to discontinue sending me your offensive publication from this date henceforward and for ever.

Yours, &c., Nessus.

---

[1] A centaur killed by Hercules, who was then killed by the poisoned blood of Nessus spread on his robe.
[2] The first part of this compound is from Tennyson, 'Locksley Hall'; the other is from *Much Ado about Nothing*.

The Hill of Illusion
(By "S.T.")

᪪

Published: *Civil and Military Gazette*, 28 September 1887.

Attribution: Scrapbook 3 (28/3, pp. 145–6).

Text: *Civil and Military Gazette*.

Notes: RK used this title twice, to the confusion of the bibliographers. This is the first instance of its use; the second is for a story published in *The Week's News*, 21 April 1888, and collected in *Under the Deodars*.

The pseudonym 'S.T.' is unexplained; besides its use here, it appears with 'Jews in Shushan', *CMG*, 4 October 1887 (*Life's Handicap*); 'The Recurring Smash', *CMG*, 13 October 1887 (uncollected); 'The Dreitarbund', *CMG*, 22 October 1887 (uncollected); and 'The Vengeance of Lal Beg', *CMG*, 3 November 1887 (*The Smith Administration*). No other of RK's many pseudonyms is used in such quick succession – five stories in just over a month. RK may have had some thought of establishing an identity for these initials, but, shortly after the last of the stories signed 'S.T.' had appeared, he left Lahore for Allahabad, and never again, so far as is known, made use of 'S.T.'

The idea that ordinary life embodies the archetypal forms of myth and legend, though with modern twists, was familiar to RK, who never doubted that all stories, no matter how new in appearance, were always old stories. As he wrote of 'The Man Who Would Be King', 'all "King" tales of that kind date back from the tower of Babel' (to Edward Lucas White, 3 January 1893: *Letters*, II, 77); in another letter he wrote that 'the blessed streets and squares and groves of today are shouting aloud the ancient tragedies' (to Brander Matthews, 7 February 1905, *Letters*, III, 176). See also the poem 'The Craftsman' (*The Years Between*).

'The Hill of Illusion' was reprinted in the *Kipling Journal*, December 2007.

᪪

When the Pandavs[1] held their last Council on the summit of aged Jacatala they laid a blessing upon the mountain so honoured; and, though the Pandavs have long since fought their way into Heaven, and a meaner generation has taken possession of Jacatala, defiling it with smoke and sewage, and calling it Jakko, the blessing remains. Once in the year, by day or by night, the Pandavs move among the pines, and to one man among the twelve thousand folk of Simla declare the secrets of the hills. It is characteristic of these Antique Essences that the percipient of the revelations of which they are the agents should see phantasma of the more gracious golden ages of belief.

On the fated day of this year there walked round Jakko a man smitten with a grievous catarrh, and filled, in vain hope of cure, with whisky and honey, strongest and sweetest of their kind, boiled together and absorbed at the highest temperature that the human inside may endure. High over head, where the monkeys chatter round the old faquir, the Five Pandavs, in the form of five fleecy clouds lay stretched upon the mountain-top, and, far below in the valley, the barking of their great dog echoed among the gorges like the roar of a hundred rain-fed streams. And the Pandavs, in their great and primeval innocence believing that the man had drunk *soma*,[2] showed him the truth of so many men and women as passed under the shadow of the five fleecy clouds that day; and they were all who walked or rode round Jakko – mean people and of no importance except to fill Government House lists and to crowd ball-rooms.

First – and the hollow road rung under her horses's hoofs – came Cleopatra robed and crowned in a riding habit and terai hat,[3] mourning that Antony, with whom she could have bowed the world to her feet, had escaped from her power, and meditating how best she should convey the asp to his breast. But all that she said, to Cæsar riding on the off-side, was:– "I think my horse is a little tired. Let us pull up." This then was the first insight granted by the Pandavs, and The Man who saw wondered, for he knew Mrs. Toveney for an insignificant and homely woman with four children in England.

The lamentation of Andromeda calling upon Perseus, for help against the Monster, came as loud and as shrill as the wind, from under the Infernal Rocks; but all that could be seen were two figures seated on a bench looking towards Sanjaoli, and there was no sign of Perseus on hill or road. Nor was Miss Derring clothed like Andromeda, and the man with her was pink and newly shaven.

"So sorry you were out when I called" said The Man to an approaching 'rickshaw; for decency and custom demanded the apology. It was heard and acknowledged by none other than the most terrible Jael herself, fresh from the slaying of Sisera, straight-browed, firm-lipped and heavy-eyed.

The Man stammered and fell back, being almost minded to ask the Pandavs what Sisera Mrs. Vannessay, model of all wives, could have killed. But he knew that a word spoken to them would destroy the charm.

So he passed on, and was nearly ridden over by Penelope and all her suitors – for the most part untrustworthy Greeks, standing in great awe of Ulysses. "This is as it should be," quoth The Man, "and needs no interpretation." Out of the shady glades beneath the Convent spurred Paris, "evil-hearted Paris,"[4] with a smile on his lips, and in his heart the knowledge that Helen for whom he had burnt and wasted his city had, all the while, been safely shut up in a far town, the Gods giving him a wraith of a woman in her stead. "I'm sorry for you," said The Man aloud; but Paris took the remark to refer to an abortive call just made, and, merely saying "Yes. It *is* a nuisance when the box is up," went his way.

A little farther on, Orpheus was striving to rescue Eurydice from Hell; but Eurydice preferred to stay where she was, and poor Orpheus' pleading was of no avail. "She'll go down-hill fast enough" said The Man, but Orpheus answered from the back of his waler mare:– "No she won't. Her forelegs won't stand it;" and The Man was angry with himself and the whisky and honey within him. Later his eyes opened with horror, for, in the full sunlight, Lancelot was patting King Arthur between the shoulders and calling him "old fellow;" while Guinevere watched him with wicked, wicked eyes. When Arthur turned and looked at Lancelot the great knight did not fall down and die, but cantered away singing a song and Guinevere waved her little gauntleted hand after him. To these, rightly enough, succeeded Tristram with the ruby carcanet for Iseult's throat in his left coat-tail pocket. Mark had passed him hurrying to office, and Tristram's sinful soul was at ease.

A light after dark and unpleasant things, walked little Ruth the newly chosen of Boaz with a smile on her lips. "My best congratulations Miss Cassaty," sputtered The Man. Ruth turned a delicate carmine. "It was only settled half an hour ago, and isn't to be made public till the cold weather" pleaded Ruth. The Man departed hastily with jumbled allusions to the Scriptures and the Pandavs, all luckily lost upon Ruth. "It's a most inconvenient faculty," thought The Man as he came upon the broader and more populated Mall. The first glance overwhelmed him. Médea was giving Jason a clue to some tangled maze in which that young hero's feet were hopelessly blundering. Dido, in a doolie by the

Bandstand, was mourning for Æneas as she looked towards the desolate grey seas of the plains; Althœa, watching Meleager's flirations with Atalanta, was nervously fingering in her bosom the *billet* that was to destroy the happiness of both boy and girl.[5] "It isn't fair" said the Man hastily, "you aren't his mother and the play says nothing about any other woman's lighting the blaze." Mrs. Blandershin, favoured the rash speaker with a look of unutterable scorn and contempt and withdrew herself statelily. "Cut for the rest of the season and no wonder," murmured The Man ruefully. "I wish I hadn't spoken." The Mall seemed to choke with all the grotesqueness of classic, mediæval, and scriptural history, as Simla flew abroad to call on its neighbour.

Boadicea, Queen of Men, hurrying from Peliti's,[6] all but collided with Delilah, and the look that passed between the occupants of the 'rickshaws showed that there was no love lost between them. Orson and Thersites, a worthy couple, trotted side by side behind fair Rosamond bending over her list of calls, and Galahad, fresh from Lower Bengal, was learning anything but innocence from the bright eyes of Lamia. "This is depressing," said The Man. "Never again will I take whisky and honey – at least not equal bulk." Final and crowning horror of all, rattled round the corner the car of Draupadi,[7] and as the man saw the face within he collapsed. "Five! Two or three I believed in, but five husbands! Oh, it's too horrible. Let me die or get sober." And as one word of death breaks every charm woven by the Pandavs, who are immortal, the spell was snapped, and the one day, on which the Hill of Illusion reveals the utmost truth, came to a premature end.

[1] The five warrior sons (nominally) of Pandu in the *Mahabharata*, endowed with various powers and virtues.
[2] In Vedic ritual a divine drink that confers immortality.
[3] 'A sort of double felt hat, worn when the sun is not so powerful as to require the use of a sola topee' (Hobson-Jobson).
[4] *The Iliad*, Book III.
[5] Meleager, who was assisted by Atalanta in the Calydonian boar hunt, has been cursed by his mother Althœa; she burns the fatal log (billet) that had been snatched from the burning because Meleager will live only while the log is unburnt. 'Billet' here has both the French meaning of 'note' or 'letter' and the English meaning of 'a stick of wood for the fire'. RK has altered things in the story, as he has done with most of the other myths in the article; if the old stories are repeated in modern life, they are repeated with a difference.
[6] The favourite café and confectionary of Simla.
[7] Wife of the five Pandavs.

Le Monde ou L'On S'Amuse
(By the Prompter.)

‰

Published: *Civil and Military Gazette*, 1 October 1887.

Attribution: In Scrapbook 3 (28/3, p. 147).

Text: *Civil and Military Gazette.*

Notes: Unreprinted. RK had himself just acted in a play at Simla, taking the role of 'Brisemouche' in a farce called *A Scrap of Paper*, an adaptation of Sardou's *Les Pattes de Mouche*. The performance, in the first week of September 1887, was at the new theatre in Simla, but it was, RK later wrote, 'a dull play which fell flat' (*Letters*, 1, 239). In the *CMG*, 'Le Monde ou L'On S'Amuse' is printed in run-on form to fit the restricted column space; for convenience I have put it into conventional play form, with a new line for each successive speaker.

‰

*Scene:— A damp cellar, anywhere in the Himalayas, tastefully
ornamented with stale scenery, slides, traps and hidden pitfalls.
Enter, tumultuously, procession of amateur actors, headed by
Affable and Energetic Stage Manager.*

A. &E. S. M.:– "Is everybody here? Where's Hortense?"
Voice from Prompt Side:– "She's tired and she told me to say" . . . .
Contralto, R.C.:– "Oh! How *can* you! I saw her going to Jelliti's with"
. . . .
A. & E.S.M. foreseeing a storm:– "Well, anyhow, we'd better begin."
Decisive Soprano:– "At the second act of course."
A.&E.S.M.:– "No! The first, without books."
Chorus, seven feminine voices:– "How horrid!"
A.&E.S.M. (apologetically):– "I told you so last week."
Mezzo-Soprano tartly:– "Yes! But I haven't had a minute to call my own for the last ten days; and there's a dance to-night and to-morrow I'm dining" . . . .

Voice from L.:– "And I had it guipured on the bias, with a good tuck in box-pleats over green *chevelure*, and green *boutons* of purple *je ne sais quoi* at the gathers where the breadths are taken in, and a sacque over the left shoulder, and chenille *pompons* all down the back."

A. &E. S.M. hopefully:– "Well, now, I think we'd better begin. Ermintrude, you come in first."

Ermintrude hastily:– "Oh! do I? What do I say?"

A. & E.S.M. wearily:– "That is for you to decide."

Ermintrude viciously:– "Well, if you're going to be rude of course –"

A. &E.S.M. penitently:– "On my honour I didn't mean anything. Only please go on."

Ermintrude sulkily:– "'Since first I saw your face' – but surely this chair is in the way."

A. &E.S.M.:– "Of course! take it out."

Mezzo-Soprano:– "Hah! You mustn't. It's wanted for *Barber Jim*. It's the chair I faint in."

Baritone from behind scenes:– "*Barber Jim* doesn't come off for three weeks, and that chair spoils my entry."

A. & E.S.M. struck with a happy thought:– "All right, we'll make it do for the chest of drawers in the murder scene."

Baritone:– "Man can't climb over chest o' drawers, and I'm not going to make my entry buck-jumping."

Tenor to Contralto in remote box:– "Don't you believe me? I never was more in earnest in my life."

Contralto behind muff:– "Yes! But, but – I know you repeat everything I say and besides" . . .

A. & E.S.M. sarcastically:– "When you've *quite* finished those tender confidences, might I ask you to take your places for the entry in the first scene?"

Contralto:– "T'wasn't tender confidences."

Feminine whisper from stage-box:– "Well it *looked* like a flirtation."

Contralto sweetly:– "If any body ever flirted with you, dear, you would know that men don't."

Basso, behind cigar-smoke:– "For Heaven's [sake] stop the women sparring, or we shan't do a stroke to-day."

Enter Hortense breezily:– "Begun already! I thought the rehearsal was for 3 o'clock."

Contralto:– "Oh! we all thought you were tired dear!"

Hortense icily:– "So I was."

Contralto venomously:– "Or at Jelliti's."

Hortense:– "Yes, tired at Jelliti's and now let us begin."

A. & E.S.M.:– "Yes, I think we'd better begin now. Ermintrude! ERMINTRUDE! Where's Ermintrude?"

Voice from prompt side:– "Gone home. 'Said she came to act not to squabble."

Basso sotto-voce to cigar:– "She's the most sensible woman of the lot."

Soprano to Basso:– "*Very* well! I'll never speak to you again as long as I live."

A. & E.S.M. to Basso and Soprano:– "Never mind Ermintrude's part. You two come on for the love scene."

Basso coming down centre and glaring into chandelier:– "'There are passions which however strongly repressed, strongly repressed'" . . . .

A. & E.S.M.:– "Look at her, man! Look at her!"

Basso turning three quarters right face, and staring over Soprano's shoulder:– "'Strongly repressed.' What comes next?"

Soprano scornfully:– "I don't know. *I'm* nor responsible for your part. It's bad enough having you to make love to me."

Basso:– "Look here! I didn't mean what I said about Ermintrude."

A. & E.S.M. from body of house:– "Aren't you two going on? I can't hear a word from here."

Shrieks, yells and giggles from behind scenes.

Mezzo-soparano:– "Oh! We've upset the red paint, and my boots are covered with it. Will it ever come off?"

A. & E.S.M.:– "Yes! a long time before the play, if we go on at this rate. Why couldn't you leave the red paint alone?"

Mezzo-Soprano:– "It looked so funny in those little jars, and I gave it the *least* little push with my toe. I'm so sorry, and it's all over the hem of my dress. I must go home and get it out."

Voice from behind scenes:– "She said if I gave her the material she could baste the *pastiches* and herring-bone the busk in two days – just in time for the dinner. So I gave her the *cornichons* and most of the quilling and the lace-tabliers at once. And, would you believe it my dear, she *volte-faced* the whole of the pannier with yellow surah! It was positively indecent."

A. & E.S.M.:– "It was! It is! It is!"

Basso, who has been explaining things to Soprano:– "For Heaven's sake, don't begin sparring with the woman."

Baritone:– "I say. *Is* that chair coming out of the way or is it not? I don't intend to fall over chairs to please any one."

Feminine whisper from stage-box:– "Not to please—— ——?"

Laughter from wing to wing.

Baritone, with attempted unconcern:– "I'm awf'lly sorry. I've got a call to make. Can't stay any longer."

A. & E. S.M.:– "Awf'lly sorry but you'll *have* to stay."

Baritone in indignant growl:– "D'you suppose I'm going to wait while that woman howls over my mashes over the footlights?"

Exit Baritone fuming. Feminine whisper under raised eyebrows:– "Did any thing I said make him angry?"

A. & E.S.M.:– "No! He said you howled! That was all."

Collapse of F.W. with accentuated titter.

Basso, from remotest box in house:– "Do you know we've been here two hours without doing a thing? It's five o'clock."

General female chorus:– "Good gracious, we must go. It's been a delightful rehearsal but, of course, a little bit unsettled. We shall be right on the night."

Chorus of all voices:– "All right on the night of course."

Exit company in pairs.

A. & E.S.M. looking off, and between closed teeth:– "Oh you little—— angels!"

An Intercepted Letter
(Authorship Unknown.)

⁜

Published: *Civil and Military Gazette*, 12 October 1887.

Attribution: In Scrapbook 4 (28/4, pp. 3–4).

Text: *Civil and Military Gazette*.

Notes: Unrecorded and unreprinted. The Third Anglo-Burmese War of November 1885 and the work of 'pacification' following into 1887 were without drama or grand spectacle, as one officer here reminds a fellow officer – one 'General' to another – pointing out that where no drama exists it is necessary to invent it.

⁜

* * * My contention is, and of this I feel sure your calmer judgment will approve, that there was no "fizz" in it; and "fizz" – as you ought to have long since learnt – is everything in these days of war correspondents. Gus Harris gave me the tip, that is to say, communicated the information to me, privately before the Egyptian business, and I think I made good use of his advice. But that is neither here nor there. What I want to impress on you, old man, is the disgracefully thick-hided way in which you threw away your opportunities. I doubt now, if one single allusion to *Bohs* and *Dahs*,[1] or what ever you call them, would raise a titter on a London stage; whereas – but you were at home I think when "Arabi"[2] was a safe draw with any gallery. You may answer that it is not exactly professional for a General in Her Majesty's Army to popularize his enemies. As I have always said, your Afghan education has spoilt you completely from the point of view of the G.[reat] B.[ritish].P.[ublic]., who, after all, is your master and mine. I had only sand and rocks to work with. They made a dull background, but I contrived to raise some very fair scenic effects notwithstanding. You, on the other hand, had all the luxuriant wealth of tropical or sub-tropical greenery – I have forgotten which, but the *Daily Telegraph* knows all about it – to help you forward; and, best of all, a river which, I should

conceive, would be absolutely unrivalled in the opportunities it offers for a torch-light procession of steamers with their flats – *quorum pars magna fuisses!*[3] You see I have not yet quite forgotten my latinity. Your only disadvantage, and this, I admit, was a serious one, was the absence of any decent ground for cavalry to manœuvre over. You could not have borrowed any of the Household Cavalry. They are, I flatter myself, kept for me; but, always assuming that there had been open space, you could have done an immense amount of effective work with the "thunderous charges, ringing of steel, and champing of bit" trick. Never mind *whom* you charge at. The great thing is the moral effect on the public at Home. But this is a digression.

My complaint and the complaint of most of my lot at Home – they are really not half so evilly disposed towards you and yours, as some of your set seem to imagine – our complaint is that there was no style about the business whatever. I admit that the place is twice the size of France; I admit that there were more men in it than we employed in the Crimea, but can you blame me if the public are not as much impressed with these two facts as I am? In the first place, they don't know the size of France, and in the second they do not remember the Crimea. They know that, to the best of their knowledge, there were "no bloody battles." I'm sorry for you. You preferred to go for the enemy as you found them – here twenty, there a hundred and so on – and according to your lights you did your work thoroughly. But, on my honour, – as the first General of the day, it would have *paid* you to have dragged the jungle with seine-nets, to have got ten thousand of them together in one place somewhere in the open and polished them off in style.

One public engagement, something on the lines of Tel-el-Kebir, with a Kassassin cavalry charge to wind up,[4] and the correspondents allowed to squib off their revolvers when they felt inclined, would have brought down the house – it would indeed! Lastly, though this would have required an amount of diplomacy rather beyond you, I am afraid, you should have borrowed a Duke – a naval one this time, and sent him up in command of a flotilla, or given him some light work of that kind and then have made arrangements for a twelve-hundred word telegram to the *Times*. You would have taken precedence of every one else on the wires and, by this time, have been very nearly anything you please. The public would have been impressed with the size of the country then.

As it is, the Exeter Theatre's burnt,[5] and they have something else to think about. You see I am now writing as a man and a brother, but for Heaven's sake don't leave this letter lying about anywhere. Want of style has been the log on your foot from the beginning.

From the chances of effect you threw away in Afghanistan, I could have made the reputation of half a dozen Generals. Harris knows as much about things as most men, and he says that even a flight of rockets and star-candles fired into the banks of the Irrawaddy as you went upstream would have passed any demand you could have made. You might have called it "shelling dacoits," and the result would have made a simply divine two-page supplement for the *Graphic*. But instead of this, you and your men rooted like ferrets in a rabbit's burrow and did your work out of sight. *I* know the use of the work, though you may say I'm jealous; but what am I to do? You missed your cue, the time has gone by, and the G.B.P. has forgotten all about Burma. Theebaw's massacres were the only thing that interested them.[6]

My advice to you is briefly to start any small Frontier expedition that you can think of, and if properly managed – there is a great deal of virtue in an *if* – you will win over that, all that you should have won down South. But you seem more concerned about your men than the Peerage. The men can wait. Waiting on a full stomach never harms a soldier. *Vide* next edition of my *Pocket Book*. Besides, there are wheels within wheels here that would prevent our giving way in the matter of your despatches, for fear of loosing on us a whole host of fellows who think that they were badly used – in one or two matters I have been connected with. Remember what Scripture says about promotion not coming from the East;[7] and try to explain that to your set.

I am hideously pressed for time; but I trust I've been able to make my meaning clear. From *our* point of view, and from the point of view of your own interests, you've mismanaged the entire business from the taking of Minhla to the Viceroy's visit[8] – Great Me! What could I not have made out of that procession up the river! – and thenceforward to your most *maladroit* announcement about "police duties." Man alive! The public don't understand that the "thin Red Line" does police work! What on earth made you go and tell them? Who is interested in the Police? Cooks[9] perhaps, but an intelligent public never. You should have held your peace and dwelt on the losses from "sickness and the

sword." That's one of Forbes' alliterations, and very effective I think. But you have no notion of effect.

The failure to get a Duke to look on from the prompt side, and the bad entry from the centre for the Viceroy, besides the absence of any comic business and the lack of a transformation scene – blood-thirsty dacoit, peaceful cultivator, private soldier playing with the babies, blue fire, "bless you my children" and so on – would have ruined even a better show than yours. . . .

---

1 Burmese titles; as in RK's 'The Ballad of Boh Da Thone', a Burmese guerrilla leader (*Barrack-Room Ballads*).
2 Arabi Pasha (1841–1911), leader of a revolt against the European control of Egypt, was defeated by the British at the battle of Tel-el-Kebir in 1882: see note 4, below.
3 Quorum pars magna fui: 'In which I played a great part': Virgil, *Aeneid*, 11, 6.
4 Episodes in the war between the Egyptian and British armies, first at Kassassin, 28 August, and then at Tel-el-Kebir, 13 September 1882, when the Egyptians under Arabi Pasha were decisively defeated with a loss of more than 2,000 men to the 57 of the British. Victoria's son, Prince Arthur, Duke of Connaught, was involved in the fighting.
5 The Theatre Royal, Exeter, burned on 5 September 1887; 186 people died in the fire.
6 See 'Le Roi en Exil' for Thebaw.
7 'For promotion cometh neither from the east, nor from the west, nor from the south' (Psalms 75:6).
8 The fort at Minhla, on the Irrawaddy, was taken by a combined force of river steamers and soldiers on land, 17 November 1885. Dufferin made a formal visit to Upper Burma shortly thereafter.
9 The travel agency of Thomas Cook & Son.

The Recurring Smash
(By S.T.)

Published: *Civil and Military Gazette*, 13 October 1887.

Attribution: In Scrapbook 4 (28/4, p. 4).

Text: *Civil and Military Gazette.*

Notes: For the initials 'S.T.' see the headnote to 'The Hill of Illusion'.
Reprinted in the Martindell–Ballard pamphlets and in Harbord, III, 1615–17.

In himself, Penhelder was not striking. His worst enemies did not call him ugly, nor his best friends handsome. But friends and enemies alike were interested in his Fate, which was unique. When he was three years old, he interrupted some mowing operations with a pair of chubby mottled legs and bled, as his nurse said at the time, "all round the hayfield in quarts." In his sixth year, he started on a voyage across the horse-pond; his galley being a crank hurdle, which, in mid-ocean, turned turtle, and but for the pig-killer, who happened to pass that way, he would certainly have been drowned. At nine years of age, he sat upon a wall like Humpty-Dumpty – a high wall meant to protect an apple-orchard – and, like Humpty-Dumpty, fell; fracturing his collar-bone. About this time, his family noticed the peculiarity of his fate and commented upon it. Three years later, being at a public school, Penhelder dropped from the trapeze of the gymnasium and broke one of the small bones of his leg. It was then discovered that every one of his previous accidents had occurred between the months of May and June. Penhelder was apprized of this and bidden to behave more seemly in future. His conduct was without flaw or reproach till his fifteenth year, when the school dormitories caught fire, and Penhelder, escaping in his night gown, was severely burnt on the back and legs. He enjoyed the honour of being the only boy who had been touched by the flames. This saddened him and his family, but more especially his old nurse, who maintained that "her boy," as she lovingly called Penhelder, was "cast" – a provincialism for bewitched.

At eighteen he found himself in London. What he did there does not come into this story. The end of a thirsty summer night, and indulgence in waters, to Penhelder, of entirely unknown strength, was, for some hours, a felon's cell and –"forty shillings or a month." With the guile-lessness of youth, Penhelder had given his real name; and had the satis-faction of seeing it not only in the police-reports of the *Times* but – and here the type used was much larger than his modesty demanded – in the market-town weekly newspaper as well. It may be mentioned that Penhelder was the only one caught of a riotous gang. At one and twenty Penhelder set foot in India, a solemn and serious boy, whose mind had been darkened by the shadow of his Fate. He was overheard, by a man who afterwards came to know him intimately, muttering, as he set foot on the Apollo Bunder[1] in the blazing May sunshine:– "I hope it won't be anything *very* serious." It was not, but the Doctor said that it might have been *most* serious; and that young men who paraded Bombay in small black hats deserved instant death instead of severe sunstroke merely.

Penhelder crept up-country to his station, and, in a weak moment, told the story of his Fate even more circumstantially than has been set forth here.

From that day, he became an object of unholy interest to the gilded youth of the Army within a two-hundred-mile radius. They looked, like the islanders of Melita, that he should "fall down dead suddenly"[2] but their watch was in vain. Late June of his twenty-fourth year saw Penhelder almost the sole occupant of a deserted station. But there were witnesses to attest the strange tale that follows. At dinner at the Club, one of the glass shades of a hanging lamp cracked with the heat, and a huge fragment fell hatchetwise across Penhelder's left wrist, cutting it to the bone. "I told you so" said Penhelder drearily, as the blood spurted over the table-cloth. The rest of the company held their peace, for they remembered that for the past month Penhelder had been prophesy-ing disaster of some sort to himself. The wound was a serious one and nearly ended in blood-poisoning.

Three years later, Penhelder took warning in time, and as May drew near, retired into his own house and lived there the life of an eremite. "If anything happens now," said he, "it will be the roof falling in, and I don't mind that. It will put me out of my misery." But Penhelder had miscalculated. In summer it is necessary to drive to office. Penhelder hired an enormous ticca-gharri of dutch galliot beam, and unquestioned solidity, and yoked thereto the soberest horses that he could find. The turn-out something resembled an ambulance in search of wounded, but Penhelder was deaf to the voice of sarcasm. What he demanded was safety. He secured it. It took him half-an-hour to reach his office, but he secured it. June had nearly ended, and, in his delight, he stopped, ere going into office, to pat the neck of one of the horses. There is a hideous description in "*Lorna Doone*" of Great John Ridd tearing out the muscle of his enemy's arm as though it had been orange pulp.[3] The horse, indeed, tore out nothing; but he clung like a leech to the inner arm of Penhelder, high up and close to the armpit.

A lighted match forced him to open his jaws, but Penhelder had fainted, and it was three months before he mixed with his friends – a moody, melancholy man, perplexed with foreshadowings of his next visitation. "It's not murder I object to," said Penhelder, "it's mangling."

Time, Chance and the Government parted me from Penhelder for many years, and he gradually faded out of my mind. But we met at Bombay a few weeks ago. I was introduced to Mrs. Penhelder, a large lady. My friend's face was drawn and haggard. I learnt that he was going Home for his health's sake. "Have you – have you," I whispered, "had any return of – broken your run of bad luck that is to say?"

Penhelder hesitated for a moment. Then he drew me aside. "I've broken it," he said, "but I married *her* on my thirtieth birthday. May the twenty-second it was."

And since that date I have in vain been trying to discover what on earth my friend Penhelder meant.

---

[1] Passenger quay in Bombay, traditional point of entrance to India.
[2] Acts 28:6.
[3] 'I grasped his arm, and tore the muscle out of it (as the string comes out of an orange)'
(R. D. Blackmore, *Lorna Doone*, ch. 74).

How Liberty Came to the Bolan
(By "M.")

※

Published: *Civil and Military Gazette*, 19 October 1887.

Attribution: In Scrapbook 3 (28/3, p. 150).

Text: *Civil and Military Gazette.*

Notes: Unreprinted and unrecorded. The Bolan Pass, now in western Pakistan, is one of the two main passes through which traffic from Afghanistan to India moves, or moved; it lies far south of the Khyber. This piece appears to be pointedly topical, but I am unable to identify any occasion for it. RK ventured into strict allegory only rarely – e.g. in 'The Children of the Zodiac' (*Many Inventions*) or the poem 'A Legend of Truth' (*Songs from Books*). This is one of the items from his Indian journalism that RK selected for inclusion in the never published 'Book of the Forty-Five Mornings'. The cutting in Scrapbook 3 has been lightly corrected by RK, no doubt in anticipation of its reprinting in 'The Book of the Forty-Five Mornings'.

※

Very long ago, before there was a beneficent *Sirkar* or a *Kumpany Bahadur* – even before Sir Thomas Roe got drunk at Ajmir for the good of his country,[1] and when men killed their neighbours as often and as cruelly as they knew how – the four Very Important Sisters, Wealth, Wisdom, Strength and Liberty, turned their backs upon Europe and went into the East to seek their fortunes. The reasons of their departure were never made public. Perhaps it was an annual pleasure-trip, or perhaps some one on the Continents had insulted them. At any rate they all walked away. Wealth, as everybody knows, goes quickly. She led the way. Strength walked behind her; Wisdom made her progress with difficulty, and little Liberty trotted last, for she was weak and undeveloped, and the stones of the Persian bridle-paths cut her feet terribly.

It is said that, as they travelled, Wealth and Wisdom stayed to flirt with the Parsees and some of the Persians; while strength went on and spent a day in the black tents of the Turkomans. The results of that interview have been disastrous to the Persians up to the present hour. Little Liberty had no time to waste. It was all that she could do to keep her sisters in sight; for Strength, Wealth, and Wisdom were self-ish and wanted to move quickly. Her only amusement was − after a great dust-storm from the north had blown out of their track, towards Nishapur − a meeting with a dissolute tent-maker who preferred get-ting drunk to making tents, and, not satisfied with altering the proper course of the year, said the most awful things about Time and Life and Death generally.² He learned several things from Liberty's lips, but they were not fit for publication, at least by the standard of those days. When the Sisters had recovered their line of march, they moved on to Berjand and thence to Nasirabad, where there are great plains of horse-mint and camomile that smell sweetly as you crush them in walking. A little further, they came to the Helmund,³ and Liberty being a frivolous child − she grew more sedate afterwards − sat down to wash her feet which were still rather bruised and sore.

The other three sisters were so anxious to move on, that they never even looked behind, and left Liberty altogether; for the stride of Wisdom and Wealth is just as much ground as a man can cover in forty years; and of Strength as much as can be reached in twenty-seven. So Liberty was left alone on the Helmund, all among the horsemint, calling to her sisters who had gone towards India. When the night came, she crossed the Helmund and wandered about in the dark, going, according to her custom, exactly as fast as an unencumbered man can walk.

Next morning she found herself among the thorny "shinalak" bushes, in a rough and unpleasant country. She moved on, following the trail of her sisters, very tired and unhappy till she came to the head of a great pass in landscapes nastier than she had ever before seen.

Therefore she sat down and cried for she was too wearied to go a step further; and, as she wept, she was turned into a little tree, called *the* tree of Sir-i-Bolan, because there was no other near it.

But Wealth, Wisdom and Strength crossed the Indus at Rohri and, after separating, spread themselves all over the face of the country in the form of forests, as being the most permanent institutions of those days. Now, therefore, wherever the forests exist, you may be fairly certain that they are the work of the Three Sisters − the Simla forests excepted. *They* came of themselves and mean nothing in particular.

If the railway people haven't used her for fuel,[4] Liberty should still be standing, in the glare, near the Sir-i-Bolan, for this is a true story.

---

[1] Roe (1581–1644) was ambassador to the court of the Great Mogul, Jahangir, at Ajmir, 1615–18. He was able to obtain recognition for the East India Company, in part, it is said, because he was Jahangir's drinking partner.
[2] Omar Khayam is meant.
[3] The longest river in Afghanistan.
[4] The first railway through the pass was completed in 1886.

"Under Sentence"
(By Such an One)

Published: *Civil and Military Gazette*, 20 October 1887.

Attribution: In Scrapbook 3 (28/3, p. 149).

Text: *Civil and Military Gazette.*

Note: Unrecorded and unreprinted.

In an access of unprofessional candour and wearied, it may have been, by the continual importunity of the patient, the Doctor broke through his established rule of always keeping his clients hopeful to the last gasp, and announced, solemnly as befitted his office, that Such an One had not six months to live. This was said, in a lowered voice and to the face of Such an One, who had so earnestly desired the information, at noon or a little later, on the 19th of September. The nature of Such an One's complaint concerns nobody. It may or may not have been heart-disease, some obscure affection of the nerves, or a score of other things. The main point is, that on the date aforesaid, Such an One was formally sentenced to death by his medical attendant – cast overboard, while yet living, from the ship of life, to find his way as best he could to the ferry where Charon waited. He had asked for certain news; and if he discovered the certainty well-nigh unendurable, had only himself to blame. But, curiously enough, he did not find the foreknowledge a horror – that is to say, after the first day and night of it had passed. Of that season of terror and despair it is better, perhaps, to say nothing. Had the Doctor said: "at the end of six months you will surely die," the minutes and hours in the one hundred eighty-two days could have been calculated, and their number would have been, for a time at least, a comfortable hedge against the black darkness of the night to come. But the Doctor said "within six months," which haziness of date left nothing to cling to. Hence the great fear that unnerved Such an One, who had sworn to the Doctor that he was strong enough to bear any news, and endure any suddenness of fate.

After the terror, came the reaction, because it is mercifully ordained that a man cannot go in extreme fear of his life for so long as a week without a break. He becomes callous or reckless.

But Such an One was directed into a middle course. He thought, and by degrees brought himself to believe firmly and beyond any chance of doubt, that he would die a little before midnight on March the 19th; thus taking almost every hour of his days of grace before payment of the last bill. By what process he had brought himself to hold this idea as an article of faith is a matter of no interest. Having contracted the horizon of life so far as it concerned him personally to the 19th of March next, he sat down and took stock of the situation, forcing the reluctant spirit to regard it; as a horse is, by an unskilful rider, forced to look at the stone-heap that has made it shy. The result of his meditation was that he should not meditate at all. The mind refused to have any thing to do with the phantasm of fixed and known death directly ahead. It veiled the fact in an impression, a presentiment, that gradually crystallized into an It – an It that was to happen on or about the date that most people would be going up to the Hills. Further than this the mind of Such an One could not go. The first shock of the announcement had blunted its receptivity. The peculiar feature of Such an One's case was that his malady in no way confined him to his bed or even to his house. Indeed he enjoyed, to all outward appearance, the health of any ordinary man, or at least so slightly impaired that only a close observer would have noticed the fatal flaw. He was under sentence, but permitted even more liberty than is granted to a French prisoner, where the prisoner can play dominoes with the jailer till the dawn of the last day. This unfettered freedom and license to move among his fellows imparted an element of the grotesque into the case; which, after the terror and the short struggle with the jibbing mind was ended, Such an One perceived and enjoyed. The privilege of being with, but not of, men is one reserved for genius and those under sentence. To assist at an Autumn Meeting and to hear the prospects of the Spring canvassed, with the absolute certainty that yourself will be completely and irrevocably "out of it;" to listen to the grievous tale of house-rents for the forthcoming year with the knowledge that neither the lowest of rents or the most central of situations will tempt you any more, affords a pleasure of a peculiar kind, not to be tasted twice in a life-time. That pleasure Such an One enjoyed to the full. Its immediate effect was to unsettle him.

Having paid the total of his outstanding debts, there yet remained, since no one but himself and his Doctor were in the secret, the necessity for working at the business which gave him his daily bread. But Such an One rebelled at this necessity and would have preferred complete idleness, the idleness that marks the day before the break-up at a school, or the departure on leave of later life. Knowing that his own fate was fixed, he did not in the least see why he should concern himself in the fates of others. He demanded, illogically enough, a holiday from work. There was nothing he particularly desired to finish, and certainly nothing that he particularly desired to begin.

The moral irresponsibility that attacked him in the second month of his waiting, spread rapidly from the details of his office-work to those of his daily life.

In sheer wantonness, he refused, without explanation, invitations to dinner and forebore to recognize his friends when he met them in the ways. While not in the least wishing to quit his hold on the things of this life, he found that men and women who were ignorant of the date of their death, ceased to interest, and even irritated him. Excess of knowledge had made him arrogant, idle and discourteous. As the allotted period drew to its end, these vices grew upon him, rendering him a nuisance to his acquaintances. In the last week of his waiting, the old terror returned and remained with him day and night for days. Then he shook it from him and stayed in his own house, watching the hands of the clock race round the dial.

But the hour that he had fixed in his own mind passed, and he lived. A month passed and he drew breath, and another doctor who knew not the first, saw Such an One and told him light-heartedly that he was "good for thirty years." So, Such an One became a mere ordinary mortal again, ignorant of the day of death like the others; but, with his joy at the reprieve was mingled – though no one but himself and the first doctor knew the secret – a sense of humiliation and almost disappointment, at valuable emotions wasted, deadly fear of nothing, and the return to the necessary, yet meaningless, labour of life on earth.

The Dreitarbund
(By S.T.)

Published: *Civil and Military Gazette*, 22 October 1887.

Attribution: In Scrapbook 3 (28/3, pp. 149–50).

Text: *Civil and Military Gazette.*

Notes: Reprinted in the suppressed *City of Dreadful Night*, 1890, in the Martindell–Ballard pamphlets, and in Harbord, III, 1618–21, The German of the title is presumably RK's own.

As a conspiracy it was infamous, and in the hands of unscrupulous men might have been dangerous; seeing how foolish women folk are.

But, worked with circumspection, as Houligan, Marlowe and Bressil worked it, it secured to three dear sweet girls with money, the right of paying Houligan's, Marlowe's and Bressil's bills for the rest of their days; and, as every one knows, all is fair in love or war. Houligan claimed and was allowed the honour of the Inspiration; Marlowe put fifty rupees into the pool, because he chanced to be the millionaire of the month; Bressil, like Mr. Gigadibs, was a "literary man"[1] with no morals but exquisite tact, knowledge of fitting opportunity, which was more than the money or the idea. He was the Napoleon of the Bund, and his contribution was a book, in two volumes, *"Phantasms of the Living"*[2] written by some of the members of the Psychical Research Society. Houligan had an Indian Telegraph Guide, and on this library and the fifty rupees, the Bund opened the campaign. Two men united can do a great deal, but a threefold cord can draw Heaven and Earth together.

The Bund was desperately poor, and, collectively, had not enough good features in it to make up one handsome countenance to go wooing with. It was unlucky in its love-affairs, for it failed to interest young women; and, even when it did, the parents said it had better work and earn twelve hundred a month before calling again. On occasions like these, the Bund used to smoke vehemently and arrange for a revenge.

Houligan's ambition was to drive over Miss Norris's father in his dog-cart; Marlowe desired to poison Miss Emmett's mamma; and Bressil, like Job, wished that Miss Yaulton's brother-in-law had written a book.[3] But what they wanted most was honourable matrimony with Miss Norris, Miss Emmett and Miss Yaulton. All their angry feelings died away when the Bund was formed, quietly and without ostentation, on strictly practical lines, and in thorough accordance with the principles laid down in *Phantasms of the Living* – *vide* the chapter on Thought Transference, Brain waves, Percipients and people of that kind. Houligan said that it was one thing to tell a girl that you were fond of her, when you were by her side, but that it was quite another, and a much more startling, thing to prove that you were fond of her when you were miles away. Once started, at Bressil's instigation the Bund quarrelled violently and in public, broke up its chummery, and was dead cuts to the great Interest of the Station. Everything, even down to the perverted English to be used for the communications, was cut and dried, and there was no further need of personal intercourse. The Bund devoted itself to laying siege to its chosen maidens in a dark and mysterious sort of way that made the latter laugh.

Houligan was transferred to a Station three hundred miles away, and Miss Norris laughed when she said good-bye. The type of Houligan's love-making has not been made public. Miss Norris said that he used to talk strangely. She held to her opinion till she was attacked by a rather severe fever, after over-exertion at tennis, on a Friday afternoon. Twenty-four hours later, being then in bed. she received a hurried letter from Houligan, explaining that an "overmastering presentiment" – that was the wrong word, but Houligan could never make head or tail of *Phantasms of the Living* – compelled him to write to her and ask if any trouble had overtaken her on Friday evening. He had had a feeling, an idea that she had suddenly fallen ill – had put the feeling from him as absurd, etc., but it had returned, etc. He was her devoted slave, and apologized for thus troubling her. From that date onward, Miss Norris never referred to the strangeness of her lover's talk. She only wondered; told her parents, who wondered too, and thought a great deal of Houligan. Miss Emmett was of a different type from Miss Norris. She was nervous and hysterical by birth, and Marlowe always thought that her parents might have been won round in time. But another man appeared and began to make love to her – he was a man from the North-West – and the Emmetts were going to spend the summer at Naina Tal. Time and propinquity in a case like Miss Emmett meant everything. By this time, it should be explained, the pool stood at nearly four hundred rupees – the result of monthly contributions. There had been a drain upon it for Houligan's benefit, in "private deferred" wires sketching the daily life of Miss Norris by the words of the Code – a lithographed M.S. of seven hundred and thirty-two pages, compiled with extraordinary care. None the less, the pool kept up to an average of four hundred. Marlowe took it all and thrust it into Bressil's hands, begging him to go Naina Tal for ten days and draw on the pool if the money ran out. Bressil went when the Emmetts moved, and Marlowe had said farewell to Miss Emmett, who was hesitating between her two admirers. Bressil was a genius in his ideas of combinations. After four days, he sent Marlowe a huge telegram, giving him the outlines of the action to take; and then began to beg and beseech Miss Emmett for a dance, at the next ball, which he well knew was a running one, given for the season to Marlowe's rival. This sort of petition can be renewed at any time and hour, and unless she is bored to death, the petitionee is always pleased. Bressil renewed his request twice in one day. At dinner, his seat faced the door, he said, *apropos* of nothing in particular, for the third time:– "Will you give me number seven, Miss Emmett." As he spoke, and as Miss Emmett was bridling, a servant put a telegram on her plate. She read it, and began to scream, for the telegram was from Marlowe and it said:– "No. To me, and I'll sit out with you in the spirit." Miss Emmett did not go to that dance. She was afraid – afraid of everything, but of Marlowe most of all. He followed up the telegram by a letter, many pages long, and was accepted by return of post. Miss Emmett was nervous and hysterical, but she made a good wife; and her parents were very respectful to Marlowe. They quoted a play called *Ingomar and Parthenia* [4] and also said that there were "more things in Heaven and Earth than were dreamt of in their philosophy."[5]

Houligan never had the heart to indulge in another "presentiment." He wooed on his own merits after Miss Norris's fever; but was accepted chiefly on account of the presentiment. Miss Norris was a healthy young lady, but she was deeply touched by the idea of a man who watched over her from afar. So were her parents. Then these two couples married, and

Bressil was left to make his way with Miss Yaulton, who was a most difficult maiden. She believed in "missions" and "spheres" and "destinies," and held that her destiny was to drift away from Bressil and become a "woman working for woman" at Home. She was different from the average of Anglo-Indian girls. She said Bressil was " a very dear friend," but she could never marry him; for his work lay in India and hers in England. They met on a high and spiritual platform; which was not what Bressil wanted. Then they parted for no earthly reason, except Miss Yaulton's ideas; and Bressil was miserable. Houligan and Marlowe had taken their wives Home, and were beginning to be loved for themselves and not for their mediumistic attainments. Bressil assumed that the Dreitarbund was dead. He had helped Houligan and Marlowe to their wives, and Fate had not put them in a position to help him. That was all. The pool was empty, and the codes were lost. All that remained to him was Miss Yaulton's address. But the Dreitarbund was only suspended for a while. The Houligans met Miss Yaulton at a big country house in Wiltshire. She had not found her mission or sphere, nor had she forgotten Bressil. There was a riding-party over the downs, and Miss Yaulton, being, as you will have seen by this time, as obstinate as a mule, insisted on riding a big black horse that was not fit for a lady. In consequence, she was bolted with and nearly thrown.

For this reason she announced her intention of riding the brute next morning, though all the house tried to dissuade her.

Houligan was not a clever man, but he fancied that he recognized in this the finger of Providence. He went away to the nearest town – a small one – and paralyzed the local telegraph office by pouring in a Foreign Telegram, the like of which had never been seen by the telegraph officials before. He spilt his words like water that nothing should be misunderstood, and paid for repetitions in a princely style. Altogether he spent £15.10 on the telegram, and alluded to many things beside the horse. No one knows what Bressil thought on receipt of it. He may have struggled with himself against the meanness of the trick, or he may not. He delayed several hours in sending his answer. At breakfast next morning in the Wiltshire country-house, Miss Yaulton, booted and habited, received Bressil's message:– "For Heaven's sake don't ride *Dandy*." She did not. She took the telegram into her own room and recast her ideas on all "missions and destinies" independent of Bressil.

149

She also was awed; but her awe was different from the nervous dread of Miss Emmett, or the frightened bewilderment of Miss Norris. She sent back a three-word telegram to Bressil that drew him back to England and then . . . . and then the Dreitarbund really died.

Houligan admits the immorality in the abstract of the work of the Bund. But he says that other Bunds have been much worse, and that "if the Psychical Research Society pops a good notion into your head, why on earth shouldn't you work it out?"

1 The auditor in Browning's 'Bishop Blougram's Apology'.
2 Edmund Gurney, Frederic W. H. Myers and Frank Podmore, *Phantasms of the Living*, 2 vols., London, 1886, reporting on hundreds of cases of 'spontaneous telepathy' and other psychic phenomena.
3 Job 31:35: 'my desire is that the Almighty would answer me, and that mine adversary had written a book'.
4 Ingomar, the barbarian, is tamed and civilised by Parthenia. Originally *Der Sohn der Wildnis* (1842) by Friedrich Halm, the play was popular in England and America in an adaptation by Maria Lovell, first produced in 1851.
5 Cf. *Hamlet*, I.IV.

In Memoriam
(By the Survivor.)

***

Published: *Civil and Military Gazette*, 27 October 1887.

Attribution: In Scrapbook 4 (28/4, p. 6).

Text: *Civil and Military Gazette.*

Note: Unrecorded and unreprinted.

***

Today, an old and trusted friend is dead. His corpse was carried out from my presence at noon, but I did not weep over him as he lay in the casket, placid and unmoved. What was I to him, or he to me? Our roads lay apart henceforward.

As the friendship of David towards Jonathan, so was the friendship of my friend to me. He was stronger in every way than I, masterful and overbearing at times, but I loved him none the less. I was not fitted to walk alone; help and counsel were as necessary to me as the breath of my nostrils – help for the hand to execute what the brain had, after due advisement, conceived. I took both gifts from my friend, lightly and without heed; never imagining for a moment that he would be called away.

Sitting now, opposite the empty place by the table, and reviewing his virtues dispassionately, I am inclined to think that, perhaps, my friend was hardly judicious in all the advice he gave me. For a contained character, his enthusiasm and buoyancy, amounting almost to spiritual effervescence, were startling and threw outsiders, unacquainted with his merits, off their balance. They were incapable of forming a just estimate of his character; but succumbed at once to the irresistible *verve* and *élan* that he threw into the conversation. I myself have been carried away by this peculiarity, and, under its influence, have lent myself to actions of which my isolated judgment can hardly approve. To do him justice, my friend never failed to read me lectures on the folly of my proceedings – generally in the early morning when I could have best dispensed with his presence. My friend was hardly logical, seeing that the deeds whereof he bade me repent had been committed when he was at my elbow – at his direct instigation in fact.

But for how much of good am I not indebted to him! It was he who whispered in my ear the outlines of a great Work that should make me famous for ever; and it was he who spurred me on towards its achievement through the long hot days and the longer hotter nights when the sick brain beat on the door of its prison-house and demanded a little rest. "Be firm!" quoth my friend. "I am with you – go on!" Together we went forward, he and I, the helper and the helped, till the work was near its end. For reasons which I could never satisfactorily explain, but which my friend said were due to my not having followed the outlines of his scheme in its "first fine careless"[1] entirely, the work was not so great a success as I could have wished. The bones of an idea were there, but they lacked the flesh. "Your fault entirely," said my friend. "Yours wholly," I answered, but my response lacked conviction; and in a little time I was converted to my friend's view.

We saw a good deal of each other, till a certain lamentable evening when my friend left an ill-assorted menagerie in my room, and, though I appealed to him several times, refused to take it away. There were, among other things, a bat with a horse's head, a shot-silk cross between an umbrella and an octopus, a ferret with a woman's teeth, a fat-tailed ram with a tapir's trunk and the scream of a dying child, an eyeless *langur* and a clockwork snake with a broken back that progressed in a series of jumps and clicks. I mentioned my friend's singular want of good manners – he was chumming with me – to a gentleman of the medical profession who agreed with me entirely; and suggested that the least I could do was publicly and privately to cut my friend dead.

So infirm is human nature that, once the menagerie was out of my house, I began to yearn for a sight of my friend. I lacked the stimulus of his fresh, inventive mind. He never sought me it is true; but I used to meet him frequently in public places, and on these occasions there was a mute appeal for reconciliation in his eye that I found very difficult to disregard. But I was firm. A friend who presumes on long acquaintance to introduce obscene animals, of no known species, into your bed chamber is untrustworthy; besides being mannerless. Often and often, late at night or very early in the morning, I was shaken by a strong impulse to visit my friend and condone the past, but I withstood the temptation. By the memory of the clock-work snake with the vertebræ like casta-nets, I put the idea from me.

Late in the year, yesterday evening to be accurate, my friend died. I could have wept for the sake of the merry days we had spent together; but in respect to the forgotten menagerie my feelings were not those of grief. Last night I put him into the casket, and watched by him through the great part of the night for any sign that should betray life. None came. In the morning I looked again, but my friend was still dead.

I gazed on him unmoved and bade the bearer – take the glass and throw away the contents.

[1] Browning, 'Home Thoughts, from Abroad'.

On Signatures
(By————*)

※

Published: *Civil and Military Gazette*, 2 November 1887.

Attribution: In Scrapbook 4 (28/4, pp. 7–8).

Text: *Civil and Military Gazette*.

Notes: Unrecorded and unreprinted.

※

* Our correspondent's name is written "Anjuolin Ihadam." But he seems to be an Englishman, and may possibly be styled Augustus Maclean by those who know him.

Sir, – The following is the kind of thing that greets me at the end of most of the letters which I daily receive:– "I have the honour to be," &c. &c. followed by a design in ink which might be meant to represent three snakes' tails and a set of triangles. "Very sincerely yours" – a felled fir-tree with a shower of chips about the stump. "Yours sincerely" – a Greek Theta, and a thing like a dead cat.

And that is one portion of my morning's *dak*. The snakes' tails and triangles represent Lee-Scuppersley, who will live and die an official prig, under the delusion that he is over-worked. He is a small man, of no earthly consideration in the eyes of his Government or his friends; but were he a Lieutenant-Governor, his signature could not be more illegible. I scorn Lee-Scuppersley. I have a genial contempt for him. I would bonnet him if he were made Viceroy to-morrow. By what right does Lee-Scuppersley then vex me with hieroglyphs? Because he is a beast.

The felled fir-tree with the chips, is new to me. It may be McCormac's name; but when he last wrote to me, his device was a house on fire with rolling clouds behind. McCormac is a firebrand in the Commission, and the totem is not inappropriate, though puzzling to strangers. Withershin again used to draw a big black fuzzy caterpillar on a boundless prairie – he was a slow worker, was Withershin. Perhaps he has sent the fir-tree to show that he has come to grief at last. But the style of the letter is not Withershin's. I can read every single word except the signature. The writer wants to know when I am "going to look him up." Now I promised on my journey to see Blougram; but Blougram never uses R.A. notepaper. Besides I can sometimes decipher his signature – the post and rail, not the shovel and dustpan one. *Who* in the world is the fir-tree man? Let me put the letter aside and go on to Theta-and-the-dead-cat. This is easier, for Theta adds that he is "Bd. Conar Cold Pork." "Bd. Conar" must be Lieutenant-Colonel – but Cold Pork? There is nothing about Cold Pork in any Army List that I know of. It may be in some G.O. regarding rations, but Hart and the Bengal, Bombay and Madras Lists know it not.

Theta-and-the-dead-cat entered the Army before the abolition of purchase. There is an excuse for him, but there is none for the expensively educated Lee-Scuppersley. Theta-and-the-dead-cat demands information about a horse "which I understand you are willing to sell." Like Lee-Scuppersley and the fir-tree-man he is perfectly intelligible till he reaches his own abominable name. Stay! He has made one mistake. He puts the price of the horse one hundred rupees lower than was advertised. In addition to being a scribbler of nonsense, this Lieutenant-Colonel of the "Cold Pork" is a fraud – a designing thief. I wish I could write and tell him so, but the Cold Pork regiment are stationed at "Ngamuk," and the post-mark shows that the letter did not come from Burmah. Where is "Ngamuk" or "Ujunivl," for it reads both ways, and what are the Cold Porks – Lord Pinks – Jilt Rams – when they are at home? Infantry, white or black, cavalry, mountain battery or what? There is no station that remotely resembles "Ujunivl" or "Ngamuk" in any Army List. And this man – this Theta-and-the-dead-cat – has doubtless been placed by Government in command of nine hundred and sixty-two, or six hundred and thirty, or nine hundred and twelve men, all with, presumably, immortal souls! He is unfit to be trusted with the control of a conservancy bullock-cart when the driver has gone to dinner. The fir-tree man is just as bad, and Lee-Scuppersley, who is actually proud of his signature, is the worst of the three. One of them I know, and the other I suspect, to be a ruler of men. The fir-tree man uses Government of India paper for private correspondence. He is evidently an official and a hardened thief. All this comes of writing signatures badly. If Lee-Scuppersley had been taught to write "Lee-Scuppersley" in his youth, he would have risen to higher things, and in time, perhaps, to a knowledge of riding [*sic*: writing?]. If the fir-tree man had begun life by writing his name so that every one could read it, he would have scorned the detestable meanness of defrauding an innocent Government of stationery supplied to him in the interests of Empire. If Theta-and-the-dead-cat, Bd. Conar, Cold Pork, Ngamuk, – to stick to the first reading – had learned his alphabet, he would now be a Commander-in-Chief instead of a grey-haired old horse-jobber, despised, I make no doubt, by the rank and file of the "Cold Porks," and the object of public derision, of this I am *quite* certain, in Ngamuk, which may also be Ujunivl.

The man with an unintelligible signature may prosper in this world, but he will assuredly be punished in the next, for causing his brethren to blaspheme. The man who, out of wilful affectation, writes himself down a wriggling worm, a *mehter's* broom, a fir-tree, a slug, or Theta-and-a-dead-cat, is unworthy of the respect, friendship or obedience of his fellow-men. He is always a potential forger, in nine cases out of ten a shirker; and when he is neither forger nor fraud, he is a wanton scoundrel. Even as I am writing these lines, comes in a letter from Blougram who, I see from the envelope, is pleased to be facetious. He has cut out my signature and gummed it on the envelope; and an army of post-marks shows that the dolts who have charge of our letters have "tried" Cherrapunji, Kohat, Jubbulpore, Nandgaon, Batala, Karachi, Trichinopoly, the Dead-Letter Office, and Aden. Now my signature is a model of caligraphy. I can read it myself ten yards off.

Blougram writes:– "Dear old man, I fancy that some letter or other came from you lately, but I'm not sure. In future, think of my years and spare my eyesight. The section of a fly's thorax under the microscope which you enclosed was a very clever drawing. I return it on the envelope just to see what will happen."

Section of a fly's thorax! My signature by [*sic*] everything perspicuous. Print here, very plainly indeed, that the one man viler and more despicable than the man with an illegible signature, is the crass and bat-blind crawler who fails to decipher so clear a name as that of

Anjuolin Ihadam.
(Qy. *Augustus Maclean?*)

The Great Strike
A Tale of 1910

Published: *Civil and Military Gazette*, 5 November 1887.

Attribution: In Scrapbook 4 (28/4, pp. 9–10).

Text: *Civil and Military Gazette.*

Notes: On the decline of the exchange value of the rupee, see also 'Les Miserables'. 'The Great Strike' was reprinted in *Kipling's India: Uncollected Sketches*.

The remedy was simple – so simple that when all was over and the rupee stood at 21-2*d.* once more, every one wondered why it had been overlooked so long. Men had devasted [*sic*] the country with meetings to protest against the "present serious inconvenience arising out of the fall in silver" or the "semi-pauperised condition of the European population"; but no one paid any special attention to their words, and subscriptions in aid of the "Cause" could not, when the rupee stood at 11 ¾*d.*, be very large. There was an impression abroad that "this state of things could not continue much longer"; but no one dreamed that it could ever be set right by juggling with the currency. All had passed from the argumentatively philosophical frame of mind to the irrationally determined – and this is the much more dangerous mood. They had decided that something must be done and that all the cheap production in the empire did not console them for having to drive in bamboo-carts and send their children to Hill-schools where they picked up curious accents and learned a great deal too much of life. At home, when the Masses wanted anything new – a day's ration or the stock of any tradesman's shop – they just assembled in their might and hammered at the Lions in Trafalgar Square or threw brickbats into the windows of the *Times* Office, and all their wants were immediately gratified. This hurt the feelings of the poor wretches in India, and they held a conference on their grievances. The Army, of course, stood aloof, but it grinned cheerfully, and said that it would be most happy to march against the mutineers. Some of the more anchylosed spirits at the conference said that the steps proposed would be absurd, but others held that a mere hint of the steps proposed would be enough to bring the Secretary of State to his bearings. There would be a stupendous novelty in the move. It was decided to exempt the lower grades of society from taking any part in the campaign. They were to attend to the railways and things of that kind without heeding. The Army also was not to be mixed up the affair at all; but the Civil Engineers rallied round the standard as one man.

There was a certain natural hesitation in being the first to begin; but a Deputy Commissioner leaped into the gap, and – he was a bachelor – said that he was ready to sacrifice himself for the good of the community. He led off, alone and unaided, and when he informed his Assistant that there would be no more work done in the district, that young gentleman telegraphed into the capital that his chief was insane. Now the strike of a Deputy Commissioner being absolutely new in the annals of Indian administration, the Government at first wished to send him Home on Medical Certificate, but he declined. He wished it to be distinctly understood that he was sane but on strike till the rupee was nearer two shillings than one. He would be delighted to resume his executive duties when . . . . but at this point the Government "broke" him in the *Gazette*, and he was ordered to go away. He went into the capital and was supported by his friends. The case appeared in the English papers and excited a certain amount of comment.

A few days later, an Executive Engineer in charge of about 230 miles of rather important railway, lost interest in his labours and went on a prolonged shooting tour, picking up an Assistant Commissioner *en route*. There was no trace of soreness in their letters to Government. They thanked it for its uniform consideration and sent it some teal; but they intimated that the section of line and the sub-division of the district had better be looked after; a few hundred thousand cubic feet of stone and a few tahsildars required supervision – at least that was their humble opinion. They were "broke" promptly, and a wing of a British regiment despatched to bring them in as deserters. They were brought in in chairs on the shoulders of the officers – and this time the proceedings were telegraphed Home. The London journals were not facetious.

They said that English gentlemen were not in the habit of striking for nothing. Then a Commissioner – camp, salute and all – went out on strike. He said that he had been sacrificing himself to the Empire for about half a century, and that it was getting monotonous. He admitted that his duty was to set an example, and he considered that this example would be largely followed. He went into the hills and lived on the prestige and the balance of his current account, while the Government wrote agonizing letters to him.

Then the blaze broke out. A Border Deputy Commissioner led off, by shutting up his kutcherry and smoking on the roof. He said that he was the only human being who knew how to soothe the Haramzada Kheyls, and that he would be most happy to talk to that turbulent tribe when the rupee was one-and-ten-pence, say: for he was a moderate man.

A Southern Deputy Commissioner followed suit, and the whole country was pitted with districts in what the native papers called "the *statu quo*", and the Persian Gulf telegraph broke down under the strain of the telegrams from Simla to the India Office – "Urgent, State, Bearing".

Now the beauty of the arrangement was that it was impossible to send troops against a man in *pyjamas*, smoking on a housetop. He always received them kindly and asked the officers to breakfast. The troops enjoyed these expeditions.

Another interesting feature of the case was the incompetence of the substitutes for men on strike.

It takes twelve years to make an average Deputy Commissioner, and the *badlis* were rather too raw from the hands of the Civil Service Commissioners. The third strong point was that the strike affected the very axle of the administration. A district may struggle on without a Judge or a Forest Officer, or even a District Engineer, but without a Deputy Commissioner it cannot work. After fifteen "breakings" some one at the India Office began to feel afraid, and suggested that enquiry be made into the grievances of "the gentlemen who have so summarily abrogated their Covenant." The gentlemen in question stated that a man could not live on paper, and that they would be very pleased to see the rupee at two shillings. They had, for the last twenty years, heard every conceivable and inconceivable scheme for restoring its value. They now suggested that one, some, all, any new scheme or schemes, be put to the test. They were not in the least concerned as to the mechanism of the change. This was their only answer; it was followed by renewed demonstrations on most of the State Railways. Every strike was timed to cost the Government lakhs in money and more than lakhs in loss of confidence. The Army stood firm, but it grinned horribly, and when off duty sympathized with the strikers.

What measures were taken by the Secretary of State for India will never be known. It is currently believed that he set every "silver scheme" he had ever heard of in action at the same time, and caused a compact little army to smash its way into China. Whether the schemes or the silver suction of the Chinese Empire, for the hole left by the Army was never again plugged, worked the rise, is a unfathomable mystery. The rupee rose steadily, and at 1s. 10d. the men on the strike began to come in; at 1s. 11d. they were once more dispensing justice as usual; and the curious thing is that all the "breakings" were rescinded in the *Gazette*.

No one knew where the business might stop, for no one had ever imagined it possible that English gentlemen should go on strike just like common labourers.

"The Biggest Liar in Asia"
(By One who knows Him.)

Published: *Civil and Military Gazette*, 7 November 1887.

Attribution: In Scrapbook 4 (28/4, p. 10).

Text: *Civil and Military Gazette.*

Notes: RK was not distinguished for an interest in music, as is suggested by his reference here to a non-existent 'C' string on the violin; nor do solo violinists play 'overtures'. 'East of Suez' in the first sentence is the earliest known occurrence of the phrase in RK's work.

Reprinted in *Kipling's India: Uncollected Sketches.*

The title carries great honour and glory east of Suez and is much sought after. It is strictly personal; being neither hereditary nor transferrable. Unlike Knighthood, Orders and the like, it must be won through a man's unaided exertion, and, when attained, is by no means a secure possession, for another and a more fluent tongue may, at any moment, ravish it from the happy owner.

As virtue lost can never be recovered; so the proud name of "The Biggest Liar in Asia" once forfeited is gone for ever. Men have essayed to regain it with fifteen years' mountainous mendacity, but they have failed. In the Illustrious and Most Dishonourable Order of the Bonnes Fortunes, the Grand Cordon is known and revered by all his associates. Equal honour is shown to "The Biggest Liar in Asia" when he condescends to do battle in public places against all comers for the honour of his name. Men flock round him three deep, or slide their chairs towards him, and, when occasion serves, thrust forward some local liar, a bantam of yet unproven beak, to engage with the adversary. Such encounters are worth travelling across an Empire to hear. They occur but seldom.

Almost as much instruction may be gathered from a meeting between Presidential Liars – squires, as it were, striving towards the full glory of knighthood. Such a tourney these eyes have been privileged to witness.

The honour of Bengal and Madras was concerned, and the betting ran high. The meeting was strictly private, and if ever man was brought to the post – the smoking-room after dinner – in fit condition, the Bengal Representative was that man. But his very fitness went near to be his ruin. He spoke too quickly, covered too much ground, and the effect of his epoch-marking inventions was in a measure lost. The Madras Man was tubby in person and slow of speech, but an artist in delivery and intonation. He capped his opponent's anecdotes with apparent effort and an assumed halting of memory; but his words sank one by one into our appalled ears, and the pauses between sentences were devoted to listening for "the feet of the young man without".[1] They never came, and the Madras Man continued the awful tenor of his way.

At the critical moment, after the twenty-seventh anecdote, when Bengal was beginning to show signs of exhaustion, the door opened and there entered "The Biggest Liar in Asia". No need to tell him what was going forward. His practised eye took in the situation without winking. On principle the Grand Master objected to any unauthorized lying, as tending to weaken his sovereignty. He struck and struck hard – this Abdur Rahman[2] of Ananiases.

"What was that you were saying about a horse, you fellows? I remember when I was at Chittagong –" and then and there, without an instant's hesitation or weakness, he delivered the most stupendous, complete, and colossal lie that has ever been told of anything carrying four legs since the Primitive Man saw the Three Toed Horse, and attempted feebly to fabricate his first untruth. Observe the magnificent originality of the idea! Not a word had been said of horses; the conversation at the moment of his entry running on railway collisions. He had taken, of design, the oldest theme in the world, and from it evolved a melody unapproachable and unique. Paganini playing overtures on the C string was a suckling compared to "The Biggest Liar in Asia."

There was a moment of silence that might have been weighed in the balance; then Madras and Bengal rose to their feet and saluted. It was their tender of submission, of admiration, and awe. The sovereignty of "the Biggest Liar in Asia" was assured. The strain on his brain must have been tremendous, but he betrayed no emotion beyond asking for a "peg". This disposed of, he left the room amid thunders of applause – every inch a king. All bets were declared off, for public opinion felt that after such a display, any financial transaction would too closely resemble betting in a Church.

But a doom hangs over "The Biggest Liar in Asia", and he knows it and trembles. In a far-away, desolate, by-white-men-forgotten-district, the Government have locked up a little wizened man with a voice like the cleaning of a file. In his banishment, he has heard calls and dreamed dreams, and he feels that Destiny has designed him to supplant "The Biggest Liar in Asia". He has struck out a new gospel – one absolutely untramelled by facts of *any* kind. His stories will be unearthly in their mad prodigality of invention. A mystic and dreamer, he will presently descend upon India, and, in that day, "The Biggest Liar in Asia" will go down. He feels it himself, for he has spent a week with the little man and sees in him his Wellington. So transitory, alas, is human fame, and so unstable the foundation upon which human glory is builded!

But when the two meet it will be a perfectly gorgeous fight.

---

[1] Perhaps Acts 5:9–10 in the story of Ananias.
[2] The Amir of Afghanistan in RK's day. RK covered the meeting between Abdur Rahman and Lord Dufferin, Viceroy of India, for the *CMG* in March–April 1885.

Deputating a Viceroy

※

Published: *Civil and Military Gazette*, 8 November 1887.

Attribution: In Scrapbook 4 (28/4, p. 11).

Text: *Civil and Military Gazette*.

Notes: Unreprinted and unrecorded. 'His Excellency' is the blasé, courtly and unflappable Lord Dufferin. The occasion of RK's comic piece is the state tour that Dufferin made to the frontier stations in the west of India (now Pakistan), including Karachi, the Bolan, Lahore, Peshawar and other points, from 3 November to 15 December. At Karachi, Dufferin received several deputations concerning the railway then being sought by the Karachi merchants. Lady Dufferin, who accompanied the Viceroy, wrote that Karachi 'has a railway question ... The address at the station was full of it, and all other addresses have continued to be full of it' (Marchioness of Dufferin and Ava, *Our Viceregal Life in India, 1884–1888*, new edn, London, 1893, p. 324). What was said to the Viceroy in Karachi is reported in more detail in the *CMG*, 14 November 1887. He was presented with 'an address of welcome' in which the municipal authorities referred to the falling off in the trade of Karachi, and to the fact that, for want of more extended railway communication, the trade of Karachi was doomed to recurrent periods of stagnation. They regretted to learn that their representations regarding the Hyderabad–Pashpadra Railway had not been favourably received by His Excellency's government.

No doubt the immediate impulse for the piece was given by a telegraphic item in the *CMG* of 7 November describing an excited meeting in Karachi and its resolutions regarding the railway question, the first of which resolved 'That the Viceroy be requested to receive a Deputation on the subject of railway extension.'

※

> They sought it with thimbles, they sought it with care
> They sought it with forks and with Hope!
> They threatened his life with a railway-share –

but there was no charming with "Smiles and soap."[1] On the contrary they held a public meeting and demanded the head of T.C.H. in a waste-paper basket.[2] The meeting were unanimously of opinion that "he who was responsible for the statement that two and two were anything other than four was totally unfit to live." This resolution together with the others, appeared in most of the leading newspapers, and was finally laid on H[is]. E[xcellency].'s table[3]

"Most embarrassing!" said His Excellency unofficially to the Keeper of the Conscience.[4] "Where's Karachi?" "Don't know. It's a second-class meeting I think, somewhere on the Bombay side. *Gin Tonic*, one of Abdul Rahman's job lots, won the –" "How interesting!" said His Excellency absently. "They are going to depute me there. Most curious people. Never seems to strike them I've work, – lots of work – of my own. What do you recommend?"

"Force the pace from the start" said the Keeper of the Conscience promptly. "Come round the home-turn before they know you've got away, spin up the straight and romp into Calcutta alone."

"That seems sound," said His Excellency. "D'you know, I really think – I do *really* think that, seeing he retires on the 21st of next month, he might have saved himself and me, this peculiarly humiliating *contretemps*.[5]

"Well, I had a charger once," said the Keeper of the Conscience, "who used to bolt cross-country to stables the moment the 'dismiss' sounded. He generally knocked down some one and" . . . .

"*How* interesting!" said His Excellency still more absently. "What's the quotation – 'Quem Deus vult perdere prius dementat.'"[6]

"No tat that I ever knew. But seriously, Sir, what do you intend to do?" His Excellency's eyes twinkled. "Do what your charger did. There are reasons, State reasons, why a deputation on this particular subject would be excessively inconvenient for me. And, whatever I may think, I can't call him a" –

The Keeper of the Conscience went away with a head full of orders and both hands full of telegraph drafts.

The special train tore westward at terrific speed – so swiftly that the expensive State track of the N.W. Railway curled up behind it as a shaving curls behind a jack-plane. His Excellency timed it with a stop-watch and now and then murmured:– "How embarrassing!" At Multan, in spite of red *saloo* and Officers Commanding the Station, it halted only to take in water, and fled, westward, ever westward, till it finally plunged, hissing hot, into the waters of the mighty Indus.

To leap from the sumptuously upholstered saloon to the deck of the seventy horse-power Indus liner "*Pannikin,*" to buckle on his revolver, and bid the captain cast off, was the work of an instant for His Excellency. A howl of baffled rage rose from the bank where a deputation of Prominent Citizens waving sheaves of paper, might be descried capering against the turquoise-blue of the evening sky. "How interesting!" said His Excellency watching the performance though his monocular. "And now I think we'll have some dinner. Moor us in the middle of the stream, Captain, please, and tell the 96th Land Crabs who have so kindly furnished the Guard of Honour and with whose stalwart appearance I wish it to be understood that I am specially impressed, to row round this spacious and excellently-designed steamer all night."

Alas for the precautions of the Land Crabs! Day broke upon the *Pannikin* ploughing madly through the limpid waters of the Indus at a speed far exceeding the one and a half knots provided for in the "Army Regulations." The seventy horse-power boilers "primed" and kicked till planks flew from the promenade deck and a wall of white foam stood up in front of the box-like prow of the *Pannikin*. A short fifty yards in the rear, using the long swinging side-stroke that had so often filled the stevedores of Clifton and the lodgers of Keamari[7] with envy, toiled the Deputation. Under cover of night it had run the blockade of the Land Crabs and almost boarded the *Pannikin*. The sheaf of papers was between its clenched teeth, and there was fire – a fine commercial fire – in its eight eyes.

"How interesting!" said His Excellency. "Now if T.C.H. were here I would throw him over and let them deal with him."

Speech carries far over water. The words reached the Deputation who puffed like grampuses and cheered faintly. They were in the lightest of attire, but loyal to the backbone. "Loyalty," said His Excellency, "is an excellent thing, but there is a loyalty which becomes a nuisance. Captain, will you kindly direct the able and zealous engineer of this singularly well-appointed vessel to increase what I believe is technically termed the 'head of steam'?"

But the *Pannikin* was doing her utmost. Hand over hand the Deputation overhauled her and finally laid hold of the stern-wheel. "The crying want of Karachi" said the spokesman as the revolution of the wheel brought him up to the hurricane deck, "is"_____

"Clothes" interpolated the Keeper of the Conscience politely.

"Gentlemen," said His Excellency as the four rubbed the water out of their eyes. "I am delighted to make your acquaintance in the unconventional garb of Lower Sind, a Province which is to me, I assure you, one of exceptional interest, and, I am inclined to believe, of equally exceptional commercial promise."

In a lengthy and eloquent speech, subsequently reported in eight columns by the *Bombay Gazette*, a feat claimed by that paper as "unique in the annals of earthly journalism," His Excellency reviewed the socio-political, military-social, political-administrative history of Sind and Beluchistan, including a masterly *resumé* of the course of frontier politics between the years 1837–62, while the Deputation shivered and one by one wrapped themselves in the double, elephant folio memorials they had borne so bravely down the raging Indus. "Turning now," said His Excellency, "to the commercial future of the greatly blessed land of your adoption, I need only say, gentlemen, that there is Hope."

Four sullen plunges were heard from the deck of the *Pannikin* where, in place of the goose-fleshed Deputation, lay in picturesque confusion the scattered sheets of the memorial. The Deputation had gone. Their spirits had been broken. Cold and exposure, and the mention of the hated name produced, as His Excellency had foreseen, an uncontrollable yearning for suicide.

"File these papers" said His Excellency sweetly. "His was indeed a name to conjure with. I must write and tell him."

The four corpses, a dreary row, floated past the *Pannikin*. His Excellency adjusted his monocular.

"How interesting!" said His Excellency.

---

[1] Lewis Carroll, 'The Hunting of the Snark: Fit the Third', slightly modified to fit RK's story.

[2] Sir Theodore Cracraft Hope (1831–1915) was currently the Public Works Member of the Viceregal Council. He was an effective promoter of railway building in India. According to *The Times*, 14 November 1887, he was 'not popular' but succeeded in 'pushing

forward the frontier railway system in face of much opposition'. But the Public Works Department over which he presided had recently rejected the demands of the Karachi merchants for a railway over the Sindh desert.

3 The public meeting on the railway issue is reported in the *CMG*, 7 November 1887. The meeting resolved to appoint a deputation to the Viceroy and instructed it 'to bring to the notice of His Excellency the errors in figures and facts conspicuous in the reply of the Public Works Department'.

4 Lord William Beresford (1847–1900), military secretary to three successive viceroys, 1882–94, and a notable rider, 'boasting a record of eight broken collar-bones, four concussions of the brain, and contusions innumerable' (Charles Allen, *Kipling Sahib*, New York, 2009, p. 229).

5 Hope's resignation took effect in December; he left India early in 1888.

6 'Whom God would destroy he first sends mad': proverbial.

7 Waterfront sections of Karachi, one commercial, one residential.

A Merry Christmas
(By the Reveller.)

๛

Published: *Civil and Military Gazette*, 31 December 1887.

Attribution: In Scrapbook 4 (28/4, p. 44).

Text: *Civil and Military Gazette.*

Notes: RK had left the *CMG* and Lahore for the *Pioneer* and Allahabad around mid November 1887, but he continued to contribute stories to the *CMG* regularly through the next year and irregularly thereafter.

RK used the pseudonym 'The Reveller' three times in quick succession in the *CMG* for the following stories: 'A Merry Christmas', 31 December 1887; 'A New Year's Sermon', 1 January 1888; and 'The Luck of Roaring Camp', 17 January 1888.

'A Merry Christmas' has been reprinted in the Martindell–Ballard pamphlets and in Harbord, III, 1629–32.

๛

Everyone who, by hook or by crook, could get an invitation to dine with a friend was dining out, and the big Club dining-room was thinly speckled with six men – to wit, Pelletbough, the Judge, who is an old man, Markin, the barrister, who is middle-aged and fat, Goyle, the veterinary surgeon, and Saulez, the man doctor, old Colonel Cassanade, and I myself. We were – we felt it as we foregathered round the fire in the smoking-room – the outcastes of Kalanaghar on Christmas Eve 1887 – men deemed unworthy of an invitation to any family circle. Cassande stared into the fire and grinned horribly at something he saw in the embers. Then he pulled his moustache and ordered a sherry and bitters. A cold wind came in with the *khitmatgar* and made Goyle, who is a singularly vituperative man, swear fluently. Otherwise the silence was unbroken except by the flapping of the leaves of the *Pink 'Un* in Markin's hands.

"*Sirwa inez par*"[1] said the *khansamah*, and we trooped into the dining-room, which echoed our footsteps and was not too warm.

169

There was an air of unusual splendour about the table and a profusion of frost-nipped roses in the center-piece. Cassanade grunted and tucked the napkin into his collar. Then he began to turn purple and to point to the center-piece. "What in the world" – but he used a much worse expression – "is that doing here?" "That" was a piece of mistletoe procured, from goodness knows where, by the *khansamah*, who explained to the horrified Cassanade that it was a *phul*, which had some connection with Christmas. "It's Christmas Eve, you know," said Markin drearily. "D— it, so it is," said Goyle.

Pelletbough was handling the dingy sprig of mistletoe in a dreamy way. He has the reputation of being semi-idiotic when he is not on the Bench. And, in truth, I think he is.

"I recollect the first time I kissed a girl under this," said Pelletbough, "It was in Jersey when I was home on leave – I mean home for the holidays, or else before I went to school, but I've forgotten which" – – .

"That remind me," said Saulez, "do you know the story of the man with the inkstand?" He told it. It was a more than doubtful tale, and in the barn-like dining-room fell very flat. Goyle laughed a little; but Goyle would laugh at anything if it were only bad enough. Cassanade pulled the inside out of his roll and stared at the table-cloth. I tucked up my legs to avoid the draught along the ground.

"Where's everyone gone to-night?" said Markin. "Dining out, I suppose, and playing children's game afterwards. What fools!"

Cassanade, who had been making faces at the centre-piece, roused himself.

"Children – children! Biggest curse in life. Look at my son. Brackenbury's and a hundred and fifty pocket money. Young whelp's failed for Sandhurst. Got the letter this mail: second time. What am I to do with him? Make him a clerk, hey?" None of us took an interest in Cassanade's son, so nobody answered the question. He went on, half to himself. "My only son too – only son. What the deuce am I to do with him, hey?" He finished his champagne and called for more. It was really very cold, and we all needed a good deal of wine of sorts. We drank quietly without talking – all except Saulez, who insisted on telling us stale tales. He was drinking Club sherry. Old Pelletbough wrapped himself up in his napkin and shivered. "This time last year," he began feebly, "I was at Home." Then he chuckled succulently, as if he had enjoyed an unspeakably immoral furlough. "I met Kiddle there – he's dead now – cut up in Burma." "Was that Charlie Kiddle?" said Goyle – "the man who belonged to Mrs. Battersby – Rocket Kiddle they called him in the Peshin."

"What can you do for a youngster who won't work?" asked Cassanade of the company generally.

"Let him drive a cab," said Saulez. "Do you know the story of the four-wheeler and the two lamp-posts?" "No, it wasn't Charlie Kiddle," said Pelletbough. "It was his brother and he was cut up in Burmah – crucified." "Nonsense," said Markin., "None of the Johnnies in Burmah have been crucified. Look at the papers."

"Crucified," continued Pelletbough blandly. "No such thing," said Markin hotly. "Well, they were much worse in Afghanistan," said Saulez. "Did you ever hear how a couple of Afghans treated Peppers when he was chucked from his horse and had his thigh btoken? We found him two days afterwards." "'Tisn't as if he couldn't work," said Cassanade, chewing his moustache. "He can work when he likes – that's what makes it so hard."

"Anybody going to play Poker?" said Markin, who is really a first class player. His own set were all dining out, and he wanted to loot some of us. "Not good enough," said Goyle; and took a cheroot. "By the way, what came to that Johnny who was here about two months ago – red-haired man who used to play with you a good deal – Curtess or Cutter, or something like that, was his name." "Oh, he! He went out with typhoid somewhere down south the other day; owed me four gold mohurs – confound him." "Was that Courtase of the Hundred and Fiftieth?" said Saulez. "Yes, that's the man – I recollect now," said Markin. "By Jove! I wonder what will happen to Mrs. Courtase and the children? I knew her in Simla about two years ago. Used to paint a good deal in those days." "S'pose they'll raise a subscription and send 'em Home," said Markin, "But isn't anyone going to play?"

"Don't tell me that these crammers look after the morals of their youngsters," said Cassanade, bringing down his hand upon the table. "I tell you they let 'em go to the devil, Sir – go to the devil about town."

"That reminds me," said Saulez – "do you know the story of the man with the plush overcoat. It's awfully good. A man brought it up from Madras the other day; come into the smoking-room and I'll tell you."

We had lingered very long over the dinner table, chilled to the marrow, but too dispirited to stir. The smoking-room was warm and well lighted. Saulez stood upon the hearthrug and began his tale. He was half-way through – and even old Cassanade had given up thinking of his son, and chuckling and leering like the old Satyr he was – when from the darkness without came a clash of bells and the high-pitched treble of children's voices:–

"Noel! Noel! Noel!
This is the salutation of
The Angel Gabriel!
Tidings true we bring to you
Brought from the Trinity
By Gabriel to Nazareth,
City of Galilee!
A virgin pure, a clean maiden,
Through her humility!
Hath conceived the Person
Second in Deity!"[2]

"Confound those Orphanage brats. The Mother Superior, or whatever she is, ought to keep 'em indoors," said Saulez. "Well, after the overcoat had been lost as I was telling you. . . ." But Markin rose in his place and said, "Oh! That's enough! What a beast you are, Saulez!" "What beasts we all are!" said Goyle. "I'm going to bed; it's Christmas Day." There was a long pause while we were all lighting our cheroots. Then Pelletbough said, "Well, isin't anybody going to say anything!" "Oh!" said Cassanade, "M'yes! Merry Christmas, I suppose."

But Saulez had gone away in a huff, because his best story had been spoilt; and no one took up the Colonel's greeting.

That was how I spent my Christmas Eve.

---

[1] 'The soup is on the table' (Harbord).
[2] 'The Salutation Carol', traditional, perhaps from the fifteenth century.

The New Year's Sermon
By the Reveller

Published: *Civil and Military Gazette*, 2 January 1888.

Attribution: Signed by 'The Reveller', a pseudonym also used at this time on 'A Merry Christmas', *CMG*, 31 December, and on 'The Luck of Roaring Camp', *CMG*, 17 January 1888, as well as on 'The New Year's Sermon'. The first two stories are positively identified as being by RK (Scrapbook 28/4, p. 44). The evidence of circumstance and style makes RK's authorship nearly certain.

Text: *Civil and Military Gazette.* The story as reprinted in 'Turnovers' shows a number of small variations from the text in the *CMG*, some of which I have recorded in the notes. They are, perhaps, evidence of RK's participation in the editing of 'Turnovers'; the publication of this series of reprints was an enterprise of the *CMG*. The alterations are, in my judgement, such as only an author might make.

Notes: Reprinted in 'Turnovers', I, 1888, and in Harbord, IV, 1945–7.

With a punctuality[1] that did them infinite discredit, the Sind, Sagur and S. P. and D. Bank sent home the balanced bank-book on the night of December 31st, to the house of the owner. By a curious coincidence the year and the last page of the bank-book ended together with the sumptuous total in hand of Rs. 46-3-9 only,[2] as the cheques say. The owner and his Familiar Imp took council together. But there was no New Year jocoseness about the Imp. He sat himself comfortably upon the top of the reading-lamp, where the heat best consorted with his ideas of the fitness of things, and coughed politely. The Bank-Book was still lying in its wrapper. "You had better open that interesting publication,"[3] said the Imp suavely: "you'll find it better fun than the newspaper." "I shan't," said the owner. "I know all about it, and this is my New Year's holiday." "Don't think that you know everything[4] though," said the Imp. "Permit me!" There was a rustling of torn paper, and in another minute the Imp had returned to his place on the reading-lamp with the book balanced on his knees. "You'll forgive a stranger meddling with your private affairs, won't you?" "It's gross insol—" "Not at all – you know nothing about it: we'll begin at the beginning." He adjusted a pair of red-hot spectacles on his nose and turned over the pages. "Now we'll see what you've been doing the last five years. 'December '82, to cheque favouring self, Rs. 170.' That wasn't the cheque for house-keeping, you know. That was your first horse – you were awfully stuck over him too – in the days when you meant to be economical. Let's see, Rs. 170 for a beast that would have been dear at Rs. 50. You began well, at all events. 'By cheque from T. Sharpe, Rs. 39.' That was what old Sharpe gave you for him – that and an old fox terrier. I suppose you know Sharpe doctored him up and sold him for Rs. 200 – a buggy-horse. That's comforting to remember. 'January, February, March, '83.' H'm – nothing very wrong there. Housekeeping, horse feeds, servants – I can account for it all. Here's a curiosity, though:– 'To cheque favouring Amir Nath, and Durga Dass Rs. 155.' Faith, you began before you had been long in the country. That was a bit of Jeipur enamel (Do you remember?), and Mrs. Golightly said it didn't match any dress she ever wore. Also that it was clumsy and barbaric. You took the hint, for next time you tried Baker and Shelvey Rs. 210. It's down here, you know, and it was all you could do to pay it. As a bracelet I don't think Mrs. G. appreciated it much. She swapped it with a Simla *bunnia* for a double sapphire ring, because she wanted to cut out Mrs. Spreadbrim's opal and her husband wouldn't give her any more money. She told you that her ayah stole it. Do you recollect that? She told you a good many untruths, and I don't think you gained anything from her, except a knowledge of Messrs. Baker and Shelvey's wares. Hey?[5] When did she cast you off. Let's see. Here's an interval of impecunious sanity and accounts overdrawn after three months of Baker and Shelvey tempered with Cameron, Gordon & Co. 'October, November, December '83.' Yes, you had to recoup yourself somewhere; but I shouldn't have taken to Black Pool at the Club if I had been you. They know how to play, you know. 'By cheque favouring Honorary Secretary, 'Skindize Club, Rs. 270, Rs. 215, Rs 431?' That 'March'[6] bill made you draw in your horns, *mon ami*: If it's any consolation to you to know that Wrest lost it all at Lucknow in the autumn you have that satisfaction. Nine hundred and sixteen rupees chucked into a bottomless billiard-pocket. All your fault for beginning with eight anna balls and going on to chick⁷ ones. You 'didn't know when to stop when once you got started?' My dear Sir, if noble sportsmen of your type *did* know, my business would be gone altogether. Nine hundred and sixteen rupees. That's cheerful! What's the next item? Sheer, stark folly this time. The billiards never taught you wisdom. 'August, 1884, to cheque favouring Lala Durga Dass Rs. 750.' No need to ask what that means. Limpsey was a *very* nice man to know, but I don't think his signature would raise sixteen annas in the bazaar even if you wrote it on a ten rupee note. It's cheaper to let a lame dog die than to help him over the style in the way you did. You'll never see one pie of that again. That's comforting, isn't it. Almost as comforting as the extra premium you had to pay in December for renewing your policy which you couldn't pay in June because of – well never mind. My best business is done in a small station in the hot weather when there are too few to talk scandal and quite enough to make it. I've omitted all the 'horses' you've been swindled over in '83 and '84 because I thought it would hurt your feelings. Roughly, you've thrown away Rs. 1,300 on things with four legs within two years and a half."

"*Now* we're coming to something interesting. Cheques favouring self by the score. You were learning wisdom in '85, weren't you? But I don't think you ever knew how thoroughly Mrs. McVortex despised you, even when she couldn't pay her bills at Tooke's, and you thought it a privilege to be allowed to help. Rs. 760 (pity you got the increase of pay), Rs. 341, Rs. 219, Rs. 132, and Rs. 284. Small wonder you had to borrow that thousand, pay three hundred for the use of it, and forego your journey home. *Entre nous,* – I may tell you that you'll never go Home. Put it down to yourself or Mrs. McVortex, just as you please, or to me if you like. I don't mind, bless you. Here's '86. Spent in trying to pay back the thousand with money won at Poker. I wouldn't recommend you to do it again. That 'By cheque from T. Doddles Rs. 103', the only receipt in the whole volume, besides your regular pay, cost you, approximately, Rs. 1,100. I won't be ceartain to a fraction. You thought you knew the game? So did Tommy Doddles when you fleeced him on the frontier; but the Frontier isn't all India, as you found out when you came south. You can't grumble, you know.

"Let's see what '87 says. By Jupiter, your personal vanity woke up this year! Nothing but clothes, and boots, and ties, and guns, and gloves!

I don't know, whether it was more harmful than Mrs. McVortex or backing Limpsey's bills; but the great question is, after you have paid off Duncan's account, which is nearer three hundred than two, and settled with Trodda for the new Express, which, by the way, is far too accurately sighted for your needs – the question, I repeat, is, *what* have you to show for five years' pay? You did not run away with Mrs. McVortex, for which you may be deeply thankful. The escape is more than you deserved. You may, five years hence, recover your loan to Limpsey, though that is extremely unlikely. Setting these things aside, my very intelligent, virtuous, temperate, self-denying friend, what have you got to show for". . . . .

There was a smash of broken glass, and the reading lamp, smitten by the bank-book which, somehow, had not been in the Devil's hand at all, crashed on to the carpet. The Devil was gone, and the owner sat in darkness, enlivened by the fitful gleam of the lighted kerosene as it pranced about the hearthrug and the stench of burning wool.

[1] With punctual sarcasm ('Turnovers').
[2] 'only' ('Turnovers').
[3] volume ('Turnovers').
[4] Every thing ('Turnovers').
[5] wares, hey? ('Turnovers').
[6] March ('Turnovers').
[7] Slang for 'rupee'.

New Year's Gifts

Published: *Pioneer*, 2 January 1888; *Pioneer Mail*, 4 January 1888; *The Week's News*, 7 January, 1888.

Attribution: In Scrapbook 4 (28/4, p. 46).

Text: *Pioneer*.

Note: Reprinted in Harbord, IV, 1947–52.

Time, Old Time, is not really half so awe-striking as artists and writer-folk try to make out. In private life, and when he pays an unofficial visit to anyone, as he did to me last night, he is a well preserved old Parsee gentleman, only distinguishable from the common herd by the length of the lock of hair on his forehead. "You see," said Time, as he took off his high lacquered hat, "I have to wear it long for people to catch hold of when they feel inclined. You've heard of taking Time by the forelock? Well, there's the whole *sub chiz*. I can't say that it's much used, in this country at any rate. and it's a great nuisance in the hot weather, but I must keep it up in case of contingencies." "Do you smoke?" I asked politely. "A little," said Time with a glance that froze me to the marrow. "I've used up a good many Empires that way, as you may have heard. I don't eat up cities: that's a popular delusion. I burn 'em – put 'em in my pipe and smoke 'em." "And what brand are you smoking now, Sir?" "Oh don't be afraid, It's Russian – very strong and a good deal of it, but I shall get through it in time. I've called to ask your advice in a sort of way." This was immensely flattering, and I said as much. "I can't altogether keep abreast of myself, and I've been so hard-pushed on the Continent, making arrangements for some fire-works, that I have rather lost touch of this country. Would you mind telling your servants to bring in my portmanteau? I've got some things in it for the men about here, and I want to ask you if they'll suit. You've heard of Time's Gifts and Time's Revenges of course. I've left the Revenges at the Station, but the Gifts are lighter and came in the compartment with me."

The trunk, a big black one, marked cunningly "Thambusjee Rerumbhoy Edax",[1] was brought into the dining-room. As he unstrapped it, Time explained:– "You see, I'm largely dependent on my staff of Days for information as to men's peculiarities. You've no idea of the amount of work I have to trust to others, now population has increased. I recollect when Adam and Eve started house-keeping I could give my whole attention to that interesting young couple; but now – humph, the subordinate staff are fearfully overworked, and, of course, there's no trusting the Hours. They come and go too quickly. The Days are the best stamp of clerks; though I *have* known some of the Hours do average work when there was an earthquake or a battle on the programme." He opened the trunk and rummaged among the packages with which it was filled. "Don't look into it!" he said. "Your time, that is to say, your day, hasn't come yet, and no man can see what the future holds and live y'know. I've got everything upside down here. What do you think of this as a present for Lord D—n?"[2]

He stripped the wrappings off a small "First Persian Grammar" and threw it across the table. "One of the November Days, I think it was, reported that that was what he wanted most." "Who am I," I said, "to dispute the verdict of Time? But do you give him nothing more for the next twelve months?" "He doesn't want it" said Time. "The year after this, I may attend to him.[3] Well, we'll let it pass then. There's a package here for his Secretary[4] I think. Can you make head or tail of it? It comes from Watts's, and smells like new saddlery." I ripped up the sewn canvas cover and saw, oh shame! – a gag-snaffle and a ring-saddle. "Your Days must be a frivolous office, Time," said I laughing. "Young man," said Time slowly, "you may thank your stars when Time jests with you. And yet, you cannot tell, nor can I. I never know whether I am a jest or a ter-ror. I follow the reports of the Days, and a good deal of my supervising power is merely nominal. But it *does* look rather quaint, doesn't it?" He polished the snaffle on his sleeve and laughed.

"Disgraceful habit you have in this country of using nick-names," said he, bending over the trunk. "I wish you'd get 'em to drop it. My Days pick up the trick. Here's a thing labelled 'Bobs,' or 'Jobs' is it? You look. Who's 'Bobs'?"[5]

He took up, and my heart died within me, a sword-case, the flap over the hilt unbuttoned. I put out my hand hastily, and was going to feel if the blade were sharp, but Time stopped me. "That sword is not for *you* to draw," he said, with quiet scorn. "But is it sharpened?" I pleaded. "Is it ground?" "What on earth are you so troubled about? Oh I forgot. You look at things from a subjective standpoint. There is nothing to worry over. A good sword is a good thing to have whether you want to draw it or not." "But how am I to know that you have given him a good sword? It may be hoop-iron for aught that I can tell." "No fear," said Time blandly, puffing at his pipe. "Men say I'm rather mean occasionally, but I've dealt fairly by this man, and I don't intend to let him down. Stop playing with the hilt-flap and tell me what you think of this for T.C. H——e."[6] He winked and held out a dirty, yellow, Board-School multi-plication table.[7] "Oh Time!" said I, "this is worse than the ring-saddle. Why can't you let him have a rest? It was a one blunder at the end of a long life, and he has been so thoroughly basted for it." "Must I tell you that the consequences of an act extend through all Time? I know some-thing about him personally, and I intend sending this Home to him." "But it will make him so savage." "Never mind," said Time, "'Hope springs eternal in the human breast',[8] as one of your poets wrote, and I've got something good in store for him later on."

He continued his search into the trunk, and in a little time stood up, with some sort of rattling anatomical specimen in his hand. "It's early to give J. B. L——l[9] a backbone, but the Days have reported that he wants it, and I can only follow their advice. How am I to rail this to him?" "Coil it up in a hat-box," I said, "if you must. Surely that would be a better gift for some of the Secretariat in those parts." "If I listened to everything the Days said about *them*, I should be sending a consign-ment of bowstrings in that direction. But they're all little men and not worth the expenses of postage. J. B., however, deserves consideration. I don't expect he'll appreciate it in the least. I think I'll send it in an office-box. 'Twould be more appropriate y'know."

There was silence broken only by the rustling of paper-wrappers. Time laughed to himself as he fished out another sword – a Japanese one this time. "'Tisn't often that I care to own myself beaten by a man; especially one I know something about. D'you see this? It's as good a sword as any Damio[10] would wish to let the life of himself out with. Tsu-Koto, great among Japanese artists, designed it, and I've got it specially for the *hari-kari* of the Gryphon,[11] as you call him, a few months hence.

But hang me – I mean kill me – if I know whether the man will use it or not! He's so desperately uncertain. I believe he's quite capable of making a fool of *me*! What do you think?" "Not knowing can't say," I said. "Strike a mean, and let him have half-bound copies of all the Bengal newspapers for the year." "That would never do," said Time. "If he doesn't take the *hari-kari* sword, and on my honour I don't know whether he will or won't, I should like to give him a good muzzle and drive him on leading-strings. But they'd have to be of silk you know," said Time, rubbing his chin, "and I haven't got any silk ones – at least not good enough or light enough. I'll trust to the *hari-kari* coming off, and send him the sword. Ten to one he'll return it, though. I wonder what I shall have to do with or for him next year? Here's something for the Bombay side and a man called R—y.[12] I haven't heard of him, but I suppose the Days know. They've packed up a hobby horse painted black. Does he ride much or badly?" asked Time. "Don't know what they do on the Bombay side," I said. "What's the next?" "Another man I don't know about Lord something or other in Madras[13] – a copybook with moral headings and '*The Art of Oratory*', one volume, three-and-six, with a coloured picture of Daniel Webster. Really, my Days might give better presents. Earth knows, I have money enough. I'm all Creation's residuary legatee."

There was a jingle of bells as he thrust back the packet. "Aha! That's an idea of my own!" said Time. "This is going to Hyderabad. It's pea-green, you'll observe, in delicate compliment to a creed I made once upon a time." He pulled out a sumptuous cap and bells, and shook them gleefully on the top of the bladder and stick attached to the outfit. "But Time!" I said, "this is disgraceful – this is libel by parcel-post! He's no end of a success."[14] "Did you ever hear of a man called Belshazzar?" said Time. "He was a little before your time though. Now, if Belshazzar had had similar warning to the one I am posting to-day, he, in all probability, would have escaped with credit, as being a first-class administrator, before the 'Mene, Mene, Tekel Upharsin'[15] came out in the daily press of those days. Belshazzar had his uses as a stop-gap y'know, but he came to grief when he began to take himself in earnest. A good many men do. I recollect a youngster of the name of Chatterton,[16] I think." –

Interesting as would have been the reminiscences of one whose memory went back to the birth of Time, I was filled with curiosity to see more of the contents of the trunk, and I said as much to my guest. "Ah!

I forgot," said he. "Now I could have gone on talking for fifty years. You would have been dead when I finished. I forgot that." He renewed his researches, and found a printed list. "Here's the invoice," he said. "I've wasted myself looking for it. What do you think of these for presents? Hm! Hm! Hm! L—d W—m B—d,[17] wadded arm chair. Well, well, it had to come sooner or later! Sir A. C—n[18] silver-mounted coach-whip, rhino-hide *sjambok*, gown and mortarboard with pins stuck into it. He's well provided for. That's better than last year's begging gourd and a mutilated Colenso.[19] Sir S—t B—y,[20] suit of ink-proof dittoes and an empty cash-box. I couldn't do anything better for him. Sir C—s and M—rs P—c S—s C—n,[21] Lowther Arcade Sphinx inkstand, two and thruppence. When you pull off the Sphinx's head, you find the ink inside. *I* call that chaste and elegant. Sir C—r P—m,[22] single passage, first class, from Bombay to Gravesend, with Cook's *chota hazri* coupons only. Mr. A. O. H—e,[23] a certificate of some kind, (my eyes aren't what they used to be) signed by a couple of doctors." "Mr. H. M. D.—d."[24] Time dropped the invoice and looked at me. "I am not going to say what I have brought for him. You wait for six months if you can live so long and see. He's rather a pet of mine, but I could wish!". . . The rest of the sentence was lost in the flutter of the leaves of a mighty book that Time dragged up from the very bottom of his trunk. "Here's a curious thing," said he pensively. "Just shows how the Days never forget a man, though I may. Do you remember the Sir W. W. H—r?"[25] "He's out of your jurisdiction now; you can do nothing for him," I said. "O yes I can. I'm mailing him a blank book for corrections of his B—l G—r. He's taken unspeakable liberties with me in his days, and I shall send one of these a month to give him something to do. If he doesn't use the pages for corrections, they'll serve him for the first draft of his first novel.[26] When that is out, I shall give him . . . . But wait and see, as I said in D's case. Here are a lot of things for a lot of men who ought to interest you. I wonder what made the Days pack up a new quill pen for G—d C—y,[27] and a scalping-knife and a copy of *United Ireland* for O'C—r.[28] Here's another P. & O. passage to Gravesend for Sir C—s A—n.[29] By Jove, I hope for his own sake he'll take the hint! What on earth is this? Who's P. D. H—nd—n?[30] I've got an auburn wig, two sticks of grease paint, a lady's fan, and the duplicate of a lease of a little house in Bath for her. She's evidently some old lady well known in your part of the world."

I bit my cheroot to prevent myself laughing, and Time went on.

"J. D——e,[31] whoever he may be, has another wig – a white one – a twitch, and a colt's bit, with printed directions for using all three. Stop! Here's something more for the same man. Illuminated text: – 'Ask and it shall be given',[32] in a border of horse-shoes and hares' feet. Evidently he's a parson of sporting tendencies, this J. D——e; and I think that's nearly all I've got in this trunk. The Revenges are at the station, but they are far too heavy to lift."

"And have you nothing for me?" I asked. "You!" said Time. "Who on earth are you to ask me for a present?" "Well, you've done your *duftar* in my house and seeing that you must sooner or later take me and everything that I have, you might as well give a fellow something." "Try these," said Time grimly, heaving on the table a pair of magnificent ten-tined deer-horns. "If you can't wear 'em yourself, you can give 'em to some other man. Don't think you're robbing me. I keep hundreds of 'em for current use. You never know when you may want a pair."

"Thanks, no," said I. "I'll wait till I'm married and then I'll think about it. I should like something lighter."

"Oh! very good; but remember, you'll have to keep whatever I give you for the next year at least. Shut your eyes." I shut them, and when I looked again, Time and his trunk were gone. I turned my head and heard the jingling bells.

Wicked, wicked Time! He had dowered me with the pied cap of the fool.

[1] An Indianised form of *Tempus edax rerum* ('Time the devourer of all things'): Ovid, *Metamorphoses*, xv, 224.
[2] Lord Dufferin, the Viceroy.
[3] Dufferin retired as Viceroy at the end of this year.
[4] Sir Donald Wallace: see 'An Official Secret'.
[5] Field-Marshal Frederick Roberts, 1st Earl Roberts (1832–1914), then Commander-in-Chief in India. 'Jobs' alludes to the charge that 'some of Roberts's military appointments ... verged on nepotism' (*Something of Myself*, 44), a charge taken up in RK's uncollected poem 'A Job Lot' (*Pioneer*, 1 September 1888: *Poems*, III, 1901). The question about the sharpness of the sword to be given Roberts alludes to the matter of defending India's northern borders against Russian aggression, an urgent political question at the time.
[6] Sir Theodore Cracraft Hope: see 'Deputating a Viceroy', note 2.
[7] Hope was accused of 'errors in figures' in his rejection of Karachi's petition for a railway: see 'Deputating a Viceroy', note 3.

8   Pope, 'An Essay on Man', line 95.

9   Sir James Broadwood Lyall (1838–1916), Lieutenant-Governor of the Punjab, 1887–92, the brother of Sir Alfred Lyall.

10 Japanese feudal lord.

11 The Gryphon: not identified.

12 Donald James Mackay, Baron Reay, Governor of Bombay, 1885–90. His particular interest in native affairs was education. RK would automatically have seen him as suspicious since he was appointed to the Bombay post by Gladstone.

13 Robert Bourke, Baron Connemara, Governor of Madras, 1886–90.

14 Not identified.

15 Daniel 5:25.

16 Thomas Chatterton (1752–70), 'the marvellous boy', forger of old poems and other documents before committing suicide; his story was a favourite among the Romantic poets.

17 Lord William Beresford: see 'Deputating a Viceroy', note 4.

18 Sir Auckland Colvin (1838–1908), Lieutenant-Governor of the North-West Provinces, 1887–92, and financial member of the Supreme Council, 1883–8.

19 The begging gourd alludes to Colvin's financial policy, satirised in RK's 'Rupaiyat of Omar Kal'vin' (*Departmental Ditties*); 'Colenso' refers to the popular *Arithmetic* by Bishop John Colenso.

20 Sir Stuart Bayley (1836–1925), Lieutenant-Governor of Bengal.

21 Sir C—s and Messrs P—c, S—s, C—n: not identified.

22 Sir William Cromer Petheram, Chief Justice of Bengal.

23 A. O. Hume (1829–1912), Indian civil servant, demoted in 1879 (a controversial case), retired 1882. A founder of the Indian National Congress and a Theosophist.

24 Sir Henry Mortimer Durand, Foreign Secretary in India.

25 Sir William Wilson Hunter: see 'The History of a Crime', note 2, above. Hunter had left India in 1887; back in England, he wrote a weekly column for *The Times* in which he was free to criticise the work of his former colleagues; his sympathetic treatment of the Indian National Congress was especially offensive (see 'In Wonderland'). Wilson's major work in India was the editing of the *Imperial Gazeteer*, 14 vols., 1885, which included a *Bengal Gazeteer*.

26 RK's long satiric poem on Hunter ends by urging him to 'bring out your novel!' (*Poems*, III, 1885). Hunter complied by publishing a novel called *The Old Missionary*, 1890.

27 G—d C—y: not identified.

28 O'C—r : not identified

29 Perhaps Sir Charles Aitchison (1832–98), Lieutenant-Governor of the Punjab, 1882–7.

30 Colonel Philip D. Henderson (1840–1918), Superintendent for the Suppression of Thuggee and Dacoity. He had been involved in a quarrel among the amateur actors in the Simla production of a play called *An Unequal Match*: see *Letters*, I, 233.

31 J. D—e: not identified.

32 Matthew 7:7.

Mister Anthony Dawking
(By "The Traveller.")

※

Published: *Civil and Military Gazette*, 11 January 1888.

Attribution: In Scrapbook 4 (28/4, p. 43).

Text: *Civil and Military Gazette.*

Notes: There is no reason to suppose that this is anything other than fiction, but in this month RK was travelling (hence the pseudonym 'The Traveller') all over India on assignment from the *Pioneer* and writing the sketches collected as 'Letters of Marque'. In the course of his travels, as he wrote to his cousin Margaret Burne-Jones, 'I saw and heard all sorts and conditions of men and they told me the story of their lives, black and white and brown alike, and I filled three note books' (25 January–24 March 1888: *Letters*, I, 151). The germ of 'Mister Antony Dawking' may have come from such encounters.

Reprinted in 'Turnovers', I, May 1888; in the suppressed *City of Dreadful Night*, 1890; in the Martindell–Ballard pamphlets; in the *Civil and Military Gazette Annual*, 1936, in Harbord, IV, 1958–61, and in Charles Allen, *Kipling's Kingdom*, London, 1987.

※

"When I comes to a gentleman and says, 'Look here! you give me a drink,' and that gentleman says, 'No I won't neither; you've 'ad too much,' am I angry? No! What I sez is".…

At this point, without word or warning, he went deeply and peacefully to sleep in the long-chair in the verandah. The dak-bungalow khansamah eyed him fearfully from afar. "He has come again," said the dak-bungalow khansamah, "and God knows when he will depart. I must get dinner." Towards dusk, Mister Anthony Dawking woke up and demanded refreshment. "The last time I was 'ere," said he pensively, "that there *khansammah* 'e ran away down the road and wouldn't give me no *khana*. So I took a leg of the bed and I broke open the cook-' ouse and I made my own *khana*. And now 'e don't run away no more. *Hitherow tum!* Just you *khana lao* and I'll have the same whiskey as I had last time." While the khansamah was preparing the meal, I turned over the pages of the dak-bungalow book. They fairly bristled with the name of "Anthony Dawking," and opposite each entry were that gentleman's comments on his entertainment. Once he had written: "the food is getting better but their wiskey is dam' bad. I am not plesed with this Dork-bungalo." A month later he had come again and written: "This day I bete the carnsarmer for his beesly cheek and broke two chares. The wiskey is better now." As I looked, he came and leaned over my shoulder, and there was a spicy fragrance in his breath. "You never saw such a 'ole," said he. "I've written some things there that shows you what you has to expec' but its worse since I come here last. They've got no good lamps now. I took and chucked the last one into the canal. It wouldn' burn proper. I know this bungalow. It's my reg'lar 'alten' place between Ammedabad an' Bhurtpore. My name is Dawking − Mister Anthony Dawking, and I was born in Southsea.[1] I'm none of your measly arf-castes I aint. I'm a true-born Englishman I am and I aint afraid of anybody.

> Anthony Dawking is my name,
> Hengland is my nation;
> Injy is my dwellin' place,
> An' work my occupation.

That's me! a 'onest pore man who 'as worked on the Hindus State, I've bin there, an' the Rajputanna-Malwa. I've bin there too, an' the Hindus steamers, an' the Southern M'ratta, an' the Dacca Daily Despatch steamers, I've been there too, an' the Injan Midlan' I was there too, an' the Irrawaddy Flotla I've been there too, fitter, engineer, foreman-fitter, pilot on the rivers that I didn't know, − anything you please, − for my name is Anthony Dawking and I'm a 'ard workin' man." All this was delivered, apparently, in one breath. Then Mister Dawking swayed on his heels for a moment. The khansamah peeped in at the door and announced that dinner was on the table.

"Come an' 'ave a snack," said Mr. Dawking genially. "You come an' 'ave dinner with me. Gor blesh you. If I was partic'lar who I spoke to an' 'ad dinner with I wouldn't be the pop'lar man I am now. 'Aven't you 'eard tell o' Anthony Dawking − the fitter? You ask old Beazeley who was a Permanent-way Inspector on the Punjab Northern. You say to 'im: 'Beazeley who's Dawking?' an' he'll begin to laugh, laugh 'imself blind. Beazeley was a pop'lar man an' so am I. Many's the time I've said to Beazeley: 'Beazeley come an' 'ave a drink, an' many a time 'as Beazeley said to me: 'Dawking, you pay for no drinks 'ere this evenin' while Jack Beazeley is 'ere'. That was old Beazeley all over. A fine free 'earted man was Beazeley. Tell 'im you've seen me an' 'e'll give you a good dinner. Better than this muck. Hi! *Khansammah*. Kisivasti 'ave you brought this *brab goshe*?" "Mister Dawking," said I meekly, "do you ever pay for your dinners?" "Do – I – pay – for – my – dinners?" He looked as though he were about to assault me. "What d'yer take me for? Me pay? I've bin from Gwalior to Kurrachi on foot an' railway pass an' I've never been asked that yet? Me pay? I'd like to see that *khansammah* ask me. Why on'y the last time I was 'ere the *khansammah* – 'e complained to the Resident because I wouldn't pay and broke all the crockery, an' the Resident 'e said 'e would send a police guard o' six to look after me. But they never came though I was entitled to 'ave them. So I deducted the cost of that police guard, six men at a rupee a day I made it, from my bill and I stayed four days an' my bill was only twenty rupees. So now I'm waitin' here for the four rupees that the police cost, an' if the *khansammah* complains again I'll 'ave 'is ears off over the top of' 'is 'ead. Me pay! of course I don't."

"That is quite true," said the *khansamah*. "This sahib never pays. I have never seen a sahib like this sahib. My bhai, who keeps the dak-bungalow at — says that he is *dewanipagal*, and so, your honour, I pay myself. He is a very poor man and he is always drunk." Mister Anthony Dawking was drinking while this explanation was offered. He roused at the word "drunk." "Who says I am drunk?" he asked with terrific gravity. "I am sober. Not a drop o' drink has passed my lips to-day. Chalk a line on the floor! Chalk a line on the floor and I'll show you whether I'm drunk or not." There was no chalk, but Mister Anthony Dawking took a juiceful capsicum out of the pickle-bottle and with it smeared an uncertain line upon the floor. This accomplished, he fell flat on his face along the line. "That's all right," he said with deep satisfaction, as he lay. "I knowed I wasn't drunk, *khansammah*, if I catch you I'll cut your head off for my name is Anthony Dawking and I am a man of my word." Still prone, he commenced to sing lustily a song that was new to me, beginning

There was a man whose name was Saul,
An' 'e died in Inji-a.
But 'e left 'is wife a Kashmir shawl
Before 'e went away.

He chaunted ten or twelve verses, and then stopped to explain. "Me an' old Scott made up that song when we was building the Sone Bridge. You go and sing it to old Beazeley and 'e'll know you've seen me." The pleasure of gazing on the dirt-grimed, liquor-blotched face of Mr. Dawking did not strike me as an overwhelming one. It was nearly time to start for the station. I gathered my traps together and left Mister Anthony Dawking fast asleep on the floor, with the *khansamah* timidly trying to thrust a pillow under his head.

※

A month later I stood in a great down-country factory worked by water-power and full of excited English foremen. "What's wrong with Number Four Shaft?" "Nothing much, only some d—d loafer has gone and hampered the turbine – with all these orders to be worked off before Wednesday too!" Strictly speaking Mister Anthony Dawking had done nothing worse than tumble into the dam above the turbine-hatch. They fished him out, as slovenly and unhandsome a corpse as could be desired, and he was buried by order of the Cantonment Magistrate. But in that far away dak-bungalow between Ahmedabad and Bhurtpore, the swindled and maltreated *khansamah* picked a bunch of yellow desert-flowers and sent his son by rail to lay them upon Dawking sahib's grave.

The son never found the grave, because there was no mark upon it; but the story is a sufficiently remarkable one, all the same.

---

[1] Where RK spent his unhappy childhood in the 'House of Desolation', 1871–7.

"The Luck of Roaring Camp"
(By The Reveller.)

※

Published: *Civil and Military Gazette*, 17 January 1888.

Attribution: In Scrapbook 4 (28/4, p. 44).

Text: *Civil and Military Gazette.*

Notes: The American writer Bret Harte's 'The Luck of Roaring Camp', 1868, is collected in *The Luck of Roaring Camp and Other Stories*, 1870. RK's various references to Harte show that he knew Harte's work well and that he was pleased to be compared to him; see, e.g., *Letters*, I, 151.

   'The Luck of Roaring Camp' was reprinted in 'Turnovers', I, 1888; in the suppressed *City of Dreadful Night*, 1890; in the Martindell–Ballard pamphlets; and in Harbord, IV, 1962–4.

※

Our Club is profanely called a "cock and hen" one – that is to say, it is open to all the ladies and gentlemen of the station. Sometimes the ladies keep to their own wing of the building, but more generally they stray elsewhere, and it is positively dangerous for a man to say what he thinks of things in general, in his own language. The Colonel's wife always manages to overhear, and then there is friction, because she asks her husband what the funny words mean. I do not say that the Honorary Secretary, who first threw the Club open to ladies, ought to be hanged, because no other living man in the station would or could manage our Club. I only want to point out a few things about Mrs. McGinnis and the baby and Bret Harte. It is too late to destroy Bret Harte's reputation; the baby hasn't got any, and Mrs. McGinnis is only an ordinary frivoller; but as Mrs. Nickleby said, "the principle remains the same".[1] Bret Harte once wrote a thing called *"The Luck of Roaring Camp,"* that I have known people cry over. It is all about a child who turned a miners' digging-town into a little heaven and then killed the best man in it. I believed in that story till the night before last. Now I see that it was all made up – fudged and compiled just like a Government report, and I desire that everybody else should see this also.

Flutterby of the Gunners was talking to Mrs. McGinnis in the tea-room. He is supposed to turn the heads of all the women he talks to. He turned Mrs. McGinnis's head to such an extent that she went home and forgot the baby. To be sure it was her first, and perhaps she did not understand that the little animals require feeding and tending every twenty minutes; but Goyle, the Vet, says that its firstness was all the more reason she should remember. Anyhow she forgot and left it in a chair, and Towser coming in from tennis nearly sat down upon it. When he had recovered from the shock he picked it up by a sort of girth-thing round its waist and took it into the smoking-room.

There it slept until the tobacco began to tickle its lungs. Then it wriggled about in the arm-chair and coughed a croaking little cough. Towser had gone out without telling any one about the affair, and the room was full of men waiting for dinner. If a shell had been exploded among them they could not have been more astonished. They all crowded round the chair, and said that the Honorary Secretary was totally unfit for his post. Babies in the tea-room were bad enough; but babies in the smoking-room were disgraceful. Goyle said if the place were going to be turned into a Kinder-Garten he, for one, would take his name off the books.

The baby wriggled so frightfully that we were afraid that it would fall off the chair. Saulez, the doctor, had never treated anything more tender than a Tommy in his life, but we felt that he was the proper man to put it back again. He shunted it into the chair with the flat of his hand, and it turned over on its stomach just like a frog. Then it began to strike out with its arms and legs as if it were swimming, and that brought it to the edge of the chair again. It was breathing through its nose like a young grampus, and all its clothes had got rucked up nearly to the level of its ears. We said Saulez was the proper man to put them straight again, but he said he was not going to touch the little devil. He was going out to dinner. Then four men took up a position in front of the smoking-room door, and they said that, dinner or no dinner, Saulez would have to mount guard over that baby till somebody relieved him. He was the only doctor, and if anything happened to it he would be held responsible. When he saw that we were in earnest, you should have heard Saulez swear. He wanted to take it up with the tongs and throw it into the verandah.

All this time it was striking out towards the edge of the chair, and Saulez had to shove it back again every few moments. Once he caught it by the head, and it bit his fingers. Goyle said that the upper and lower tushes were fully developed, and by horse law it ought to be much older than it really looked. Saulez said to Goyle that if he knew such a lot about the little beast he had better look after it instead of sniggering.

Then the baby grew tired of swimming and began to cry. It led off with a wail that grew to a sort of dry scream, just like the noise that a heavily-braked train makes when it is coming into the station. Vanderdee, who is a musical German, was trying to read the papers, and the noise upset him. He said it must be taken out of the room, and we said that he might do it himself. That made him angry, but the screaming made him nearly insane. He swore in English at first, but later in German, so that we missed the point of his remarks, which seemed to have a "Verdamnt Spitz-bub" for their object. Other men got angry too, and we sent a bearer to look for the Honorary Secretary; but whatever we did the baby cried just the same. Saulez shovelled it over on to its back, but that only seemed to open all the pipes, and the row was amazing. It drew old Cassanade from the billiard-room, and he came in snorting with anger. After he had used all the bad words he could think of, he said: "What's that!" and put on his glasses to look at the baby, who, by the way, had been dropped by Towser into Cassanade's pet particular chair. When the baby saw his face it stopped crying, said: "*Goo! Goo! Goo!*" turned over on its stomach (it really could twist like a screw propeller) and was violently sick. Every thing Saulez and Vanderdee had said up to this point was pious and printable compared to what Cassanade delivered himself of. There was a suspicion in the station that Cassanade had been a ranker, and his performance proved the suspeicion.

He wanted the Honorary Secretary's blood, he wanted Major McGinnis put under arrest, and he wanted the baby taken out of the room He commanded some of his subalterns to do this, but they refused point blank. Vanderdee, who is not in the Army at all, backed him up; and then he asked Vanderdee what on earth he had to do with a Colonel's orders. Then Saulez tried to bolt out of one of the doors, and was hauled back just in time to prevent the baby falling out of the chair. Saulez called us all names, because his dinner engagement was an urgent one, and the baby began to cry just as strongly as every body else was swearing. When the Honorary Secretary entered five men turned on him and he lost his temper, and Cassanade continued to shout orders to his subalterns; and Vanderdee ran out of his German into French, and back again to English; and the baby brought all its clothes over its head, and the clamour was something awful when * * * *

Mrs. McGinnis dashed into the room and asked what we brutes were doing to the baby. You might have heard a pin drop as she took it up and smoothed it out, and mumbled it all in the middle of the smok-ing-room, looking at us as though we were vampires or Thugs. When she left, the disturbance began. It ended in five closely written pages in the complaint book, two resignations, two quarrels, one apology, three coolnesses, and the attempted resignation of the Honorary Secretary.

Bret Harte's baby, as I have said, turned his temporary resting-place into a little heaven. But perhaps we had not got the proper sort of baby.

[1] Dickens, *Nicholas Nickleby*, e.g., ch. 37.

The Wedding Guest
(By the Traveller)

Published: *Civil and Military Gazette*, 16 February 1888.

Attribution: In Scrapbook 4 (28/4)

Text: *Civil and Military Gazette.*

Notes: Like 'Mr. Anthony Dawking', probably suggested by RK's travels through India in January and February, 1888. Reprinted in 'Turnovers', 1, 1888; in the Martindell–Ballard pamphlets; and in Harbord, IV, 1970–2.

⚹

An unkindly fate has cursed me with a Curse. It is ordained that wherever my unfortunate feet tread, there has been found a man with Something on his Mind. Like the Ancient Mariner he is unhappy until he can catch a Wedding Guest to whom to tell his tale. I am that Wedding Guest. I am sick of it. I am a repository of confidences and begin to suffer from indigestion. I will unload and scare off the Ancient Mariners.

Observe! I am, on the authority of Tipsley, the only living soul – Tipsley has no regard for dead souls – who knows that Tipsley is a married man. I am sorry for Mrs. Tipsley because Tipsley is always drunk. He caught me alone and undefended in an Intermediate Compartment near Rupaheli, and he wept when I offered him a cheroot. He was a platelayer, but what he felt most was his marriedness. "As true as I'm a-settin' here," gulped Tipsley, "I'm a married man. An' you're the only soul as knows it. Lord! Lord! How strange it all do seem. A Married man!" I had known Tipsley exactly one hour and forty minutes and it seemed very strange indeed. But I wasn't interested in his matrimonial ventures. He might have kept a harem for aught I cared. He told me that he had "never loved but one woman and her he didn't marry."

Then he cried anew. I'm sure I don't care; every man only loves one woman and generally marries the other. All the Punjab is at perfect liberty to know that Tipsley the platelayer – he is out of employment now,

192

but he thinks he will get work soon – is a married man – married to the wrong woman. She drinks like a "sanguinary ganger." I don't know what a "ganger" is, but it must be something very like Tipsley. If you meet an "orful fat woman with a bonneck that I paid for on 'er head, drinking like a sanguinary ganger" you will know that she is Mrs. Tipsley. Tipsley is not responsible for "any debts that she may contrac'." He said so three times openly, and that means "let it be law as it is desired." Tipsley told me so. He appears to make his own laws just like a king.

Again, only I and Mr. D'Silva and a woman with red sunflowers in her bonnet know that "Mary broke her heart over the mate of the *Blenkindoon*." Mary was a girl with a squint "but otherwise a lady in every respect." Mr. D'Silva is a contractor and he was "much impressed with Mary." He said that "her movements was so undulating." The woman with the red sunflowers in her bonnet told me this. I was flourishing in a second class compartment, which was extravagance, but it was a long run. The woman with the red flowers in her bonnet said that she always travelled first and she wouldn't have anyone know for the world that she was travelling second. However, she seemed to know all about the second-class refreshment tariffs right away from Chukabad to Bitsaur. Mary was her niece on her sister's side and a "great catch". She had ninety rupees a month "in her own right, from another aunt" – not the red sunflower one but one in the Railway – and, you see, the mate of the *Blenkindoon* thought that it was a hundred and ninety. The way he went on with Mary in the Eden Gardens was "most scandalous" said the red sunflower woman. Then she died – Mary died after the mate of the *Blenkindoon* had sailed away "to China on seven pound ten a month." He was a particular mate. If Mary had had a little more money he would have married her. If Mary hadn't "took up with him", Mr. D'Silva would have married her. He was a "most genteel young man," and he "turned over" a thousand a month. But "Mary she would have the mate of the *Blenkindoon*, and he seeing how things was with the money he went away to China, and Mary, that was my niece on the sister's side, she broke her pore heart and Mr. D'Silva he paid for the funeral most handsome. It was a most delicate thing to do, all things considered, because he was the only one except me who knew why pore Mary was dead. He had a marble tombstone with gilt letters and a text and then he married a sort of Jewish woman: young men will be young men, and it would have been too bad if Mary had broken his heart besides her own." So now you know all about Mary and Mr. D'Silva and the mate of the *Blenkindoon*, and the tombstone.

Once more. I know where there's a "gloating gold mine," and if I had five thousand rupees I would be "as rich as Crissers." A man in a striped waist coat told me this. He said he would like to have me as his partner – if I had five thousand rupees. He said all the capital requisite was only two Kabul tents, a fossicking knife and a coal shovel. It beat Dolgelly. It beat Aregona and Bolivia and Per-nam-bu-cow.¹ The man in the striped waistcoat is responsible for the statements and for the geography. He said that he wanted the five thousand rupees for "contingencies" and to "foreclose the market". What "foreclosing the market" is I do not know, and I am absolutely certain that he does not. But it sounds well. The gold mine is in Rajputana on the top of a hill.

The reason why Castries retired from "Asher, Straight and Dacree" was not because he went off his head from overwork but because he embezzled money. The firm hushed the matter up, and it would be an awful thing if people generally knew the real facts of the case. A man with two trunks of samples told me this. He said that he could confide in me. It had been a weight on his mind for some time. He told me all the story in the Rosicrucian Boarding House where there are lodgings for seamen, and strange ladies put their heads in over the half-door and whoop like fox-hunters.

But the landlady of the Rosicrucian told the longest and quite the strangest tale. It was all about her cousin who clandestinely married a corporal and came to great grief. The landlady cried three times while she was telling the tale, and sipped little liqueur glasses of rum between whiles. She cried so much that I lost the point of the disaster. Either the corporal or his wife was hanged for something or other; and after that nobody would call upon the landlady. They said "she kept the halter in her house" which is a polite way of saying:– "You've had a relative hanged." However the little stiffness wore off in time; and, when the landlady told me this story, the house was full of custom.

One of the strange ladies who whooped told me in strict confidence that she was engaged to be married and I wasn't to say anything about it for a week. No names were given, and so I kept my secret.

Then there was a mother with a blue baby – indigo blue and insane; there was a man who had invented a new pulley and was trodden down by the Government; there was an old man with a young wife who made him miserable; there was a man from Yokohama who had "got into a mess in Borneo." He repeated this phrase about once every five minutes. All these people, besides the men in the tramcar, told me their stories. They poured their woes into my ears, and I was forced to listen and pretend to like it. But I will have my revenge. I will let all the Punjab know what these people said, and next time perhaps they will not be so anxious to confide in me.

---

[1] All sites of gold mining.

The Tracking of Chuckerbutti
(See Tuesday's "Pioneer.")

᙮

Published: *Pioneer*, 1 March 1888; *The Week's News*, 3 March 1888; *Pioneer Mail*, 7 March 1888.

Attribution: In Scrapbook 4 (28/4, p. 53).

Text: *Pioneer*.

Notes: In his copy of Chandler's *Summary* RK has written against this title 'not mine RK'; a note in another hand questions this with the statement: 'in cutting book'. Since 'The Tracking of Chuckerbutti' was published forty-two years before RK could have seen Chandler's *Summary*, published in 1930, he had ample time in which to forget the story. The presence of the story in RK's Scrapbooks is decisive evidence for his authorship.

The story has been reprinted in the suppressed *Smith Administration*, 1891, in the Martindell–Ballard pamphlets, and in Harbord, IV, 1979–93.

᙮

Chuckerbutti[1] did not understand the working of the Police Department. All he knew was that, at the *thanas*, the Inspector was wont to put a charpoy gently but firmly on a witness's tummy, while his men, beginning with the slimmest *naique* and ending with the fattest *constabeel*, sat down upon it, one by one, until the required evidence had been extracted. Chuckerbutti's uncle had heard this from a Mahajun who once made the pilgrimage to Benares. So there was no doubting the truth of the tale. "It is an unmitigatedly burglarious department" said Chuckerbutti, but he did his best to get his cousin's nephew into it all the same.

One day Chuckerbutti found a Paper. The pressman gave it to the *durwan*, to whom he owed five annas for *pan*, and the *durwan* sold it to Chuckerbutti for eight annas. Chuckerbutti read it all through twice – once forwards and once backwards. Then he threw up his head to the silent stars and gave tongue, calling on his friends to help him. "We are betrayed!" said Chuckerbutti. "Lend me the *Webster's Complete* with the illustrations. The Empire is tottering to its fundamental base."

He ran his finger down the pages, "amazement, anarchy, brutality, bul-
lying, cowardice, distrust, despotism, espionage, fury, gall, hate, infernal,
justice, loathsome;" and so on, down to the end of the alphabet. The
resources of the office did not allow him to transfer the illustrations
also; but he made arrangements to have these lithographed later on. He
turned on the lycopodium lightning[2] and the tin thunder to an estimated
pressure of 75 lbs. per square inch, and painted L—d D—ff-rn red.
The *Holi* powder came in very handy here. "Oh! Alcibiades, the Seven
against Troy, Theocritus on Biology, Mister Seymour Keay,[3] Aristotle,
Demosthenes, Mister Cotton and the reverberating soup-tureen of the
Impartial Heavens, can you look down on this unmoved?" That was
the first sentence in the leading article. Chuckerbutti passed Aristotle
in the proof with three "t's", but the beauty of the opening was in no
way spoilt. "That will horripilate their crania," said Chuckerbutti; for
he was a first class classical student. "Hi you *duftri*! Where is *Maunder's
Treasury of History and Biography*?[4] Also *Pope*. Can't do anything without *Pope* now. *The Sunderbunds Semaphore* has used up the school-edi-
tion of *Bacon's Essays*."

Chuckerbutti got his books round him and started afresh with:–
"Hope for a while did bid the world farewell, And Freedom shrieked
as Kuski-uskin fell."[5] There was a misprint in the last word, but the
principle was just the same, as Mrs. Nickleby said. The *Maunder's* supplied unlimited Historical Comparisons, from the Fight of the Three
Hundred to Poland and St. Petersburg.

Having finished his work, Chuckerbutti went out stealthily into
police-ridden Calcutta, and wrapped a blanket round his head to avoid
detection. This ended in his nearly being knocked over by a Scaldah
tram. "Assassination in broad daylight," gulped Chuckerbutti as he
picked himself up. "They have read the article already." O he went from
house to house saying in a whisper: – "Hist! We are observed! The hell-
hounds of the law follow my slightest movement. When his friends
said:– "*Arré bap!* – what have *you* forged?" Chuckerbutti smiled mournfully, as one who already felt the leg-irons on his ankles, and gave them
the Paper to read. Then he departed, as he had come, with gigantic
strides, copied from the "stars" of the Parsee theatre, and the blanket all
over his head. It was an exhausting progress, but Chuckerbutti enjoyed
it down to his patent leather boots. Never had he had such a good time.

O'Brien's breeches were nothing to it. The policeman at the corner of Bentinck Street nearly arrested him for a lunatic. Chuckerbutti felt that he was dying for his country by whole feet at a time.

The day wore on, but nothing special happened. The sun did not turn blacker than usual, nor were the gates of Government Place thronged with *mouchards*. The loafers in Beaden Square were rude to Chuckerbutti; but even his luxuriant imagination could not transform them into emissaries of the Police.

"Never mind," said Chuckerbutti, "the convulsion will begin to-morrow. " But to-morrow was as colourless as to-day, if we except the article that Chuckerbutti wrote, with one eye on *The Voice of India* and the other on the *Pall Mall Gazette*, entitled "Come over and help us!" It nearly broke down the establishment in large type, but that was all. By this time all the other levers of the Universe were jammed "hard down" on the Espionage question, and the demand for *Popes* and *Juniuses*[6] made the fortunes of two *bickree-wallahs* in the Chandney Chowk. Chuckerbutti enjoyed himself hugely. He had changed the heavy blanket for one of lighter material, but, on the other hand, his strides were six and a half inches longer; so the disguise was still impenetrable. Next week, seeing that the Police were still backward, he abandoned the blanket and stood ostentatiously outside Twenty-two Lal Bazar with bound volumes of the *Sunderbunds Semaphore* in his hands. A brutal mounted sergeant nearly rode over him, and then abused him for obstructing the traffic. Chuckerbutti strained this into an article headed:– "The Beginning of the End", with the quotation:–

> "Let Honours, Arts, Matriculations die,
> But leave us still our old Morality."[7]

This was no good, and Chuckerbutti grew desperate. Hiring a first class *ticca gharri* he, after duly debiting the fare to the office, thundered up to Twenty-two Lal Bazar, and rushed into the office crying:– "Arrest me! I am the great Chuckerbutti. I avow it. I glory in it. I demand permanent accommodation in your deepest dungeon!" Then he struck all the attitudes of all the statues on the *Maidan* that he could recollect. He had no horse to help him out, but the effect was gorgeous. It brought a committal for house-breaking to an end. "Who," said the gentleman in the chair, – "Who the Dickens is that?" Then said the Sergeant briefly:– "Chuckerbutti." "What does he want?" "Instant arrest," said Chuckerbutti who had finished his Outram[8] attitudes. "I have lived under the galling burden of embittering espionage till death itself would be preferable to the agony that I endure. Arrest me! I am the author of –" "That'll do," said the gentleman in the chair, "we know all about you. Editor of the *Sunderbunds Semaphore*, isn't it? What's the trouble?"

Chuckerbutti handed him the Paper and restruck all the attitudes, winding up with the Municipal Demosthenes one.

"Umph – I see," said the gentleman in the chair, "Is this man a sect or has he any political doctrines Mr.—?"

"Arya Samaj,"[9] said the Assistant briefly. "National Congress. Cusses the Government and Us like the rest of 'em. File in the godown."

"Is he a suspicious foreigner or a criminal tribe?"

"Sir," said Chuckerbutti indignantly. "I am a Bengali of the Bengalis."

"Does he publish rumours disturbing the public peace, or comment on laws and Government measures?"

"Now for the holocaust!" thought Chuckerbutti.

"File in the godown," said the Assistant and killed a fly with the paper-cutter.

"Illicit trade in arms and ammuniation?"

"Never owned a gun in his life and wouldn't know what to do with it if he had."

"Affairs in independent Native States?"

"Diwan – bakshish – highest bidder. File in godown."

"Political Societies?"

"About six. Secretary of two. President of three. Schoolboys slanging Professors in Universities *and* Government."

"Mass meetings? Agrarian excitement?"

"Won't spend money. Landholder."

"I *don't* think we need ask the last question. Now Mr. Chuckerbutti, are you satisfied?"

But Chuckerbutti was not satisfied in the least. He demanded incarceration.

"You are more likely to get it for purloining than politics. May I ask you how you got hold of this paper?"

"There are no witnesses," said Chuckerbutti. "I defy you to bring any witnesses and the law lays down" . . . .

"Never mind the law at present, Mr. Chuckerbutti. You are at perfect liberty to go. But if you will take the advice of one who dabbled a little in the classics in his youth, you will spell Aristotle with two 't's'. It looks better. *Good* morning." Chuckerbutti departed.

"We must have that *durwan* dismissed," said the gentleman in the chair. "I've suspected him of trafficking before. Our routine work is heavy enough without this sort of nonsense. You were saying, Superintendent?" . . . .

Next morning, the *Sunderbunds Semaphore* appeared with a double-leaded article describing the heartless cross-examination of Chuckerbutti by the Police, the Head of which "purse-proud Department" had given Chuckerbutti "ultra-Draconian orders" as to the conduct of his paper in future. But, even while he wrote, there was sorrow and impotent anguish in the heart of Chuckerbutti. So ended the tracking.

It was all due to Chuckerbutti thinking of himself the most important person under Heaven.

India is still calm.

---

[1] Hobson-Jobson explains that 'this vulgarized Bengal Brahmin name is ... a corruption of *chakravarti*, the title assumed by the most exalted ancient Hindu sovereigns'.

[2] Lycopodium powder, from the spores of the lycopodium moss, was used in flash powder.

[3] John Seymour Keay (1839–1909), banker and merchant in India, founder of cotton spinning mills in Hyderabad, and then a supporter of the Indian National Congress. He was now active as a Liberal in English politics.

[4] Samuel Maunder (1785–1849), *Biographical Treasury*, London, 1838; *The Treasury of History*, London, 1844, and other such compendia.

[5] 'Hope, for a season, bade the world farewell, / And Freedom shrieked – as Kosciusko fell!': Thomas Campbell, 'The Pleasures of Hope', lines 381–2.

[6] The pseudonym of the author of a series of letters, 1769–72, attacking contemporary politicians from the Whig position; the identity of the author is not certainly known.

[7] A parody of Lord John Manners, Duke of Rutland, *England's Trust*, Part III, 227 (1841): 'Let wealth and commerce, law and learning die, / But leave us still our old nobility'.

[8] After Sir James Outram (1803–63), general in the Indian Army, known as the 'Bayard of India'.

[9] 'Noble Society', Hindu religious reform society founded in 1875.

"Bread upon the Waters"[1]
(By R.K.)

Published: *Civil and Military Gazette*, 14 March 1888.

Attribution: The story is signed 'By R.K.'

Text: *Civil and Military Gazette.*

Notes: At the end of the story in his copy of the suppressed *Smith Administration* (British Library, file 462, p. 87): RK wrote: 'I do not remember this thing as mine at all – at all. Rudyard Kipling'. In his copy of Chandler's *Summary*, RK has put a question mark after the entry for this story. Against these doubts the initials 'R.K.' with which the story is signed in the *CMG* are decisive: they could not have been used by anyone else in that publication.

The story was reprinted in both the suppressed edition of *The City of Dreadful Night*, 1890, and in the suppressed edition of *The Smith Administration*, 1891, in which all the stories but this one are certainly known to be by RK.

The story is not to be confused with the story of the same title originally published in *The Graphic*, Christmas 1896.

'Bread Upon the Waters' has been reprinted in the Martindell–Ballard pamphlets and in Harbord, 1, 1991–3.

There has been a good deal of discussion in the Helanthammi barracks lately. Chewser began by flourishing round the canteen with a copy of the *C. & M.* in his hand and fire in his eye. Chewser is the best boxer in the garrison, now that poor Mullane is doing his hundred and sixty-eight days for larking. The men weren't anxious to cross him because he was in the habit of hitting out on slight provocation. Spightly was there, too, and so was Snooker Clarke, who keeps the snakes. Chewser puffed about the canteen, breathing angrily through his nose, for at least five minutes. Then Spightly said, "Wot's on!" Chewser waved the newspaper like a flag of battle, and answered "Bobs is on." "Then there's something goin' to come off," said Snooker Clarke. "Which is it? Sik-kim or the bloomin' Paythans. Chuck us over the paper." "Garn 'ome," said

Chewser. "Tain't neither one nor t'other. Bobs sez I must keep sober."
"Faith, then, you've been movin' in the best o' society, that Bobs takes
you walkin' an' tells you what to do." Said the Canteen Sergeant, "You'll
be above mixin' in ord'nary p'rades after this." "Look at that," retorted
Chewser, sending the paper flying into the bar. Half a dozen heads
bent over the journal, deeply scored by the thumbnail of the indignant
Private Chewser. "Tain't a row after all. Fancy Bobs awastin' of hisself on
Te-emperance!" squeaked Snooker Clarke with deep scorn. "Spit it out,
Spightly." Spightly sat down on one of the tables and proceeded to read,
slowly and deliberately, with immense importance. "S'elp me! Does he
mean to do away with Canteen," shouted Chewser. "Tea an' eggs is it?
Wad-shop! Gareen!" "Don't int'rup the Honourable gentleman who 'as
the ear of the 'Ouse," said Spightly. "It's too long to read, but Bobs sez
Chewser is goin' to be eddicated on tea – with plenty o' sugar an' milk;
an' Chewser isn't to go hout on pass never no more because Chewser
can't be trusted not to make a beast o' hisself." "Climb down out of that,
Spi, or I'll knock the face o' you silly," said Chewser. "I've read it myself
a sight better than you could read it. Bobs don't say that." "Well he
meant it anyhow." "He don't," retorted the contradictous Chewser fil-
lilng his pipe. "No dirty little snipe like you's goin' to tell me what Bobs
is drivin' at. It's as clear as mud. We's goin' to have the Blue Lights[2] in
Canteen to teach us our drill." "Then I'm more than a little sorry for the
Blue Lights," said Snooker Clarke. "'Twas only the day before yesterday
Cassidy told me that I was layin' up for myself treasures in the wrong
place. Cassidy's a pet Bull Bison, or somethin' fine in the Blue Light
Lodge now. That's what Cassidy is, an' I remember him only last month
whipped on the peg all but whistlin' for being drunk as a hog trough."

"Cassidy's in D Company," said Chewser with dark significance,
"an' so t'wasn't a comp'ny thing at all. What did you do?" "Cussed him
back." "Bobs sez we mustn't swear never no more," murmured Spightly,
who was still deep in the Meerut speech.[3] "Was that all?" said Chewser.
"Twasn't enough – an' him a Blue Light. I take shame for you, Snooker
Clarke. Come outside with me, an' we'll look into the matter as the
Adjutant sez."

Spightly followed the unwilling Snooker Clarke, and outside the
Canteen was struck with a brilliant idea. "See here, Chewser! Don't
you tuck in. You'll more than 'arf kill 'im. Get hold ar [sic] Cassiddy

an' turn the two together. Bobs sez a Blue Light can lick *our* heads off. Let's see." Spightly had translated the Meerut speech[4] with a freedom which His Excellency the Commander-in-Chief had never intended. "Are you willin'?" said Chewser grimly to Snooker Clarke. "Ye-es. It's better nor bein' belted by you any waeys. Wher'll we have it out?" "Back o' the cavalry *rukh*. Spi, you go an' get Cassidy an' tell 'im wot for." Whatever the principles of the Blue Lights may be, fighting apparently is not prohibited, for Cassidy accepted the challenge with an avidity which Snooker Clarke considered absolutely un-Christian. The little procession wended its way to the back of the cavalry *rukh*. "Strip," said Chewser, "an' mind you, only body-blows. Neither of you two is worth knockin' the face of. One's Canteen and t'other's Wad Office, and now go in all you know."

Long and furious was the battle behind the Cavalry *rukh*, and deep the delight of Spightly, who, acting as referee and time-keeper, cheered the combatants by reading fragments from the Meerut speech. "Bobs sez swearin's a filthy habit. Cassidy's knocked off swearin' in reason. Smash his chest in, Snooker. Bobs sez a man who drinks ain't fit to be a bloomin' sweep. Cassidy ain't lushed for ten days. Smash him on the gullet plate, Snooker! 'Struth! Wad Office[5] 'as won! *Bote acchy*[6] wad shop!" And in truth, the unhappy Snooker was knocked clean out of tune – was hopelessly defeated.

"Wad-shop's won," echoed the burly Chewser, and hauled up the defeated. "Now you remember, Snooker, from this day on, henceforward for ever a man [*sic*: a-men?], you're a temperance advokit, an' into the Blue Lights you goes if they'll 'ave you. *Will* you 'ave 'im?" he asked Cassidy. "Ask the Master," returned Cassidy, putting on his coat. "His eye's out with lush, 'relse he'd a had me as near as winky more than once." "Very good," returned Chewser judicially. "Now you're a bloomin' Blue Light, an' you go an' be a Pet Bull Bison or Fringed Aprin as soon as you can. An' look here! If I ever catches any bloomin' bad words comin' out of your bloomin' sacrifunged lips, I'll – I'll – try – I'll attend to you myself." "It's bl— it's rather 'ard on a – on a man bein' cut 'is liquor 'cause of a bl— *blessed* fight," said Snooker Clarke mournfully. He had no thought of appealing from the decision of the bully of the company. "You'll do it – that's all!" said Chewser, and the big man walked away – to the Canteen.

"Now you look 'ere," said Cassidy to his newly found convert. I'll tell you something."

Snooker Clarke looked inexpressibly doleful. "Your body guard's all right, but you ain't got no eye, and you ain't made up your mind before you lets out, where your fistes are goin' to land. I'll learn you that on the quiet, an' if *he*" – he jerked his head towards the retreating form of Chewser – "sticks to canteen beer, as he's stickin' now in another month I'll learn you how to hang him up an' paste him agin a wall in little bits." "D'you mean that?" said Snooker jubilantly. "I do."

"Then I'll be a Blue Light straight off, an' I'll put a head on Chewser wot his own towney wouldn't know from a squashed tomata."

About thirty days hence there will, in all probability, be another conversion in the ranks of the Tail-Twisters; and when Chewser falls, Spightly is sure to come in.

---

[1] Ecclesiastes 11:1.

[2] Temperance workers.

[3] Roberts established an Army Temperance Association in 1887; it was given a room in each Soldiers' Institute 'where alcohol in any shape was not admitted' (Frederick Roberts, *Forty-One yeas in India*, London, 1897, II, 421).

[4] *Bahut accha*: very good

[5] 'Wad' means 'gunner'.

[6] Bahut accha: very good.

A Free Gift

Published: *Pioneer*, 19 March 1888; *Pioneer Mail*, 21 March 1888.

Atrribution: Not in the Scrapbooks, but the story clearly follows from 'The Tracking of Chuckerbutti', published eighteen days earlier, which is in the Scrapbooks.

Text: *Pioneer*.

Note: The story has been reprinted in the Martindell–Ballard pamphlets and in Harbord, IV, 1994–7.

⚘

If his worst enemy had been at his elbow all the time Chuckerbutti could hardly have mismanaged things more thoroughly. He had a splendid chance too. All that he wanted was just the least little bit of reserve – the "judicious impartiality" trick. But he threw his chance away. And in this fashion.

Chuckerbutti had been permitted to call his Viceroys pet names – such as "George Samivel" or "Freddy."[1] When they pleased him, he slapped them on the back familious-fash, and said:– "Shabash! Babu how he can make eshlave!" Some Viecroys rather winced, but some of them liked it awfully. When they didn't please him, Chuckerbutti used to dance in front of Government Place and snap his fingers at them. "We're the salt of the Earth and you're a dilettante mediocrity. We'll pull the scalp about your ears," shouted Churkerbutti. Then the Viceroys, who were not altogether unknown men, used to put on their collective eye-glasses and say:– "*How* interesting? Is it possible that this – ahem – gentleman has never been beyond the Ditch?" Then they would go on with whatever work was most urgent, and Chuckerbutti jumped with indignation. Some years before a man[2] had come along and stroked Chuckerbutti on the head, saying:– "You haven't taken any scrip in railways or mills or any single commercial enterprise: you don't know what cleanliness means, and you keep *rayther* too tight a hand upon your women folk; but you're a great man – you're the Heir of all the Ages." Chuckerbutti had been living on that certificate ever since. When he came across a Viceroy who recognised that there were other people in the world besides Chuckerbutti, he naturally ramped. But that was his blunder. If he had said:– "I'm a down-trodden Aryan groaning under a brutal heel. Observe my bleeding chest!" and *stopped there*, the hat would have gone round for pice, and Chuckerbutti would have secured unlimited pity. He preferred the "rumbutious periwig-pated style"[3] because it filled more space and amused the subscribers who were absolutely devoid of any sense of humour.

"See me slang Freddy!" said Chuckerbutti; and his friends sat down on the pavement and said: "Ya-as! Go on, ole bhai! Win, and blow thee necessary expenditure." Chuckerbutti went full steam ahead and slanged "Freddy" and "Freddy's" friends and most of his ancestors, and all his ways and works and manners and thoughts. It was gay while it lasted. It was gaudy and turned up with crimson at the edges. Two or three friends who had taken an interest in Chuckerbutti's career had hoped he would do something one of these days, said, – "Does the boy know what he is doing?" They remonstrated feebly with him, but he answered:– "I'm a patriot, and anyway, your mother was no better than she should have been; all thee bazaar knows you drink wine privately." Then the friends said:– "For pity's sake don't put this stuff into print. Abuse us verbally but don't put it into print." "Aha! you terremble!" said Chuckerbutti. "I'll hold you up to thee odium of a justly incensed nation of patriots. You buy to-morrow's issue and die!"

Chuckerbutti was resolved not to spare them. He ran in a stereo-block about the "necessities of this vast country demanding the sacrifice of personal and private feelings," because he wasn't sure about the filling in of the two columns, and, anyhow, it looked better. Then he pulled out all the stops and made the music play, and chaunted the pæan of Regenerated India, trampling on the battered mediocrity of "Freddy." It was a royal production, and it ran thus:– "Babu Behave yourself Betha[4] is a beast and a Thug in disguise. His uncle's son expects to be made a C.S.I. What more do you want? Is he not heavily in debt, and will not this connection give him a longer lease of credit. Oho Babu-ji, if you have recovered from your last big drink, or can tear yourself away from the low-caste woman you married in Orissa, listen to our pure and self-sacrificing council. Raja Harun Shiad should really be called Raja

Haramzada.⁵ He is a lick- spittle and his father was a *coachwan*. We beg
all patriots to remember that Raja Haramzada has been unfaithful to his
country as he has been unfaithful to his domestic relations. But a poor
man seeks pice even in the dunghill. Any man who disagrees from us is,
ex officio, base-born, married beneath him, an eater of forbidden flesh,
a chastiser of the priests, a despiser of Brahmins. All true men who
cherish cows should believe in political regeneration, the emancipation
of the masses, the Growing Light, and above all, the surpassing vileness
of Freddy."

"Freddy" turned his eye-glassed eye on to the effusion and said:–
"How interesting! Cows and the Caucus, Brahmins and Brummagem,
Puranas and Politics – all together. How interesting! I suppose they
mix in this curious country." Chuckerbutti drew breath and went on
anew, and there was woe and lamentation among a lot of worthy men
whose ears were nailed to the pump. When he had finished one leading
article he began another, repeating all the old abuse backwards – it read
equally well both ways – and the unhappy Rajas and Babus squirmed.
They objected to this sort of publicity, especially when they read statements that had been supplied by the dismissed *durwans* and cashiered
coachwans. Chuckerbutti called his system "Pride's Purge"⁶ – he had
found the name in a book, and it looked beautiful in burgeois [*sic*]
capitals.

When he had quite finished the mangling of "Freddy" and his friends,
and had suggested the burning in effigy of about every native gentleman with a head on his shoulders, he looked round to the benches for
applause. But there was a ghastly silence – broken at last by a laugh.
"For what are you now laughing?" said Chuckerbutti. "Is this not pure
patriotism? Take a care that you do not laugh in thee backside of your
physiognomy." And the laughter grew louder. Even Bombay, that rich
grass-widow who sits on Malabar Hill and dreams about cotton-shares
as she jingles the keys of the Empire – even calm-eyed, Scotch-blooded
Bombay – laughed. Even Madras, sleepy semi-religious, *passée*, Madras
laughed; and the Punjab, a Princess among the Provinces, poorest,
proudest and prettiest of them all, laughed merrily. And the burden of the
words that underlay the laughter was:– "O Chuckerbutti, Chuckerbutti,
now you've gone and done it!" "I know it," said Chuckerbutti, "This
will prove that in future thee Viceroy of the country must not only

content himself with unsympathetically administering, but he shall also be in keen accord with thee legitimate aspirations, &c." – "Bosh," said Bombay, "even I – I with my money and my cotton-shares and my charities – I who could buy you a hundred and fifty times over – shouldn't be justified in going on in this way. You're cutting your own throat, Chuckerbutti." "Bosh!" said Madras, "if you had punkahs up all the year round, and no Viceroy to play with, you *might* talk. You're overfed, Chuckerbutti, and she turned round and went to sleep again. "Bosh!" said the Punjab, "if you have your own box of lucifers and choose to play at Hell with it, you can't expect *us* to pretend to be scorched as well." "You are subservient traitors," said Chuckerbutti, "and I shouldn't at all wonder if your Mammas were. . . . "

About this time the Englishman, who was a down-trodden *janwar* of sorts, allowed to do all the hard work for Chuckerbutti if he gave Chuckerbutti the credit, pricked up his ears. He was underpaid and overworked, and once a week all his friends at Home slanged him for not being more enthusiastic over the "gorgeous, budding East." He was considerably in the background, and when Chuckerbutti was rusting for something to do, he used to accuse the Englishman of riding over natives for choice, and beating *sheristadars* with polo-sticks, and making women scream. "See here," said the Englishman, "you've had three beautiful chances and you've chucked 'em away. The first was in '83, and I didn't mind your going mad then, because it was your first trial; the second was in '87 and you mulled that by your ignorance of proportion.⁷ This now about 'Freddy' is the third, and you've given yourself into the hands of your enemies, bound hand and foot. You've got no head, and your language is the language of a *khitmatgar*. You're as spiteful as a woman, and as foolish as a little child. When anyone touches you, you scream; and if anyone differs from you, you fall back on the *gali* of the *bazar*. You've scared half your following by your abuse; and how on earth do you expect men to back you up when you may turn on 'em any minute and call 'em sons of *mehtranis* or paupers? You've used up about three hundredweight of type in proving that you have no *ukal*, no manners, no foresight, precious little organization, and as much sense of responsibility as a fox-terrier pup. That all comes from your want of proportion. You've given yourself away, Chuckerbutti, my son. I knew all about you before, but some other people didn't." Chuckerbutti was angry:– "You're a hide-bound bureaucrat," said he. "A bird of passage, spending thee money you wring from the sweat of thee ryots in alien countries. I'll appeal to the Holy British Elector and all thee Houses of Parliament!"

"I shouldn't do that if I were you," said the Englishman. "if the Holy British Elector gets hold of some of your files, he'll be asking questions in the House, and then I shall have to answer 'em. You won't like that, Chuckerbutti. Much better keep on slanging me. I'm paid for it, you know, and I can't hit back. Look here, we'll make a bargain. You can call me a thief. A bureaucrat, a ravisher, an unsympathetic alien, and anything else that you like, every day except Sundays, and I won't say a word if":– "If what?" said Chuckerbutti.

"If you'll only help me to clean up a few sewers now and again, and prevent your bhai *bund* from going out at the rate they do."

"Sewers!" shrieked Chuckerbutti. "You foist me off with sewers when my spirit aspires to a pure elective system of Representative Councils, eminently calculated to put thee administration of thee Empire on a fundamentally constitutional basis and unite all creeds and denominations in that profound and unflawed loyalty which" – He dashed off to his office, to finish the leader there. The Englishman looked at him ruefully and scratched his head.

"I *do* believe the creature believes it all. What a product!" said the Englishman.

---

[1] George Frederick Samuel Robinson, Lord Ripon; Frederick Temple Blackwood, Lord Dufferin, the latter succeeding the former as Viceroy.

[2] Perhaps Lord Ripon is meant; his policies towards the natives created violent resistance from the British in India. He is treated with unvarying hostility by RK.

[3] *Hamlet*, III.II: 'robustious, periwig-pated'.

[4] Not identified.

[5] That is, 'Raja Scoundrel'.

[6] Colonel Pride turned out the Royalists from the House of Commons in 1648, an episode that acquired the name of 'Pride's Purge'.

[7] Allusions not identified.

A Hill Homily

✠

Published: *Pioneer*, 30 March 1888; *Pioneer Mail*, 4 April 1888, *The Week's News*, 7 April 1888.
Attribution: In Scrapbook 4 (28/4, p 56).
Text: *Pioneer*.
Notes: RK was looking forward to his fifth and final visit to Simla (21 June–July) when he wrote this piece. It is reprinted in the Martindell–Ballard pamphlets and in Harbord, IV, 2005–9.

✠

Dilsukh, 25th March

Dear Jack – Your handwriting is strange to me, and the contents of your letter stranger still, for, nowadays, few young men consider it necessary to ask the advice of their seniors. You have put in two years of Indian service, and by this time, you should have sold some seven or eight ponies, screwed two or three more, written once at least to your father for an increase of allowance, lost your heart to several pretty girls – I trust, for your own sake, that they were girls – thought seriously about entering the Staff Corps, and backed a friend's bill. To these experiences you now intend to add a season at a Hill station, and demand rules for your conduct there from the 15th of April to the 15th of October.

The latest photograph of you – sent by your mother, for you evidently did not think it worth while to waste one of Bourne and Shepherd's shiniest cabinets[1] in my direction – shows me that, when he is knitted together a little more I shall have every reason to be proud of my sister's son – as a fine animal. You look as if you knew how to wear your clothes, and there is an excusable touch of affection [*sic*: affectation?] in the strapped watch at your wrist. When you are a little older, Jack, you will know that, in uniform, an officer should be independent of time. But let that pass. You are not a bad-looking boy, and you are extremely satisfied with Lieutenant John McRanamac. I envy you.

To return to your questions. You ask for "tips" about "getting-on" at Hill stations; but I notice that you are particularly careful not to mention the sanitarium which you intend to honour by your presence this hot weather. Shall I hazard a shrewd guess? Remember your letters are not the only ones that bring information from Ajaibgaum. Mussoorie of course you will not dream of visiting. That may do for the Staff Corps or the P.W.D.,[2] and though Bohemia is pleasant enough for a while, six months of Bohemia are demoralizing, Naini Tal is provincial: tell Judge — that if he ever asks you to dinner. Dalhousie as a nursery has its charms, but neither you nor I, dear boy – you will notice that in deference to the Spirit of the Age I treat you as an equal – are fond of nurseries. Muree I know now, as a halting stage into Kashmir, and a place where the average price of the muddy gruel called bath-water is about eight annas a *mussuck*. In my time the best whist in upper India could be found at Murree. But whist is not your forte and I do not for an instant believe that you are quitting the Plains for the sake of your health. Your mother appears to have some notion that you were coming Home for the year. I will not ask who gave her this belief or who has changed your plans. I assume that you are going to Simla as "claimed property" to quote the words of my esteemed little friend Mister Wilkins of the Jammabundi Moguls, who occasionally slaps me on the back and does me the honour of calling me "old boy." Jack, *never* slap a man ten years your senior on the back, and avoid familiarity of address.

But this is beside the question. Read my minor "tips" first, and try to avoid the use of slang in writing. You, in all likelihood, have one pet and particularly corky polo pony; perhaps more. Leave him or her at the foot of the hill, and while you are at Simla confine yourself to one horse of at least fifteen hands, and a second handy galloway, as little below that height as possible, for excursions along the narrower bridle-paths. The best and neatest fitting gaiters, and the most irreproachable breeches will not carry off the incongruity of a heron-legged subaltern like yourself straddling a thirteen-three on the Mall — more especially if your companion be riding a large waler. So mount yourself well, Jack, and mount yourself *large*. You believe that you can ride – most men of your age do – but do not let this belief seduce you into dispensing with a double bridle. Call me an old woman if you choose, and follow my advice if you can.

I fancy I hear you thinking:– "But I don't need to be told how to turn myself out." Perhaps you do, perhaps you do not; and perhaps I *am* an old woman. I must beg the forbearance of your immense experience and knowledge of the world for the rough notes hereunder.

The primrose path of dalliance marked out by you for the next six months looks, I know, specially bright and alluring; the more so since you have a sympathetic soul to share it with you. But it may be well to bear in mind that there are as good fish in Simla as ever came up to it; and that in no station does even the most sympathetic and constant woman-friend develop more quickly and surprisingly. The admiration which was grateful and comforting on the dusty roads of Ajaibgaum may – observe, I do not say will – become a bore in the city – for Simla is in no sense a station – where there are so many men willing and anxious to burn incense at the shrine of any passably pretty divinity. I do not suppose that you are worshipping an austere Minerva. It is just possible, my dear Jack, that you will find yourself cast adrift within a fortnight or a month of your arrival. In which case, you will probably be pained and a trifle astonished. Remember that you enter the tourney as a knight with a blank shield, for I do not consider that your year's dacoit-hunting in Burma is an experience peculiar to yourself. You will meet men with manners (those too you possess, if you have not abandoned them for the *faroucherie* of the modern Mess) and reputation, and a tale of achievements behind them. Many of them will be as good-looking as yourself, some will have more money, and all a wider knowledge of life. If you, with the insolence of youth, pit yourself against these, you run the risk of being ridden down. Lancelot was "often vanquished, victor at the last."[3] You are as little of a Lancelot as you are a Galahad, but even you may learn experience from being thus worsted. Neither Ajaibgaum nor Upper Burma contain all the fascinating men in the world; and though a pair of handsome eyes may do much they are not everything. Some women worship success. For your own peace of mind I hope that your fair friend is an exception.

If you *do* learn a rather unpleasant lesson, take your schooling like a gentleman, Jack. Petulance, reproaches, appeals, and expostulations carry little weight coming from young lips which are too prone to be rude when they should be severe, brutal when they should be cynical, and pitiable when they should be pathetic. Do not appeal from the sentence of dismissal, spoken or implied. Go – and go with a good grace; and, above all, let no half hints of reconciliation, or compromise, lure you back to the bait when the hook is once shaken clear of the jaw. I know that in saying this I am asking you to do the impossible, but, believe me, there is no sadder sight in the social world than the spectacle of a young man, of your age we will say, being retained for purposes of vivisection. In this case, and this only, you may acquire your experience vicariously. This, my dear last of the batch, means in your speech:– "Watching some other Johnnie kick."

And now I come to the more serious portion of my homily. At an Indian hill station, unless they have completely changed within the last two years, you will find yourself, as regards your male intimates, in one of the most unhealthy moral atmospheres in Asia. The causes of this I need hardly explain to a man of your immense penetration and sagacity. Thank Heaven, your conduct has never given me reason to believe that it was other than natural to you to behave as a gentleman. But the task is – I say it advisedly – a hard one. Disregard anything else that I may have said but remember this. As you hope for consideration among women and the respect of men whose respect is worth having, let nothing – neither jealousy nor pique nor the *abandon* of the "last supper" (I am not too old to forget [*sic*: remember?] what that means), the idle talk of the Club, nor, most deadly of all, the pleading of another woman, lead you into *talking*. Silence is more than golden. It is, by reason of rarity, diamond. Yet there are many silences more deadly than speech. How can I make the old, old story clear to you, my boy, to whom life is as new as it was to Adam? Let me put it on the ground of personal advantage. You must know, even in your limited experience, how – men of a certain class – go away on Hill leave and return with a hundred foul slanders on their lying tongues. You know too, how their friends ask mysteriously:– "Is there any biz?" – tailors, clerks and shop-boys that they are! – and you know what sort of answer is given. Nine-tenths – what am I writing? – the whole of the thing is untrue. It may, I hope it does, not do more harm than further polluting the souls of these scrattels – for, if you notice, Jack, the "weeds" are the greatest offenders; but there is always the chance of its ruining some woman's reputation. They say that the type of man at Home is changing. Neither you nor I can reform it, but you at least, with your five foot eleven muscularity, can make it unpleasant for some. Have nothing to do with them – you are too big and too good-looking for degrading folly. Drop your best friend as soon as he begins to talk – put his crime away from you as you would theft or desertion. I write strongly. Perhaps this maundering Polonius in pyjamahs, the hot weather has begun with us, is digging into his own old heart for your benefit, you graceless young scoffer. Perhaps I sinned and fell in this way years and years ago when I was your big "Uncle Davy"; and perhaps I am repenting of it bitterly still. Talking is cowardice, and the meanest form of cowardice, because the perfectly innocent victim, in nine cases out of ten, is a woman who has done her best to be polite to the gutter-souled beast . . . . Who is writing slang now? Never mind what I was going to say. Neither in word, deed, wink, implication, or failure to deny promptly and on the spot – a man who talks is always a cur, and you can frighten him into silence – ally yourself with the babblers who ought to be flogged – no, birched – an honest flogging would be too great an honour. And you shall find your reward. But it will *not* be in the anecdotes of the messroom, or the laughter of the club.

One matter I would put before your vastly experienced mind for consideration. Do not express admiration too hastily; and be sure of your ground. Some women – I do not know how the sets run this year or I would indicate their gathering-grounds – talk quite as much as some men; but in a different fashion. Has it ever struck you, my boy, that the rapturous and impassioned compliment stuttered out overnight under the combined influence of respect and Rœderer,[4] let us call them both, may be dished up, next morning to amuse the grim-visaged *Monsieur le Mari*, whom you take so little into your reckoning, as he reads the *Pioneer*? Has it ever struck you that the unfortunate little sentence that sounded so well under Chinese lanterns, may go the round of half a dozen feminine gatherings, growing on each stage, till it comes back to you in a form that makes you blush hotly and wish you were buried under Jakko? Reflect on this, my boy, ere you give yourself away with the family impetuosity of the McRanamacs.

In conclusion, learn a respectful *camaraderie* in your first season and – refrain from practising it. You will be sure to overdo it, and then the anguish of the colt brought to his bearings by the breaker's bit will be yours. If I thought that there was the least chance of your listening to me, I should say devote your first season to standing aside and watching.

Get into as good a set as you can. Follow Mrs. —'s lead in this matter and you will find that you cannot go very wrong. Do your duty calls as though you enjoyed them; always give Peliti one clear day's notice when you want a tiffin there, and take the left-hand room, the table *away* from the window. Leave nothing to Chance in your arrangements, and Chance will be your friend. Never forget to tip a servant, and never quarrel with your own or any one else's. Burn every note after reading it, and let no consideration prompt you to couch a written suggestion for a ride or a walk in any but the most formal language. Allow the second admirer, but be sure that he *is* the second, to get the *rickshaw*. It will please him while you will avoid a chill and secure ten minutes more conversation with the Goddess of the hour. Four dances in an evening are quite enough: more than four come under the same head as "talking"; and are reprehensible. Your partner will thank you later for your consideration. Make one khansamah your own for all the dances of the season, and you and she will be well attended to. If there is any poker, and you wish to keep within the paternal allowance, avoid it. Simla is not Ajaibgaum, and you will find that all I have said about better men than yourself is doubly true at the little green tables.

Have as good a time as youth, health, and spirits warrant, and send the mother a letter – *not* this one – occasionally. They would be glad to hear from you at Home; and a glimpse of your hieroglyphics will be always acceptable to

Yours affectionate Uncle
David.

P.S. – Are you too old for "tips" of another kind? The enclosed may interest you more than the letter and help words [*sic*: towards?] those wonderful clothes in which you will soon blossom out on Mall. Spare the Sex of which you know so much, my very dear boy!

---

1 A large portrait photograph from one of the leading photographers in India, with studios in Simla, Bombay and Calcutta. Several of the photographs of RK in India are from the Simla studio of Bourne and Shepherd.

2 Public Works Department.

3 Not identified.

4 Champagne Roederer, one of the *grandes marques* of Champagne.

The "Kingdom" of Bombay

Published: *Pioneer*, 10 April 1888; *Pioneer Mail*, 11 April 1888; *CMG*, 12 April 1888; *The Week's News*, 14 April 1888.

Attribution: In Scrapbook 4 (28/4, p. 44).

Text: *Pioneer*.

Notes: Making fun of the self-important style of the Bombay *Times of India* and the administration that it served was a regular amusement for the *CMG*.

'The "Kingdom" of Bombay' has been reprinted in the Martindell–Ballard pamphlets and in Harbord, IV, 2013–17.

All classes and creeds are alike interested in a policy
(the transfer of Sind to the Punjab) which strikes a
mortal blow at the future growth and prosperity of
the Kingdom of Bombay.
                    —*The Times of India, April 5th*.

Who are they that bluff and blow among the
    mud-banks of their harbour?
Making mock of Upper India where the High Gods live
    alway?
Grey rats of Prince's Dock – more dull than oysters of
    Colaba –
Apes of Apollo Bunder – yea, *bacilli* of Back Bay!
                    Swinburne (adapted).[1]

They met with one accord and a simultaneous gasp on the Central Indian plateau: each one carried gingerly and at arm's length a cutting from the *Times of India*. Together they cried:– "Have you seen this?" And a second time:– "*Have* you seen this?"

Bengal was voted into the chair. And the Punjab supported, but the Punjab was hot-headed. "There's only one course open to us," he said buckling on his sword. "We must court-martial him." "Better send a set of resolutions," said Bengal. "I don't think resolutions would touch the peculiar mental condition of my esteemed neighbour," said Madras dreamily. "Prod him with a pen," grunted the North-West savagely. "At any rate, get him up here and ask him what in the world or out of it he means by it."

So they made a long arm and picked Bombay out of his office, the cotton-waste in his hair, by the slack of his ducks, and set him down on the table with a thump. "What's that for?" said Bombay sulkily, for Bombay is quick to think his dignity scratched.

"For!" said the Punjab. "For impertinence – dashed impertinence, Sir." "You frontier men are *so* coarse," said Bengal; "let us preserve the decencies of debate. Bombay, you are charged by this assembly with – 'pon my honour, gentlemen, I can't hit on the proper word." "Exaggerated estimate of personal worth," suggested Madras, who was always polite. "Yes – thinking yourself a small sun and moon and universe combined," said the North-West. "Yes, and saying that your quill-drivers were better than my Civilians – *mine* d'you hear – men who were making history when you were gambling in cotton shares, you dissipated *dalal*," said the Punjab. "Yes – and calling yourself a Kingdom, you fluffy, stuffy little provincial," said Bengal with awful gravity. And they all shouted together:– "Calling yourself a Kingdom. Who made you a ruler among men?"

"Gentlemen," said Madras, "let us conduct the trial without heat. It is possible that the prisoner's brain may have been unhinged by the peculiar circumstances of his environment. On one side we have a Governor[2] who feeds it with" – "*Qoorma*,"[3] interrupted the Punjab. "What's that?" said Bombay. "Talk the vernacular to your Goanese boys and then you'll know. Go on Madras."

"Who feeds it with butter, and on the other a Royal Duke[4] for a Commander-in-Chief. These things, I submit, may have conduced to an intensification of the self-esteeem which" –

"Bosh!" said the Punjab. "I know the man you mean. He was with me at Pindi for a while, but he didn't disorganise *me*. *I* didn't say I was a Kingdom." "It can't be Lord Reay," said Bengal. "Now if the Viceroy had been down there, telling every one that they were the finest men in Asia I could have understood it." "It's just Bombay's blessed conceit," said the North-West. "I went through there the other day and they wanted to know what Simla thought of their Municipal Bill." "I wish you up-country men would talk in a more dignified way," said Bengal. "We're in the presence of a Kingdom, you know."

"'Hear I pray you this dream which I have dreamed,'" quoted Madras who had always taken an interest in Missions. "'And his brethren said unto him: shalt thou indeed reign over us?' Oh! Bombay, Bombay, we've been next door neighbours for a longer time than I care to think about, and I never expected to find you making such an exhibition of yourself."

"It's the amazing imoralilty of the creature that bothers me," said the North-West. "'Future growth and prosperilty of the Kingdom of Bombay!' Are you mad or what?"

"That is not the way to discuss an important public question," said Bombay angrily. "I base my claims to superiority on the fact of my being, in short, Bombay."

"Thank Heaven there's only one of 'em," said Bengal. "Fancy the Empire filled with us fellows calling ourselves Kingdoms! Well, my King, what next?" "I *am* Bombay and I'm not going to be laughed at," reiterated the prisoner.

"Yes, you *are* Bombay, and considering your pretensions, you own some of the worst hotels in Asia" answered the North-West. "You can't talk the vernaculars; you say: 'Hi! Got it?' when you ask for anything; your servants are bad; your capital could be blown into the blue by a decent sized iron-clad; and your Army List could be put into our Bengal one without increasing the postage; your districts are as quiet as water-gruel and about as interesting; you have the worst climate in India, and excepting you yourselves, not a soul east of Ahmedabad cares what you say or do or think unless you happen to be quarrelling with your Magistrates. You're useful to us, as a half-way house on the road Home."

"I go to Karachi," said the Punjab, "and when I've got Sind . . . never mind what I'll do. Look here, my King, in addition to everything my honourable friend here may have said, I want to point out to you that you are as naked as a pigeon-squab. I, and Bengal here, own the troops, and do the rough work. I and Bengal deal with the tribes on our frontier – 'EHA's' tribes are good enough for you. I and Bengal are the two people who are listened to when there is anything to be done, and I and Bengal are the people indented upon. Now we've never called ourselves more than Province or Presidency, but, when we speak, people stop talking and say:– 'What's that?' You aren't the Boston of the Empire, though you may be if you live long enough and grow humble. You aren't the Washington either. Simla is that and *I* own Simla. You *are* the Saratoga if what they say about Poona is correct; but even Poona, and the Duke, and an academical L.G. – I beg his pardon 'Guv'nor' – doesn't justify you in making such an outrageous ass of yourself. You and your 'deadly blows!' Aren't you ashamed of yourself, Bombay? You'll never hear the end of this – my uncrowned King. It's such bad form too. What would you say if I called myself a Kingdom? I'm the warden of it. You're only the stevedore – the underwriter."

"I don't care," said Bombay sulkily. "I abide by what I have said. You in the Mofussil can't be expected to understand the enormous advantages which I possess. Turning to the study of my most recent piece of civil legislation" –

"*That's* what has turned his head," said Bengal. "Listen, King, I've got a municipal bill *fifteen* times as unworkable as yours. Do I call myself a Kingdom on the strength of it? No. I write to the *Englishman*."

"The Press of Western India has long led the public opinion of the Empire," said Bombay.

The assembled Board looked at each other and groaned. "What *can* you do with hide-bound crassness of this sort? That comes of filling the Educational Department with Scotchmen," said Madras. "Bombay, do you recognise the enormity of your offence?" "No." "Nor the absurdity of it?" "No." "Nor the lunacy of it?" "No."

"Very good," said Bengal. "The sentence of this Court is that the Kingdom shall abide by his words if he can and they will. He shall eat the issue of the *Times of India* of the 5th April, 1888. . . . advertisements and all. The Court will carry the sentence into effect."

"But, gentlemen," pleaded the prisoner, "this is not *the* manner to approach a great public question. There is a levity – a lack of statesmanship. It is *not* argument."

"Can't help that. If you behave like a bumptious schoolboy you must be treated as such. Will you begin on the inner or the outer sheet?"

"In referring to the Kingdom of Bombay, the intelligent reader will at once understand," said the prisoner –

"Hold his nose, he's speaking between his teeth! Now!"

"That it was a misprint – a misprint – a *lapsus pennae* – regrettable incident! Gentlemen! printer's ink is a deadly poison," shrieked the maltreated Presidency.

"Let him go," said Bengal. "We'll accept that as an apology."

"What I hate about Bombay," said the Punjab, as he slued his Sam Browne belt straight, "is the way he wriggles out of everything. Why couldn't he have said that at first?"

"Wanted to see whether we'd stand it or overlook it, I suppose," said Bengal.

"Well," said the North-West grimly, "he's got his answer."

1 Adapted from Swinburne, 'The Commonweal', first stanza.
2 Lord Reay.
3 Variant spelling of 'korma', a curried dish of braised meat and vegetables.
4 Duke of Connaught.

Bombaystes Furioso

※

Published: *Pioneer*, 16 April 1888; *Pioneer Mail*, 18 April 1888; *The Week's News*, 21 April 1888.

Attribution: In Scrapbook 4 (28/4, p. 56).

Text: *Pioneer.*

Notes: The title puns on that of W. B. Rhodes's *Bombastes Furioso*, 1810, a popular burlesque. A follow-up to 'The "Kingdom" of Bombay', to which the *Times of India* had imprudently replied.

'Bombaystes Furioso' has been reprinted in the Martindell–Ballard pamphlets and in Harbord, IV, 2018–21.

※

> Oh! What will Your Majesty please to wear –
> Shoddy or fustian or piebald down?
> Will Your Majesty look at *our* bill of fare?
> Will Your Majesty wait till we take you down?
>
> *Bombastes Furioso* (adapted).[1]

Once more the Presidencies and the Provinces gathered upon the Central Indian plains to discuss the day's *dâk*. For half an hour no sound broke the silence but the ripping of dockets and the fluttering of newspapers. At the end of that time Madras chuckled audibly: "Joseph objects to being pitted," he said. "Who? What? 'Nother scandal? I beg your pardon, Madras," said Bengal. "No, Bombay, my brethren." Madras plunged into the paper afresh and laughed. "Just as I expected. What a nickel plated prig it is!"

"Let's hear. Don't keep it all to yourself," said the Punjab, who was fresh from a long parade and was rather sleepy. "Any more Empires been born lately in Mazagaon or the Mahim woods? What is the matter with our Thrice Puissant Sovereign now?"

"He says," began Madras, clearing his throat. "He says:– 'Don't you think yourself awfully funny neither?'"

"Doesn't *sound* exactly like a leading article," said the North-West, "give us the *ipsissima* – no, *imperialissima* – *verba*."

Madras read:– "The refined women and educated men who read the *Pioneer* must appreciate the delicate wit of 'lifting a man by the slack of his ducks'." "What did I tell you," said Bengal. "You up-country men behaved shamefully at that Court-martial. Of *course* he goes on the 'culchaw' tack and the *Saturday Review* lay. You gave him an opening." "Gave him a good deal more than that. It was a shutting up," said the Punjab stroking his moustache. "Never mind. Let him have his little morality. Only a strong sense of mental superiority can console a king when he is" – "Hsh," said Madras, "he can hear every word from here. Listen:– 'Hold his nose he's speaking between his teeth' is also another example of the cultured humour of the writer! There! *Saturday Review* again." "Cultured humour!" said Bengal. "It was the sentence of the Court and it was all for his good. What base ingratitude! What will he say next?" "Hold on to your chairs. I'll tell you," went on Madras. "'The expression' Kingdom of Bombay 'was no *lapsus pennæ*, but it was deliberately used because considerable mischief arises from regarding the Provinces of India as mere petty districts.'"

There was a long awe-stricken hush. Very far away, the roar of the Jubbulpore train came faintly to the astounded Provinces and Presidencies as the murmur of a shell in the ears of a child. "Well," said Madras, "is nobody going to say anything?"

"'Considerable mischief'," murmured the Punjab; "Yes! John Lawrence, and Herbert Edwardes, and Van Cortlandt,[2] and all the old heroes – I suppose *they* regarded me as a 'petty district'. They did 'considerable mischief' didn't they? I'm the apple of Bobb's[3] eye; the Frontier Force would die for me; I suppose I've had as much English blood spilt on my fields as most places; and, and – Oh! I say, you fellows, it's a shame to pull the thing's leg any more. Let him alone or goodness knows how he'll give himself away next."

"No, we won't," said the North-West. "I like the 'cultured humour' of this King. Hasn't he a fine grip of history? Doesn't he know his India? It needs a Kingdom to give mouth to views as broad and enlightened as those."

"And see the practicalness of the remedy!" said Bengal. "Call us 'Kingdoms' all round in print and people will get out of the habit of thinking of us as 'petty districts'."

"*Quem dues vult*,"⁴ said Madras, "and he can't see the microscopical pettiness of it all! I have yet to learn, as my Secretariat boys say, that the fountain of honour is shifted from the keeping of the Provinces concerned to" –

"To the composing room of a daily paper. Yes, it's rather a revelation, isn't it? Go on," said the North-West. "I wouldn't trust this King with the management of a collectorate. He'd call it a Province, to increase its *izzat*." "The best comes last," said Madras. "Some one has lent Joseph an atlas. Now for the statistics to crush us:– 'Bombay and Bangalore are the same in extent as Spain'."

"There! He admits that, and yet he objects to be handled as the King of Spain is treated by his *ayah*,"⁵ said the Punjab.

"Don't be Rabelaisian," said Bengal, "this isn't a Mess. Wish he wouldn't bracket me with himself, though. Well?"

"Now for some really startling information: 'Bengal contains twice as many inhabitants as the United Kingdom, and Bombay a million and a quarter more than Austria. The Punjab and Madras are each nearly the same size as the United Kingdom and Greece put together. When the *Pioneer*'" –

A triple roar of laughter cut short the reading for some minutes. "By Jove! He doesn't really mean all that, does he? Picture it, think of it, dissolute man!" said the Punjab to the North-West, wiping his eyes.

"I've known ordinary people go nearly mad over the E[ast]. I[ndian]. R[ailway]. time-tables," said the North-West, "but I've never known a King getting intoxicated over *Whitttaker*,⁶ before."

"*Whittaker!* He couldn't have got those revelations out of *Whittaker*," said Bengal. "They've been overhauling the Bombay State Records lately. That's where he found it. Why, I haven't known what he says about me for much more than seventy years. There's enterprise and salesmanship for you. A regular torpedo-boat of a Kingdom is our P & O principality. It's simply dizzying. Now for the peroration, Madras. He can't beat that."

"Yes, he can. Here's something to your address, North-West. 'When the *Pioneer* realizes that it is the leading paper in the North-West Provinces, which form a Kingdom.'" –

"Oh! Come. No! You're making that up, Madras."

"On my honour as a 'petty district' I'm reading as it's written – 'which form a Kingdom nearly the same size as Italy and contain a population nearly as large as the German Empire' – there's richness for you – 'it may become less Provincial in its tone and more refined in its painful efforts to be humourous.' Now do you feel properly sat upon?"

The North-West smoked for a long time without answering. Then he began slowly:– "I'm sorry, – awfully sorry we ever began the business." "Hullo! Has he hurt your feelings?" said Bengal. "No, not quite. I've used that *Saturday Review* trick myself in my time and – I know what I know. It's this way. Anyhow you look at it, he's one of us and we've got to stand or fall together, and when one of us makes an exhibition of himself, the rest feel uncomfy. Don't you think so? I know when Bengal had a touch of liver the other day I was sorry for him."

"You aren't going to make excuses, are you?" said the Punjab. "I want to loot Sind from our King on the ground that he's incapable of managing his own affairs. He has given me a beautiful chance. Don't take it away."

"Nonsense," said the North-West. "The more I think over it, and that stuff we've just heard, the more convinced I am that we haven't got the right man. Some one of the Bombay side has swallowed a *Whittaker*, and a Chamber of Commerce report, and some municipal papers, and they've disagreed with him. It is *his* whooping that we hear. Bombay *can't* be so idiotic."

"Don't know about that. He's in office all day, and he's got prickly heat half the year, and he hasn't open country to ride in. That *must* tell on his constitution one way or another," said the Punjab, who believed in exercise and wanted Sind.

"No," said Madras, "I think the North-West is right, Bombay carries too much side; but he has his points, and he's generally sane if you take him the right way."

"*A la* King of Spain for instance," said the Punjab wickedly. "Well, I'm off. Bobbs is wearing my life out with parades. I'm more *Greece* than United Kingdom these days." And the Piffer Province[7] mounted his charger and turned northward across Rajputana.

"Well, I'll go back and look after my Italy and German Empire," said the North-West stretching himself. "It's aggravating to have school-primer facts heaved at your head to bolster swaggering griffindom,[8] but we've had our laugh out of it, and it's no good taking it seriously. I go to kiss the hand of King Colvin,[9] by the Grace of Government Defender of the Allahabad University."

"And I, to see His Serene Majesty Stewart Bayley,[10] Kaiser c Calcutta," said Bengal.

"And I, to King Connemara,[11] Monarch of Madras, Autocrat of the Utakamund and Emperor of Assisted Education," said Madras.

And the peace of the twilight settled over the Damoh hills as the Four Great Brethren departed laughing.

[1] *Bombastes Furioso*, opening lines. The original runs thus:
> *1st Attendant.* What will your Majesty please to wear?
> Or blue, green, red, black, white, or brown?
> *2nd Att.* D'ye choose to look at the bill of fare?
> *Artaxaminous.* Get out of my sight, or I'll knock you down.

[2] Heroes of the Indian Mutiny, 1857: John Lawrence, Baron Lawrence (1811–79) was Chief Commissioner of the Punjab in 1857, afterwards Governor-General of India; General Sir Herbert Edwardes (1819–68), Commissioner of Peshawar, 1856-59; General Henry Charles Van Cortlandt (1814–88) raised a field force in the Mutiny

[3] Lord Roberts.

[4] 'Whom the gods would destroy they first make mad' (*quos Deus vult perdere prius dementat*): proverbial.

[5] Alphonse XIII was King of Spain from his birth in 1886, his father having died before the birth.

[6] *Whitaker's Almanac*, a popular reference work since 1868.

[7] The Punjab, so called after the initials of the Punjab Irregular Force, formed in 1865 to protect the frontier.

[8] 'Griffin' was Anglo-Indian slang for a new arrival, a greenhorn.

[9] Sir Auckland Colvin, Lieutenant-Governor of the Punjab.

[10] Stuart Bayley, Lieutenant-Governor of Bengal.

[11] Robert Bourke (1827–1902), Baron Connemara, Lieutenant-Governor of Madras from 1887.

A Day Off
(By One Who Took It.)

Published: *Civil and Military Gazette*, 4 May 1888.

Attribution: In Scrapbook 4 (28/4, p. 60).

Text: *Civil and Military Gazette*.

Notes: Late in 1909 the American publisher B. W. Dodge brought out an unauthorised collection of RK's early work under the title *Abaft the Funnel*. At RK's direction his American publisher, Doubleday, at once (December 1909) brought out an authorised edition of the same collection under the same title at a price of 19 cents, intended to undercut the sale of Dodge's edition. In January, 1910, RK's agent, A. P. Watt, sent to Doubleday a list of titles from RK's file of early work to be kept in Doubleday's safe 'pending any further action on the part of Messrs Dodge or other pirates' (1 January 1910: copy, Watt UNC 122:14). 'A Day Off' was among the titles on the list, but Dodge presented no 'further action', and thus 'A Day Off' did not appear in any authorized collection of RK's work.

Reprinted in 'Turnovers', 11, 1888, in the Martindell–Ballard pamphlets, and in Harbord, iv, 2032–5.

"'And on the seventh thou shalt do no manner of work. Thou and thy servant.'¹ –

Kadir Buksh is that bath ready yet?" Body o' me! I have slept till ten o'clock. That comes of one, two – no, four whiskey-pegs after dinner. But it has the great advantage of eating into the "long, hot Indian day."² In common decency one cannot go to bed again till ten. There still remain, therefore, twelve weary hours to kill. Outside, the sun has baked the roses brown, and the dust is whirling furiously down the garden paths. It has got into the morning tea, and the day opens auspiciously with the taste of gritty dust in my teeth. Decidedly, the weather is warming up, and gives one headaches – for those four pegs cannot account for the crisp and crawling sensation in the hair of the scalp, and the pain through the temples.

Now, in England, when a man rises on Sunday morning he looks forward to a day's pleasuring – by river, rail or road. Let me think – Loughton, Virginia Water, Datchet, Richmond, with something to eat at a place called the Star and Garter isn't it? Putney, a boat and someone else in it; blissful idleness á *deux* in the Parks – that is humble, but heavenly, – oh there are a hundred things that one can do. And here? "*Sahib, Sahib, gusl thanda hojaiga.*"[3] Kadir Buksh, you are an irreverent ruffian – and I am just going to dream a beautiful dream all about Putney tow-path. With the best will in the world a man cannot spend more than half an hour over his toilet – And such a toilet! Is it worth while dressing at all? Is it worth while doing anything?

Murchison of the Gunners decidedly thinks that it is. His tum-tum is scattering the Olympian dust of my compound. He is bravely attired in cow-hide boots, cord breeches, and a *jharun* coat. His nose has been peeled by the sun; he is hot and thirsty, but jubilant. "Hi! are you up? Give me something to drink. I'm dead!" shouts Murchison, and enters my humble apartment gaspingly. . . "Pilsener! For pity's sake – Pilsener! With oceans of ice in it. Such a morning as we've had! Riding *nilghai* with hog-spears down the river. Big as bulls and twice as festive! I got pipped twice, and the brutes got away; and I b'lieve I've screwed my tat, and – I say, *have* you got anything to eat in the house?"

Murchison is stoked up with fish, half a dozen curried eggs, two chops, *kichri* and omelette about a *seer* and a half, another big bottle of Pilsener, two-thirds of a tin of smoked salmon accompanied by unlimited bread and butter, six purple plantains, and a final instalment of Cape gooseberry jam. I look that he should drop down dead suddenly; but he lights a cheroot, fights for twenty minutes against a manifest desire to go to sleep, and then departs. "See you at the Club in the evening, I suppose," says he.

Now all the blights in all Rabelais light on that young barbarian! His disgustingly healthy appetite has taken away mine, and the silence of the house is more strikingly oppressive, now that he has gone.

The clock-hands are close upon mid-day. At six it will be cool enough to crawl out. How are those six hours to be murdered? What will tobacco do? I have been smoking since ten without knowing it, and my palate is blunted.

One consolation gone. The Library peon comes with some books – *videlicet* Hubner's *Through the British Empire* read six months ago; two French Doctors on Animal Magnetism, and *The Silence of Dean Maitland*.[4] Cheerful literature for a Sunday afternoon! Hubner shall be heaved to the other end of the room, and the terrier may read him if it likes. The French Doctors will do admirably to prop up the leg of a ricketty table; and *The Silence of Dean Maitland* shall come along to the sofa with me.

Unfortunately, a mosquito comes with him, and the *kenching* of the unfortunate punkah coolie out-side will not drive the pestilent creature away. My left eyelid is the one on which his heart is set, and it is impossible to read and to wink continuously at the same time. I will bend all the forces of my massive intellect towards the capture of this one wee vermin.

At the end of ten minutes I catch him. He is dead, but I am hot, dank, and uncomfortable. He will have his revenge in death: for if I lie under the punkah in this state I shall assuredly get chilled, and if I get chilled I shall have liver. Liver! And a certain number of years ago, if any one had asked me where I kept my liver, I should have said, in all good faith:– "By the Gods, Philoctetes, I cannot tell." Still the breath of the punkah is very pleasant, and the wind rustles in its fringes like the far-off murmur of the sea. The murmur gets nearer and nearer, and louder and louder, and at last I stand on a great clean wind-bitten English beach Yellow sea-poppies stick out of the sand, and inland the wind is rioting among the dried bents.

I stoop down and scoop up in my hand the clear bright salt water, that makes one sneeze. Who said that I have ever left the sea? I have been there all my life – for the taste of the salt water is familiar to my lips.

The sea-beach slides away and – oh horror! – I am sitting in my pyjamahs in a first-class compartment of the E.I.R., flying towards Jubbulpore. Nobody seems to notice my attire. They are all going Home by this week's steamer. So am I! On my word and honour so am I! I join desperately in the conversation to show that I belong to their set, and strive to prove that pyjamahs are my usual travelling kit. Nobody takes any notice of me, in spite of my enquiries about berths and luggage. I have no ticket either for train or steamer; but I am going Home somehow. If I can only look unconcerned they will land me at

Tilbury a few minutes after we have reached Bombay. The great thing
is to make the train go quicker before anybody can come to interfere. I
run behind and push. Then I jump in again, and we arrive at the Apollo
Bunder. No one has noticed me so far. In another five minutes I shall
be safe. I hurry to the steamer, fly into a cabin and shut myself up.
Enter, through the roof, the Commissioner's wife, bland, smiling and
gorgeous. I am conscious of my raiment, but all that I say is:– "How
unfortunate that I missed you when I called!" I say this several times,
and hope that she will go away. She does not. She continues to smile,
and says:– "Badminton next Wednesday, and every alternate Tuesday
throughout the hot weather: Errors and Omissions excepted."

The steamer vanishes, and I am alone – miserably alone – in the centre of a gaily-dressed Badminton party. Everybody whose good opinion
I ever valued, or whose ridicule I shrank from, is there; and everybody
is laughing at my 'appearance. Then they all begin to sing the nursery
rhyme:–

"Oranges and Lemons'" Say the bells of St. Clemens."

What has happened? The bearer is bringing in the lamps, and the
bells of St. Gigadibs in Partibus – I should like to raze that place to the
ground – are sullenly booming the refrain:–

"When will that be?" Say the bells of Stepney.
"I do not know" Says the great bell of Bow.

I have slept into the twilight. It is too late to go out. The Day of Rest
is ended!

1 Cf. Deuteronomy 5:14, the seventh commandment.
2 Not identified.
3 'Sir, sir, your bath will get cold' (Harbord).
4 Alexander, Graf von Hubner, *Through the British Empire*, 1886; Maxwell Gray, *The Silence of Dean Maitland*, 1887.

The Unpunishable Cherub
(By His Friend and Partner.)

Published: *Civil and Military Gazette*, 15 May 1888.

Attribution: In Scrapbook 4 (28/4, pp. 62–3).

Text: *Civil and Military Gazette*.

Notes: This was written when RK had returned to Lahore, after half a year's absence, to edit the *CMG* in the absence of the regular editor. When the issue for the 15th came out, RK wrote that 'It's a full paper, done with a fuller heart and may the Unpunishable Cherub, whom I have thinly disguised in the similitude of an allegory, forgive me for its blunders' (to Mrs Hill, [12–14] May 1888: *Letters*, 1, 176).

Reprinted in 'Turnovers', 1, 1888, in the Martindell–Ballard pamphlets, and in Harbord, IV, 2037–9.

"Turning now to a consideration of the financial aspects of the question we find – it will be obvious – we cannot fail to be impressed by . . . . Which is the best expression?"

"Tan I tum in?"

That's the Cherub, and if he intrudes to-day, small hope of the "financial aspect of the question" ever being considered in a proper and solid fashion. If I keep quiet, perhaps he will depart. No! The idiot of a *chaprassi* has told him that "the door is shut," and The Cherub has never found door of heart or house shut in his dimpled face yet. He won't take that for an answer. He is beginning to hammer on the lower panels with his fists.

"*Tan* I tum in?"

I will sink my voice into my slippers, and peradventure scare him away. "No, you *can't*, Cherub." That silenced him; and I can hear the patter of his little feet dying away in the direction of the nursery. "But if we consider the financial view of the matter, it is obvious that, in the face of an annually increasing Imperial deficit" – that's good – "Imperial

230

deficit." Where is that fat report with the blue back? Good gracious, Cherub, what are doing here?

"I tummed in by the window."

"Oh, you did? Then go out by it again." When Love comes in at the window, I know what happens to Work. "Cherub, hump yourself!" The Cherub looks at me with grave disapproval. "I doesn't know what you means. I is tum to see you w'ite."

"Who asked you, bad child?"

The Cherub thinks deeply for half a minute. Then, with an engaging smile (I am doing all I can to hang on to the thread of the idea about that "annually increasing Imperial deficit") says:– "Nobody didn't ask me. I tummed with me myself. You can w'ite." Is this a question or a command? I will treat it as the latter. "Imperial deficit, it would be futile to expect a Provincial allotment –"

"You can w'ite?" A seraph estrayed from the clouds could hardly speak in less passionless voice. I know the Cherub's ways. He is hatching mischief. Once more, he repeats the sentence. Clearly it is a question.

"I *am* writing, Don[1] Cupid. Can't you see me doing it?"

"No, I tan't. I is too small. Put me upon a chair."

"You got in through the window. Find your own chair, Mischief, and leave me alone."

He tramps round the room and touches each chair tentatively, but all are too heavy for him to lift. He sits down on the matting with a little sigh, and an appealing look at me.

If I talk to him I am lost. Let us go forward. "Provincial contract on lines which – based on – provincial allotment" – I wonder what the Cherub will do – "liberality for which the Supreme Government is neither designed nor inclined!" The sentences are plunging about like dolphins at play. I must Arion them into order.[2]

"*Do* your shoulders always w'iggle when you w'ite, like ayah when she is going to cough?"

The Cherub is sitting cross-legged in the middle of the floor regarding me with a large and luminous stare. What a child it is! There is some Bambino in some Continental gallery which is rather like him about the nose and forehead; but the eyes and mouth of the Cherub are better, being delightfully and impishly human. He sees that I am not angry with him, for he is beginning to smile, and when the Cherub smiles, I would defy the gloomiest to remain uncheered. But how about those accursed Provincial Contracts, and the liberality of the Supreme Government?

"*Why* does you shoulders w'iggle?"

I will be adamant. "Because you are in the room, Cherub, and you bother me."

"You shoulders w'iggle when you're bovvered? When ayah is bovvered she eats *pan*? Do *you* eat *pan* too?"

"Look here, Don Cupid, if you came in through the window to insult me, you had better go before I smack you."

The Cherub thinks the question out. Then he smiles:– "You thmack me! *Kubbi, kubbi nahin!*"

That's true enough; but I did not know that the Cherub was so thoroughly aware of his power.

"If I put you on a chair, and let you see me write, will you be quiet?"

"Yes," says the Cherub; "but it must be a chair with a book for me to sit upon."

Five minutes are spent in adjusting the Cherub. I fall to afresh, and for nearly five minutes I continue my glorious career – "And, we thus arrive at a position neither sanctioned by precedent, approved by exprience, or fruitful of any good promise for the future." That *sounds* well at any rate. I read it out half aloud, the Cherub watching me with his fat chin sunk between his soft fists. And now for the closing count of the indictment. "As a matter either of policy, statecraft, or simple expediency, the transfer stands condemned." –

"Oh! I *is* so tired! Put me down please," yawns the Cherub. "Is that wi'ting?"

"Yes. What do you think of it?"

"Let me look." He pulls the sheet towards him, and his brow puckers as he turns over the pages of the fat blue-book. The columns on columns of figures catch his eyes. "Like my tin soldiers," he murmurs to himself. "All ones and twos, and twos and twos."

"Well, what do you think of it all, Don Cupid?"

He picks up the report gingerly.

"It's very heavy. What for?"

"Because it's full of weighty facts, Senator."

"Watifax. What is watifax? Is it what makes this heavy like a b'ick?"

"Yes."

"Oh!" says the Cherub. 'It's only old paper, like the paper you w'ite on, and it doesn't mean."

"Doesn't mean what?"

"Doesn't mean. *All* nothing. Doesn't you know what doesn't mean is?"

I do, Cherub. Tangle-headed despot, I know thoroughly! It's rubbish and nonsense, My Prince, and we'll get rid of it in half a minute. With a sudden frog-like sweep of both arms, he has scattered my report and all my laborious comments thereon, and has annexed my most powerful paper-clip.

"Very well," he says imperiously, for I have trifled with his authority too long. "I'll put this on your nose, and you shall be a *baloo*, and when I say '*salaam karo*' you shall dance. Tum along!"

I am victimized before I can protest, and his feet are trampling on what I assure you was intended for a leading article for your esteemed columns, while I bend down to accept the paper-clip.

Gedtlebed of the Directiod, receive the assurance of my bost distinguished consideratiod. The clib has be by the dose ad I ab dub!

---

[1] 'Don' for the conventional 'Dan' is used throughout the story.

[2] 'Dolphins' in the preceding sentence presumably suggested 'Arion' here.

In Gilded Halls

Published: *Civil and Military Gazette*, 18 May 1888; *Pioneer Mail*, 27 May 1888
Attribution: In Scrapbook 4 (28/4, pp. 63–4).
Text: *Civil and Military Gazette*.
Notes: In May 1888, RK was back in Lahore, substituting for the absent editor of the *CMG* and living at the Punjab Club. Of this he wrote to his friend Mrs Edmonia Hill: 'I have returned to the old, wearying, Godless futile life at a club – same men, same talk, same billiards – all *connu* and triply *connu* and, except for what I carry in my heart, I could almost swear that I had never been away' ([9–11] May, 1888: *Letters*, I, 171).

'In Gilded Halls' was mistakenly identified in Livingston, *Bibliography*, as the story collected in *The Story of the Gadsbys* under the title of 'The World Without'. The two stories are both dialogues set in 'the Degchi Club' but are not otherwise similar. The error was repeated in Chandler's *Summary*, in the Stewart-Yeats *Bibliographical Catalogue* and in Harbord.

Reprinted in 'Turnovers', II, 1888; in the Martindell–Ballard pamphlets, and in Harbord, I, 299–302.

In Xanadu did Kubla Khan
A stately pleasure-dome decree,
Where Alph, the sacred river, ran
Through caverns measureless to man,
Down to a sunless sea.

Coleridge[1]

Scene: Smoking-Room in the Degchi Club, ten minutes before dinner; thermometer in ante-room marking 98°. Picturesque arrangement of six deboshed men in the easiest chairs.

First Voice: Sherry bitters *lao*!
Second Voice: Khitmatgar! why the dickens isn't that punkah being *kenched*?

234

Third Voice: And what news have you of your people at the Hills? Mrs. Tomlinson quite well?

Second Voice (wearily): Yes. She's all right. I say, you're a married man, what do you think is a fair monthly average for quarters in "Purgatory".

Fourth Voice: Yes, I took him twice round the jumps– the brute ran out to begin with, but he was all right after that. 'Jove! I raised a thirst that I wouldn't ha' sold for anything.

Fifth Voice: "Rejoice, O young man, in the days of thy youth, when the silver bowl is generally within arm's reach, and the clouds return not after the rain."[2]

First Voice: Bet you a chick that's wrong. The silver bowl doesn't come in at all.

Fifth Voice (lazily): Take your oath? Confine yourself to sherry and bitters.

First Voice: Well, you needn't get stuffy about it.

Fifth Voice: I'm not. *You* are.

Third Voice: 'First sign of the hot weather, when men begin snarling like women.

Second Voice: By the way, who was that woman with Jingle this afternoon?

First Voice: Coming through on her way to the Hills. Mrs. — Mrs. — I've forgotten her name, but her husband's in the Army.

Fifth Voice: You don't say so? Fancy a woman with a husband in the Army. What will they do next?

First Voice: You want a pill. You've got liver.

Fourth Voice: Liver? You fellows talk of nothing else but liver. Never knew such a place for liver.

General Chorus: Wait a little– *that's* all!

First Voice: Well, I've got a splitting headache, anyhow.

Fifth Voice (venemously): S'pose you tried the bitters without the sherry.

Sixth Voice: *Have* you seen this in the paper?

Third Voice: How could we? You've been reading it ever since it came in. Couldn't you lend us the advertisement sheets?

Sixth Voice (jubilantly): Exchange down to one and four. Who's remitting this month? There's a chance for someone.

Second Voice: It's all very well for you to joke about it. It's no fun to me. Is that the Calcutta or the local rate?

Sixth Voice: Local. You may get one-eighth more down country.

Third Voice: It's infamous!

Fourth Voice: Aw'fly good thing when a man gets a remittance from Home, y'know.

Fifth Voice: A curiosity! Ye Gods, a curiosity! Get up and walk round that we may get a look at a *man* who gets a remittance from Home. Stand up, Curlywig!

Fourth Voice (nettled): I don't care a– blow. If I am young, I haven't got liver, and I shall be alive and enjoying myself when you are all dead or diseased.

Third Voice: O the insolence of Youth!

Fifth Voice: There's some truth to it. Never mind, Curlywig. I didn't mean to hurt your feelings.

Fouth Voice: I didn't exactly mean all *that*, you know.

Second Voice: Don't apologize, youngster. I was that way once before Exchange was one and four.

Seventh Voice (Baritone robusto in the ante-room):

> Loose, loose every sail to the breeze
> The course of your vessel improve!
> I ha' done with the toil of the seas
> Ye sailors, I'm bound to my Love![3]

(Enters Smoking-room). Good evening.

First Voice: We're delighted to hear it. What does your Love say about it?

Seventh Voice: Ah! You poor wretches. I'm off tomorrow and:

> "Ow! My Love she wears a white ca*mil*yer.
> An' gingy is the colour of 'er 'air."[4]

Fifth Voice: This isn't a Music Hall.

Seventh Voice: No, it's a Dutch oven, and you've got to fry in it. Anyone seen the big Umballa *dâk*-tariff card knocking about?

Third Voice: Ugh! Get out of this, you lucky sinner. It's in the ante-room. What's your excuse *now*?

Seventh Voice: Duty, Sir. Stern duty! This time Saturday I shall be in Peliti's. Shall I meet any of you Johnnies there? *(Sings)*

"Where was it den der Breitmann lif?
Upon der Rond Pont gay
What was der street behind his haus?
La Rue de Rabelais.
Around der gorner Harper's stands
Where Yankee drinks dey mill,
Und straight ahet agross the street
Dere lies der Bal Mabille!"⁵

General Chorus: Stop that abominable noise and go! (*Exit Seventh voice, unabashed.*)

Sixth Voice: The Russians are advancing on Herat.

Second Voice: Wish to goodness they'd take India and have done with it! I'm sick of the country.

Third Voice. Prickly heat.

Fifth Voice: No. Liver. Tomlinson always despairs of the Empire when he has hepatic enlargement. By the way, where is Murger?

Third Voice: 'Saw a *Khit* taking some soup into his room. He's seedy I suppose.

Fifth Voice: Then that soup won't make him any better. It's mulligatawny with the *nimbu* left out.

Second Voice: Mulligatawny's only fit for breakfast and not too much of it then. It catches a man on the right side like a hot iron.

Fifth Voice: Oh, Christopher! Are we a Hospital or *are* we a Club?

Third Voice: Neither. We're a second-rate collection of caged beasts waiting for the beef shin- bones, and growling to fill in time.

Fourth Voice (hesitatingly): Usen't there to be some sort of Ladies' Night here once on a time? Don't you think . . . .?

Fifth Voice: No, we *don't*. You must entertain your Divinities somewhere else, Curlywig, or I'll put you in the complaint book.

Third Voice: Nice sort of place to ask ladies to? With a stench of tobacco fit to knock you down.

Second Voice (grimly): Some of 'em seem to think it a sort of masculine paradise, though. Here's my wife writing:– "And of course the Club, which you are *quite* free to attend now, must be a great resource and comfort."

Third Voice: Yes, but just think where we'd be without it!

Fifth Voice: "Great resource and comfort." Little *de*-ars! Let 'em keep their tender illusions.

Third Voice: When I was first married, be shot if my wife would let me come to the Club at all. Said it was a dissipated place!

General Chorus: Yes! Regular Alhambra!

Fourth Voice: Oh, it's not so bad!

Fifth Voice: Wait till you've had four years of it, Curlywig, and have heard every story before.

Fourth Voice: That reminds me. I've got a new story. (*Tells half of it.*)

Fifth Voice: Protect me from Curlywig's "new" stories! That was old before your Papa cut his teeth. There's the second bell. The funeral will now fall in for refreshments. One, two, three, four, five, six.

Second and Third Voices: We're dining at home.

Fifth Voice: Four then! This *is* lovely! Friends and fellow sufferers, come along and stoke, and thank Heaven there's another day done with.

Fourth Voice: Oh, it's not as bad as all *that*!

---

¹ 'Kubla Khan', lines 1–5.
² A mixture of phrases from Ecclesiastes 12:1, 2, 6.
³ Traditional whaler's song.
⁴ Not identified.
⁵ Charles G. Leland, 'Breitmann in Paris', stanza 5, from *Breitmann in Europe*, 1871. RK's text varies in detail from the original; he is evidently quoting without the book.

"Till the Day Break"

ЯΔΩ

Published: *Civil and Military Gazette*, 19 May 1888.

Attribution: In Scrapbook 4 (28/4, pp. 64–5).

Text: *Civil and Military Gazette*.

Notes: In a letter dated a few days after this piece, RK wrote that 'The heat here is maddening and gets worse at night. In the day one can force oneself into work and not notice it but in the night there is no such relief and so one kicks and knocks about "till the day break"' (to Mrs Hill, [25–27] 1888: *Letters*, I, 194).

The title is from the Song of Solomon 2:16. 'Till the Day Break' has been reprinted in *Kipling's India: Uncollected Sketches*, 1986.

ЯΔΩ

The Brain-fever bird had a secret to tell since the earliest morning. "I'll tell you what," said he confidentially. "I'll tell you what." But he never never told. Now he has gone to bed, taking the secret with him, and the little owls have come out to play bo-peep among the *bougainvilleas* and chuckle over the folly of the Brain-fever Bird.

Does an owl feel the heat? How can an owl hang head downward for five minutes and talk politics to a neighbour at the same time. If an owl were to lose his balance. . . .

But the business of the night is to sleep. Once upon a time, there were one thousand sheep who came to a nullah, and the bell-wether jumped, and the second sheep jumped, and the third sheep jumped, and the fourth and the fifth and the sixth. . . . Whose cartwheels are those? Some man coming back from a dinner somewhere. Is it a two-wheeled cart or a four-wheeled? If the first, it may be Bathershin's– if the second, Nixey's. But *did* Nixey send his cart to be repaired, or was it Nixey's mare or Bathershin's mare that cut her hock upon the splash-board? It was a beast with two white stockings– no, one, and a blaze on the nose. Or two. But *which* was it? A stocking and a blaze, or two white stockings and without a blaze?

If she had two *why* did not Nixey or Bathershin get rid of her, for the saw says:—

One you may buy it,
Two you may try it,
Three you may doubt it,
Four go without it.

But it may be, "one you may try it, two you may buy it". That can't be correct. It must be as first stated. The punkah is flapping to the cadence in the hot darkness. "One you may" – a brisk kick – "buy it". "Two you may" – No that was too slow. The next pull is correct. "Three you may doubt it." He has altered the swing afresh. How can one go to sleep? "The seventh sheep jumped it and the eighth sheep jumped it and the ninth and the tenth." Angels and ministers of grace defend us, *what* is in the next room! Only Nixey's little terrier hunting for some cool spot to sleep in, and sniffing for rats.

He was very friendly in the day-time, but suppose he has gone mad since we last met and presently fixes his teeth in my throat, or, pattering up in the dark, nips me on the leg. Nothing will happen for weeks and weeks, months and years, and I shall have forgotten all about it. Then one fine day – a very fine day in England, most likely – there will be a funny little spasm in my throat that will grow and grow and grow, and I shall see a looking glass, just like the one that the moon is beginning to shine on now, and I shall howl like a jackal and hide myself in a corner of the room until I feel thirsty and want a drink. By the way there *was* a spasm in my throat just now. *Spoof* never bit me that I can remember, but he may have scratched me and that is just as bad.

I would throw a boot at him – he is sniffing in the next room – but for fear that when I put my hand out of the bed, I should touch a *karait* that had been waiting there since the dawn of time.

That would be even worse than feeling *Spoof's* business-like little teeth in my leg, for when a man is bitten by a *karait* he dies in twenty minutes in excessive pain. There was a cow once bitten by a *karait*, on the tongue, and she lowed without ceasing for an hour and then was dumb; and when the morning broke she was a swelled and shapeless mass upon the ground. The *gaoli* said he thought that she was crying for her calf. If a man lowed for half an hour without ceasing, no one could hear him in this place, and he would be able to swell in peace, just as the cow did.

Curious idea – a man's lowing. If any one heard him what would they suppose he was bellowing for? A khitmatgar? It would be amusing for a punkah-coolie to hear a Sahib bellowing and to know that the Sahib could do nothing, and so to fan that Sahib from this world into the next – if there is one; the punkah-stroke answering the last beat of the pulse just like the relentless *tick, tick, tick,* of the watch under the pillow.

By the way, what time is it? Two twenty-seven and the blessed sleep as far off as ever, the head throbbing like the drums behind the servants' quarters and the brain full of sick fancies. The outside world is worse than indoors. A choking dust-storm has wiped out the moon, and the air if full of flying rubbish. All the world is going down-wind together – beyond the girdling belt of trees, beyond the white road – straight into the cop-per-hued bosom of the sultry night. Everything would escape from the heat if it could – even the tortured writhing clouds of dust that must be used to it.

If a man returned to his couch and lay very still and religiously thought of nothing at all, he might surprise sleep unawares. But to think of nothing necessitates thinking very hard indeed, and this increases an already sufficiently lively headache. Not to think of nothing meant that the uncontrolled brain will tie itself up in a helpless knot of doubt, per-plexity, argument, re-argument, wonder and pain. The stroll into the open has brushed away the unwholesome cobwebs of groundless panic, but when will the rest come?

Nine hundred thousand sheep – all Australia full – tried to jump through a hedge. And the first jumped, and the second jumped. . . . and the thirty hundred and forty first jumped. Never were such dis-appointing muttons! They jumped so merrily that I took an interest in them instead of dozing off. Happy thought! One hundred and fifty Blathershins once tried to crawl through a hedge on their hands and knees. And the first Blathershin – stuck "like a fou-weltered yow". I am so absorbed in his performances that I neglect all his followers. Fancy Blathershin with his head in a black-thorn bush and his feet kicking wildly over a ditch! And that is no use. The real thing is to think of nothing – of nothing – of nothing.

5.45 A.M. – As bitter a piece of work as ever was! And here with a cessation of the dust-storm and a few drops of tepid rain, breaks the pitiless day. The Brain-fever Bird is up and across the lawn, stammering the secret that he is forbidden to divulge. Sleepless, and you who have watched through the night, all the world over, good morning!

Spoof trots round the corner, his tail in the elements and his nose on the quiver for a rat. He looks as though few ill dreams had disturbed *his* rest.

Spoofkins, come here and have your ears pulled for frightening a fool of a Sahib nearly into a fit last night!

The Fountain of Honour

※

Published: *Civil and Military Gazette*, 4 June 1888.

Attribution: In Scrapbook 4 (28/4, p. 68).

Text: *Civil and Military Gazette*.

Notes: The celebration of Queen Victoria's jubilee in 1887 had generated a stream of decorations of far greater volume than usual, yet the demand for honors did not cease. In a letter of 27 June, a few weeks after 'The Fountain of Honour', RK reports the viceroy, Lord Dufferin, as follows:

> He has just made a discovery – or pretends that he has – and tells the tale (with a somber twinkle in the one eye that he can see out of) as one who is genuinely pained and astonished. 'Do you know,' says H[is] E[xcellency], 'that there are gentlemen – Indian Civilians – who write – ah yes – *write* to me suggesting – ah yes – *asking* that they should be decorated because they have done the state some service.' Then he paused and went on gravely 'And quite the hardest part of my official labours is replying to those letters,' (*Letters*, 1, 217)

'The Fountain of Honour' has been reprinted in the Martindell Ballard pamphlets and in Harbord, IV, 2057–60.

※

They were sitting upon the "mossy banks of Jakko", – rows and rows of them – and they drummed with their heels on the mould while they sang softly to the tune of the lawyer's song in *Trial by Jury:–*

> For the Ju-bi-lo[r] cleared off you know
> The last jam-tart in the larder,
> And no one will be a C.I.E.
> Or even a Rai Bahadur

Then they wept on each other's necks copiously, and the little monkeys in the pine branches said:– "How interesting!" Far, far down the

slopes towards the Church the children of the Kindergarten were practising their innocent songs to sing before the Inspector; and the shrill
childish treble floated up on the breeze:–

"Old Mother Hubbard she went to the cupboard
"To fetch her poor dog a bone;
"But when she got there the cupboard was bare,
"And so the poor doggie had none."

"Ugh!" grunted the Chorus of the Disappointed. "If they only knew
how they were hurting us." "Is there no chance?" murmured one more
heart-broken than the rest. "No," was the dejected reply. "They've
turned off the gas at the meter. Don't you recollect? The Fountain is
exhausted – bone dry;" and again the disconsolate wail of the song
about the "Ju-bi-lo" answered the murmuring of the pines.

"There's not the least use in catching liver here, said a voice. "Let's go
and look at the Fountain. 'Tisn't the rose perhaps, but it's the watering-
rose." And the melancholy procession wound its way through the
mango topes of S—a to the place of the Fountain of Honour, which
stands, as every one knows, very nearly where the Fishponds live at the
big fêtes. It is only visible on certain occasions, and is made out of the
purest printed papier-maché and ormolu. When not in use it is covered
up with red velvet; and all around it, if you dig, you may find the bones
of those who have died in working their way to its basin.

Among the bones are fragments of the helmets, the Political cocked-
hats, the office boxes, the silver lotahs, and so on, which the dead men
brought to drink from. There is nothing like a sound brass-bound helmet to catch the water of the Fountain of Honour.

It was to this place that the procession came, and they stood on the
margin of the trampled earth dinted with the mighty heel-prints of
the giants of old days. The Fountain was dry – indubitably dry – and
on the nozzle hung a notice, which had been copied into all the
newspapers – "CLOSED FOR REPAIRS."

"What did I tell you?" said one of the crowd. "It's shut. It won't be
opened till next year. Are we going to camp round it for twelve months?"

"Drop a penny into the slit and see the model work," said another
absently. "But I forget. This isn't a French toy. Oh boys! What shall we
do? I can imagine India without the rains, without railways – yes, even

without Simla; but I cannot – I *will* not – imagine it without the B—thd–y G—tte.² It couldn't exist. It couldn't exist."

"It's no imagination unfortunately," said a third, with one eye applied to the nozzle. "I can see – I can see right through a mill-stone, and my opinion is that this creature is dead." He thrust a walking-stick down the nozzle, and the ferule rang repellently on the strainer at the bottom. Again the crowd moaned. "Don't you think that something might be done if we spoke to it prettily," suggested a hopeful spirit and cried:– "Oh Fountain, wake up! Fountain ji! Rai Sahib Fountain! Rao Bahadur Fountain! Khan Bahadur Fountain! Sir Fountain! Sir Fountain, K.C.I.E.! G.C.I.E. and all the other letters of the Alphabet – *play!*" But the Fountain made no sign, though they walked round it in Order of Precedence, shouted at it, gave it *attar* and *pan*, patted it on the head, tickled it with a feather, prodded it with a sword, burned official joss-paper in its honour, asked it to come to tea, offered to put it up for a week, and did everything that Experience, Ingenuity, Science, and Forethought could suggest.

"Well, it's a poor Fountain anyway, and I don't care," said a voice. "It'll play double tides next year." "Death and the Eumenides!" sobbed another. "Can a man live for ever? It's not that *I* care a bit, but the public have paid their shilling, and they are entitled to see the show, and the advertised time has passed. I speak on purely public grounds." And the crowd echoed with one voice, "*Pu-urely* public grounds."

Even as they spoke there was a subterranean chuckle. "What's that?" they cried, and edged in to the Fountain. "Somebody laughing in the verandah I think," was the answer. "They're always laughing at us up there. Don't tread on my toes, you behind. Close! Close into the center!"

Confused cries arose as the crowd pressed forward, for though every one was trying to believe that the chuckle came from human lips, all hoped that it might be the Fountain that had given tongue. They slipped, and stumbled, and scrambled in the gigantic foot-prints of John Lawrence; they elbowed, and sweated, and fretted, and stamped. And the subterranean chuckle grew louder.

It was the Fountain after all!

With a rush, and a guggle, and the whizz of a rocket, it spouted up to the blue sky – exactly as it had spouted in the past, and the winking spray made rainbows in the sun. Never had the Fountain looked fairer to wearied eyes. The crowd were too astonished to grumble at its manifest southerly tendency. "It's all right," they cried rapturously. "The Empire is still firm, and the world may continue to roll!"

A brisk tap on the long glass window recalled them, and they were aware of the politely – always politely – amused visage of His Serene Obscurity.[3]

· "Bluffed again, gentlemen – bluffed again," he said sweetly as he stepped on to the lawn. "You all passed, I think, did you not?" A sigh of relief was the answer.

"Ah! This is no ordinary game, however," continued His Serene Obscurity. "*I*, gentlemen have bluffed on a full hand, but *you* take the pool; and glad and pleased am I . . . ."

The roar of the Fountain drowned the conclusion of the speech, but louder than the noise of the waters rose the thundrous bass chorus round the new rapidly filling Fountain of Honour. And they chanted till the horses in the V—I[4] stables jumped with fright, this anthem of praise:–

> "Two K.C.S.I's!
> "Oh! what a surprise!
> "Why did he keep us in darkness so long?
> "Two K.C.S.I's!"

"Mother," said the child, who had sung best at the Kindergarten that day, "what is that noise?"

"It's the frogs singing because the rain has fallen, childie. They can't do without the rain – and now go to bye-bye."

The little pink cheek nestled down to the pillow, and the small lips murmured dreamily:– "I'm glad they's happy too – 'ittle fwogs. I dot my pwize this mornin'."

---

[1] Victoria's jubilee, 1887.
[2] Birthday Gazette, in which the award of honours would be announced.
[3] The Viceroy, Lord Dufferin.
[4] Viceregal.

The Burden of Nineveh

※

Published: *Civil and Military Gazette*, 6 June 1888.

Attribution: In Scrapbook 4 (28/4 pp. 68–9).

Text: *Civil and Military Gazette*.

Notes: RK treats the ignorant Englishman, especially the MP, not only in 'The Burden of Nineveh' but in the verses on 'Pagett, M.P.' (*Departmental Ditties*) in 'The Englightenments of Pagett, M.P.', written in collaboration with his father (*In Black and White*, Outward Bound edn), and, indirectly, in 'One View of the Question' (*Many Inventions*).

The lines quoted from Rossetti's *Burden of Nineveh* at the head of the story are from the first edition of that poem, 1856, and are not to be found in later editions.

'The Burden of Nineveh' has been reprinted in 'Turnovers', II, 1888, in the Martindell–Ballard pamphlets, in the *Kipling Journal*, July 1940 (in part only), and in Harbord, IV, 2062–4.

※

> Small parsons crimp their eyes to gaze
> And misses titter in their stays
> Just fresh from Layard's "Nineveh."[1]

> *The Burden of Nineveh*

It was the Patient East, but not quite as Arnold[2] has painted her. She was thinking, it is true, but there was no dignity in her attire. In the first place, they had given her a beautiful British check-pattern shawl to hide the shoulders that had driven mad Alexander and one or two other gentlemen with armies and aspirations. In the second, they had put a mortar-board atilt on her dark hair, but through some little error it was hind-side before, and the deep part was scratching her nose. There was a bundle of Educational Primers at her feet, and the Tiger, which she used to hold in a golden leash, was sitting on his hind legs snapping at flies. Altogether, the Patient East did not look her best.

"It's curious," she thought; and she pinched the beautiful British check-pattern shawl. "It's *very* curious!" She squinted at the peak of the mortar-board. "I suppose they mean well."

And the British M.P. came that way, with his head full of plans for the regeneration of all the Earth, and cuttings from the newspapers in his pockets. "And how are we to-day?" said the M.P., walking round the Patient East to see that the shawl hung straight. "Ve-ry pretty and civilized. We are advancing, madam! We are advancing to a goal which –" then he stopped, for he was not quite sure what the goal was. "A-b ab; b-a ba; b-a-b bab," repeated the Patient East wearily, for she knew that the M.P. would be pleased to find that she had been reading her Primers. "Be-autiful," said the M.P., stepping back to watch the effect of the mortar-board. "In another year or two, my dear madam, we shall be in words of three syllables; and, ere long, I see no reason we should not arrive at stand-pipes in all the main thoroughfares, cof-feeshops, omnibuses, local-option, and – and all the refinements of civilization, including a complete dress of Liberty's fabrics. You shall walk, my dear lady – ah-h'm – you shall walk down Westbourne Grove exactly – er-hmm – like One of Us; and I'll introduce you to my wife who will, I am sure, be delighted to make your acquaintance. My wife takes a great interest – ah-hmm – in the heathen."

"How kind of her!" said the Patient East without a smile; and her thoughts wandered away to some other wives that she had known. "Is it not?" said the M.P. blandly – "But then she is a Vicar's daughter of Enlarged Sympathies. Still, I think, she would not quite approve of your walking about – pardon my saying so – bare-foot. We must have boots – sound, stout walking-boots."

"What is the matter with my feet?" said the Patient East putting out a shapely gold- ankletted foot that had been set on the neck of some few not altogether undistinguished persons. "Well," said the M.P. "I observe that you adhere to that poetical, but still barbarous, custom of dying the soles. Lac dye, is it not?"

The Patient East smiled inscrutably. "No – not quite," she said. "Yes – in a sense; for it is the dye of *lakhs* and *lakhs*." The M.P. made a note of the phrase, and continued:– "I would suggest that you remove it, though it is undeniably picturesque. My wife wouldn't like it." "I'm sorry for that," said the Patient East gravely. "Is there anything else?" "Yes," said the M.P. "We cannot be too careful, my dear madam, just at present. My wife and I heard, with considerable regret, that you – ah – allow more intoxicating liquids to be drunk among your dependents than is prudent."

"Ah," said the Patient East with a queer look in her eye, "I have drunk strange drinks in my time – *very* strange liquors," and she quoted, half to herself –

> "We drank the midday sun to sleep, and lit
>   Lamps that outburned Canopus, O, my life
> In Egypt! O the dalliance and the wit –
>   The flattery and the strife!"[3]

"Glad to see that you read Tennyson," said the M.P., though I cannot approve of all his sentiments. It shows an interest in our glorious literature – inheritance of ages y'know, and all the rest of it. But you'll remember about the drink, won't you? And – ah – there's another very delicate question." The M.P. blushed.

"Don't mind me," said the Patient East. "These eyes have seen a good deal since they were first opened."

The M.P. began rummaging in a bag, and pulled out a double-handful of books on grey paper with bold black titles. "Why do you let these things lie about the bookstalls? They – they corrupt the morals of youth, y'know – Not fit to be read. 'Fraid it's our fault – doing you serious injury; but you might help us to stop it. Where there's no demand there's no supply. Law of trade, that." He mopped his forehead nervously.

The Patient East turned over a few pages of some of the books – they were bad Yank translations of Zola's novels.

"Aren't they dreadful?" said the M.P. "My wife says so." But a smile was dimpling over the face of the Patient East, and it spread till it ended in a burst of mirthless laughter – deep as a man's, and terrible as a Djinn's. She threw the pied volumes from her, leant back in her throne, and laughed anew. "Shocking depravity!" murmured the M.P.

"And you bring your penny-farthing suggestiveness to *me!*" said the Patient East. "What have I to do with it? Before your ancestors knew what woad was, my Zolas". . . .

"Oh! this is positively awful! What shall I tell them at home?" said the M.P. picking up his despised and dispersed library. "No, it is not shocking," said the Patient East. "It is you who are so young – ah, *so* young! When you go home, tell them that you have seen me wearing their shawls and mortar-board gracefully. They will believe you. Tell them too,". . . . She broke off suddenly, for the day was dawning; and there beat up to the stale, hot sky the noise of her servants going to work. They filed past to the tramp of booted feet, the ring of spurs, the rattle of horse-hooves and tum-tums, the thunder of railway trains, the chipping of grave-stones, the bubbling of camels, the cries of the children who were suffering from prickly heat, and the wails of the mothers who watched their babies dying in lonely out-stations – one by one, swaggered, galloped, crept or crawled, her captains, councillors, administrators, engineers, planters and merchants – and each as he passed her throne, said briefly – for he had no time to waste – "*Ave Imperatrix! Te morituri salutant!*" But in the M.P.'s ears it sounded like "Humph! Another beastly hot day to pull through!" The Patient East pointed to the crowd. "Tell them that," she said simply "and don't bother." "But they have nothing to do with the important political considerations". . . . began the M.P.

"Little man," said the Patient East quietly, "if you don't go back to your vicar's daughters, and your muffin-struggles, and your important political considerations, I shall – kiss you."

"Oh!" gasped the M.P., "and what would happen then?"

"You would never for the rest of your life be able to see anything as a respectable, middle-class, antimacassar Briton should!"

The M.P. took up his carpet-bag and fled over the seas to his wife.

The Patient East dropped her head on her hand and laughed. "After all, what *does* it matter?" she said. "They will pass away – all my lovers have. I wonder whether I shall be glad or sorry."

---

[1] Sir Austen Layard, *Nineveh and its Remains*, 1848–9.
[2] Sir Edwin Arnold (1832-1904), author of 'The Light of Asia' (1879), providing an idea of 'The East' for a British public.
[3] Tennyson, 'A Dream of Fair Women', lines 145–8: 'Libyan Sun'. RK is quoting without the book.

His Natural Destiny

㿞

Published: *Pioneer*, 10 July 1888; *Civil and Military Gazette*, 13 July; *The Week's News*, 14 July; *Pioneer Mail*, 15 July 1888.

Attribution: In a letter of [28 June–1 July 1888] RK, then at Simla, says that he has 'written a thing for the same rag [the *Pioneer*] called His Natural Destiny' (*Letters*, I, 225). The piece is not in the Scrapbooks.

Text: *Pioneer*.

Notes: RK was evidently fascinated by Sir William Wilson Hunter, the subject of this sketch, whom he satirised – 'dear delightful humbug' – and yet admired (see 'To the Address of W.W.H.' in *Poems*, III, 1885). He appears also in 'The History of a Crilme' and 'New Year's Gifts'. Hunter had left India and returned to England in 1887. He then began a series of weekly letters on India in *The Times* in which he was free to criticise Indian affairs without reserve and to express sympathy with the aims of the Indian National Congress. In a letter written a few weeks before 'His Natural Destiny' RK wrote thus of Hunter:

> Hunter my own W.W. has risen in the West and wishes to be taken *au grand* serieux. Tisn't good for Hunter to be so taken and I am preparing a little *bandillero* for him which will appear in the *Pi* and will hurt him a few ['To the Address of W. W. H.']. He'll know my skin on a bush as the Irish say for in the old days he was good to me and showed me one or two tricks of the pen and once he struck at me and got me very neatly. I like, I admire Hunter immensely but ... not as a statesman.[1]

Reprinted in the Martindell–Ballard pamphlets and in Harbord, IV, 2066–9.

㿞

And the Indian Government missed the point after all, as it always does unless it be directed properly.

They cast H—r out into the wilderness and very naturally he cursed them by Book, Pen and Candle. "This," said the Indian Government blowing its nose embarrassed-wise, "is very distressing. What more could we have done for him? We gave him a K.C.I.E. and our blessing, and said, "let us never see your face again, dear boy."

"When a steer is dead," said the Still Small Voice, "I remember that it is the custom in London to pin a rosette to the carcass and hang it up by the heels. The crowd upon the pavement stop to admire the ingenuity of the Butcher, but the steer is indubitably dead. Now H—r is not a steer, and you shouldn't have pinned a rosette upon him."

"Then he should have been dead," said the Indian Government savagely. "Odds Dockets and Files! do we ever leave anything in a man when we have done with him? Look at any of 'em – *gastados* – used up, expended. He should have gone to Bath or Cheltenham instead of flourishing about in a paper like the *Times*."

"A–men," said the Still Small Voice, "but he didn't and he won't; and *now* what are you going to do?"

"Give him another K.C.I.E.," said the Indian Government. "New sealed pattern, you know."

"That might stop another man, but he isn't built after any pattern you know and he'd only laugh."

"Couldn't we put him on to a school board or something, like that man on the Bombay side – what was his name? – who used to ride fifty miles a day and pick people's brains. Suppose we give him a *chit* certifying that he was the greatest Educationalist of the East – would that do?"

"He'd tear it up and laugh."

"Imperial Institute then?"²

"He's tried that; it doesn't seem to be quite big enough for him. He wants a large horizon with fleecy floating clouds, lots of colour and – not too much permanence."

"Let him go to the Deuce then," said the Indian Government.

"All in good time," said the Still Small Voice. "You'll meet in some council chamber overlooking the Styx I daresay. But before you get there, he'll make it unpleasant for you."

"Who's afraid?" said the Indian Government clapping a despatch box on its head and calling for more blotting-paper.

"I don't know. You ought to be."

"Why?" said the Indian Government nibbling seriously at a sheaf of aromatic elastic bands.

"Because he can write," said the Still Small Voice.

"Is *that* all?" said the Indian Government with a sniff of contempt. "Why any of us can do that and most of us do write! Lor' bless you, we've got one Province as nearly as possible brought to a deadlock because the Secretariat do nothing but write. Isn't that glory for you? There's not a newly caught up cherub of the office that can't turn out thirty folio pages a day – and call for more ink at the end of it!"

"I know what you mean," said the Still Small Voice. "Lion and Unicorn atop, ten pages of statistics, a fifty-line sentence studded with 'and whiches' and 'forwarded to the officers concerned' as a tail piece. That's not writing, that's *shikast* – what the *bunnias* keep their books in, you know. Only intelligible to the initiated."

"It's Administration, anyhow," said the Indian Government, "and he never was an administrator."

"No. He was the only one among you, though, who could write up to your level. He wrote Imperially. You admit that."

"It was Government property. We paid him for it – paid him well! He's eaten our salt –"

"And it doesn't stop his mouth. Of course it doesn't. Has it taken you all these years to find that out – you who really are so impressive?"

"We are."

"And so dignified."

"We are," the Indian Government bridled with pleasure.

"And so powerful and pathetic. Do you know that you are an epic in a Blue-book only the leaves aren't cut?"

"Well?" said the Indian Government, for it was puzzled.

"Well," said the Still Small Voice. "I suppose you have a Policy of sorts haven't you?"

"Wait a bit," said the Indian Government "and we'll see." So it ran up and down the Mall, and sent *chaprassis* to Barnes Court and Snowdon and Viceregal Lodge, and drummed on the tin roofs of the offices and shouted down the chimneys:– "Have we got a Policy!"

The answers were satisfactory. "It's all right," said the Indian Government. "We've got one."

"I knew it all along," said the Still Small Voice, "and it's a grand Policy. Why don't you explain it occasionally?"

"We do," said the Indian Government: "we're always explaining it. W-stl-nd [3] explains it like anything, so does the Serene Obscurity, [4] and so do all the others. We're a Government by explanation."

"You flatter yourselves. You're nearly as dumb as a healthily constituted Rule can be and when you speak, forgive me for putting it so coarsely, you're a horrid bore."

"What are you driving at?" said the Indian Government sulkily, for it did not like being called dull.

"This," said the Still Small Voice. "He was the only man among you who could make outsiders take an interest in you or your work. He was made for that, and you threw him away just when he was ripe for the appointment of Thrice Puissant Herald and Golden Mouthed Ambassador, Polisher of Things in General and Universal Explainer."

"No such appointment in the Civil List," said the Indian Government bewilderedly.

"There isn't, but there ought to be. You've got your little jobs to put through like the rest of us. You could be painted in scarlet and gold as befits the dignity that you are always trying to explain and fail in – and he was the man to do it. You needn't have told all the world about it."

"But how could we depend on him?"

"Surely you've been at Simla long enough to know that water runs in the trough put for it. You should have made it worth his while; have given him archives to rummage in, have asked him to write a history of your administration since the Mutiny – anything to have kept him *hazar*. He would have found out what you wanted before your spoke, and he would have done it well. Everybody would have seen that with all your faults you were a gorgeous administration."

"But that is written in books already," said the Indian Government.

"Yes, but he would have written it much more prettily, and before he had ended, he would have believed what he was writing."

"Now you're talking of what you don't know," said the Government of India. "He would *not*."

"Well, never mind," said the Still Small Voice dying away, "you've lost your chance – you who pretend to understand the capacities of men – and it will never come again. But here's the *Times*, and you can see for yourselves how he is inconveniencing you. Another time be sure that a man is quite squeezed out before you throw him away"

But the Government of India didn't see it. "We should have given him a G.C.I.E." said the Government of India, "and then it would have been all right."

[1] To Edmonia Hill, [25–27] May 1888 (*Letters*, 1 193).
[2] The Imperial Institute, planned in the year of Victoria's jubilee, 1887, was meant to gather and disseminate information about the Empire. Its site is now occupied by Imperial College of London University. RK's 'A Song of the English' (1893) was written to celebrate the opening of the institute.
[3] Sir James Westland (1842–1903), then secretary of the Indian Finance Department, later finance member of the Viceroy's council.
[4] Lord Dufferin, the Viceroy.

That District Log-Book
(By the Keeper of It.)

Published: *Civil and Military Gazette*, 10 July 1888.

Attribution: Not in Scrapbooks; it is included in the Crofts collection, though that is not decisive, since RK later denied authorship of a few items in that collection – but not this one. The story was reprinted in 'Turnovers', III, 1888 and in the suppressed edition of *The City of Dreadful Night*, 1890. In both of these collections all of the other items included are known to be by RK.

Text: *Civil and Military Gazette*.

Note: Reprinted in the Martindell–Ballard pamphlets and in Harbord, IV, 2070–3.

The *Pi* began it, and you may be quite certain that, if there is anything more than usually bothersome abroad, the *Pi* is at the bottom of it. Heatherfledge saw an idiotic leader about keeping a log-book of the district, and nothing would satisfy him except to keep it on the lines recommended. . . . As he is my Deputy Commissioner I couldn't rebel, and brought a great ledger from Lahore. "It's beautiful paper," said Heatherfledge. "Hi, bearer! Get my paint-box and we'll paint a view of the D.C.'s house to begin with." He painted a thing like a wet hayrick standing in a bed of boiling spinach. "Now you fill up the rest," said he; and promptly forgot all about it from that day forward. If there is one thing more than another that I pride myself on, it's the faculty of organization. I made the munsiff of my court copy out from Hunter[1] a statistical account of the district. It was a trifle out of date, for the munsiff got the wrong edition; and then I put the book on the table in the verandah, with a printed notice atop, requesting "Gentlemen and Officials connected with the district to write down anything connected with the district that might appear to be connected with anything." I had this done in Gurmukhi, Hindi, Nagri, and Ak, and in case any one shouldn't quite understand, I pasted the *Pi's* leading article on the wall;

giving special instructions_that any Sahib who might drop in while I was on tour should be shown the book. When Heatherfledge asked me whether I had "taken steps", I told him of the arrangement, and he said that, with proper sifting every three months, he had no doubt that we − and I had done everything − should accumulate a most valuable mass of local information. So I went into the district and forgot about everything but my work for ever so long.

In the fullness of time the L[ieutenant]-G[overnor]. came down. He had been a Settlement Officer, and understood a great deal more about districts than any L.-G. has a right to know. Heatherfledge had to entertain him, and there was a small Darbar in the Station, and several venerable sinners were given turbans and dishcloths for building *serais* on some other man's property with a third person's bricks and forced labour. In the evening, after dinner, Heatherfledge told him about the log book. He said:− "My log book, Sir;" but later on he tried to give me all the credit of the work. Heatherfledge is too generous to his assistants sometimes. I had noticed that the book had been filling up very satisfactorily; but I was always far too busy to look into it.

"Excellent idea," said his Honour, quietly opening the book. "Yes, it keeps the unrecorded records of a district together," said Heatherfledge, who prides himself on epigram. He quoted about half the leader in the *Pioneer* and purred softly.

"Excellent idea," repeated His Honour, looking at the picture of the D.C.'s house. "'Hiranand has run away with my wife. O just Almighty, is there no redress? She has taken her anklets too.'" Heatherfledge opened his eyes rather, but said: "Yes, it's a sort of informal complaint book too, Sir." "H'm," said His Honour:− "I should imagine that the *chuprassie* in charge made a fine thing of it Here is another complaint:− 'Dear old man, − Missed you on my way to Sidoontha, and stayed here the night. For Heaven's sake, make your *khit* get some decent Whiskey. Seeing how often I have assisted you to get tight, do this for, yours thirstily, Tom Pyecroft.'" Heatherfledge turned blue. "I assure you, Sir," he began. But His Honour was laughing, and I couldn't catch the end of the sentence. "It throws a valuable light on the unrecorded records of the district," said His Honour. "Who is Tom Pyecroft?" "A friend of mine, Sir," I said. "I think he misunderstood the object of the book." "Seems to know what he wants though," said His Honour. "What does this mean:− 'A cure for sore toes?' Take three green lizards in the full of the moon; steep them in water infusioned with chillies, and swallow while repeating the name of the Commissioner.' No – Creator. 'The toes will then drop off. Glory Glory-Hallelujah – to Heatherfledge, Sahib Bahadur.'"

Then I knew that old Ardasir Pestlejee, in charge of the dispensary, had been making use of the book too. "Local simples;" said Heatherfledge feebly – "accumulated knowledge of the countryside." But from the glare in his eyes I felt that I should have a bad time when H[is].H[onour]. was gone to bed. H.H. showed no signs of moving. He appeared to appreciate the book, and began reading out the second page, which ran thus:

"I swear on the cow's tail that, if Ram Kishen lays a complaint about his mango tree before the Huzur Stunt Sahib Bahadur, he is a liar and possessed of grown-up unmarried daughters who do not behave as they should. – (Sd.) Daulat Ram."

"Whiskey as bad as ever. Old man, it's really past a joke. Ride over some day and I'll give [you] something decent. – 17-7-'88. Tom Pyecroft."

"This district is favoured by Heaven because it is ruled by Heatherfledge Sahib Bahadur – just, chaste and wise – who drives in his chariot and regards the people as his children exclusively. I do not know anything more about this district – (Sd.) Makhan Lal, Student-at-Law."

"'Rats in the Record-room. Sanctions occasional presence bull terrier. Services debited to State. – (Sd.) Piari Lal, Deputy Assistant, in charge Record-room."

"This day a Sahib in the Railway sat upon my trolly, and requested to be trollied to Jehannum. What action do I take? He is there. – 9-7-'88. – Pundit Esha Nath Dass."

"There's a district due north of the Jumnear
"Which I wish I had never come near,
"For I find to my grief
"That the beggarly thief
"In charge don't keep whisky nor rum near."

(Sd.) *Ernest Houligan, P.W.D.*

"This the most damnable district to move troops through that I ever wish to find. The one-eyed owl at the Ferry is mad, and I can get no help from the local idiots. – (Sd.) J. Matherby, 145th *Pindarris*."

"How doth the festive Heatherfledge
"Delight to bark and bite,
"And murder common law by day,
"And common tunes by night."

Anon.

At this point His Honour gave up, for it is notorious that Heatherfledge is *not* a good musician, and better on the executive than the judicial side. Shortly afterwards he went to bed, saying that there were seemed a lack of comprehensive system in our log-book, but he had no doubt that it might, in an abridged form, be worth publication. Then Heatherfledge turned on me and swore that I had made a laughing-stock of him and the district, and that the log-book was no better than a pot-house complaint-book. I said a pot-house complaint- book had its points, and Heatherfledge said that he'd get another assistant. So I have put in for transfer, and merely lay the case before you. It was all the *Pi's* fault; but if His Honour had only turned over the next page he would have found this written in red ink by McKenzie Doule, who really doesn't care *what* he says, and belongs to the Imperial Government:–

"There's a province that's governed on tick,
"And it's bound to collapse with a click,
"For what they call Finance
"Is the workings of chance
"And it's making our Government sick!"

Perhaps it's just as well that His Honour didn't see that.

[1] The *Imperial Gazetteer of India*, edited by Sir William Wilson Hunter.

An Unequal Match

꙰

Published: *Pioneer*, 11 July 1888; *Pioneer Mail*, 15 July 1888.

Attribution: In Scrapbook 4 (28/4 pp. 72–3).

Text: *Pioneer*, 11 July 1888.

Notes: *An Unequal Match*, by Tom Taylor (1817–80), originally performed in London in 1857, was performed at Simla on 6 July 1888. RK wrote of his review of the play: 'Have attempted a new and slightly audacious form of criticism of The Unequal Match. Instead of writing a laboured review vowing that every one could not have been better I stuck four people into Peliti's balcony and made 'em talk over the play as they naturally would. I fear, as I said, that the result is slightly acid and I fancy that G. W. A[llen]. won't be over and above anxious to retain me as a dramatic critic' (to Edmonia Hill [7–8] July 1888: *Letters*, I, 241). The female lead in the play was taken by Mrs G. W. Allen, wife of the proprietor of the *Pioneer*.

Reprinted in the Martindell–Ballard pamphlets and in Harbord, IV, 2074–9.

꙰

Simla, 8th July.

First Voice.– Two coffees, and two vermouths: and this is the nicest table. Well, what did you thnk of it Mrs. X——?

Second Voice.– Oh de-lightful. Especially the dancing. How *could* they do it?

Third Voice.– No, no. Not *Bluebeard*[1] – the *Unequal Match* last night.

Second Voice.– I didn't go. Was it amusing? I hear that –

Fourth Voice.– If we begin by listening to what we *hear*, we shall never finish anything at all. I went, and I thought it would have been much better if it had not been played when it was.

First Voice.– Mrs. Y— is pleased to be oracular. How do you mean?

Fourth Voice.– And yet after all we *cannot* kick our legs over each other's heads eternally.

Second Voice.– Heaven forbid! It would make me nervous. You think – that it –

260

First Voice.– Didn't "bite" exactly after *Bluebeard*. I thought so, too. It's an old play. We played it here six years ago and it was a great success then.

Third Voice.– Before our taste had been vitiated by burlesques I suppose. Poor little Simla!

Second Voice.– *Please* don't go back to the Dark Ages! I wasn't born then. Mr. —, tell me what it was all about, and Mrs. Y— can tear the actors to pieces afterwards.

First Voice.– Let me reflect. There was a lovely village maiden called Hester Grazebrook who lived with her father, a Yorkshire blacksmith. And the local doctor, Boerhaave Botcherby, loved her. But a gilded youth, Arncliffe, who had been lately refused by a fascinating widow, came down with his comic servant, Blenkinsop, to the village and fell in love with Hester; the comic servant nturally falling in love with Hester's servant, Bessie Hebblethwaite. Is that clear? Hester refuses the local doctor, and the fair widow drops into the village after her carriage has broken down and sees some of the love-making between Hester and Arncliffe. Then matters become complicated. Arncliffe's uncle dies and Arncliffe becomes a baronet, so Mrs. Montressor, the widow, naturally wishes to marry him. But in the presence of all the available characters he swears to marry Hester.

Second Voice.– And does he?

First Voice.– Yes. Lady Arncliffe prefers romping in the hay-fields to doing the honours of the Baronial Hall, which is filled with friv-olous guests who sneer at her and make her husband miserable. Mrs. Montressor of course re-appears and adds to the trouble. And Hester's unkempt papa pops in to breakfast with agricultural mud on his boots. This makes Arncliffe so sick that he flies on medical certif-icate to a German watering place called Enosfruitsalstrasse.

Third Voice.– No! Seidlitz stinkenbad. Be accurate.

First Voice.– Something nasty anyhow. Of course the widow goes after him after a scene with Hester, and Hester weeps. You can guess the rest. Sir Harry and the widow recuperate at this Pyreticsalineabad for a year; then the despised and persecuted Hester descends on them, a lovely and accomplished woman of the world, immensely admired by all the Dukes of Germany; and the designing widow is routed and the curtain comes down on a moral rhyming "tag". That's only just the rough outline, because there's the servants' love-making; and the local doctor becomes the high priest of a hydropathic establishment, and so on – but that's the idea.

Third Voice.– Well done; another vermouth and bitters after that?

First Voice.– No thanks. I'll wait Mrs. Y—'s verdicts. The first act depressed me and I couldn't form judgments – so I talked.

Fourth Voice.– Simla all over! *Why* is it so absolutely necessary that you should grin when you go to the theatre?

Second Voice.– When I want to be preached at I go to church. I heard the play was full of morals.

Fourth Voice.– And good acting. I've known Simla for – don't ask me how many seasons – and, so far as my poor opinion goes, the company was far above the average.

Third Voice.– There was any quantity of new blood in it. The companies are changing very much this year. But what did you really think of Arncliffe's love-making? It seemed flat to me.

Fourth Voice.– Have you ever tried to make stage-love, Captain Q—?

Third Voice.– Well, h'm! Not on the stage exactly.

Fourth Voice.– Never mind about your *other* failures, try a *jeune premier's* part and see how crushingly difficult it is. Arncliffe might have been more various in his wooings.

Second Voice.– But one man only makes love in one way, and that's what –

First Voice.– (*lowered*). Makes one man so monotonous. *Thank* you.

Fourth Voice.– There! You've shown the main difficulty in criticism. You import the personal element at once. That's Anglo-Indian.

First Voice.– Arncliffe might have done better, but seeing what he had to do he did it uncommonly well. I played that part in my youth and –

Second Voice.– Made love infamously I'm quite certain. I heard that Blenkinsop made them laugh very much.

Fourth Voice.– Yes, Blenkinsop and Bessie Hebblethwaite were as good as could be. But Mr. —, did you see how he fell into temptation after the first act?

First Voice.– In forcing the effects d'you mean?

Fourth Voice.– Yes. He took the house with him at first and then the house took him with it and he overdid the study.

Third Voice.– But it was first-class work, and even the best actors can't help emphasizing what they can feel the house likes. You're too critical.

Fourth Voice.– Not in the least. Let us take the Doctor – I think he was the best of the men.

Third Voice.– Oh surely not "A'm Yorkshire and Stingo." "Grazebrook" was awf'ly good.

Second Voice.– But they said the dialect couldn't be understood.

Third Voice.– So much the worse for the poor Southrons. But I've interrupted you Mrs. Y—.

Fourth Voice.– The Doctor is blessed with a couple of low-comedy knees.

First Voice.– Witness "Blore" in *Dandy Dick*² last year and "Modus" the other day at the A[mateur].D[ramatic]. Club.

Fourth Voice.– Exactly; but last night he ironed them out, and he ironed out several other mannerisms and gave a new part. I respect a man who can subordinate his understandings to his understanding. He was the best, the most carefully worked out, and the most level of them all. Isn't that a typical woman's criticism? Three superlatives in a row. Well, he knew how to make his rough love-making effective.

Third Voice.– Still Grazebrook was really pathetic; don't you think? Goodness knows, I hate pathos on the stage but – Oh you ought to have understood his dialect. It was a treat. "Dom tha comfort!" Did you see how he got through that?

Fourth Voice.– Personal element again. Why can't you be impartial? To be sure no one is impartial in Simla.

Second Voice to First.– There's a *most* impartial woman riding by now. Look! You know you'd give your boots to be with her instead of up here.

First Voice.– Not my boots. That's where you've sent my heart these past few days. Wouldn't my head do? I've lost *that*.

Second Voice.– So the head doesn't go with the heart? But you mustn't be silly. . . We sit and gather wisdom, Mrs. Y—. Tell us what the women were like. Mrs. Splurgerris called this morning, but she only spoke about their dresses.

Fourth Voice.– I liked Hester best in the first and third acts, and she would have been better had –

Third Voice.– Arncliffe played up to her. I liked her entry in the second act, when Arncliffe was explaining things to the widow, and I liked the way she made her husband unhappy when "Feyther" dropped in to breakfast.

First Voice.– I think the sparring match between Hester and Mrs. Montressor was the best bit in the play – only it might have been written up.

Fourth Voice.– What a Vandal it is! You can't "write up" Tom Taylor. I confess Mrs. Montressor startled me in that scene. Frankly, I didn't think she could do it – wasn't that charitable?

Second Voice (lowered).– Wasn't that *Mrs. Y—*? Always so charitable. Somebody told me that the scene struck them as brusque and unnatural. But I remember it was a man who spoke.

Third Voice.– Do women stab at each other as bluntly as the widow did at Hester? – "You know, I refused your husband just before he married you." That seemed rather over-brutal.

Fourth Voice.– It depends. Mrs. Montressor carried that scene through wonderfully, but I think she should have been sitting down all the time.

Second Voice.– How *very* critical you are, Mrs. Y—! It's only the "Duke sitting down and the Duchess standing up." And really in scenes like those one would hardly think of attitudinizing, would one?

Fourth Voice:– It seems to me that it is a matter in which experience would be the only guide – though some people might find it better to sit with their backs to the light.

First Voice (aside).– Now, what *has* happened?

Second Voice.– Ah! You see, I never talk about my experiences. It leads to complications. Don't you think so?

First Voice (aside).– That's drawn blood! Why doesn't Q— say something?

Fourth Voice.– Ye-es. I suppose it would if one habitually dealt with second-rate men. But I have no knowledge.

Third Voice (aside).– Neatly parried, indeed! If we could get this on the Gaiety Boards! (*Aloud and quickly.*) Yes, I'm like the Devils, I believe and tremble, and prefer to watch a *rixe* between woman and woman with the footlights between. As you say, Mrs. Montressor was startlingly good, especially at the end. Altogether the play improves as it goes on.

First Voice.– I never believed much in the conscience of the Simla stage until last night. Did you notice how the minor parts were filled by first-rate people – Miss Leech for instance? Hardly twenty lines, and the heroine of *Dandy Dick* to take it. Chillingham, too – another *Dandy Dick* star.

Fourth Voice.– Simla was never so full of good amateurs before. The A.D.C. are finding that out. Tofts and Honeywood – but who in the world made him up with that livid stare? – and Lady Honeywood, all new and both good. They could have given us a *lever de rideau* with the minor parts alone.

First Voice.– There speaks Simla! – "Can you do this or that to amuse us? Then do it and do it better." Do you know what the end will be?

Second Voice.– Collapse? Surely not.

Third Voice.– A permanent band of actors. A stage subsidized by Government *á la* Theatre Français. Department of Histrionics. We officialize everything.

First Voice.– Something of the sort – somewhere in the nineties.

Second Voice.– Then I hope that they won't let the actors preach at us. I heard that, last night, they positively hurled morals across the footlights, and someone called it "The Church and Stage Guild."

Fourth Voice.– Really it wasn't that, but we are so irreverent and frivolous.

Third Voice.– Hear! Hear! "Behold the conclusion of the whole matter!" Mrs. Y— shall declare it.

Fourth Voice.– A not too lively play, well acted by a first-rate company and handicapped by being sandwiched between two burlesques. A house – are you willing to hear your noble selves condemned? – a house that sniggers at sentiment, chuckles at pathos and yawns at the other sentiments because – because –

Second Voice.– Oh, our poor little society! Spare us Mrs. Y— and I'll go to the second night.

Fourth Voice.– Because we are all so busy with our own little farces and – next year they will be forgotten, and so it really doesn't matter.

Third Voice.– How truly magnificent! It's half-past seven and I shall be late for dinner at Welsh Mountain. Good night! You come my way Mrs. Y—?

Second Voice to First.– What did she mean by farces being forgotten?

First Voice.– Nothing, or at least, it only applied to the Simla stage. We'll see what the *Pioneer* says about it.

But the *Pioneer* said nothing whatever, and only gave the cast as below:–
Harry Arncliff (Mr. R. A. Dick); Blenkinsop (Mr. E. Hemming); Sir
Sowerby Honeywood (Mr. A. J. Swiney); Captain Loftus Chillingham
(Col. G. de C. Morton); Dr. Boerhaave Botcherby (Mr. G. Williams);
Tofts (Mr. H. Irwin); Grazebrook (Major Tidy); Hester Grazebrook
(Mrs. G. W. Allen); Mrs. Topham Montressor (Miss Lound); Lady
Honeywood (Mrs. Beauclerk); Miss Leech (Mrs. Deane); Bessy
Hebblethwaite (Mrs. Westland); Lieschen (Miss Gambier).

---

[1] A burlesque by Colonel Arthur Hobday, ADC to Lord Roberts at Simla. RK attended
the first production of *Bluebeard* on 24 June 1888 and wrote a long review of it for the
CMG, 30 June (uncollected).
[2] A farce by Arthur Wing Pinero, 1887.

A Horrible Scandal
(*See "The charges against the* "Pioneer" *in another column.*)

❉

Published: *Civil and Military Gazette,* 24 July 1888.

Attribution: In Scrapbook 4 (28/4, p. 75)

Text: *Civil and Military Gazette.*

Notes: A native newspaper, the *Hyderabad Record,* printed a story claiming that an agent of the *Pioneer* was in Hyderabad to collect a bribe of 40,000 rupees from the Nizam for the paper's support of the Nizam's cause in something called the Deccan Mining Scandals. To this charge the *Pioneer* made no reply, since, according to the report ('Charges' Against the *Pioneer*) in the *CMG* of 24 July 1888, the *Pioneer* 'has cultivated a habit of hearing its critics and disregarding them'.

'A Horrible Scandal' has been reprinted in Harbord, iv, 2081–4.

❉

> The eldest oyster winked his eye
> And shook his heavy head,
> Meaning to say he did not choose
> To leave the oyster bed.
>
> *The Walrus and the Carpenter.*[1]

There was, as the poet says, "a shine in the tents of Ham."[2] All the *Pi's* friends and enemies and acquaintances assembled with copies of the *T—s of I—a* [*Times of India*] of the 13th July in their hands and wagged their heads dolorously; "Oh, *Pi!*" they groaned. "Profligate old *Pi!* And has it come to this?" "Come to what?" said the *Pi*, shortly, for it was busy. "Shock, shock! fie, fie!" cried the crowd; and they intoned the following in jerks:– "English newspapers being subsidized to take sides in the keen controversy which has been created in the Deccan Mining Scandals. . . Most grave allegations made against such papers as the *Pioneer* and the *Bombay Gazette.*"

"Yes" said the *Pi*, abstractedly. "They said five thousand dibs was its price. No wonder it took steps. Five thousand! Just about the price of a new machine! But go on." "Gross slanders reproduced in a number of journals. . . . naturally looked for a prompt and indignant denial . . . *Pioneer* has seen fit to sit silent under the imputation. . . . We still urge upon our contemporaries that they should give the *lie direct* to their traducers."

"'Traducers' is distinctly good," said the *Pi* shamelessly. "The style of the indictment seems familiar to me. Is it by any chance my little friend, the Kingdom of Bombay?" "It's the *T–es of I—a*," said the crowd, shocked at this display of levity, "and it's very angry."

"Ya-as" said the *Pi*. "I don't wonder. The poor devil has been out of it since the beginning, and I think it owes me one or two. It is *very* virtuous."

"'The honour of Anglo-Indian journalism'," quoted the crowd, "'demands that the plain, blunt, and unmistakeable course should be followed. The Native Press'" –

"Dear Creature!" said the *Pi* sweetly. "'The Native Press have been indulging in bitter and sarcastic allusions to the manner in which, according to them, the Nizam has been bled by unscrupulous Anglo-Indians.' Now what *have* you to say to that?" The crowd looked at the *Pi* under its eyebrows, and the more tender-hearted proffered it tracts and oranges to keep up its spirits.

"It's very pretty," said the *Pi* reflectively – "ve-ry pretty. Especially that touch about the 'honour of Anglo-Indian journalism'. Is there any more in the same strain?"

The chorus began anew:– "'That such statements, however false, carry weight with natives, if allowed to pass without emphatic contradiction, is incontestable. To ignore the grave charges, or to gloss them over, is a serious mistake, involving much wider issues than even the fair fame of the journals involved. The charges are categorically made. They should be categorically answered.' That's all," said the crowd. "Now go and hide your diminished circulation."

"It's much too kind of the Kingdom of Bombay," said the *Pi*, wiping its eyes. "Any time during the last twenty years I've been branded as a hireling organ of a brutal Government, a subsidized mercenary, a deliberate liar, a bloody contemporary, and everything else that was nice and complimentary – and the dear little Kingdom took no notice. It's really overwhelming. My 'fair fame' is safe – it is in the keeping of the *T—s of I—a*. Let the world roll!"

"But, *Pi*, this is disgraceful. You should take steps – you really should," said the crowd "Think so?" said the *Pi*. "Do you happen to remember who was the 'traducer'?"

"It was the *Hyderabad Record*," said the crowd. "Ah!" said the *Pi*. – and a grin of introspective reflection stole across its expressive countenance. "H-mm!" said the *Pi*, chuckling softly. "The *Hyderabad Record* – excellent paper – extended knowledge – first class information. Says that the *B—y G—e* [*Bombay Gazette*] would take a five thousand rupee bribe. I *like* it for that. It must have made the *G—e*. wild."

"But it says that you have sent a representative with a bill to the Nizam for services rendered of forty thousand rupees," said the crowd.

"How much?" shouted the *Pi* indignantly. "Forty thousand! That's a clever hit – worse than the slur on the *B—y G—e*. For-ty thousand rupees at one-and-four-pence each! My *dear* friends, if ever I sent in a bill to the Nizam it would not be for thousands but for *lakhs* – five at least. Forty thousand rupees! What does he take me for?"

"Oh! what cynical and blatant immorality," said the crowd, "You admit that you can be bought?"

"Yes – for four annas a copy – back numbers half price," said the *Pi*. " Would you like some? They will explain exactly how I came to be bribed, you know."

"We don't want your back Numbers. We want a categorical explanation," said the crowd.

"Plain, blunt, and unmistakeable? You shall have it – though you have no right to it. In the first place, you are – not wise."

Here the Kingdom of Bombay sailed into the discussion, breathless and panting. "Oh, the arch-deceiver!" it cried; "and we never had any news at all. Hit him hard – he's got no friends! We had to borrow his telegrams! Gouge his eyes out! Make him confess! Alone we did it. I myself and the incorruptible *Englishman*! Smash his head in! Think of our fair fame and – those telegrams."

"You'll hurt yourself, my little man, if you go on like this," said the *Pi* tenderly. "I admit it *was* irritating to be left in the cold."

"Don't impute motives," said the Kingdom of Bombay sulkily. "You're always making fun of me, but I've got you now. Deny the imputation or die the death."

"It will need a bigger man than you to kill me. Listen, my Breach Candy³ Bantam. I led, and the *B—y G—e* followed, and together we did what – forgive my being personal – you couldn't do. You admit that?"

"It was with other people's money," snarled the *T—s of I—a.*

"That's foolish – and insolent. But, never mind. Out of Hyderabad, where I have been working, and whose workings I know a great deal better than you ever will, comes an 'imputation' that a representative with a till is knocking about the State. You know the paper that makes the charge? If you don't, I can tell you all about it."

"I don't want to be told," said the *T—s of I—a.* "I *hate* you. Let me go."

"Now you're talking sense," said the *Pi.* "You and Calcutta have no reason to love me – I know that. And it suits you – bless your innocent heart – to run the *Record* as a first-class journal for this occasion only. Do you know that the *Record* has withdrawn its wild statement about our bill-sticker?"

"Then you bribed it to do so," said the *T—s of I—a.* "I hate you. You're a bully."

"Sweet child – perhaps I am – perhaps I'm not. But you are impertinent, and too clever, by half, with your 'honour of Anglo-Indian journalism', and your 'Native Press'. Since when has the Native Press believed that the *Pi* is anything but bribed to the gullet, that its good opinion should be so desperately important? You precious little Pharisee! Go home for a few months and live in wholesome surroundings for a while. Do you suppose that any moderately sane man believes that the first paper in Asia risked its reputation by peeking about for bribes. And if it *did*, do you suppose that it would look at half a lakh? No – nor twenty half lakhs. If you can't understand honesty try to comprehend expediency at least."

"But we do hate you so," said the *T—s of I—a.* "You swagger, and you bully, and you're generally offensive."

"When you are as big as I am perhaps you'll be able to do it yourself, and perhaps you'll do as good work as I have done. But, at present, my advice is, don't you try to ram a ship that carries twice your metal. Go and hit the *B—y G—e* and see what happens."

"But you haven't denied the charge," persisted the *T—s of I—a.*

"*You* made them," said the *Pi* graciously. "After you will come the *Englishman*, after the *Englishman* all the Native Press, calling Heaven and Earth to witness that the *Pi* is no better than it should be. Then some madman may ask questions in the House of Commons, and then perhaps I'll attend to it. You certainly won't be paid the compliment of a direct denial here. You aren't worth it; and – forgive me for making fun of you – I want to see what you'll do if you are left unanswered."

"I'll smash you. I'll go and tell everyone that the *Pi* takes bribes, hand over fist."

"Quite so," said the *Pi* gravely, "anything from postage stamps to blank cheques. The smallest contributions thankfully received! You really have no knowledge of my perfidy – my avarice and my want of principle. It will give you material of a much finer business than the Deccan Scandal. Run along and convulse India with it."

But the *T—s of I—a* went away in a pet, and the *Pi* returned to its work. The convulsions are maturing.

---

¹ Lewis Carroll, 'The Walrus and the Carpenter', lines 45–8.
² I have not identified the poet. 'Tents of Ham' comes from Psalms 78:51 (in some translations).
³ A district in Mumbai.

An Exercise in Administration
(According to Onandorf.)

‌‌‌‌‌‌‌‌‌‌‌‌

Published: *Pioneer*, 14 August 1888; *Civil and Military Gazette*, 14 August 1888.
Attribution: In Scrapbook 4 (28/4, p. 77).
Text: *Pioneer*.

Notes: Onandorf ('on and off') plays on the name of Heinrich Godefroy Ollendorf (1803–65), deviser of a popular 'step-by-step' method of foreign language teaching.

The subject of this burlesque is the case of Arthur Travers Crawford, C.M.G. (1835–1911) of the Bombay Civil Service, who in 1888 was charged with having received bribes from natives and official subordinates. Evidently it was first intended that he be tried in the regular courts. He was tried instead by special commission, which held sixty-seven public sittings reported at tedious length in the press. The commission's report did not find Crawford guilty of corruption but did confirm the charge of borrowing from natives in the division that he administered. After further reviews of the case, Crawford was removed from the Civil Service at the end of March, 1889, some weeks after RK had left for England. The case raised several legal difficulties and excited great public interest. It is reviewed at length in William Wilson Hunter, *Bombay 1885–1890: A Study in Indian Administration*, London, 1892, pp. 414–20.

'An Exercise in Administration' has been reprinted in 'Turnovers', III, 1888, and in Harbord, IV, 2099–101.

‌‌‌‌‌‌‌‌‌‌‌‌

Q.– What is that Thing over there?
A.– That is a Bombay Government attempting to administer a Presidency.
Q.– But why is it hunting the elderly gentleman with the grey hair[1] among the trucks of the G.I.P.[2] terminus?
A.– Oh it has a notion about him, and I think that the constables rather enjoy the fun.
Q.– But the old man is mad – anyone with half an eye can see that. Look! He has attired himself in a fez and gaberdine and is dancing sarabands

in front of the Inspector of Police. Ah! They have caught him by the collar! He must be a distinguished burglar in disguise

A.– On the contrary, he is a civilian of thirty-three years' standing, a C.M.G.[3] and one or two other things which are generally considered respectable.

Q.– And what has he done?

A.– The Bombay Government believe that he has taken bribes and prostituted his office. You may read the indictment in all the Bombay papers. He has been arrested on the strength of that indictment.

Q.– Who are those men with second-hand shirt-collars and pencils pointed at both ends?

A.– Those are the Reporters. They are going to report the trial for all the Indian papers, especially the Bombay ones, who are discussing it in great detail. With reminiscences of the elderly gentleman's early career.

Q.– But isn't that rather – improper?

A.– What *does* it matter? He is only a civilian of thirty-three years' standing, &c., &c., and the Bombay Government have got a notion about him. All Poona knows that.

Q.– What do you think they will do?

A.– They will first draw all the eyes of all India in this direction by allowing the utmost publicity to the indictment. They will later put the elderly gentleman, who by the way has engaged solicitors, in the dock, and will try him on criminal charges under certain sections of the Penal Code. The jury will then retire to consider their verdict and . . . .

Q.– Why do you stop?

A.– Because the Bombay Government have changed their mind.

Q.– Why?

A.– Possibly because they have another notion. They are taken that way occasionally.

Q.– What are they going to do this time?

A.– They are not going to prosecute the elderly gentleman in Court.

Q.– But they have hunted him down and grabbed him by the hair, and published all the indictment and put some new varnish on the dock-rails. They must surely go forward.

A.– Wait a moment. Lord Reay is sucking his thumb. He will presently say something.

Q.– What is he saying?

A.– He says:– "False start. We won't count this time. Let us begin again from the very beginning."

273

Q.– Are they going to turn down the elderly gentleman and hunt him afresh?

A.– Oh no. They will merely catch a Commission to sit upon him – if they don't change their minds in the interval.

Q.– What is a Commission?

A.– A thing that commits itself – like the one which sat on Mr. Wilson; or does *not* commit itself – like the Public Service Commission.

Q.– But the elderly gentleman seems displeased.

A.– He? Oh he is only saying that he has been arrested, indicted, ruined, shown up, damned beforehand and all but brought to a trial, and he has some narrow-minded wish to go through with the business for his own vindication. He seems to think it is his right.

Q.– But, look here, *hasn't* he a right to be tried?

A.– Not a bit of it! If he were a Bengali schoolboy with a taste for fish-stealing, or a Rungpore deer or a *mela* case he might talk. Being only a Civilian of thirty-three years' service, a C.M.G., a builder of markets, and so on, I assure you he has not a leg to stand on.

Q.– What do you think they will do with him?

A.– Wait a moment. When Lord Reay has finished sucking his thumb I'll tell you. Ah! Now I see. They will really try him by a Commission, if they don't think of something newer and more entertaining.

Q.– And if he is innocent?

A.– The Native Press and some of the Indian papers will declare that that Commission has been started to hide the truth.

Q.– And if he is guilty?

A.– Every one who is on his side will say that he has not had a fair trial.

Q.– That is an interesting situation.

A.– Yes. It reflects the greatest credit on Lord Reay's sagacity, prudence, forethought and knowledge of mankind.

Q.– Happy thought! Suppose we hang Lord Reay.

A.– Oh no. Let him suck his thumb. He will come to sufficient grief through his own unassisted intellect.[4]

---

[1] Crawford was then only 53 years old.
[2] Great Indian Peninsula Railway.
[3] Companion of the Order of St Michael and St George.
[4] Witnesses in the Crawford case were promised indemnity from punishment, but some were afterwards dismissed; a special act had to be passed in order to deal with the contradiction. Reay received some public censure for this situation and offered his resignation, which was refused (see Hunter, *Bombay Administration*, 416–20).

My New Purchase
(By the Victim.)

Published: *Civil and Military Gazette*, 27 August 1888.

Attribution: In Scrapbook 4 (28/4, p. 78).

Text: *Civil and Military Gazette.*

Notes: Unrecorded and unreprinted.

Don't do it! Kind Christian friends, whatever happens, don't do it as you value your peace of mind. Get a *tikka* – a second class *tikka* – from day to day, or buy a cart and a caster, and keep them in the cool of a well, using them stealthily at night.

I only wanted something to move about in – a bathtub on wheels would have suited my purpose admirably. But I demanded four wheels – that was the fatal mistake. I never knew before how strong is the current of public opinion in an up-country station.

"Four wheels!" said Botcherby. "What on earth do you want with four wheels. Beastly affectation *I* call it. Here! Much better buy my dog-cart. Seven feet high, black lacquer, red mare – carry you from one end of the station to the other in ten minutes, but you mustn't cough, or smoke, or take off your hat, when you're behind her. She's nervous, but as good as gold."

"Thank you, Botcherby," I said meekly. "I have religious objections to driving any animal. I always manage to hurt their feelings."

"Huh!" said Botcherby, "better get a bassinette then."

"The very thing," I said. "I will procure a bassinette."

Then Botcherby drove his ramping red devil of a mare all round the station to spread the news that I was suffering from paralysis brought on by evil living, and required a padded carriage and a keeper.

Sigala was the next torturer. "You must get a Lavengro bassinette," he said, "and be sure that it has a swingle-gaff dissel-boom."

"Amen," said I; and went to the Equine Emporium trying to look as if I knew all about it:— "Lavengro bassinette please, and be sure it has a swingle-gaff dissel-boom," I said.

The proprietor looked at me reproachfully. "We can *build* you a Lavengro bassinette if you *insist* upon it," he answered; "but I feel it my duty to inform you that a hind-lock quarter-bar is the only absolutely safe appliance, and I should be very sorry of the public knew that *this* establishment turned out swingle-gaff dissel-booms."

I knew that if I talked any more I should expose my ignorance.

"Look here," I said, "I'm a stranger in a strange land. All I ask is peace and quiet. I desire none of your Longacre[1] lectures. Get me something to go about in — go-cart, rattle-trap, war-canoe, car of Juggernath, — anything you please, — and I will reward you. All I insist upon is that it shall have four wheels and a box."

The Proprietor of the Equine Emporium threw open eighteen godowns and two barns. He talked for an hour and twenty minutes on coach-making, and for another fifteen minutes on hind-lock quarter-bars.

"Man," said I faintly, falling into the nearest vehicle, "this will do. Bring me water — I am dying."

He sent me home with a note informing me that I was the possessor of a patent scear-spring Landaulinka; but I am prepared to swear in a court of law that a *mistrie* made it out of the ends of cigar-boxes. Botcherby, Sigala, Van Trump, Dennison-Howker, and Pole-Katte paid it a formal call — at least they all tramped into the verandah to tell me that they were going to "have a look at the thing." They did more than look. Botcherby crawled underneath it and said the iron work was "sham-dam-skelp." I said something of the same nature, but I left out the sham and the skelp. Van Trump and Pole-Katte each took a wheel and waggled it for five minutes, while Dennison-Howker held up the shafts and told my fat bearer to sit on them. They stayed for half an hour, and nearly dragged the whole trap to pieces.

"Well, I don't think much of it," said Botcherby. "Haven't you the decency to offer us a peg?"

I couldn't tell the bearer to put arsenic in the whisky, but I gave them the Liniment Brand — twelve annas a bottle — and they were not pleased.

The real agony began when I got a horse – a large live horse – to pull the Landaulinka.

Every single soul in the station had something to say about that horse and something to do to him. Even "Baby" Podd, who has been exactly six weeks in the country, thought it incumbent upon him to feel the brute's legs for five minutes. He stopped at the one sound leg of the four, and told me that there was "something wrong with the back sinew." The old horse sneezed.

"Podd," said I, "he has not only got back sinews, but the most virulent form of glanders, coupled" – here I pointed to a collar gall – "with farcy." And Podd actually had not sense enough to know that glanders are highly contagious.

I suppress the honours [*sic*: horrors?] of the next fortnight; the comments of all my friends, acquaintances, and enemies; the production of the "other traps" which I "might have bought for half the money, and of the "other horses" which were ten times better than my fossil. I endured it all. I even laughed occasionally; but deep in my heart I meditated revenge. I dared not put scythed blades upon my wheels, for that would have been too obvious.

I hired a convict-coachman, who had no sentimental clinging to life and a weird power of getting speed out of the horse. Then I crawled about the station exposed to the derision of Botcherby and his gang, who enquired about the paralysis, and asked for pieces of the horse – on skewers – for the use of the bobbery pack.[2]

My day came at last. Botcherby in his trap was talking to Van Trump, Dennison-Howker, and Sigala, who were on foot. Podd and Pole-Katte were on horseback. They all stood in a clump at the turn of the road to the Club.

"Yes," I heard Botcherby remark, "it's a solemn fact that the old animal lies down the road every half mile and wallows. He has a great deal of buffalo blood in his veins."

"*Coachman*," I whispered, "into those *Sahibs*. Five hundred rupees for each corpse and – go!"

The convict lashed the horse to madness, and we whirled round the corner. I heard a shriek, an oath, and the scream of a wounded mare. The wheels jarred horribly and a shaft snapped.

There was no other damage. Next moment I was a quarter of a mile away, and behind me, in the Club porch, lay Van Trump with a broken ankle, Dennison-Howker with a scalp wound, Podd breathless and bleeding from the nose, and, under a heap of lacquered match-sticks, Botchery white and still – his mare with her shoulder torn open heading across the tennis-courts.

They say Botcherby will never have the use of his lower extremities again. I take him out occasionally in my patent scear-spring Landaulinka. He is very grateful, and seldom alludes to the infirmities of others.

¹ Centre of carriage building in London.
² 'A pack of hounds of different breeds, or (oftener) of no breed at all' (Hobson-Jobson).

Exercises in Administration
(Devised and Compiled for the Use of the Simple.)

Published: *Civil and Military Gazette*, 15 September 1888.

Attribution: In Scrapbook 4 (28/4, p. 86).

Text: *Civil and Military Gazette*.

Notes: Reprinted in 'Turnovers', III, 1888.

I.

(*Of Things in General*)

Q.– What is India?

A.– A plain country, continually in debt, whose centre is Simla and whose circumference is hazy, populated chiefly by gentlemen with ideas.

Q.– Who governs the same?

A.– His Majesty the Secretary of State, hampered by His Excellency the Viceroy and certain Councils.

Q.– Which are they?

A.– Two for the most part, – excluding those which are divided – to wit, that of the India Office and that of the Indian Officers.

Q.– Why that of the India Office?

A.– For the better performance of contracts and the housing of the aged.

Q.– Who are the aged?

A.– Administrators who have been returned to store condemned, impotent, or expended.

Q.– Their function?

A.– To intercept messages from East to West and from West to East, to call Sir John Gorst[1] from labour to refreshment, and to obey the commands of the Secretary of State.

Q.– Why that of the Indian Officers?

A.– For the occasional benefit of the daily papers and the permanent delight of the Red Chuprat.[2]

Q.– Its function?

A.– To obey the command of the Shrieking Sisterhood, to listen with fear to the preaching of the Anti-Opium Society, to behave with humility and reverence to the Native Press, and to support the Baal Butcha of the Red Chuprat.

Q.– How to obey, &c.?

A.– By repealing the C.D. Act as ordered, and entrusting the talk thereupon to the man who most shrinks from the task.

Q.– How to support, &c.?

A.– By individually keeping eight or more Red Chuprats in their verandahs, *duftars*, and nurseries.

Q.– What is a Viceroy?

A.– The Head of the Council, if not otherwise employed or guided; a valuable name upon a Poster, and, in some cases, an enthusiastic Collector of Beetles.

Q.– How is he regarded?

A.– According to the taste and fancy of the Indian Nation, to imitate which is forgery.

Q.– Of what is the Indian Nation composed?

A.– Of those who eat the Viceroy's dinners, and dance his dances, and of those who do not.

Q.– And how does he regard India?

A.– As a hot house.

Q.– For what plant?

A.– The orchid of His Excellency's reputation, found in Ireland, grown in Syria, budded in Canada, grafted in Egypt, and now to India transplanted.

Q.– Why does he so regard it?

A.– Because he possesses a reputation which he is anxious to take Home intact.

Q.– In what condition will it reach Southampton?

A.– Blown – full or fly. Consult the papers of next year.

Q.– You have several times alluded to newspapers. What is a newspaper?

A.– A periodical publication created to control the Destinies of the Universe, but more generally used to stick a stranger with a vicious pony.

Q.– Has it any other uses?

A.– Several. The dissemination of the merits of Pears' Soap, Naldire's Worm Tablets, and British Rule. It has been known to contain news.

Q.– Has it any bearing upon the administration of India?

A.– It is considered an efficient substitute for a napkin at a Seepee picnic, a cork at a Conference, and stimulative blister on a debilitated constitution.

Q.– On what does it subsist?

A.– Dry bones chiefly, varied by exchange quotations and domestic occurrences.

Q.– Are there any other factors in the Government of the Empire besides the three set forth above?

A.– Excepting the weather and the crops, there are none officially.

Q.– Name the unofficial factor in a whisper.

A.– The Army – but don't say I told you.

Q.– Whence this coyness?

A.– Because the Army is a relic of barbarism incompatible with the Spirit of the Age.

Q.– What is the Spirit of the Age?

A.– "If I kill you it's nothing, but if you touch me it's murder."

Q.– And what is the Army?

A.– An inadequate collection of elderly gentlemen with grievances, married men in civil employ, juniors with unschooled ponies, and a few persons suffering from Martini-Henri rifles and autumnal fever.

Q.– What is the function of the Army?

A.– To give tennis parties and at Homes, to lend the Regimental Band when so required, and to go to Levées in full dress.

Q.– In what estimation is it held?

A.– It is justly condemned by the educated, because it is entirely devoid of political influence and may be trusted not to agitate. The unenlightened regard it as the Court of Ultimate Appeal, superior to all Civil and Criminal jurisdiction under the canopy of Heaven.

Q.– What is its treatment?

A.– It is used shabbily, treated carelessly, and hurried into the background as soon as its work is accomplished.

Q.– What is its work, other than what you have specified?

A.– To furnish guards of Honour when required, to mount guard over three honey-combed guns and a pile of obsolete shot when not required, and to win more victories and drink more liquor than the state of its internal economy justifies.

Q.– And are you prepared to say that it has no direct concern with the Government of India?

A.– The Spirit of the Age forbids, inasmuch as the work of the Educational Department and the prestige of the Civil Power are amply sufficient for all needs.

Q.– What are the Educational Department and the Civil Power?

A.– Products of a glorious civilization which we will discuss at our next meeting.

---

[1] Gorst (1835–1916), Conservative MP, Undersecretary of State for India, 1886–91.
[2] Not identified.

The Dignity of It.
(Awful Results of Action on Part of B—y M—y)[1]

✺

Published: *Pioneer*, 6 October 1888; *Pioneer Mail*, 10 October 1888; *The Week's News*, 13 October 1888.

Attribution: In Scrapbook 4 (28/4, p. 87).

Text: *Pioneer*.

Notes: RK wrote on 5 October 1888 that 'I did this morn horribly oversleep myself and eat too heavy a breakfast which led *me* to write a pasquinade in the *Pi* on the text of a telegram from Bombay' (to Edmonia Hill: *Letters*, I 256).

The telegram reads: 'The Bombay Corporation being anxious to secure a greater measure of dignity for their newly constituted body, resolved to apply to Government for sanction to their President being termed "the Honourable" or "Worshipfull"' (*Pioneer*, 6 October 1888: RK evidently saw the telegram before it appeared in the *Pioneer*).

Reprinted in the Martindell–Ballard pamphlets and in Harbord, IV, 2109–11.

✺

Board Room of the Purkeshaditvarsubhana Municipality. Revenue Rs. 3,671: population 22732: local death-rate 39.4 per mile.

Babu Chuchundra Bandra Sen, President (addresses his colleagues).– And how shall fair flower of this our local self-government flourish not ingloriously in all the divisions, sub-divisions, *pergunnahs*, *mahals*, and general auditoriums if she is left in naked barrenness unadorned with raiment which well becomes, as Shakespeare says, "this mortal trick before high heaven?"[2] I pause for a reply.

Municipality (generally).– *Shabash*! How a peroration!

Babu C.B.S. (waving copy of "Englishman").– I observe in this truly inimical journal, injurious to best interests of nature's gentleman that on Bombay siding such a flower doth *not* so flourish. (*Thunders of applause.*) I repeat categorically she doth not so flourish, and why? Because the just and benevolent Lord Reay, truly actuated by high motives that always will and always shall govern all political crises and contingencies, has been graciously pleased, in response to the humble memorial of the Bombay Municipality, to abrogate excessive titular distinctions upon native gentlemen, who at vast sacrifice in time and personal predilections steer the organ of State to its destined haven here below. And if Bombay, how, my brothers and sisters, not Bengal? And if Bengal, how not Calcutta? And if Calcutta, how not our own hearths and altars – aries et *phooka* – the sheeps in the fields with enormous agricultural interest on their backs and the cow upon – the *band*? Must Purkeshaditvarsubhana thus lie ingloriously upon its stomach under repeated obloquy? (Shouts of *Kubbi, Kubbi nahin! Bravo!* and *Hi! Yi! Jai*).

To be brevity, which is the soulfulness of Attic salt. Lord Reay, that just man and true Radical reformer, has enhanced the dignity of municipal administration in general, and the Bombay Municipality in particular, by conferment and preferment of a Title of Honour upon the laborious and high-minded President. Now, henceforth and for ever, Bombay Committeedars rising in cerulean [curulean in text] chairs shall say "Your Washup" before presuming to make financial, statistical, poliltical or religious remarks in the eye of the President.

Babu Barumber Gumber De.– Chuchun Babu, I move amendment.

Babu C.B.S. (pathetically).– How I have just said, you now see consequences in noxious overflow! I am elect of all the wards, *not* Government nominee swayed hither and upside by fawning speciousness of a *ma bap*, but representative of *full* people, and I am called in obliviousness my high officialism only Chuchun Babu! Can I work so in this manner sacrificing my time and endearments of domestic toils . . . .

Babu B.G.D.– Ho! Ho! Ho! Since what time endearments? (*lapsing into vernacular*). Husband of a noseless wife!

Babu C.B.S.– I name that member under the Penal Code. Barumber Babu, you are a damn! (*lapsing into vernacular*) Son of a *Mochi*, what do you among *bhadra log*?

(Alarums and excursions stifled by rumour that the Stunt Sahib may turn up any minute.)

Babu C.B.S. (with portentous gravity).– Wherefore, unprotected by the Fountain of Honour, *exempli gratum*, oppressive and unsympathetic Government, how I *can* conduct debates on all subjects in fitting way of work? Now under more recent auspice and by *parwarna* from On High, you call me Your Washup or Most Honourable, accelerate all despatch of public affairs and gratify instincts of the people towards Political Enfranchisement. When I move prepration of a memorial upon similarly identical lines of these of the Bombay Municipality for grateful submission to His Honour the Lieutenant-Governor. You think how?

Babu B.G.D.– I move amendment so that proposed honorification must not apply to present President.

Babu C.B.S.– But in the interests of State can you not stink [*sic*: sink?] sectarian animosity?

Babu B.G.D. (in vernacular).– Flesh eater! Your father was a lizard. Your mother was a one-eyed dog of imperfect virtue. (*In English*) How are you so Worship? Pokul Nath's *chabutra* all across my roads.

Babu C.B.S.– There was no money. I swear on the cow that Suruj Bal spoke a lie! The two rupees. . . .

Babu B.G.D.– Who said two rupees? Guilty conscience putting its tail in the trap. Chuchun Babu, where is the octroi book? I move amendment of full examination of octroi book.

Secretary to Municipality.– White ants and monsoon – only backside binding left. Shall I produce?

Babu C.B.S.– No! Draft Memorial! May it please Your Honour. How much will hold up their hands? (*In vernacular*) Bastard of the Gringi Mohulla, what does your brother the conservancy darogah give you out of his pay?

Babu B.G.D.– Who sold his ringstreaked cow to Ashraf Khan? Give answer Your Washup.

Babu C.B.S. (shouting) – Original motion passed in total entirety. Draft memorial shall be submitted next special meeting, which shall be duly notified by *tom-toms*, and I shall promulgate *most* severe censure of Barumber Babu.

Babu B.G.D.– I shall, I will – veto memorial and hold indignation meetings in the brick pits! It shall be sent to Calcutta.

Editor of the "Sachi Durpan" (aside to Babu C.B.S.).– *Babuji, ap ki municipality kuch lêta dêta hai?*[3]

Babu C.B.S.– To me in my house – to-night at nine o'clock. Hon![4] (*aloud to Babu B.G.D.*) Municipal meetings all strictly privileged and *I will* be Honourable Warship!

[1] Bombay Municipality.
[2] Cf. *Measure for Measure*, II.II.125: 'plays such fantastic tricks before high heaven'.
[3] 'Sir, your municipality, some give and take.'
[4] The word is not clear in the *Pioneer* text. According to Hobson-Jobson a "hon" is a coin worth 20 rupees.

Exercises in Administration

꧁꧂

Published: *Civil and Military Gazette*, 12 October 1888.

Attribution: In Scrapbook 4 (28/4, p. 88).

Text: *Civil and Military Gazette*.

Notes: 'I've sent to the C & M a second section of my exercises in administration' (to Mrs Hill, [8] October 1888: *Letters*, 1, 263). The satire makes plain the grounds of RK's objection to western education for Indians: by forcing educational 'beef' upon a nation that eats none, the result is a 'horrible intellectual indigestion'.

Reprinted in 'Turnovers', iv, 1888.

꧁꧂

II.

Of Things in Particular.

Q.– At our last Conference, holden at least a month ago, you referred to the Civil Power and the Educational Department as factors in the Government of the Empire and superior to the army. Be good enough to explain the nature of the Civil Power.

A.– The Civil Power is bounded on the north by the District Officer's tent and baggage camel, on the East by the irresponsible Vakil, on the south by the Indian Ocean, and on the West by the interests of the Bombay Chamber of Commerce. In the centre is the Brown Man, its organ is the *Pioneer*, and it is kept humble by the Secretariat.

Q.– What is the Secretariat?

A.– The most uncivil power in the world, devised for the benefit of the bilious civilian who is too clever to live.

Q.– Is there then no conscious existence in the Secretariat?

A.– None. This may be proved by reference to the Resolutions composed therein.

Q.– What affinity has the Secretariat for the Civil Power proper as by you described?

A.– The affinity of the brake for the train and of the gadfly for the hide of the buffalo. The Secretariat being born of the District is immeasurably superior thereto: both being the coat and the lining of the Civil Power.

Q.– On what does the District Officer subsist?

A.– In ancient days the upon the *prestige* of the White Man, at present – upon the *mehrbani* of the Secretariat.

Q.– And what was the prestige of the White Man?

A.– It has been officially proved never to have existed, and I am therefore unable to expatiate upon it.

Q.– And what is the *mehrbani* of the Secretariat?

A.– To call "for all the papers connected with this case," to write comments upon them and supplementary comments upon the comments aforesaid; the whole being overlaid with additional notes and countersigned according to the Penal Code.

Q.– And is that all?

A.– To file all papers connected with this case pending further consideration, to cut razors with grindstones and to split hairs into fourteen separate pieces for the glory of the Service.

Q.– And in what Province or Presidency is its *mehrbani* most felt?

A.– In the Punjab.

Q.– And on what side?

A.– The Revenue and Judicial, though it strays occasionally into the Executive.

Q.– With what result?

A.– In the hampering of work invariably, and very frequently the madness of the Executive officer.

Q.– What is an Executive officer?

A.– An ass between two burdens – a highly educated pauper doing the work of two men on an income one third less than it is written.

Q.– What are his duties?

A.– To refer matters to higher authority, to rule without powers, and maintain the dignity of his race without help, comfort or recognition.

Q.– Has he independent power?

A.– One only.

Q.– What is that?

A.– To die when he pleases – so long as his death does not interfere with the interests of the Service.

A.– The *Stunt*, the *Diply* and the Commissioner *Sahib*. The *Stunt* is
ridiculously young, the *Diply* is ridiculously old, and the Commissioner
Sahib is always ridiculous.

Q.– Why?

A.– Because he considers himself a person in authority.

Q.– And is he not so?

A.– By no means. He is walked upon by Members of Council, Lieutenant-
Governors and Viceroys under pretence of extreme friendship.

Q.– What is the ultimate end of a Commissioner?

A.– He may die from heat apoplexy caused by excessive tennis in the hot
weather; he may occupy an eighty-pound tenement at Southsea, Bath or
Dulverton, or he may be made a C.S.I.

Q.– What is a C.S.I.?

A.– A Completely Spent Indian. As the caster of the bounding battery is
branded with an R. under the saddle; so is the ancient official labelled
on the left shoulder as an outward and visible sign that he is "cast."

Q.– These being the props and cupolas of the civil power, we will pass now
to the Educational Department always genteel and superior to the army.
Kindly define the meaning of education.

A.– "Damn it, Sir, you *shall* have mustard with your beef!"

Q.– Beef being avoided by the bulk of the population of India, the definition
cannot be held to apply to education in this country.

A.– A slight modification only is necessary, "Damn it Sir you *shall* have beef
with your mustard."

Q.– Who said that in the first place?

A.– Sir Charles Wood,[1] with the professed object of conveying "useful and
practical knowledge suited to every station of life in the great mass of
the people, &c., &c.."

Q.– And did he so convey?

A.– Read the native newspapers.

Q.– Are they the result of the system aforesaid?

A.– Absolutely, entirely and without reservation; the said system being
grafted on the Character Unsaid?

Q.– Why Unsaid?

A.– Because never enquired into by those who supplied the beef.

Q.– Was the supply regulated by prudence, forethought or statesmanship?

A.– By all three, but of the purest British type. Beef with mustard being
good for the European abdomen it was instantly assumed, and is even

now by some consistently believed, that the same food is preeminently suitable for the Asiatic *pét*.

Q.– On what grounds do you base your objections to the use of such food?

A.– On the horrible intellectual indigestion now visible from one end of the Empire to the other; and the complete absence of any sign that the food has been naturally and healthily assimilated by those upon whom it has been forced.

Q.– Kindly explain?

A.– In the non-existence after thirty years of stenuous endeavour, of one solitary original thinker, writer, poet, novelist, artist, engineer, or savant among the two hundred millions of the Brown Man.

Q.– Are you prepared to affirm this on oath?

A.– I am willing to abide by a reference to the history of the land for the last three decades. The matter is not worth swearing over.

Q.– Your mood of mind being at present of a distinctly flippant and cynical character, I will allow you an interval for reflection and repose ere we pursue our investigations further.

---

[1] Wood (1800–85), later first Viscount Halifax, as President of the Board of Control sent a celebrated 'dispatch' outlining a plan for state-supported education for Indians to Lord Dalhousie, the Governor-General in 1854; RK quotes from that.

In Wonderland

Published: *Pioneer*, 20 October 1888; *Pioneer Mail*, 24 October 1888.

Atrribution: In Scrapbook 4 (28/4, pp. 87–8).

Text: *Pioneer*.

Notes: The 'Interminable Muddle' is RK's term for the Indian National Congress, founded in 1885. It became one of the chief engines leading the drive for Indian independence. At this stage it was still a new thing and therefore the object of official uncertainty, but RK's treatment of it is uniformly hostile.

Besides the satiric 'In Wonderland', RK wrote brief, untitled items about the Indian National Congress in the *CMG*, 14 and 30 December 1886, and 'A Study of the Congress', *Pioneer*, 1 January 1889.

Reprinted in the Martindell–Ballard pamphlets and in Harbord, IV, 2112–15.

"Will you walk a little faster?" said the whiting to the snail,
"There's a porpoise just behind us and he's treading on my tail;
"See how eagerly the gudgeons and the whip-tailed rays
    advance:
"Will you, won't you, will you, won't you, won't you come and
    join the dance?" [1]

The Interminable Muddle had advanced one step further towards the Embarrassing Jam. Far away in the West. Sir W. W. Hunter spread his wings on the blast and skimmed the new found path of Earnestness which his enemies called his Milky Way. "Treat them, O treat them seriously," fluted Sir William, and the echo of his cry came back, a hundredfold multiplied, from the ever silent spaces of the East.

"Treat us, O treat us seriously!" clamoured the Proprietors of the Interminable Muddle; "We love you with a love that threatens to destroy our reason, but at the same time we desire nothing more than your complete reorganization, subversion and effacement – always by genteel measures. Just, worthy, sublime, oppressive, brutal, unsympathetic

Government of India, extend to us the shadow of your protection while
we go about to improve you! O thou, sitting upon the hill-tops adorned
with red-tiled roofs, girt as to the loins with a girdle of red-tape and
daily drunk upon ink, be kind to us! We desire only freedom of discussion. Let no man be permitted to disagree with us, or bloodshed
will ensue. Those holding contrary opinions are *chamars* and the sons
of *bungis*, grey-muzzled apes and eaters of forbidden flesh. Above all
things, do we desire temperate discussion. We will discuss and thou,
advancing with the clatter of a thousand office boxes, shining painfully
on account of the C.S.I. and the C.I.E., do thou keep thy temperature. Wise, merciful, tyrannous, far-seeing and most easily to be hood-
winked, protect us while we govern thee!"

This was the prayer of the Proprietors of the Interminable Muddle,
and it went up day and night amid squabbles, altercations, recrimina-
tions, abuse, tears and whimperings. But loud and clear above all rose
the voice of Sir W. W. Hunter crying:– "Be of good cheer. Give the
drum a oner!"[2] and each cry was accompanied by a new boom.

The Government of India said no word for good or bad, though it
was credited with evil actions, intrigue, fraud and wrong. So the cry
went up afresh:– "We will distribute the fruits of the land; we will clothe
the widow and the fatherless and bind the sickness with green withes.
We will raise the *bunnia* to lie down with the *bazugar*, the *nat* with the
Nawab, and the B.A. with all four; and we will give to each a Maxim
gun and two revolvers. We will secure too the privilege of saying to
the Viceroy:– 'Well, old man, how are things in office to-day?' We will
make a new heaven and a new earth, for we are the created jay-hawks of
Aryavarta one and indivisible, if the Government whom we adore will
only keep the *Jathis* down; but we are certain that it intends privily to
destroy us and is even now arranging disturbances to discredit our Holy
Mission. Pigs, we preach you love! Dogs of the *bustees*, our watchword
is Brotherly Affection!"

And the Government made no sign,

It sat with its chin on its hand and murmured: "Same old people, same old *bundobust*. Same old everlasting suspicion. Must borrow a
hazur-ki-parwasti even when they want to turn us upside down. Leave
'em alone and they'll go Home, dragging their tales behind them"

And this was exactly what the Proprietors of the Interminable Muddle did. The brutal Anglo-Indian shut his left eye and said:– "*Connu,*" so they fled afar, screaming like gulls, westward down the Line of Least Resistance, straight to the bosom of the Holy British Elector who knows everything, believes everything, and does – nothing.

But or ever they launched themselves upon the Black Water they cast a jibe at the Man of Feeling[3] who controlled the destinies of Bombay. "You're another of them – a hidebound bureaucrat!" they groaned, and departed leaving the Man of Feeling disconsolate.

Alone of all the Stewards of the State, he possessed an Educational Policy worthy of the name; and therewith culture to the tips of his finger nails. "O Heavens!" gasped the Man of Feeling. "Have they known me for three and a half years and am I still misunderstood? Lend me an ink-pot!" Wisely, profoundly and unreservedly did the Man of Feeling indite a manifesto[4] setting forth how he approved of Principles, advocated Theories, and honoured Notions; and by those Principles, Notions, and Theories considered the Interminable Muddle an excellent idea partaking of the nature of the Lyceum, Augustus Harris's pantomimes (and this was truth) and an Alhambra ballet.[5] "How dare you think of fearing me. You ought to love me, man," wrote the Man of Feeling, and the Manifesto was made public.

Sir S. B—y, Sir A. C—n and Sir J. B. L—l[6] read it at breakfast together. For a while nothing was heard save the heavy breathing of the red khitmatgars behind their chairs. Sir A. C—v whistled the *Nunc dimittis* softly, being of a devotional frame of mind. "God gie us a gude conceit o' oorsel," said Sir S. B—y. He was thinking of his darling Municipality. "*Hakim do jane-valon men ek anjan,*"[7] said Sir J. B. L—l, for he had been a Settlement Officer in his day and knew the wisdom of the country side. There was another pause.

"Well?" said Sir S. B—y wearily; "You see what that means? Climb down and take sides, *mes amis*. Sail into it – ahem – bald-headed!"

"Never!" said Sir J. B. L—l with a shudder.

Sir A. C—n read the Manifesto a second time. "For the Man of Feeling excellent. For His Excellency the Governor a little premature, eh?" said he; "What one might call Hunterian. Is it possible that he thinks that a Governor has a character? He governs."

"No, he does not," sighed Sir S. B—y, "he is governed. They will be making a pronouncement from *you* next, C—n. They will ask you to declare on oath whether you really hid *lathials* in – what's that reeking village in the centre of Allahabad? – Colonelgunge, or suborned a Telegraph clerk to mutilate the Congress telegrams. You will have to write manifestoes on politics – and *such* politics!"

Sir A. C—n dipped his fingers daintily in the "bowly glass" and dried them carefully. "I *hope* not," he said simply; "I am supposed to look after a Province. It's quite a big Province, and you have no idea what a lot of things have to be done it from day to day. Strange as it may appear to you, I'm, to put it shortly, a Governor."

"I too had some dignity once," said Sir S. B—y; "I wonder if that will help me when they request my reasons in writing for not shouting 'Congress ki jai' from the top of the Ochterlony Monument."[8]

Sir J. B. L—l took up the Manifesto. "He thinks he is misunderstood after three and a half years. *I* think they understand their man perfectly. They have taken the measure of his foot to a fraction. On my word it's a beautiful draw!"

"You can laugh," said Sir S. B—y, tho' Sir J. B. L—l was doing nothing of the kind; "*Your* Province doesn't cold [sic] *suttee* with one hand and constitutionally light fireworks with the other. It will be some years before we see you on the hustings."

"It will," said Sir J. B. L—l. "By the way, C—n, I hear that the boys in your Muir College are upset with this little business and are working badly in consequence. Is that true?"

"Can you ask?" said Sir C. C—n. "Can you object? When Governors – Governors who are supposed to be responsible to some one or other – throw themselves into the scrimmage, why in the world should school boys stand out of it? As B—y says, take sides, gentlemen, and d—n administration. Off with your coats and come into the arena! The Man of Feeling has been three and a half years in the country and *he* sees the wisdom of it. Why should we, mere Civilian hacks with only thirty years' service, be wiser than he?"

"Because," said Sir S. B—y slowly, "we are not fools."

"Hm," said Sir C. C—n, "there's a great deal to be said on both sides. They called Dickey the Apollo Bandar;[9] what can we call the Man of Feeling? I want some adjectives."

There was a twinkle under the penthouse of Sir J. B. L—l's eyebrows, as he entrenched himself behind a chair.

"Call him? – why The McCaucus Reayus[10] of course, and keep Sterndale's[11] hands off me."

The *sederunt* broke up in confusion before the only jest that the Warden of the North had only perpetrated in his long and meritorious career.

But the occasion justified it.

[1] First stanza, slightly misquoted, of Lewis Carroll, 'The Lobster Quadrille' (*Alice in Wonderland*). RK has invented the gudgeons and whip-tailed rays.
[2] A 'Oner' is a shilling. According to Harbord, the phrase comes from a once popular party entertainment burlesquing the patter of a barker at a country fair (Harbord, IV, 2115).
[3] Lord Reay, Lieutenant-Governor of Bombay. *The Man of Feeling*, by Henry Mackenzie (1771): the hero exhibits an unfailing benevolence and tender sensibility, often to his own cost.
[4] Reay's manifesto: I have not identified which of Reay's official statements about Indian education is meant.
[5] The Lyceum Theatre, then managed by Sir Henry Irving; Harris (1852–96), of the Drury Lane Theatre, produced popular pantomimes and melodramas; performances at the Alhambra, a music hall on Leicester Square, ended with a ballet (Harbord, IV, 2116).
[6] Sir Stuart Bayley, Lieutenant-Governor of Bengal; Sir Auckland Colvin, Lieutenant-Governor of the North-West Provinces; Sir James Broadwood Lyall, Lieutenant-Governor of the Punjab.
[7] 'Of every two knowledgeable *hakims* one is ignorant.'
[8] A monument on the Calcutta Maidan to General Sir David Ochterlony (1768–1825).
[9] Dickey is unidentified. 'Apollo Bandar' means 'Apollo Monkey', punning on the landing place in Bombay called the Apollo Bundar.
[10] Alluding to the Caucus Race in *Alice in Wonderland*, ch. 3; the contestants run in circles, and everyone wins.
[11] R. A. Sterndale (1830–1902), civil servant in India but better known as a sportsman and author of books about big game and other Indian animals. His *Seonee* (1877) is an important source for the *Jungle Books*.

In the Year '92
The Evolution of the Missing Link

Published: *Civil and Military Gazette*, 8 November 1888.

Atribution: In Scrapbook 4 (28/4, p. 91).

Text: *Civil and Military Gazette.*

Notes: Unrecorded and unreprinted.

The Bombay Municipality meant business, and there was joy in the hearts of Hunt and Roskell, Rundle and Bridges, Garrard & Co., and T. Lamb, the masonic regaler.

"What we want," said Major S—lb—y,[1] "is dignity—dignity, gentlemen, proportioned to the stinks of the beach and matching the status of the wandering leper who is as yet unlegislated for. Suppose we were some day called upon to form a procession – suppose we were suddenly overtaken by a Royal Duke upon a pier-head, such things have been and may be again? I, gentlemen, possess a uniform which, though I say it who should not, is remarkably effective. But you, where would *you* be?"

"Very true," said the Bombay Municipality, "we will do the job in style. 'A stitch at the time saves nine,' as our Honourable and Worshipful native colleagues remark. Let us begin by dressing up the President." They swaddled him in a silk tabard, embroidered with bullion and blazoned as to the back with the arms of the Corporation – *videlicet parly per pale* a sewer *cassie*, on a field of town sweepings *improper*, in chief a sitting Bull, *gules*; supporters a bag of assafœtida *ouverte*, and a shovel, both of the cheapest; motto:– "He Injun, he big Injun, he heap big Injun, he mighty big heap Injun; he dam mighty big heap Injun. He Jones!" They further provided him with an all-oak, platinum clamped, Tantalus lock, ivory inlaid civic chair, with three-pile velvet cushions of six inch sterling fringe, and an open work back of Limoges enamel. Round his stomach they festooned a repoussé gold work chain of four Strands, and upon his bosom they placed a *plaque* of Doulton-ware mounted in silver and pourtraying the superiority of Bombay to all other places in the world.

"I – I fancy this wadded white silk lining is a trifle warm," said the President nervously, "but there's no denying that it is dignified."

"*Il faut soufrir pour etre swell*," said Major S—lb—y. "Don't you think he'd look better with a hat on?"

"The very thing," said the Bombay Municipality, "what sort of hat shall it be? A fireman's helmet with plumes, or a bearskin with a water-proof cover?"

They sat upon the question for a week, and ended by giving the contract to the Municipal Engineer; the design to be left in his hands entirely.

He perpetrated a Delight and a Wonder. It was a Tusco-Doric D.P.W.[2] hat with an allegorical peak, a clap-board ventilator, and patent reversible feather top. The total weight was only seven pounds and four ounces. When the sun shone on it, it could be seen from the Prongs Lighthouse, for it was made of crystal and *cloissonée* work.

The President winced a little bit when Major S—lb—y put it on his head and saluted him as Thrice Puissant Bottlebhoy, and gave him the sign of the Holy Archimandrite Degree. He said it was premature; and would the Corporation supply him with funds for raising the roof of his brougham eighteen inches? The hat always stuck in the doorway. Otherwise he was moist but happy.

"It seems to me," said Major S—lb—y after three blissful meetings, "that there's a lack of preparation in this assembly. His Holiness the President's Urim and Thummim puts us all in the shade. The question before the meeting is, shall we level up or level down?"

With one voice the Municipality cried:– "Level up, of course. That is the watchword of India."

"Exactly," said Major S—lb—y; "Let us strike while the iron is hot." He disappeared for a moment and returned arrayed in the most delicate pink silk *pyjamas*.

"Now this is my notion," said he, turning round slowly for the benefit of his colleagues, "I do not say that it cannot be improved upon, but I flatter myuself that for temperance and chastity the line cannot well be surpassed. I believe it to be an article of feminine attire in use in the Punjab, and I observe that it is no less than twenty-four feet in the waist. Hence the fullness of the pleats. *Isn't* it a beauty?"

"I am not going to wear a Hindu woman's how-do-you-call-'ems," murmured Pestlejee Mortarbhoy Bashit." It's not becoming."

"In private life, possibly not," said Major S—lb—y softly, for he was of a conciliatory disposition, "but, my dear friend, you will see that, as the – ahem – garment need only be worn on the Municipal side and at processions, there can be no reason for not instantly adopting it, by God. Anyone here going to contradict me? – I'll throw in a gold stripe down each leg, and a string of silver bells round the ankles, if you insist upon it, but don't irritate me further. There are six-and-thirty pairs of this perfect colour in the robing-room. Go and put 'em on!"

"Anything for the sake of peace," said the Municipality, and the pink *pyjamas* were unanimously voted and, which is more, worn. In order to get round any religious objections to their use it was found necessary to give a masonic touch to the meetings, and that meant all the fittings of a Blue Lodge, a Chapter, and a Consistory. The Board of General Purposes met in the Blue Lodge to the strains of the Dead March in Saul and passed all the estimates blindfolded. Supper was "holden" in the chapter-room, and all the fighting – there was a good deal of fighting, by the way – came off in the Consistory. You have no idea how many throwable articles are to be found in a well regulated Consistory. There was some confusion about the official titles which came in with the *pyjamas*. Thus a man who in the Blue Lodge was only a Howling Hiram, became, in the chapter, an Archdiaconal Wanderoo, and in the Consistory refused to answer to any name save that of "His Extreme Senility St. Simeon Skylights." This multiplicity was imposing and the Municipality enjoyed themselves immensely. They sat three days a week on a Board of Sumptuary Eclecticism, which was Municipalese for altering the design of their robes of office; and the fame of the city of Bombay spread throughout the world, and Globe-trotters used to pay the janitor of the Hall of Assembly – his real name was Panchoo and his pay was six rupees – enormous sums for the privilege of looking at the Municipality in its war-paint. Occasionally weak-minded members protested against the rules of the Board, but they were always reminded that Bombay was a city of three quarters of a million people and that it behoved her to consider her dignity – which was the dignity of her Municipality.

※

And a young man appeared – a very young man, in drill riding breeches and cowskin boots, and a *Jharun* coat, smoking an evil cheroot. "Do you know the First Great Pass word" said Panchoo janitor of the Hall of Assembly. "I do" said the young man. "The first syllable is *Mar* – and the second" – "O!"[3] said Panchoo, for he had been smitten on the head; and the young man passed through the Blue Lodge and the Chapter to the domed hall of the Consistory, led by the tinkle of the chandelier drops which fringed the hem of the President's robe of office. He stood all unabashed, the cheroot in his mouth, before the Great Curule Throne of *repoussé* silver work.

"Sacred Estimates!" said the President and all the members; "What do you here, rash introuder?" And they waved the banner of the Municipality under his nose and chanted the Municipal Hymn.

"I'm an Assistant District Superintendent of Police, and my orders are to turn you out of this. There has been a public demonstration in Rampart Row and a new municipal election and the kingdom of Bombay sends his love and says you'd better go. You're too beautiful to stay here!" said the young man.

"Go?" said the President. "Where to?"

"Mr. Ph—ps—n[4] has made *all* the arrangements," said the young man, "and the new Municipality are going to give you a subsistence allowance and ten per cent of the gate money. You will retain your dresses and – your future titles will be Honorary Members of the Ethnological Section of the Zoological Gardens." There was a howl of despair, a shrill whistle, and twenty grinning blue jackets from the *Bacchante* suavely but firmly conveyed the members of the Municipality to the padded vans that waited below, while Mr. Ph—ps—n ticketed each gentleman as he settled down, and smiled with glee.

So now, my child, if you go to Bombay Zoological gardens and take the second turning to the right after passing the Aviary, you will find them all in a spacious cage "replete with every modern convenience," the envy of the wandering Raja, and the delight of the little boys of Marine Lines.

The present Municipality wear just common clothes and are universally respected.

[1] Not identified.
[2] Department of Public Works.
[3] 'Maro', strike, hit hard.
[4] Not identified.

"A Free Hand"

❧

Published: *Pioneer*, 10 November 1888; *Pioneer Mail*, 14 November 1888.

Attribution: In Scrapbook 4 (28/4, p. 91).

Text: *Pioneer*.

Notes: Lord Lansdowne (Henry Petty-Fitzmaurice, fifth Marquess of Lansdowne, 1845–1927) succeeded Lord Dufferin as viceroy at the end of 1888. What Dufferin in 'A Free Hand' is imagined as saying to Lansdowne is developed at length in RK's dramatic monologue, 'One Viceroy Resigns', published in the *Pioneer*, 7 December 1888, and collected in *Departmental Ditties*, 4th edn, 1890.

Reprinted in the Martindell–Ballard pamphlets and in Harbord, iv, 2119–21.

❧

While we cannot recommend that the mother-country should run any serious risk in altering its system of currency to assist its dependency, we think that the Government of the latter should be allowed a free hand to deal with the problem as it considers best in its own interest. *Vide Minute of Dissent of Currency Commission.*

"How interesting!" said L-d D-ff-r-n as he read the telegrams of the *Pioneer* of the 9th. "Even I could hardly have said, 'Go to the Devil!' in more graceful terms." He threw open the window and looked towards the blue haze of the plains of Umballa, and the land he was shortly to quit for ever. "Free hand, indeed!" he said, contemptuously. "A free dinner would be more to the point, as L-nsd-wne will discover." Then he fell a-musing upon his successor, and the Aide-de-Camp who was cording up the boxes in the hall heard something that sounded like a quotation from *Plot and Passion*.[1] "L-nsd-wne! L-nsd-wne! after *me*!" said H-s Exc-ll-ncy, and sighed deeply. A few days later he was on his way to Calcutta to give over charge, and had a man been daring enough to clamber upon the Viceregal "Special" as it fled southward he would have seen H-s Exc-ll-ncy dancing a weird and wonderful saraband in the saloon carriage, while Sir D. M. W-ll-ce[2] smiled an austere smile and beat time on the lid of his office-box. It was not altogether joy at returning to England that moved our Viceroy to this unusual demonstration. Sir D. M. W-ll-ce could have enlightened the world had he chosen to open his lips; but he was mute, as a Private Secretary should be.

And L-d D-ff-in fell upon Lord L-nsd-wne's neck and wept over him. "You are young," said the retiring Viceroy, "twenty years younger than I. It is possible, therefore, that you have a stronger belief in yourself than I have in myself. Cultivate that belief. You stand on the threshold of new experiences – most of which will disgust you and a few amuse. You are the centre of a gigantic Practical Joke. Strive to enter into the spirit of it and jest temperately. There is a man called Roberts[3] whom I commend to you. He is little but good, and he alone makes the joke a practical one. There is also a man called Westland[4] from whom you will draw your pay, and once a week you are expected to be at home to half-a-dozen elderly gentlemen whom you will have great difficulty in distinguishing one from another, and much – much greater in extinguishing. Decorate them tenderly. They come in the rain and mean well. Wear flannel next your skin, avoid the sun, and above all things remember that you have a Free Hand, Heaven bless you, dear boy! It is about all you will have."

L-d D-ff-rin went his way humming. "'Tis the most disthressful country that ever yet was seen",[5] while Sir D. M. W-ll-ce was closeted with Lord L-nsd-wne from breakfast to dinner. No man knows what passed at that conference, but when the doors were throw open there was a thick haze of cigarette smoke in the room and an air of triumph on the face of the new Viceroy. Sir D. M.W-ll-ce was fast asleep. He had talked for eight hours without cessation.

"Is there a Finance Minister anywhere about the premises?" asked the new Viceroy in a tone studiously calculated to disarm suspicion. And men brought up Mr. Westland. "Leave us alone," said Lord L-nsd-wne; "and, by the way, be good enough to send Sir F. Roberts here, in full canonicals."

The doors closed anew and all India listened at the keyhole. There was a murmur of voices, and then a wail of despair from Mr. Westland. "But I am a financier – a financier with a reputation! I tell you, Sir, you *can't* do it. It's impossible! It's political lunacy! It's" . . . .

"One gun of Z.24 is now on its way from Fort William," said Sir F. Roberts crisply. "I have sanctioned the expenditure of one round of ammunition in expectation of orders from your successor." Mr. Westland wailed anew and there was the sound of a prolonged yawn as Sir D. M. W-ll-ce woke up from his slumbers. "Very well," said Mr. Westland sullenly. "I didn't come here to be blown from a gun" – ("As you certainly will be," said Lord L-nsd-wne suavely) – "and if I must, I must, though it's absolute insanity."

The murmur of voices ceased and was followed by the scratching of pens.

A howl of rage rang through the City. India was paying interest on her loans in silver! "But you can't," shrieked the City. "Who ever heard of paying interest on gold loans in silver? 'Tisn't legal tender. We must speak to the Secretary of State!" And they spoke to him by deputations and phalanxes and platoons, and when he fled to Scotland they clamoured at the doors of Lubbock, Herschell, Freemantle and Birch. "It's all your doing!" they snarled.

"But the most elementary considerations forbid" – began Sir John Lubbock.[6]

"D—n your financial considerations!" cried the City. "All we know is that we are getting ten of their dirty rupees for a sovereign. Ten of 'em! Wrapped up in paper, and weighing *tons*! What are we to do? It's blanked Repudiation that's what it is! Tell 'em they mustn't."

And England set itself to argue with its dependency, and the City screamed at both. "Are you all mad over there?" said England.

"Not in the least," said Lord L-nsd-wne, "we're having a lovely time. Come and look at our new railways and bridges and roads, all native capital. If men don't subscribe we forbid 'em to come to durbars and deprive 'em of their titles. If they are still reluctant, we appoint native magistrates and refuse to listen to petitions. Nothing like a Free Hand."

"Be serious," said England. "You're disorganising all our financial relations."

"We can stand it if you can," said Lord L-nsd-wne, shutting the telephone with a click. "Ten dibs to the pound are our terms, and if you don't like it, you had better appoint a fresh Currency Commission and do something."

And that was exactly what England did. The City wished to stand Sir John Lubbock head down in one of his own bee-hives,[7] but the Blues dispersed the rioters and peace came in with the adoption of a bimetallic standard.

Which proves that if you do what is manifestly impossible and absurd, no one will tell you to go to the Devil.

---

[1] *Plot and Passion*, a play by Tom Taylor and John Lang, acted at the Railway Theatre in Lahore in December 1883, by an amateur group, including RK, who played the role of Max Desmarets, head of the Secret Department of the Paris Police. See RK's 'Preadmonisheth ye Ghoste of Desmarets', *Poems*, III, 1709.
[2] Sir Donald Wallace: see 'An Official Secret', n. 8.
[3] Lord Roberts, then Commander-in-Chief.
[4] Westland: see 'His Natural Destiny', note 2.
[5] From the first stanza of 'The Wearing of the Green'.
[6] Lubbock (1834–1913), prominent banker, MP and distinguished natural scientist.
[7] Lubbock published *Ants, Bees and Wasps*, 1882.

Susannah and the Elder
(With Apologies to the Shade of Lawrence Sterne.)

§

Published: *Pioneer*, 12 November 1888; *Pioneer Mail*, 14 November 1888.

Attribution: Signed 'R.K.'

Text: *Pioneer.*

Notes: 'Susannah and the Elder' was reprinted in the October 1940 *Kipling Journal* by Captain E. W. Martindell, but, according to Harbord (IV, 2125), the pages of the *Journal* containing the story 'had to be destroyed (in most cases) by order of the Owner of the Kipling copyrights', i.e., by Elsie Kipling Bambridge, RK's surviving child. My copy of the *Kipling Journal* for October 1940 contains the story, as, I imagine, do most copies.

The story is a close and skilful imitation of the narrative method in Laurence Sterne's *Life and Adventures of Tristram Shandy* (1759–67), from which RK has also taken the names of the characters. Incongruity, apparent inconsequence, and shows of odd learning are the rule.

'Yoreayke' mimics the name of the parson 'Yorick' in *Tristram Shandy*; he is also the narrator of *A Sentimental Journey* and a pseudonym for Sterne himself. The modified spelling identifies Lord Reay, the governor of Bombay, as the object of the satire. I have not identified what particular statement or publication by Reay is in question, but Reay's main interest in his term as Governor of Bombay was in education, especially in promoting technical and practical education. The subject has been presented at length in W. W. Hunter, *Bombay 1885 to 1890. A Study in Indian Administration*, London and Bombay, 1892. RK was evidently unimpressed by Reay (see, e.g., 'An Exercise in Administration').

Nothing else that RK wrote for the Indian papers shows such confidence in the high literacy of his readers.

'Susannah and the Elder' has been reprinted in the Martindell–Ballard pamphlets; in the *Kipling Journal*, October 1940 (suppressed); and in Harbord, IV, 2122–5.

§

"Men's insides is made so comical, God help 'em."

George Eliot.[1]

Aha, *elucescebat* quoth our friend
No Tully, said I, Ulpian at the best

The Bishop Orders His Tomb[2]

Chapter XXVII

The city of B-mb-y, the siege of which was begun by your honour's self, lies in the middle of a devilish strange country. 'Tis quite benighted, said Corporal Trim. Then I wish the Faculty would follow my advice, said Yoreayke. But it cannot, said Corporal Trim. But it must, said Yoreayke. It never will, said Corporal Trim. It shall by G— said Yoreayke. The Recording Angel vaulted the celestial barriers with a smile of scorn.

'Twas by Gl-dst-ne that Yoreakye swore.[3]

Chapter XXVIII

Three and a half years with a bib under his chin.[4]

Three and a half years travelling from M-bl-shw-r to B-mb-y and again to P—na. A hellish quandary at P—na.[5]

Three years and a half at his probations and negations and nothing done for his statue upon the market-place. No wonder, then, when they heard he was still disputing about *wisdom* men asked:– If the old man be still disputing and inquiring concerning wisdom, what time will he have to 'make use of it?

'Twas at Butler that he checked, on his north-west passage to the intellectual world, and Dr. Slop could make neither head nor tail of it.– Butler, said my Uncle Toby, was with the Danish regiment at the siege of Limerick, and he was a good auxiliary.

It is a work that troubles me, said Yoreayke. You should get it done then and say no more about it, said my Uncle Toby. 'Tis an immoral work, said Yoreayke. The more reason for getting it done, said my Uncle Toby, and the less for talking of it. The first part only is immoral, said Yoreayke.– La! said Susannah 'tis all wrong from beginning to end, and left the room in a flame. Yoreayke sat down sighing.

He has sat on the pap bowl, said my mother.

Chapter xxix

Wherefore what manner of government he hath created let him and his coun-scillors consider, said Dr. Slop . . . .
. . . . said Yoreayke.

Dr. Slop was reading by the book, I assure you.

Chapter xxx

Dr. Slop looked upon the floor. . . . . Butler, as truly as ever Pharaoh raised one to honour said Dr. Slop, – Locke, said my father. That's as you please, said my Uncle Toby. Shut the book, said Yoreayke. Dr. Slop held it as wide open as before – that is to say upon the broad of its back. Would you desire to teach Tristram an abomination? said Yoreayke. God forbid, said my mother, he will learn all too quickly. Then shut the book, said Yoreayke, the first part is immoral.

Whether the word attracted the wench or whether it was that Trim had prevented the action, certain it is that Susannah looked in with a dish-clout.

Chapter xxxi

Did I say that Dr. Slop was stubborn – stubborn as the Abbess's mules? I have done an injustice – at all times abhorrent to my nature. When the Abbess and the novice shared the oath betwixt 'em in the fear of blas-phcmy the mules went their way.[6] So did not Dr. Slop, – But Tristram is as black as my shoe, said Dr. Slop. 'Twas no fault of mine, said my mother on a sudden. Pish! said my father, look at the calendar.

And on my reputation there had been an eclipse of the moon!

All this while Yoreayke was sitting in my pap-bowl.

Chapter xxxii

I am a Turk if I had not remembered the *Analogy*. Thus:–

The Eclipse ——————————Tristram (which is myself including my blackness).

The Dish-clout ——————————Yoreayke (which has no correlation with the pap-bowl).

Now what the devil had the dish-clout to do with Yoreayke? A dish-clout is no savoury gift for any man, but a man should not come into a nursery and sit upon a pap-bowl.

It is all in that, says Susannah, and surely she should know.

Chapter XXXIII

The education of a child, cried Dr. Slop, is a serious matter, and should be conducted by his own father. Nay, said Yoreayke, by the stranger within your gates. . . 'Tis a poor philosophy, said my father, for the burden and heat of the day were mine.– I start for Antwerp in the summer, said Yoreayke. It is the mercy of Providence, said Corporal Trim, who was in the shadow of the door, near Susannah.– Trim, said my Uncle Toby, wait without.

Trim bore Susannah with him lest he should be lonely on the road to the kitchen.

In the meantime, said Yoreayke, the book must be shut.

Dr. Slop opened it very wide and drew a blue line round the margins –

Chapter XXXIV

A distinguished personage had condemned it, said Yoreayke, and fell a-musing upon the pap-bowl. That may well be, said my Uncle Toby, does your honour know the gentleman's name? He commands my immediate confidence, said Yoreayke. The pap-bowl lay upon the floor – Prignitz, Scroderus, Andrea Paræus, Erasmus, Hafen Slawkenbergius, Gregorius, Didius? said my father.– But my father's questions – I shall never get half of them through this year.

Dr. Slop snapped his fingers scholastically – ecclesiastically – pragmatically – judgmatically, according to all the nostrums of the Faculty, and surely that was a better way of reply. 'Tis a monstrous clever gentleman, my dear, said my mother softly, and as concerns your morals – 'twas to my father she spoke.

Madam, said my father, at forty-nine a man has no morals. He gets out of his body to think.

Chapter xxxv

Yoreayke walked down to the hedge, his arms akimbo, having broken my pap-bowl.

Was there ever such a mess! said my mother.

The wind blew Yoreayke's coat-tails abroad diffusely. Surely the breeze hath a right to blow where it listeth for all coat-tails in the world.

Courage, gentle reader, I have prætermitted, passed over and cast into the outer darkness of the kennel my chapters on coat-tails lined with blue satin and the Dignity of Man.

Seventeen chapters Master Printer – but it escaped me that I should pay for thy villainous type transmogrifications.

Chapter xxxvi

The good man has not put away his handkerchief, said my mother.

Tchk! Tchk! Tchk! said Susannah – a crowing huskiness in her throat. Corporal Trim stood to attention.

Why! 'Tis a dish-clout that has been pinned to him! said my father, he has never been into the kitchen.

Now how should my father have connected the kitchen with the dish-clout or that with the coat-tails? God knows my mother was the meekest woman that ever . . . .but in a matter of patty-pans nature will out. And, above all, patty-pans are a woman's peculiar province.

An't please your honour, said Corporal Trim, he passed through the kitchen upon going out. To the wars? said my Uncle Toby. To his work, said my father. To his craft? said Dr. Slop. To the devil! said Trim.

'Twas to make Master Tristram new pap, said Susannah.

Susannah, said my father, thou are an honest wench. Was it a clean dish-clout?

No, said Susannah, 'twas————————————

[1] Mrs Poyser's remark: George Eliot, *Adam Bede*.

[2] Lines 99–100 of Robert Browning's poem.

[3] The Liberal Gladstone had appointed Reay to the Lieutenant-Governorship of Bombay.

[4] The current length of Reay's tenure as Lieutenant-Governor.

[5] Support of the Poona College of Science was a main part of Reay's educational policy.

[6] *Tristram Shandy*, vol. VII, chs. 21–5. The nun and the novice; in order to make their stubborn mules go up the hill, each speaks two syllables of a four-syllable oath directed at the mules and so halve the sin involved. The mules do not move.

The Coming K

Published: *Pioneer*, 28 November 1888; *Pioneer Mail*, 28 November 1888.

Attribution: In Scrapbook 4 (28/4, p. 95).

Text: *Pioneer.*

Notes: *The Coming K*, by Samuel Orchert Beeton (the Mr Beeton to the celebrated Mrs Beeton), published in 1873, is a satiric poem attacking the then Prince of Wales, afterwards Edward VII, for his self-indulgent and near scandalous behaviour.

In tracing the transformations of the 'Lansdahn Chamber of Commerce and Mercantile Union', the speaker works his way through the succession of governor-generals and viceroys from 1869 to 1888: Lords Mayo, Northbrook, Lytton, Ripon, Dufferin, and Lansdowne.

Reprinted in the Martindell–Ballard pamphlets and in Harbord, IV, 2128–31.

꙾

> And George my lawful king shall be
> Until the times do alter.
>
> *Vicar of Bray.*[1]

President (*of the Dufferin Medical Fund Assistance Society, Bebusteeghat*)[2] *loq:*– Gentlemen of this so honoured institution, and alumni of First Arts, under all circumstances the question before our considerations to-night is of singularly preposterous and variegated character fundamentally complicated because of spelling. How you spell Lansdahn?

Secretary.– This question demands explicacity and is not at all before the meeting. Financial difficulties pave the way as registered in minute-book of last proceedings. Dufferin Medical Fund Assistance Society, pre-eminent factor in national progress but no subscriptions paid.

President.– *Gorah ko lât, admi ko bât!*[3] Are you all mud heads? Dufferin Medical Fund Essistance Society dead as Queen Anne's hair-ring on account of funds. How does this matter? Not a swear – not a two-annas swear! Gentlemen, I have honour to be connected with this and kindredly

311

similar enterstutions ever since my connection with service of gorgeous and beneficent Sirkar, and continued honour in public service and this, in my o-pee-nion, is fitting time for the back-slide. Ease her! Stop her! As my friend Captain Pereira on the Hughli steamer pertinently says in crossing over to our offices. I am distinguished member of local admin-istration and all known down both banks of the river for twenty years. You are so young men you do not comprehend political status in its comprehensiveness. *Lat Sahib gya!* Medical Essistance Fund Society *bhi phut gya!*[4] What use any more bother and voting addresses. When I was *ommedwar* I took deep interest in national progress marching to glory through social elevation on empty stomachs; and this society, you can see by minute books, was the Mayo Athenæum for enlightened discus-sion. Babu Ahutosh Mookerjee – alas poor Yorick! – was our president, but he is now gone the way of all flesh which is green as ghauts and in the evening is burned up; but he was Sudder Munsif and he was my true friend. I am your true friend, gentlemen, by seniority and honour you have done me in electing me president of this rapidly moribund institution. But I pause for a reply to my previous digression. When Ahutosh Babu jumped the branches I feathered my oars in my nest, and it was I suggested vital alterations in society and voted address to Lord Northbrook[5] with maximum of public spirit. Mayo Athenæum was dead by gentle process of athenasium (*very earnestly*). That, gentlemen, is a pun. And we all became Northbrook Young Men's Improvement Association, and I was Nazul Darogah and headed all the addresses. (Hear! Hear!) Gentlemen, by God we wrote addresses day and night and then Pitamber Babu took the cash-box and lavantined to Behar with ninety-seven rupees ten annas four pie. So Northbrook Young Men's Improvement Association was hit upon the hat, as the joke is, and lay in abeyance till Lord Lytton[6] came. I was possessed of all the minute-books and enormous bump of public spirit with studious bent towards the glories of oriental poetry – not Mahabharat nor other Rigs but Hafiz (*sensation*). Gentlemen, I see that you are ashamed because Hafiz was Mahomedan voluptary, but I beg you to hang your verdicts till I tell. At that time we became the Lytton Literary Society and I tell you this, that His Late Excellency came by steamer to Bebusteeghat and I personally in presidential capacity presented him with vellumi-nous address and His Excellency gave a gold medal for poesies after the style of Hafiz upon female orientals. There was no competition, but I have the medal and I was appointed being E.A.C. Gentlemen, now you remember that millennium of Ripon the Good when all was pure politics and abstract ideals, from the *Pax Britannica* at Peshawar to the Adam's Bridge at Comorin and freedom of debate! Then Lytton Literary Society became Ripon Political Club and sent addresses direct by post, advocating supreme validity of Rousseau's *Social Confessions* and other things on a similar platform of pure Liberalism. So we were re-organised in a commensurate scale and promulgated progress in all directions and *never* salaamed to the Deputy Commissioner! By God, that was elevated old period and Lord Ripon was very much pleased and our true friend. I had promise of Rai Bahadurship, but Lord Ripon went away in the centre of popular demonstrations and nobody knowing how the all and devil illustrious successor would think. Thus Ripon Political Club sank upon its ashes. But nevertheless I subsequently discovered that a medical fund was up the wind and took proper measures, so that Bebustceghat sent *first* address of this nature that ever was to Lord Dufferin, and the Political Club was re-called Medical Essistance Organization! Also, first and before any other place, I beg you will remember gentlemen that promptitude is the mother of promotion and this fool-talk over defunct corpse of effete organization *because* the *Lât Sahib* is going away, may be inimically prejudicial to our all true interests. Now this new Viceroy is most enlightened ruler, but I do not know his political proper gander and per*haps* we have been making too much political platform in these last days since, however great, however grand, however superior in aspiring, nothing *can* do without bamfoozling the *Shahib log*, which is tantamount to inviting to co-operate in stupendous labours of national elevation. And just these present times, the *Shahib log* are not so pleased as Panch. Wherefore, still retaining minute books of previous Societies, in my o-pee-nion it would be sound temporary measure capable of further expansion, that this Medical Fund Essistance Organization constute itself Bebusteeghat Chamber of Commerce and guardian of mercantile interests up and down the river and any where else. Commerce is innucuous and pleases everybody, and if Lord Lansdahn is unfortunately devoiding commercial instincts so necessary to the proper conservation of this resourceful country we will do no harm *ad interim* but only watch which way the cat runs. How so great as Commerce? How so stabile? Let us become commercial and make Captain Pereira an honorary member by acclamation, because we travel daily in his steam-boat and he may ameliorate fares. But Chamber of Commerce *certainly*; and an address will conduce to our true interests. Wherefore I move that Dufferin Medical Essistance Fund is now abrogated and Lansdahn Chamber of Commerce and Mercantile Union supersedes there sub. *pro tem.*, till alterations are necessary. But first how you spell Lansdahn, Honorary Sekuttar Sahib?

Secretary.– L-a-n-s-d-o-n. I have much pleasure to second and President shall draft address in strict commercial lines.

Extract from Sachi Durpan, December 2nd, 1888:–

"It has been truly observed that a period of rest and commercial enterprise is, after political regeneration, one of the most urgent needs of this unhappy country. We are truly rejoiced to see that a step in this kind of enterprise has been taken at Bebusteeghat which has always been foremost in all the public movements of the hour. The step has been taken under the guidance of our public spirited countryman Harindra Oko Deb, E.A.C., a veteran of all kinds of things, from whose sagacity and intelligence we hope the utmost. Commercial enterprise is lamentably backward throughout this province, but under the fostering ægis of our new ruler it should grow to immense proportions. The Chamber of Commerce which has been inaugurated at Bebusteeghat is clear proof of the intellect of the Bengali and sufficient answer to the cavillers against our nation. It will regulate commercial enterprise and encourage the development of trade and legitimate commercial aspirations. Harendra Babu will not be trodden down by the voice of public clamour. Why should not all Bengal follow his illustrious example? Why should not – *et cætera, et cætera, et cætera.*"

---

[1] Eighteenth-century song by an unknown author, the point of which is, that though governments change, the self-serving rule does not.
[2] 'Bustee' means, among other things, a slum; 'ghat' is a landing-place or quay.
[3] 'For white men, lordship and rule; for ordinary men, talk.'
[4] 'The big boss has gone. The Medical Essistance Fund Society has gone bust.'
[5] Lord Northbrook (1826–1904), Governor-General of India, 1872–6.
[6] Lord Lytton (1831–91), Viceroy, 1876–80 (the change from 'Governor-General' to 'Viceroy' is owing to the proclamation of Victoria as 'empress' at the beginning of 1877).

What the World Said

※

Published: *Pioneer*, 4 December 1888; *Pioneer Mail*, 5 December 1888.
Attribution: In Scrapbook 4 (28/4, p. 95).
Text: *Pioneer*.

Notes: Lord Dufferin, no longer the viceroy, on the eve of his departure from India, spoke at length at the St Andrew's Dinner, Calcutta, on Friday, 31 November, 1888. In the speech, a swan song, Dufferin spoke more frankly on certain subjects than he had allowed himself to do in his viceregal character, especially on the subject of the Indian National Congress. The Congress was regarded with great suspicion by most of the English in India, and in fact it led the way towards what became the movement for Indian independence. The speech was reported fully in the *Pioneer*, 3 December 1888.

But it hardly matters what Dufferin said, for the idea of 'What the World Said' is that each paper will ride its own hobby-horse whatever the news might be.

'What the World Said' has been reprinted in the Martindell–Ballard pamphlets and in Harbord, IV, 2132–4.

※

> And school foundations in the act
> Of holiday, three files compact,
> Shall learn to view thee as a fact
> Connected with that zealous tract –
> "Rome, Babylon and Nineveh."
>
> *The Burden of Nineveh.*[1]

The following will be found to be a more or less accurate forecast of the opinions of the Indian journals on Lord Dufferin's speech at the Calcutta St. Andrew's Dinner:–

The C-v-l and M-l-t-ry G-z-tte:–

Like Sarah Battle of old Lord Dufferin asks only for the extreme rigour of the game. And he plays that game with light-hearted abandon on

315

the eve of his departure. The reason for his reticence up to this point are [*sic*] explained by our Afghan correspondent and the Lord Bishop of Lahore as being due partly to religious considerations and partly due to the passage of a Toorkh Kafila through the Pariari Syed country, circumstances which those in the least acquainted with frontier policy will at once see, &c., &c.

The B-mb-y G-z-tte:–

Though our telegraphic *resumé* of his speech is a feat unparalleled in the history of Indian journalism, we should be sorry to think that Lord Dufferin's animated and picturesque description of the land whose rule he is now resigning bears any approximation to the truth. The most unobservant visitor to these shores, as he paces down Breach Candy[2] or stands upon the cupola of the G.I.P. Terminus, cannot but fail to be impressed with the almost aggressive material civilisation of the East. We in Bombay, &c., &c.

The T-mes of Ind-a:–

Our local contemporary completely misapprehends the situation. We ourselves were not long since approached on behalf of the Supreme Government and soundings were taken as to whether we would be prepared to publish an official commentary on Lord Dufferin's speech. This offer we indignantly declined, and now, wrapping ourselves in our virtue, will leave to our versatile correspondent Mr. N. S. Ginwalla the pleasant duty of criticism, &c., &c.

The Engl-shm-n:–

The overgrown Debating Society whose irresponsible chatter has of late been dragged into such undeserved prominence will now, we trust, quietly and decently subside. Lord Dufferin has gone out of his way to crush it with eloquence that were better employed in defending the disgraceful exodus to the Hills and the hybrid employés in the subordinate offices will now perhaps understand that their attempts at playing at administration are not acceptable to the State whose bread they eat. "*Hukm nahin hai*"_is a hint rarely lost on molluscous Aryanism, &c., &c.

The Ind-n D-ly N-ws:–

Beyond a passing reference, which may possibly have been dragged in for the sake of rhetorical effect, we grieve to see that the Viceroy has made no reference to the non-official class or to the pernicious habit of the young *gentlemen* of this town "purchasing" trousers from Messrs. Cutter, Ghuse and Irons and then going up country without paying. Business obviously cannot be conducted in this way, and the many Bishops at whose feet we in our youth had the privilege of sitting were entirely of the same opinion. In regard to the Congress we fear that much of his Lordship's judicious advice will hardly be acceptable to the well-meaning but perhaps over-zealous gentlemen, &c., &c.

The St-tesm-n:–

In the days of Lord Minto³ we approached the authorities with a new scheme of Government founded on the principles of statesmanlike Christianity. We can do no more than point out anew after an interval of many decades the wisdom of finding and applying that scheme. It is fatuous folly to act in any other manner, and the bare fact of Lord Dufferin's speech, an instalment of which we give to-day, is sufficient evidence of the ghastly gap now widening and deepening between the races. Had our recommendations in '43, '58 and again in '67, as reference to our files will show, been carried out in their crystal entirely it would not be our painful duty, &c., &c.

The Ind-n M-rr-r:–

The legitimate aspirations of the people have received a cruel blow. Lord Dufferin, as we have always believed was the case, has fallen entirely into the hands of high-handed officialdom. But we would entreat our brethren not to be cast down. His shadow will soon be removed from the land, and we have a just and righteous Governor in Sir Stuart Bayley. We expected no more from this Viceroy. His superficial and misleading views should be received with caution, for it must be remembered that since the Congress disowns the Pamphlets his *locus standi* is non-existent, &c., &c.

R–s and R–yy–t:—⁴

Dufferin has not an over-delicate stomach, but the Congress must blame itself if it has been "spanked". Moderation is the watchword of dynasties, and the needs of the case demand that the Pamphlets must be disowned *instanto*. Lord Dufferin is no prodigy, but he is a lord for a' that and he kicks from the shoulder. We pause for a reply.

Amr–ta B–z–r P–tr–ka:–

A new era of oppression opens before us and the *ap–ke–wastes* are jubilant. Henceforth the Congress is to be hounded down by *pseudo*-Rai Bahadurs of sycophantic C.I.E.'s. The Bengalis, whose honest criticism had done everything for our country, have fallen under Lord Dufferin's displeasure. Our portion is either the gallows, jail or starvation. Under which King, Bezonian, speak or die? But we are much afraid that we shall die. We shall return to this subject in a later issue.

H–pe:–

For ought we can see the retiring Viceroy stands exactly where he stood before he spoke. His Jubilee speech won him undeserved praise from the too impressionable Bengalis because, forsooth, he promised pleasant things. Now he is damned for showing his real hand. We shall grovel at Lansdowne and later we shall damn him and the country will remain as it was. When we are not carried off our feet by every straw we may be taken seriously, &c., &c.

N–t–n–l G–rd–an:–

No expedient is too mean, no trick too filthy to use against the natives of India. This Dufferin was crammed with official pride and then let off before he goes to Europe, where he will find his own level. But why

blame him? He had to please his masters – the Anglo-Indians – ⸱
his fiery words suited the beef and the whiskey that graced the festiv
board. We are glad that the revellers did not break off the table-legs and
beat their *khitmatgars*.

CHORUS of the FATES and the DESTINIES:–

What's all the noise about down there?

---

[1] Rossetti, 'The Burden of Nineveh', from the first edition, 1856.
[2] 'A locality on the shore of Bombay Island' (Hobson-Jobson).
[3] The first Earl Minto was Governor-General of India, 1807–13.
[4] *Raees and Ryot*, native paper in Calcutta.

An Interesting Condition

Published: *Pioneer*, 20 December 1888.

Attribution: In Scrapbook 4 (28/4, p. 96).

Text: *Pioneer*.

Notes: For the group to which this item belongs see the introductory note to 'The History of a Crime'. Gladstone, not at the moment prime minister, was political anathema to RK, as might be guessed from the statement quoted from Gladstone at the head of the piece. Gladstone's speech appeared in the *Pioneer* of 18 December 1888 and differs in some details from RK's text.

Reprinted in the Martindell–Ballard pamphlets; in *The Victorian*, April 1938; and in Harbord, IV, 2135–8.

The people of India were in a condition most interesting to every man qualified to comprehend the large principles and responsibilities of the English domains. They were desiring more and more to enter into the public life of their country which was beginning to have a public life of its own. . . . Our business is to foster and nourish that sentiment.– *Mr. Gladstone on India.*

It was the East – beautiful, unpitying and old.

It was, moreover, the East inhabited by the Englishman.

An Englishman has no sense of humour.

A man without a sense of humour is a monstrosity incroyable.

All Englishmen are monsters incroyable.

I include here the German who is almost an Englishman.

Mes amis, let us then be thankful that we are not Englishmen.

Also, that we do not inhabit the East.–

To elaborate Fiascos. . . . . .

I eliminate here Tonquin, which is not a Fiasco but an Experiment.

An Experiment does not become a Fiasco till the Englishman appears.

It then finds itself a *Dam Mess*, according to the language of the Englishmen.

The East sits upon a Throne. The West inhabits a *bureau*, a *comp.* or a *boutique*; but the Throne belongs to the East.

The reason why a Throne exists in the East is that there are no paving-stones in the streets. There is only dust and sunshine. Me, I have seen it!

You cannot create barricades with dust and sunshine.

The reason-to-be of the Throne explains itself.

In the course of time arrives the Englishman, with his *gret-coat* upon his arm, his *braddishaw*[1] in his hand and his wife upon his knee.

The Englishman supports always his wife upon his knee. It is to him an observance national. It is an obligation solemn also upon the wife. When the husband is not here she will sit upon the knee of any man. The husband upon his return sells her by auction at *Smiffel*,[2] which is the recognised *magazine central* of these goods.

Thus, then, are the manners of the English.

The Englishman confronts the East. The East does not confront the Englishman.

She regards to the above of his head, which is bald. To the Eternities, to Napoleon, to the Forty Ages which regard also. To the Vague Profound! To the Immensity!

She would also regard the Past, but there is no Past in the East.

It is only the Present – ã *bon marché*.

The Englishman says:– "Goddam. Where is an omnibuse?" – and the East says:– "I have it not here."

The Englishman is *furibonde*. He demands his ominibuse, his *rosbif*, his *roug-towel* and his *tobb*.

The East washes not herself.

The Englishman obtains these things by *force majeure*.

The *rosbif* gives to him arterial blood: the *tobb* a circulation of the most vigorous and the *roug-towel* a glow of the most generous.

Mistrust there [*sic*: then?] the Englishman when he is generous.

He will sell you a young dog.

The Englishman slaps his thigh: he whistles his *bouledogue*; he takes a stick convincing. He has those things there upon him all, as says the *chanson* of the Boulevarde.

He confronts anew the East, and says:– "I am great. I am strong. Above all I am just. Govern me or I will Sacred Blue your eyes! I desire to be governed. It is an experience."

And the East says only: "Protector of the Poor."

The Englishman kicks her children to school. They read there how the East has been misgoverned by the Englishman.

That is taught to them that they may understand the style of Macaulay; of Burke; of Pitt; of deuce an' all the authors popular.

It is further taught them for nothing. That is Policy.

The children emerge. They have notions which are wrong. And theories.

These are incorrect. But all have been taught by the Englishman.

He slaps his chest. According to the custom of the *cab drivaire*.

The children swarm upon him in the excess of an affection which has been purchased.

They become *exigeante.*

They become impolite.

They are *blageurs.*

Above all, they wish to govern the Englishman.

Then the Englishman slaps those children. Brutally and upon their softest parts. He Sacred Blues their eyes.

And for what?

Because they have been taught by him to misunderstand their teaching.

Above all, reposes the East.

She is old, but she is beautiful.

A beautiful woman is always old. As old as Beauty.

She is of a moral reputation indifferent.

A beautiful woman is always. . . . .

Let us return to our sheep.

The East intrigued with Alexander. It was a *liaison* passenger.

With the Toorkh.

It was an *affaire militaire* only.

Again with the Toorkh.

That was not constancy but a coincidence.

Again with the Toorkh!

A coincidence is permissible once only. That was a *bétise.*

With the Rajput; with the Hindou.

It was to pass the time.

With the Portuguese.

It was an aberration erotic.

With the Frenchman.

It was an affair of the heart.

But she was a woman. The Englishman came. With him the gold of Perfide Albion.

Encore – she was a woman!

Let us be merciful to women. So long as we do not possess gold.

It is now the Englishman who is kicking her children to school. She has a *ménage* of the Britannic ideal – solid, sumptuous, and wearying above all.

The Englishman believes that he has married her. By the high mass of the rope and the low mass of the sabre.

The others also believed.

And she?

Ask her. Her eyes are upon the Vague Profound where dwell the shadows of her dead Lovers.

The Englishman has taken her by the arm. He promenades with her upon the Sundays. He laughs. He exhibits his teeth. He slaps his leg. He also pats her upon the back.

These things are the marks of the husband English. But. . . . ask her.

She has seen many lovers.

A woman who has seen many lovers will see more.

This woman will exist for ever, and she will always be beautiful.

An eternity of beauty and an eternity of *liaisons*! The *liaisons* of a Nation! Pyramidal! Immense.

I, the Gaul, may return to her arms.

She may prefer to be *Cossaquée*.

Let us not try to foretell the mind of a woman. Even in Literature.

Meantime the Englishman is kicking his sons putative to school. He will Sacred Blue them if they do not go. He will Belly Holy Grey them when they emerge.

Meantime a *bourgeois* of the most respectable, who exposes indecently his braces when he cuts trees for the purposes of religion, exhorts her with tears to enter the strife political.[3]

She, the Messalina of Monarchs! The Cleopatra of the Ganges – inconstant, insatiable, shameless, old!

He, the reader of the Scriptures in the Church of Hawarden! The God of the *bourgeoisie*! The man of the collars of speckless purity. *Schoking* you say?

Situation Magnificent, but these English are fools.

They would call it a Development of Policy.

Doré is dead, and with him Gavarni.[4]

Rédacteurs of the *Vie Parisienne*, I present to you the idea of a *croquis* immortal – the Rehabilitation of the East.

Gautier[5] is dead and with him Heine.[6]

There rests M. Renan.

Author mellifluous of the *Book of Job*[7] in prose rhythmic, spread, I pray you, yourself over this subject so worthy which I, son expatriated of France, present to you now upon my knees.

You seek a title?

"Les Amours Faciles d'un ancien Réprésentant du Peuple Anglais."

Ou, *tout court:–*

"*Les Libertinages de M. Gladstone.*"

---

[1] *Bradshaw's Railway Guide.*
[2] The great London meat market.
[3] Gladstone is meant; exercising by chopping wood was among his well-publicised idiosyncrasies.
[4] Gustave Doré: see 'My Christmas Caller'; Paul Gavarni (1804–66) French illustrator.
[5] Théophile Gautier (1811–72), French poet and novelist.
[6] Heinrich Heine; RK wrote that 'I owe much to Heine' (*Letters*, III, 193).
[7] Ernest Renan, *Le Livre de Job*, 1858.

The Comet of a Season

Published: *St James's Gazette*, Supplement, 21 November 1889.

Attribution: RK to Edmonia Hill, 8–16 November 1889 (*Letters*, 1, 360): 'My notion of the literary tale for the Jimmy [*St James's Gazette*] still hot and disposed myself unto a complete day. Began at ten, stopped for lunch at two and went on till five weaving the yarn of a young man who started in a literary career in London and wrote himself out in the desire to accumulate money. He used and reused his incidents all over again till the public sickened of him and he married a rich wife just in the nick of time.' The story perhaps reflects RK's own anxiety: a few weeks before writing 'The Comet of a Season' he wrote that 'I did not come to England to write myself out at first starting – not by a very long sight.'[1] The fear soon passed and never recurred.

Text: *St James's Gazette*.

Notes: RK wrote against this title in Chandler's *Summary* the words 'not mine RK', but this was some forty years after the fact. RK denied several items in the bibliographies that he marked that are known to be his by clear evidence, most of them from his very early work.

'The Comet of a Season' has been reprinted in the Martindell–Ballard pamphlets and in Harbord, v, 2395–401.

✠

> But we, brought forth and reared in hours
> Of change, alarm, surprise,
> What shelter to grow ripe is ours?
> What leisure to grow wise?[2]

Mr. Ralph Etheredge was a young writer, and it occurred to him to write a book about a woman who had her throat cut and a horse drowned while crossing a ford. You would never suppose that these incidents and a little ink comprised in themselves the elements of glory. That is because you do not know the great British public. People had been suffering from a surfeit of shuddering kisses, or Pyramids, or purple heather, or dialects, or something indigestible, and demanded change

325

THE COMET OF A SEASON

food. They found what they wanted in Mr. Etheredge's book, and they told him so.

He was impressionable. When you praised him little twitches would crumple the corners of his lips. When you ceased awhile from praising, he would interrupt the conversation to make clear how utterly indifferent he was to praise. This, of course, re-established the current. His eyes were blue and his eyelashes were curly, and the craving of his soul was Sympathy with a gently whispered capital S. His two ideas, being direct inspirations, he naturally valued them much more than other things which had cost him time and headaches: for the sovereign picked up at the bottom of the cab is not to be compared with the shilling earned by virtuous driving. Cabmen say so. The get drunk on the larger trove; exactly as Mr. Etheredge did on easily won praise. And so he became upset, and his lips twitched more than ever, and his need for sympathy grew with his disease. Sympathy is a beautiful thing. It can best be found in the corners of second-tier boxes, between the acts, after little dinners, and in country-houses at five-o'clock teas before the candles are brought in and the voices naturally sink with the sun. Mr. Etheredge used to hunt for it in those places. There was not so much in billiard rooms or corner divans of clubs, where men warm their toes and prove that all their acquaintances are impostors. Sympathy is a God-given emotion; but when a man seeks and obtains the sympathy of eight or ten very nice ladies who would sympathize unutterably with all things new – and when he, at various times and places, squeezes their eight or ten right hands and severally assures them that they are his respective and more than respected Egerias – the mental horizon and the power of absorbing tender speech seems to grow wider and washier every day.

And with the sympathy came the publishers and the fat green cheque books. Their demands were as simple as those of the man at the telephone. They rang Mr. Etheredge's bell and shouted "Repeat". They assured him that he had struck out a line, occupied untrodden ground, developed a new field, and done several other things of the greatest possible importance to the world and themselves. He was to till that field diligently and to produce that line as far as it would run. And he was never to forget that Codlin was his true friend and Short was a brigand:[3] and when did he think that he would throw off a shilling's worth of, say, one hundred and sixty closely printed pages, etc., etc., to be followed by, let us say, etc.; which would naturally lead up to, etc., etc.? Red hot with many sympathies, deafened with the five o'clock litany that told him he had only to go forward – "and accomplish anything and everything, Frank, dear, for *I* may call you Frank" – Mr. Etheredge arranged his contracts on much the same lines as the morning sun would arrange to warm the earth. Messrs. Kilt, Milt, and Roe were the "mortgagees of the property hereinafter mentioned of the one part," and one Gallihauk was their reader. He was a brutal man, unfit for society. He modelled himself on Doctor Johnson – at least the veins used to stand out on his forehead when he ate his food and the front of his waistcoat was speckled with gravy, and his language was the language of thieves. It was he who took the trouble to call on Mr. Etheredge, who fancied he came about the rent of his chambers till he said without preface: "I was what you are. My line was mist, sea and a headland, with a girl falling from the top, and the tide bumping the body against a rock. That ruined me; but I recovered, and now bump other bodies. You won't recover. My unofficial advice to you is, Dry up. What I have to tell you is, Continue to gush till you are dry. Go on. Keep yourself *en* évidence, get two suits of dress clothes and never refuse an invitation. You can write between dinner parties, you know; and above all things, don't forget the throat and horse trick. No thanks, I should like you to remember, however, that there is no discharge in this war; and if you dip out of a bucket without putting back, you arrive at the bottom."

Mr. Etheredge took as much of this advice as related to the evidence and the dress suits, and wandered from centre piece to centre piece fantastically comparing Gallihauk to Mr. Wemmick,[4] while everybody laughed. No establishment pretending to completeness could, after the due and proper formalities, dispense with Mr. Etheredge between half-past seven and half-past eleven P.M. His theory, which he explained at length to the ladies, was that he was studying certain side-lights of society; and in the studying he learned to talk from the top of his palate and the left-hand upper canine and between his two front teeth, and to pet particular words as old ladies pet black-and-tan terriers, according to the needs and customs of his company. A young man with blue eyes, whose lips twitch and whose fingers drum in ordinary conversation can give out at a three hours' dinner party, where he has, for his unmade reputation's sake, to talk well and epigrammatically, quite as much nervous force as would carry him through six hours' desk-work and a stubborn plot. Mr. Etheredge never minded explaining how inspirations came to him, and what were the difficulties of controlling a large troop of headstrong characters, and the ladies in the alcoves to the left of the soft pink lamps used to coo, "How interesting! How wonderful! Tell us mo-oor!" Thereupon he told all over again; and Gallihauk would fluctuate on the outer rim of the hearthrug afar off and murmur, "Dam fool!"

So in a very little time – for he drove through his work like a cyclone – his shilling's worth was born. A shilling's worth is, for reasons which do not matter, an excellent – indeed an indispensable – performance for a man who keeps three dress-suits and eighteen top-hats, and studies English society by the light of pink shaded lamps. It was called "Blind Kamartha," and of course Kamartha had her throat cut through two chapters; and there was a horse who got drowned in another forty pages, beginning with his birth and early parentage and his views on life and death as he went under; and the remaining pages led up and round to those two central facts. "Ha!" said Gallihauk unguardedly at a dinner, "he has enlarged his aperture. The wine is escaping." Another man "jackalled" this on the spot, and in the chorus of praise that went up round "Blind Kamartha" the still small voice of our paper was heard repeating it. The cruelty of the thing was that it was just short enough for the public to remember; and Mr. Etheredge met it out at dinner and was sympathized with about it, and would kick the cat all round his chambers afterwards. But the book sold in its thousands, and was stolen by the Americans, and re-written to suit political exigencies in that country. And that was glory; and Kilt, Milt and Roe knew how much they gained by it.

Then there were some more dinner parties and dances, and country houses and club dinners, and first nights and other steadying influences, and Mr. Etheredge under the discovery that if he epigrammed too fluently other gentlemen would steal his ideas and sell them. This led him often to refer to himself as a walking gold mine, and later to surround himself with chosen friends, chiefly female, who would respect his words. Thereafter another book was born: in which a woman was bowstringed, and an elephant was engulfed in a quicksand and so went round roaring to the tip end of his trunk; and that was the horse slightly swelled at the extremities, with attachments. By a small oversight, due to having half heard the tail-halves of two stories, he wrote as the elephants were the natural inhabitants of Turkey, and bowstringed h woman in the one place in Europe where the yataghan – his legitimate throat-cutting – would have been employed. A disgustingly literal man found that out, and recommended him in print to return to his horses and blunt knives. Kilt, Milt and Roe wrote that, though the book was selling, it seemed to them, without presuming to dictate to so well-known an author, that a more serious reputation was to be built up by more serious work.

Gallihauk said nothing, but that he had known four and twenty leaders of revolts in Faenza,[5] and the Russians on the other side of Europe began to harry the Jews; the newspapers were full if it, and the Mansion House opened a subscription. Then rose Mr. Etheredge and bought a Josephus, an S.P.C.K. Bible in speckled calf, a Cook's ticket, and a pair of blue goggles; for he saw his chance. He loathed to leave the pink lamps; but Art was Art, as he explained to some lady friends, and he was going to "take up the dear Jews" and saturate himself with local colour between Jerusalem and the Red Sea, particularly the Red Sea. Gallihauk grinned when he heard that. Etheredge arranged to write for some home papers and sent back amazing articles depicting himself in camp with the children of the desert, and hooking up Pharoah's chariot wheels with the kedge-anchors of British India steamers.

After six months there was produced at all the libraries his "Passed Over by Azrael." And it told how one of the first born of Egypt had escaped the night of death, and tied up in a baking-trough, had journeyed with his foster-mother and the flying Israelites. There was a moral in the tale. Unfortunately the Russians had left off killing and outraging the Jews, and were doing something else when it came out; but there was Josephus in it; there were Liberty portières and Ben-Hur dialogues and high-peaked saddles in it, and, most of all, there were horses – all the horses of Pharoah's host drowning together in the Red Sea. Etheredge made one big washing-day of the event. He choked his animals by squadrons and troops and regiments against most tempestuous backgrounds of sea and foam. So greatly and completely did he drown them that there was a distinct sense of reaction in the reader's mind when he turned his Israelites loose to cut the throats of the Jebusite and Hivite women, though that slaughter was even more complete than horse-killing. The two together, with all the properties thereunto ppertaining, were called a novel, and sold at the regulation tariffs.

Do not imagine that the British public would have wearied of him on his own merits. But a man elbowed his way through the crowd, bearing blood in a horse-bucket with wild oats atop. Slit throats were fair; but this was the genuine article. Etheredge's tents were on the Red Sea. Long before he returned his public were crowding with their forefeet in the food held out by the other man.

It is not good to surround yourself with adoring friends. They may love, but they cannot foresee, and the more they know the less will they tell. Etheredge returned hungrily to his pink lamps, and related imaginative stories of adventures under the stars; while Kilt, Milt and Roe squabbled with the libraries on points of business and batches of returned books. They were large batches; for the tide was running out, and spits of sand showed. Gallihauk took it upon himself to speak the very bitter truth early one morning, when he had thrust his way into Etheredge's room and found him undressing after a dance.

"The game is up," said Gallihauk, who never wasted his words except for so much a column. "The boom is finished. How can you get clear?"

These be no cheering words to hear in the dawn. Moreover, Gallihauk had not had his breakfast, and desired to finish that interview.

"Listen here. They are tired of you – you, and your throats and your drowned horses. The new man, the horse-bucket man – you can hear the public lapping it up if you stick your head out of window. On what I have left of a reputation – and I know books better than some men know stocks – you've come to the end of yourself. You're ridden out, written out, talked out, used up – as I was. A year's rest might give you fresh material t go on with, but I doubt it; and you couldn't afford to take it."

"By what right?. . ." began Etheredge; and his lips twitched, for he knew that if his pass-book spoke truth, and bankers seldom lie, he could afford himself no rest.

"By the right of a man who has passed through it all," said Gallihauk, drumming on a calf-bound copy of "Passed Over"; "only, thank God! I had a better education than yours to go on with after my collapse. What can you do? To-morrow you'll hear the whips crack. In three months your market value will be depreciated 50 per cent., and Kilt and Co. will be running the horse-bucket man. You'll have the profits on your sales as by contract, and I know what those sales will be. You haven't even had the strength to plagiarize from yourself. The people don't take the trouble to call you good, bad, or indifferent. They don't want you, that's all. What'll you do? A year hence you may earn three hundred a year if you work hard. How far will that carry you among the sets you frequent? You haven't the stamina, if you had the ability, for journalism, and you can't give up the rotten dinner party and the pet dog demoralization that you call studying society. I care less than a tinker's curse for you – I know the way you have been sharpening your wits on me at the De Tompkinses and Van Robinsons; but I . . . . have I spoken the truth?"

Gallihauk does not often take the trouble to speak the truth, his profession being literary: but when he does he enforces belief with every flap of his coat-tails, which are weighted with a pipe or tobacco pouch.

"I believe you have," said Etheredge, after a long pause; and no one should have known better than he.

Then Gallihauk developed surprising craft, unsuspected knowledge of society, and not a little tenderness, if all be true. He was at great pains to curse the British public, which always was, and until another public arises always will be, waste of breath; but he never allowed Etheredge to forget that he must either start an entirely new line and run the gauntlet of those who would drive him back to his horses, or die the death or . . . . That was where the craft began. It was connected with banking accounts.

Etheredge waited till Kilt, Milt, and Roe had written him a letter with some enclosures, and he had read a few things not in the letters. Then he also wrote a letter, but not to Kilt, Milt, and Roe; and four hours later took a cab across town, and after dinner returned to his own place with the smile of a newly-washed baby – half pleasure and half soap in the mouth.

"You see I was right," said Gallihauk, "there must be some who believe in you – even you. But be quick and hurry things forward, for you cannot afford to wait even through a six months' engagement." The fall of "Passed Over by Azrael" is written large in many papers, but now happily forgotten in even greater falls. The public clambered over the horse-bucket man till he fell, and another gave them honeysuckles and wood-anemones; and so forth and so forth. It all comes to the same in the waste paper basket, as the love letter said to the tailor's bill.

Four months after the wedding, when Etheredge had apparently settled the problem of living with a wife some years older than himself, who told every one about "the basest conspiracy that ever disgraced the history of journalism" (she wrote things occasionally), Gallihauk was to be found chaunting Gounod's "Funeral March of a Marionette" over a small volume of poetry – an inch and a half of type, three inches of margin, with a lily sprinkled vellum back – bearing the name of Mr. and Mrs. Etheredge.

That was the nearest approach to a review that Gallihauk ever gave it.

⁂

But let us suppose for a minute that there had been no wife available?

---

1 To Caroline Taylor, 2 November 1889 (*Letters*, I, 356).
2 Matthew Arnold, 'Stanzas in Memory of the Author of "Obermann"', lines 69–72.
3 Dickens, *The Old Curiosity Shop*, ch. 19.
4 In Dickens' *Great Expectations*, clerk to lawyer Jaggers.
5 Browning, 'A Soul's Tragedy', last line, a favourite of RK's. He quotes (or misquotes) it in letters of 14 September 1886 and 2–3 March 1909, and in 'In Reply to the Amateur', *CMG*, 24 February 1887, as well as here.

Gallihauk's Pup

Published: *St James's Gazette*, 30 November 1889.

Attribution: The story is referred to as by RK in a letter from Harold Macmillan, the publisher, to A. S. Watt, RK's agent, 13 August 1929, and by Watt to Mrs Kipling in a letter of 17 September 1929 (Kipling Papers, 22/4). It is included in a list of RK's works made for Scribner's and annotated by Mrs Kipling (British Library, Add. MS 54940). Since Gallihauk had been invented by RK in 'The Comet of a Season' in the *St James's Gazette* of 21 November, only nine days before this second appearance of Gallihauk, no one else could have written the story. It is remarkable that RK apparently acknowledged authorship of this story yet denied authorship of the closely related 'Comet of a Season'.

Text: *St James's Gazette*.

Note: Reprinted in the Martindell–Ballard pamphlets and in Harbord, v, 2408–12.

> Keen was his woe; but keener far to feel
> He nursed the pinion that compelled the steel.[1]

He was occasionally called Ishmael, but more often referred to as above, his real name being Hognaston, which is just as bad and does not make a particle of difference.

Stewart-Atherley, who writes for the *Eclectic Emporium* and is arrayed in the borrowed fragments of a new creed every month, lisps that it was entirely Gallihauk's fault for taking an interest in a New Man. But Atherley would not stretch a hand to save living soul or body if he had to rise from his armchair to do it.

Gallihauk was greatly to be excused. He was a lonely soul, austere, and without any attachments, and chiefly at war with all his acquaintances. No one would have credited his taking up a New Man. No one more fiercely attacked the New men as they came up and went into the Outer Darkness where there is job-work and decay of power. It was a proverb in the Deucalion Club that whoso passed with a decent

̲ree of success the double-shotted guns of Gallihauk would go far. ̲is theory was that most new writers were possessed not with fancy but flux: and he was used to elaborate the theory offensively and medically in his own chair at the Deucalion. Hence the large surprise when Stewart-Atherley, who always knows things twenty minutes before he should, announced that Gallihauk had discovered a New Man eating the bindings off the historical sections in the British Museum Library, had fed him with raw meat behind a door, and would presently introduce him to the Deucalion. Marple – who believes in the complete selfishness of the human race, and consequently writes about its perfectibility and the ringing grooves of change – denied that Gallihauk would ever concern himself over any human being not 120 years dead. But it befell as Atherley had said; and after a season, in which the Deucalion heard much of writers and rumours of writers, Gallihauk surged down the smoking-room with what, for the sake of brevity, must be called his New Man. Atherley promptly christened it "The underhung Aberdonian" (it was of northern extraction and rattled its *r*'s like the cog-wheels of a coffee-mill); and other men, moved by their own unholy fancies, called it other names and less quotable. It was not lovely, and seemed but newly introduced to a dress coat and a white tie. Gallihauk gave all the world to understand that it was his trove and protégé, and drove Steinwürth of the *Gasometer* into a corner for half an hour while he rehearsed its perfections. "He's rough, I admit that," said Gallihauk (and when Gallihauk admits that a man is rough the subject is generally more than rugged); "but it is the roughness of the diamond in the matrix."

"Amen" said Steinwürth, "but why not leave it there? You can buy three-and-sixpenny Brazilian articles in the Lowther Arcade." Gallihauk said that that had nothing whatever to do with the case; and Steinwürth could not get away in time for his whist. Wherefore he detested Gallihauk and the New Man, henceforward to be called the Pup.

There was an earnestness about that animal which after dinner meant nothing less than indigestion – a grim and Carlylese earnestness expressing itself in copybook headings and vehement twistings of the nose. The last two inches of the Pup's nose were hinged and prehensile. They used to frighten Stewart-Atherley into blinking stupor. No man knew whence the Pup had sprung – whether from nowhere in

particular or a county paper. He was the property of Gallilhauk, the aus
tere man, and Stewart-Atherley's version of the discovery might have
been correct after all. Gallihauk never told. He introduced the Pup as
a shining and significant fact, as a sort of undeveloped Titan destined
to upheave the Deucalion and the rest of the earth as understanded by
the Deucalion, which is to say the four mile cab radius. Gallihauk, who
never believed in three pens this side of Doctor Johnson, who swore by
and at and with Smollett, who considered Prior a much misunderstood
man, and who knew Swift's soul as the Dean himself never knew it,
pinned his newly found faith upon his New Man – his own discovery.
"And hereby," said Stewart-Atherley, "you may see how much superior
is a man to a woman. Gallihauk has yet to learn how much a man
differs from a woman." Stewart-Atherley's pet vice is unsubstantial
epigram.

Gallihauk exerted himself immensely to find work for the Pup, who
really possessed the rudiments of a style and the beginnings of power.
He had been carefully educated, and had acquired at some mysterious university a degree. Yet his appearance was of one who had never
seen even the roofs of Burlington House, and his hands were rough as
with the handling of agricultural implements. Gallihauk would refer
to Burns when men referred to these blemishes; but the Pup was not
Burns. Gallihauk did his best to convert him into a sort of "Kinmont
Willie"[2] of the reviews and the lighter walks of literature, where all the
paths carry labels, saying "Please keep off the grass," and it is rigorously
defended to trample on the flowers of fancy. It is said that Gallihauk
and the Pup would together sharpen their pens on their lonely hearth-
stone and sing wild war-songs of the North for a week at a time, and
then descend upon a herd of new books and disembowel them. That
was when the Pup "devilled" for Gallihauk and was sitting at his feet
learning grim wisdom. In the evening he would come to the Deucalion;
and you could hear his voice all down the corridors, croaking to some
amazed senior. "That's all verra well; but it's not A-r-r-r-t!" And when
men, so to speak, kicked off the boots of toil and put on the embroidered slippers of fancy and the dressing-gown of *abandon* and talked
sheer nonsense, as men must for the good of the soul, the Pup would
rush out growling from under a billiard-table and bristlingly argue
with them. He could never talk without arguing, and his red-headed

arnestness irritated. Nor did he much care whom he corrected; and he had a fascinating custom of saying "Hoo!" just like an angry owl, when he differed from but despised his opponents.

Gallihauk saw no harm in these eccentricities – not even when Stewart-Atherley said "I wish to goodness you'd take your Pup out of this place and tie him up. He bites." The man honestly seemed to love the Pup and be proud of him, and overlook in his work absences of taste and temper that in another's he would have double-thonged. He should have married and had a son of his own instead of adopting literary infants late in life. He smiled at the Pup's broad-shouldered brutality and want of proportion, and very weakly trumpeted work that were better left to find its way on its own merits. He introduced the Pup to valuable commanders, who enlisted him and gave him guns and swords far too deadly for one so intemperate and earnest. In private he used to lecture the Pup, and teach him his own philosophy, which was summarized from another writer:– "Never go back, never think twice. Be alone." So the Pup throve and grew fat, and learned to scrub his nails before dinner, and was always the terror of the Deucalion on account of his disputatiousness.

It happened upon an occasion – an ordinary every-day occasion – that half a dozen men were talking nonsense, the ball flying from hand to hand round the fire, and each man developing theories wilder than the last. Tintwhistle had taken upon himself to prove the precise amount of Carlyle's teaching which was directly traceable to the rooster which crowed and disturbed him, or the baker's cart that called inopportunely. "Here," said Tintwhistle, quoting something from "Sartor Resartus", "an Eternal Verity of a costermonger came by. Here you trace the pessimistic influence of a Pickford van rumbling in the street. And here" . . . The Pup arrived, his bristles aloft on his back; for if you touched Carlyle you profaned one of his high gods. But even he might have seen that he interrupted a game of pure skittles. He dashed in armed at all points – offensive, raucous, irrepressible, and earnest. Tintwhistle tried elaborate sarcasm, and suggested the writing out of his views. Then the voice of Gallihauk, always somewhere near the Pup, fell like a rough-cut log across foaming water.

"Don't you be so dee clever! You're making yourself a nuisance over there."

The Pup flushed scarlet. To be lectured in private is one thing, to be checked across the manful width of a club-room is otherwise. Tintwhistle declared that that was the Psychological Moment. The Pup smiled furiously and with ostentation; and later, in the cloak-room, Gallihauk was overheard abasing himself before this Border Ruffian, whose raw Scotch pride was in revolt. "*I* should have kicked him," said Stewart-Atherley – "kicked him first, and reviewed him afterwards." Gallilhauk did not kick. He honestly loved the Pup, and believed in his future, and – this is quite true – he apologized when the Pup talked wild nonsense about having been insulted before he flung out of the door and – into the arms of Leftwhich. May that man die on a crowded pavement from a cab accident with a costermonger's heel in his left eye, and the only woman he ever loved audibly asking his rival "Who is that drunken person?" Knowing that Gallihauk loathed Leftwhich, the abandoned Pup quitted the club with him while Gallihauk was fumbling for his stick all alone in the cloakroom. Leftwhich does not talk about Psychological Moments; but he knows when he meets them, and he is also in charge of the *Record of Lost Endeavour*, where gentlemen and ladies – who, never having had any of their own, naturally do not believe in success – explain monthly why Shakespeare is over-rated, or in what respects they could improve on Homer, and other more nearly living folk. Only the smallness of the motive could have justified the scale of the revenge. Because he owed his little name, his every step, and (if report be true) several meals to Gallihauk – because he had been brought forward, taught, and cherished by that much misguided man – the Pup sought satisfaction from the ink-pot. As Stewart-Atherley said, "even a woman would not have done it." Very naturally Leftwhich secured the Pup for the *Record*, and thereby won a better writer than many; and in process of time – Gallihauk still roaming disconsolate through the Deucalion, and seeking his lost child – there appeared in the *Record's* "Touches in Aquafortis," a brutal, bitter sketch of Gallihauk, engendered in rebellion, developed in flippant sin, and bitten in with the malice of the intimate inferior – the valet or the pot-boy. That was the Pup's satisfaction – tasteless, tactless, butcherly, and incomplete even in its completeness. It was bad with the badness of baseness, and it grieved Gallihauk for many reasons. When Stewart-Atherley, forgotten of man and God, once called him "the tattered Thug of the more june jingles of journalism" Gallihauk laughed and said that Atherley did not understand alliteration. But the Pup's attack was another affair entirely, and I believe he was moved more by sorrow for the boy than any personal consideration. All the faults out of which he had carefully trained him reappeared in that production, the more luxuriant for having been pruned so long. The want of balance, the slovenly county-journal diction and the slack-set sentences tailing into "and whiches" were all there, with the close personal knowledge of Gallihauk's failings and peculiarities that the Pup had so recklessly employed. Gallihauk mourned over the workman more than the work; though the Pup had managed, not unskilfully, to convey the impression that Gallihauk was a Bottle-nosed Shark. Gallilhauk was sensitive about his nose, which is a fine, large, and, above all, erudite feature – a thing that suggests whole libraries in half-calf with yellow busts atop and ragged volumes of the Fathers in the lower shelves. The Pup sneered at that nose.

No man in the Deucalion said anything to Gallihauk till he broached the subject one day of his own accord.

"Have – have any'f you seen that – that thing in the *Record* – 'bout me?"

"Yes," said one man, while the rest looked every other way at once. They were all sorry for Gallihauk.

"It's no sort of Literature," he said, "but I suppose it's every sort of human nature."

Then he went out of the club looking very straight in front of him, while Stewart-Atherley quoted the immensely original lines at the beginning of this sketch.

Infamous, infamous Pup!

But the judgement of Heaven overtook him later; and to-day he writes extended leading articles in Leftwhich's *Record* proving that Mr. Gladstone is the only authority upon everything in the world.

---

[1] Byron, 'English Bards and Scotch Reviewers', lines 839–40: 'Keen were his pangs, but keener far to feel / He nursed the pinion which impell'd the steel'.

[2] Hero of a ballad in Scott's *Ministrelsy of the Scottish Border*, 1802–3.

The Inauthorated Corpses

᠅

Published: *The Author*, 15 July 1890, pp. 73–4, anonymously.

Attribution: A signed MS of the piece is at Dalhousie University.

Text: *The Author.*

Notes: The title plays on that of the Incorporated Society of Authors, of which RK was a member. British authors had no copyright protection in the United States until the American International Copyright Act went into force on 1 July 1891. Before that date piracy was unrestrained, and the authors concerned rightfully felt themselves to be the victims of robbery. The Society of Authors, founded in 1884 by Sir Walter Besant, was dedicated to changing this situation.

RK was among the loudest among those who cried out for justice: see, for example, the curse he pronounced upon the Americans when he discovered, in Japan, a pirated American edition of *Plain Tales from the Hills* (in the original letter xx of the 'From Sea to Sea' letters as they appeared in the *Pioneer*, where the pirated book is said to have been published by the 'Seaside Library'; the curse is omitted in the revised version of 1900 but may be found in Harbord, II, 827–8). On American piracy, see also the poem called 'The Rhyme of the Three Captains' (*Barrack-Room Ballads*).

'The Inauthorated Corpses' has been reprinted in Harbord, v, 2470–2, with some small variations from the text in *The Author*.

᠅

Two Congresses, fifteen Legislatures, one House of Commons, and several hundred newspapers had sat upon the question of International Copyright for years; and nothing beyond pirated editions were ever hatched of it. As the honourable member for Lower Idaho pointed out in Congress:– "If we can hike down the fruit of centuries from the moss-gnarled trunks of an effete civilization over the sea, why in Paradise should we pay a dollar for a book when we can hook it for a dime? Let the good work go on." In England every vestryman knew that there were no votes to be obtained from authors, and no one could quite understand what it was that the gang wanted, or why they should actually own what they had "made out of their heads, y'know," and the situation

339

crystallized itself into a round game of grab. The American publishers began by giving an English author ten pounds for advance-sheets of a book which they brought out for fifty cents. Then the Sad Sea Wave Library¹ would undercut the first firm, and produce a thirty cent edition; and last of all the "Bowery Bloodsucker Serials" would set a muzzy German to abridge and adapt the book and would issue the mutilated fragments for a dime or ten cents. When a man had taken some trouble over his book and put perhaps one or two ideas into it, and was feeling happy, his friends would post him American variorum editions of that book to make him happier. Later on the American publisher discovered that it was not worth while to pay the author for advance-sheets at all. The syndicates established an agency for appropriation, and their agents moved among the English printing-houses and turned the handle of a printing-press four or five times more than was necessary, and went away with the advance-sheets. That was called Enterprise, and it made both the British and American reading public laugh.

Then the authors borrowed some writing-paper and wrote a petition to Parliament asking that the fight be made if not a fair, at least a free one. They respectfully prayed that all the laws were on one side, but, they said, if the matter of copyrights were "left to be fought out by such instruments as your petitioners' resources allow they would ever pray, &c.." Parliament then being extremely busy with a new scheme for Local Self-Government in Cornwall (which county had discovered that it was Phœnician and not British) said, "Let it be law as it is desired," and it was law.

Three days after it came into effect, the London representative of the great "publishing" firm of Fibbs and Glew met an author-man by appointment in the former's rooms.

"How is the *Legend of the Spotted Death* getting on?" said the representative, with a grin.

"Gone to press," said the author. "What are you going to do about it?"

"Nothing much. One of our men photoed the MS page by page in the office, with a button-hole camera. I've mailed the enlarged films to America, and I guess we've got the drop on your English firm this time."

"But I'm going to knock the thing about in proof a good deal," said the author. "There's more bad work in the last chapter than I care to think of."

"Can't help that," said the representative. "We *must* be first in the market if you wrote a revised edition of the alphabet with twenty-six misprints. However, we've dealt with you from way back. Here's a tenner. Take it or leave it."

He turned to his desk to get the money. When he faced round he was looking directly down the barrel of a 440 Derringer. His hands stiffened above his head, the bank note in the right fist.

"Who has the drop now?" said the author. "It's a fair fight at last – with such resources as we can command. Keep your hands up, please."

"Don't be an ass," said the representative. "This isn't a theatre."

"Quite right. It's a court of law. Understand, I'm not in the least angry with you. You had a perfect right to steal my work, which is about all the property I have or ever shall have. You were entitled to insult me with the sort of 'tip' his uncle gives to a boy going to Eton, as well as to make hay of my sentences to suit your convenience. There was no law, and so you reverted to the primitive man. Quite right Now you're going to learn the law just as a horse-thief in Idaho learns it – through fear of death and physical pain." He took the bank note from the uplifted hand. "Lie down on the hearth-rug with your hands behind you. I'm going to take all the money I can find in the office. Drop!"

The representative obeyed, and the author made investigations which repaid him for two years' sales of unauthorized editions.

"Now it's not safe," he concluded, "to leave you with a fighting hand. I should be within my right if I killed you as your countrymen kill horse-thieves. And let us be moral. *Why* do they kill horse-thieves?"

"Because," said the representative, his face on the hearth-rug, "the assumption is that when you steal a horse you dismount a man, and the man may die in the wilderness."

"Exactly. How do you know where I wish to ride on these my books, and why do you try to dismount me before I dismount myself?"

"There was no law," said the representative.

"The law has come now. It's primitive for the nineteenth century, but I think it will work Hold your right hand over the fender-rim; I don't want to spoil your carpet. There! Through the right wrist. That will cripple you for life. If you can shoot me with your left next time we meet, well and good. Then you can go on stealing without fear. Let me tie your hand up. We must all learn the Law with pain and sorrow. Good bye!"

The author departed while the representative lay fainting with his head in the fender. He came of a nation eminently just at heart, so he brought neither a civil nor a criminal suit against the author, but went to the very best doctor and the best gunmaker in all London and made arrangements to bring out an edition as soon as possible of that author – in boards – limited to one copy.

---

[1] See the reference to the 'Seaside Library' in the headnote. That is what RK calls it in the 'From Sea to Sea' letter referred to, but no firm has been identified under that name.

One Lady at Wairakei

Published: *Sunday Supplement, New Zealand Herald,* 30 January 1892.

Attribution: Signed by RK.

Text: *One Lady at Wairakei,* ed. Harry Ricketts, [Wellington, NZ, 1983].

Notes: The story develops a favourite theme of RK's, how the different peoples of the Empire will produce distinctive literatures drawn from their new surroundings and conditions. The story after its original publication was reprinted in various New Zealand papers at the time. Reprinted, *Pall Mall Budget,* 24 March 1892; *New Zealand Herald,* 20 January 1936. Separate publication, edited by Harry Ricketts, Wellington, NZ, 1983.

The extraordinary thing about this story is its absolute truth.

All tourists who scamper through New Zealand have in their tours visited the geysers at Wairakei, but none of them have seen there what I have seen. It came about with perfect naturalness. I had wondered from one pool to another, from geyser to mud spout, mud spout to goblin bath, and goblin bath to fairy terrace, till I came to a still pool, where a wild duck sat bobbing on the warm green water, undisturbed by all the noises of the wonderful gorge. A steam jet hidden in the brushwood sighed and was silent, a tiny geyser gobbled, and a big one answered it with snorts. I thrust my stick into the soft ground, and something below hissed, thrusting out a tongue of white steam. A wind moved through the scrub, and all the noises were hushed for an instant. So far there had been nothing uncommon – except geysers and blow-holes – to catch the eye. Therefore I was the more astonished when from the depths of the pool, and so quietly that even the wild duck was not scared there rose up the head and shoulders of a woman. At first I imagined that I had better get away. But, since I had seen the face, I did not move. The woman flung back her long hair, and said, laughing:

"Well?"

"I beg your pardon," I stammered. "But I didn't know – I didn't – I mean – "

"Do you mean to say that you don't know *me?*" she said. "To be sure in your profession I'm more talked about than seen."

"To whom have I the pleasure of speaking?" I said desperately – for it is not seemly to stand on a bank and talk to a woman who is swimming in the water. Besides, I felt sure that she was laughing at me.

"They call me all sorts of things," was the reply. "but my real name is Truth. Haven't you heard that I live in a well? This is it. It communicates directly with the other side of the world, but I generally come here for peace and quiet on a Sunday. I have some friends here." She nodded casually up the gorge, and I heard the geysers bellow.

Natural politeness and a strong desire to see whether she was not a mermaid led me to put the next question. It came rather clumsily.

"Aren't you going to get out?" I asked.

"I can't. You'd die if I did because I'm the Truth, the Whole Truth, and Nothing but the Truth. No man can see me and live." She swam a few strokes towards the bank, and rested while the steam drifted in clouds across the pond. I sat down and stared again.

"*Some* people," said Truth, "would say they were pleased to meet me."

"I'm not," I replied. "You see, or rather I see, in the first place, that you are too unconventional, and in the second place I never believed in you – much." This was not in th eleast what I meant to say, but the words came of themselves. Truth laughed.

"Shall I go away?" she said.

"This pool is private property. I've paid to see it. You haven't. What do you think y ourself?"

"From your point of view you're quite right, but – you wouldn't care to see a fresh geyser break out just under your feet, would you? or a mud volcanoe? or a rift in the earth?" My friends would be happy to oblige me. Shall I ask them?"

"Truth," I said, jumping up, for the ground was shaking like a boiler plate; "you know as well as I do that you're making me say unpleasant things, and now you propose to boil me alive for saying them. You're illogical, because you're a woman, and I'm going back to the hotel."

"Wait a minute," said Truth, laughing. "I want to ask you a question and then I won't be rude any more. How do you like New Zea—?"

"Don't!" I shouted. "*Please* don't! Let me put the answer on paper, at least."

"Tell me now," said Truth, "or i'll splash hot water at you. Tell me the truth."

"Promise me you'll tell me anything I want to know afterwards?" I said, for I felt the answer coming, and it was not a polite answer.

"I promise," she said, and heard my remarks out to the end.

"H'm!" she said, gravely. "One big encumbered estate, is it? Folly to play at party government when the whole population is less than half the German army? All in the hands of the banks, is it? Forty thousand horse-power to drive a hundred-ton yacht, and the country not scratched? Upon my word, you'll get yourself dearly beloved if those are your sentiments, and you say them aloud."

"Well, it is absurd, isn't it, if you can run the place with three men and a boy, to start Upper Houses and Lower Houses, and pay a few hundred men to help spend borrowed money?" I persisted. I knew that I had gone too far to explain.

"I admit nothing. I'm the Truth," she said, "and I merely wished to hear what you considered the truth. It's your turn to ask questions now. I'll give you five minutes to think of them." "Tell me the truth, the whole truth, and nothing but the truth, about New Zealand," I said promptly.

"Banks – railways – exports – harbour boads, and so forth – eh?" She smiled wickedly. You will find all that in books."

"No. I want to know how the people live, and what they think, and how they die; and what makes them love and fight and trade in the particular manner in which they fight and love and trade. That isn't in the books."

"No – not yet," said Truth thoughtfully, drawing her pink fingers to and fro through the water. "It will come some day."

"That's just what I want to know. When is it coming?"

"What?"

"The story of the lives of the people here. I want to read it."

"Perhaps they haven't any lives. You said they were all in the hands of the banks. How can you expect an encumbered estate, mortgaged to the hilt, to have a life of its own?"

"Truth, you're prevaricating. You know I didn't mean that. Banks have nothing to do with the inside lives of peoples. I have not the key to the stories myself, but they are here in the country somewhere – thousands of them. When are they going to be written, Truth, and how are they going to be written, and who is going to write them?"

"My young men and my young women. All in good time. You can't fell timber with one hand and write a tale with the other. But they'll come, and when they come –"

"Yes."

"The world will listen to them. Do you remember coming through some dense bush fifty miles down the road? Well, half a mile from the road, down in a gully among the tree ferns, there lies the body of a man under the butt of a great pine tree. He loved a woman at a sheep station – one of the women who serve up the "colonial goose" to the tourist when he stops at the wooden shanties with the chemists' presentation almanacks on the walls – a red-faced raddled woman who talks about 'ke-ows,' and 'bye-bies.' He was one of three lovers!"

"Whew!" I said. "That sounds like an old story."

"Yes, it *is* an old story – otherwise it wouldn't be new. And that woman in her sloppy, slatternly house among the fern-hills where the sheep live, played with those three lovers as a Duchess might have done; and the drovers and the sheep-men came down the road and said most awful things. She took her sentiment and her heroics out of the bound volumes of the Family Herald and Bow Bells – you've seen the tattered copies in the wooden houses on the tables where the painted kerosene lamp stands, haven't you? But her iniquity was all her own. Two of her lovers were just sheep-men, but the third was a remittance-man, if you know what that is, and he had been a gentleman in England who thought a good deal of himself."

"And she killed him?"

"No, he killed himself. At least, after some things had happened, he went out into the bush and carefully backscarfed a big tree so that it would fall in one particular direction, and stood there when it fell. Now he will become a rata-vine. Remember, he had loved her for three years and put up with everything at her chapped hands."

"So she *did* kill him."

"That comes of knowing too much. He killed himself after a good think, wholly and solely on account of a girl in England whom he had no chance whatever of winning. I think that he realized that competing with sheep-men for stolen kisses behind corrugated iron sheds was not

nice; and that showed him several other things. So he died, and the ⌐
band, of course, had to get a new hand for the shearing. But *she* believ
that she killed him and – she is rather proud of it.:

"Truth, who is going to tell that story?"

"I don't qute know. Perhaps one of her children, or grandchildren, as
soon as the spirit of the fern-hills – they are very lovely, you know – and
the snow mountains has entered into his blood. Yes, it shall be one of
her children (that is to say, one of *his* children) and he shall lie under
wool drays in summer, and sleep with his back on a salt-bag, and his
heels on a bag of harness, and be frozen and sun-tanned, and ride long
rides at night, fording rivers to make love to big, round-faced girls, till
he finds that story. Then he will tell it and a hundred thousand things
with it, and the world will say, 'This is the truth, because it is written
so.'"

"And after?"

"Afterwards he may try to tell other stories as good as the first. If
he tries he'll fail, but there are thousands more. Hark! Do you hear
nothing?"

Under my very feet there was the dull thud as of a steam-hammer in
a mine – a thud that rippled the still waters of the pool and struck the
geysers dumb.

"What's that?" I asked, wondering and afraid.

"It's down in the guide-books as a Natural Phenomenon. But you
have heard of the Roaring Loom of Time, haven't you? That's the shut-
tle clicking through the web, and you know who the Weavers are?"

I bowed my head and was silent, having no wish to meet the Fates
yet.

"They are busy today," Truth continued. "It is no easy work to weave
the souls of men into their surroundings. So far, they have done little.
The men don't belong to the mountains and the plains and the swamps
and the snow passes and the fiords and the thick fat grazing land – and
the women, of course, poor dears, they belong to the men. But in time
the men will be of the land, and write of the land and the life of the
land as they have seen it and as they know it. Then the people will know
themselves, and wonder at their own lives. There is a girl-baby nearly
a thousand miles away from here. Her father found a pass through the
Southern Alps, and good grazing ground the other side. So he stole the

347

ple's sheep, drove them through that pass, and was well to do till
ople found him out and he disappeared. That girl has lived among the
mountains and the snow rivers all her days. She knows how the water
comes down cold as ice, and chokes men and horses, and tosses them out
on the shingle a dozen miles down stream. Some day, I think, she will
sing up there among the mountains, and half the world will listen. After
her will come others – women – and they will tell how women love men
in this country, and all the women all over the world will listen to *that*."

:Won't that be rather an old story?" I demanded.

"Of course it will (Eve loved Adam very much, I remember), but you
forget what the hills and the clouds and the winds and the rain and the
sun can do. Remember how nearly some parts of this land run into the
tropics, and wait till you hear them sing."

I remembered at once and sat corrected.

"But won't they imitate Shelley and Tennyson and Mrs Browning?"

"At first, naturally. When they belong to their own country you will
hear what you will hear."

"And what shall I hear?"

Truth was silent for a while, and then raising one shapely arm from
the water, said softly – "Listen now! Listen and see!" The thud of the
loom beneath me ceased, and the dead air became full of voices, thick-
ened into shadows that took form and became men and women, before
my amazed eyes.

A man with a shaggy red beard and deep sunk eyes strode forward
scowling and with savage gestures and a hundred hurrying colonial
oaths, told a tale of riotous living, risk of life, sorrow, despair, and death.
"I have suffered this, and I have suffered that, and my tale is true,"
he cried. A women cumbered with many children but in whose face
there were few wrinkles followed, and – "Our lives were very quiet in
Christchurch," she said, "as quiet as the river, and – I thought perhaps
that if I wrote just our little lives – for the children, you understand . . .
But, oh!" – she clutched my arm nervously – "it – it has just been the
saving of our house."

Truth laughed tenderly as the woman passed on, gathering her children round her.

"She will be taught through Poverty," said Truth, "but thousands of
mothers will laugh and cry over her tale."

The men came next, assured and over-confident some, crippled and doubting others, but each with his tale to tell of the land he knew, the loves he had loved, and the life that lay about him. There were tales of the building of new cities, desperate intrigue for diversions of the local railroad; of railway frauds, local magnate pitted against local magnate, both fighting furiously, first for their own pockets, and next for the interests of their towns; tales of gumdigging under the dusty manuka scrub, and dreams of lost loves and lost hopes in the dead-houses of the country pubs; stories of the breaking of new lands, where the wisdom of men said that there was not food for a rat; of Toil that began before dawn and lasted far into the starlight, when men, women, and children worked together for the sake of their home, amid the scarred and blackened stumps,; stories of unclean politics, swayed by longshore loafers drowzing at wharf-ends, and, in an almost virgin land, clamouring for the aid of a spineless Government; of money paid to three or four hundred of these who dared not work, and for each payment of a thousand pounds, twenty times that much capital scared from a land that, on its own confession, was as hopeless as an eight-hundred-year-old-island. Lastly, a change sudden and surprising, in the midst of this keen-voiced strife. I heard tales of gentle lives, as sheltered in the midst of the turmoil as the ferns in the gorge – lives of ease, elegance, and utter peace, begun under the trailing willows, where the little children go to school, two and three together, astride of the old bare-backed horse, and ended in some well-kept cemetery, looking seaward to America. They were old tales, but upon each lay the stamp, inimitable and indescribable, of a new land and of fresh minds turning the thought, old as Adam, to lights as new as the latest road across the mountains. And, Heavens! how they gambled and swore and drank in the pauses between the crises, thinking no shame of themselves, having no fear, and reverence only for that which was indubitably and provedly stronger than themselves. But there were liars, too, among the crowd, smooth-faced men who shaped their work as they conceived that other folk was best approve, and a few of those unhappy souls whose fate it is to pile up wealth of fact and fiction that stronger people may raid into it at will. I caught one wail of a weak-lipped shadow – "But I – but I wrote all this before, and another has merely re-written my work, and *he* gets the credit. It was I – it was I!"

"He will suffer," said Truth. "With his temperament he will probably die, but it is necessary. Hark to the women now. They tell the old story well."

I listened as the shades went by – of girls too early dead – sterile blossoms whose only fruit was a song, of hard-featured Scotchwomen preaching wittily and wisely with illustrations drawn from the rainy, wind-swept South, the fear of the Lord that goes to the making of home; of mothers driven by bitter grief and loss to soothe the grief of others, marvelling in their simplicity that they could so soothe; and of maidens who had never known love, and therefore told his power and his beauty till heartstrings quivered twelve thousand miles away. Since they were women they sang chiefly of the things about their homesteads, the orange-ribbed black velvet of the burnt fern-hills, the windy plains overlooked by the mountains whose scaurs are the faces of dead kings, the jade-green rivers with the only swirls in them that run through the bush and take away the lives of little children playing at the back of the house, the long breathless days when the iron roof works uneasily over the new wood framing, expanding till noon and contracting till night, when you hear the buzzing of the flies about the face of the sick one under the roof, and outside the rush of the wild horses, their twilled manes flying free over the shoulder point, with the crackling, dried swamp-bed as it peels in the sun-haze. There was always a man in their songs – a man who went away and never came back, a face seen on horseback for a day and lost for evermore, or some treachery of a man with only the black stumps for witness to the sin, or a drowned man brought up from the river-bed at night through the grass that he had planted only that spring – only that spring.

The shades passed, and the click and thud of the unseen loom recommenced.

"Well," said Truth, "you have seen?"

"It is very well," I answered. ""

"Will it be in my time?" I asked eagerly. I wanted to hear some of the tales again.

"I cannot say. Perhaps – some of it – if you live long enough. Be content to know that it is coming."

"In this country alone, Truth?"

"In every country that has not spoken as yet, and as surely as sunlight follows morning. You have seen the beginnings of it. Have faith. There is such a little time to wait."

Once more Truth was forgetting the limitations of man's life, and I did not care to remind her. I was thinking of the future, and the voices of all those shadows who had told me their tales. The more I meditated, the more magnificent did the prospect appear.

"What are you thinking of?" said Truth. "The banks and the loans again?"

"No. I'm thinking," I responded loftily, for Truth was only a woman, and could not be expected to understand these things, "of the Future of Colonial Literature!"

"What?" said Truth, with a touch of scorn in her voice.

I repeated the words, emphasizing the capitals.

"Oh, hear him!" she cried, lifting up her face to the fern-wreathed rocks around. "One short-lived son of Adam, who may die to-morrow, splitting his tiny world into classes, and labelling them like dead butterflies. What do you mean" – she looked me in the fact – "by Colonial Literature?"

"Oh – er – stuff written in the colonies, and all that sort of thing, y'know." I couldn't understand why Truth was so angry. The loom thundered under my feet till the sand by the pool shook.

"Isn't the stuff, as you call it, written by men and women? Do the Weavers down below there at the loom make anything else but men and women? And until you step off this world can you expect anything more than stories of the lives of men and women written by men and women" What manner of monsters live in your part of the world," she concluded, "that you speak so blindly?"

"Fools," I said, penitently. "Just fools, Truth. I'm one of 'em, and you're right. It's only men and women that we have to think of all the world over. I said [But,]" I added, remembering another country across rhe seas, "these people will be quite as foolish as myself when their time comes, won't they?"

"I'm afraid so," said Truth, with a smile, "they will only be men and women."

"Ah!" I said triumphantly, "they will talk rubbish about a Distinctively Colonial Literature, a Freer Air, Larger Horizons, and so forth They'll vex 'emselves with unholy comparisons between their work and other people's work. They'll flatter each other and write of the Oamaru Shakespeare and the Timaru Tennyson and the Dunedin Dryden, and the Thursday Island Thackeray, won't they?"

"They will," said Truth. "(When did you leave America, by the way?) Some of the people here will do all those things, and more also. What else can you expect? They are only men and women, but those who make the noise will not be the people who tell the stories."

"Thanks. That's all I wanted to know. The banks can look after themselves. You are sure that the tales will come?"

"I have said so, and you have heard. Good-bye!"

Truth nodded and disappeared under the water. I watched the ripples stupidly, and not till they died away did I remember that I had a hundred questions to ask. Only the wild duck at the far end of the pool did not look as if it could answer them.

That same afternoon, riding in the buggy with Sam the Maori, across a new land teeming with new stories to which, alas, I had neither clue nor key, it occurred to me that I had largely discounted the future. But when I came to the sea coast and found a ten-thousand-soul town up to its tree-ferns in debt for a quarter-million pound harbour, the sand faithfully following each pile of the futile break water, and a sixty-thousand-soul town with municipal offices that might have served Manchester or Liverpool, I perceived that I was in good company.

You see, New Zealand is bound to pay her unwritten debt. Truth said so, and I have seen the assets. They are sufficient securities.

The other things are not of the slightest importance.

The Princess in the Pickle-Bottle

※

Published: *The Princess in the Pickle Bottle*, [n.p., n.d., New York City, 2006].

Attribution: MS signed 'Rudyard Kipling'.

Text: Published edition.

Notes: This previously unpublished story was published in an edition limited to 100 copies by David Alan Richards, the then owner of the manuscript, on 16 December 2006. It is an earlier version of the story 'The Potted Princess', published in *Saint Nicholas*, January 1893, but not collected by RK until the Sussex Edition. The MS is an undated letter to Serena Marshall, daughter of Henry Rogers Marshall, the architect of 'Naulakha', RK's house in Vermont. It was written, according to Richards, in the 'autumn of 1892' (*Bibliography*, p. 352).

A reduced facsimile of the MS was published in the 'Books' section of the London *Daily Telegraph*, 9 July 2005.

※

I

Once upon a time there was a Princess who lived in a Pickle-Bottle because fairy-land was full. Now there was only one way to get out of that Bottle and the King who was the father of that Princess said that any one who rescued the Princess should first be compelled to marry her and secondly to govern half a Kingdom. As the Princess was very beautiful and the Kingdom was very large, 10,764,302 Princes, all of Unblemished Reputation tried to open the Pickle Bottle. 8,763, 824 Princes consulted Court Magicians, Astrologers and Old Men whom they met in the Woods. 264, 230 Princes took the advice of Fairy Godmothers, White Witches, Magic Foxes, Enchanted Horses and Faithful Servants.

Consequently they killed

10765 Red Dragons all supposed to guard the Pickle-Bottle.

45689 Trolls   }

1765 Dwergs   } all supposed to guard the Pickle-Bottle

3764 Lame Dwarfs   }

189 One eyed Giants   }

And they said 846,729 Infallible Charms and Incantations any one of which was warranted to split Mountains of Glass and open the most Secret Treasures in all the World.

But the Pickle-Bottle would not open and they all went away very sorrowfully taking the heads of the Blue Dragons, and the Trolls and the Dwergs, and the Lame Dwarfs and the One- Eyed Giants along with them and looking back over their shoulders at the Princess in the Pickle-Bottle.

II

But there came along just One Prince and he was so poor that he could never afford to keep a Court Magician and his only Faithful Servants were his Two Hands. He walked on his feet because he had no horse to ride and he whistled as he walked.

When he came to the Pickle-Bottle he walked round it and nodded to the Princess inside and put his head askew and shut one eye and whistled as the other Princes told him about the Blue Dragons and the Dwergs and the Charms that would not work. The Princess looked at him between her fingers and blushed for he was the Most Beautifullest of all the Princes.

At last he put his hand into his pocket and said:– "What is the matter with pulling out the Cork of the Pickle-Bottle?" And the other Princes said "Ah!" for they had not thought of that.

Then he pulled out the cork with a Corkscrew and it came out because it was just an ordinary cork in a common bottle which did not know anything about Charms and Incantations. And the Princess came out of the bottle at the open end and all the other princes cut off the heads of the Court Magicians, Wizards, Witches, Faithful Servants, Talking Foxes and Enchanted Horses because they were annoyed.

And the Prince married the Princess and they lived happy ever after.

The Moral of this Story is, Next time you find a Princess in a Pickle-Bottle never try to open the Bottle with charms and Blue Dragons.

Take a Corkscrew.
Rudyard Kipling.

Why Snow Falls at Vernet
(A Legend of St. Saturnia)

※

Published: *Pages from 'The Merry Thought'* [Vernet-les-Bains], May 1911.

Attribution: The story is accompanied by a letter from Kipling, 16 March 1911, to the editor of the magazine enclosing 'a contribution to your valuable paper' (story and letter printed in *Pages from 'The Merry Thought'*).

Text: Typescript copy, Kipling Papers, Special Collections, University of Sussex (SxMs 38/2/8/1/6/1). This text is preferred to the printed version in *Pages from the Merry Thought*, since RK evidently saw the typescript. No copy of the issue of the magazine for April 1911, in which the story was first published, appears to have survived. *Pages from 'The Merry Thought'* is a selection from the issues for February, March and April 1911. For a description of this pamphlet, see Richards, *Bibliography*, pp. 389–90.

Notes: The magazine was published in Vernet-les-Bains, a spa at the foot of the Pyrenees, to 'amuse' the patrons. RK and his wife stayed at Vernet on three occasions, in 1910, 1911 and 1914. They arrived at Vernet on 20 February 1911 when 'the snow lay in two foot patches beside the roads'. After an interval of 'glorious weather' it 'snowed again and thawed. Since which the weather has had worms' (to Stanley Baldwin, 18 March 1911: *Letters*, IV, 25).

Reprinted in the Martindell–Ballard pamphlets and by H. Dunscombe Colt, December 1963, in an edition of fifty copies (Richards, *Bibliography*, p. 339).

※

I had this legend from the Rock which rises behind the laurestine bush and the loquat tree, in the winter garden. Shortly after the end of the first crusade, so the Rock told me, there came to Vernet, wearied by war and seeking a quiet life, two English knights – Sir Brian and Sir Gilbert, the one round and reddish, the other long and dark; the one limping from an inveterate sciatica, the other bowed in his saddle by an ancient lumbago. They arrived separately: Sir Brian on a Monday, Sir Gilbert on a Thursday.

Sir Brian, after the simple usage of those days, possessed himself of the ground, where the Vernet hotels now stand; Sir Gilbert, the later

355

contenting himself with the pleasant fields round Casteil. Here, ˌlence as profound as that of the mountains above, each devoted ˌself to the planting of vines and fruit trees, and the cure of his ˌlment. On Tuesday, for example, Sir Brian betook himself and his leg to the sulphur-scented pools behind his modest hut, bathed for one hour, drank half a helmetfull of heady Vaporarium, and returned to his vineyards. On Friday Sir Gilbert, descending from Casteil, sat for two hours in the rock-cut basin which is now the Piscina, drank a full helmet of strong Barara, and fished the left bank of the river on his homeward way. On Sundays the two would meet exactly below the great Rock and exchange exactly seven syllables – one for each day of the week.

Sir Brian would say to Sir Gilbert: "Ha! How's back?" Sir Gilbert would reply: "Better thanks; how's leg?" So punctual were the performers in this ritual that the simple inhabitants of Vernet who, till then, had not much concerned themselves with the flight of time, used to set their church clock to twelve noon on the instant, that the seventh of these words had been spoken.

Now there lived beside the church a holy man, destined afterwards to become a bishop and the patron-saint of the town, none other, indeed, than St. Saturnia himself. His virtues as a silent and sympathetic listener, together with the excellencies of his cooking, so profoundly impressed the two knights, that very soon Sir Brian made it his habit to dine with Saturnia every Saturday, while Sir Gilbert dined with him every Wednesday, nor were there lacking to these meals, the wines of the rich countries round about – wines which awakened in the knights' memories anecdotes of the most variegated and interesting.

At one of these little dinners given about the time young asparagus comes to perfection, Saturnia grew bold to speak intimately to Sir Brian.

"My son," he said at dessert, "do you, by chance, live in mortal hatred of any of your neighbours?"

Sir Brian reached for the flask of Burgundy. "As for that", he replied, "I am at peace with all men. To be otherwise would be bad for the sciatic nerve."

"You are at peace then," Saturnia hazarded, "even with Sir Gilbert?"

"But certainly", said the knight. "I have known and respected him for three and twenty years. It is true he is a bit of a bore if you let him talk about the siege of Antioch, but otherwise he is, as we say in England, not half-a-bad sort."

"Pardon", said Saturnia, "It is not then a challenge to mortal combat which you address to each other every Sunday, exactly at noon beneath the great Rock?" Sir Brian removed the flask of Burgundy to his own side of the table.

"My father", he murmured respectfully, "may I recommend you to try white wines in place of red? You will find them less fatiguing. I remember, for example, at the Siege of Acre," and he delighted his host with another of his incomparable and illuminating anecdotes.

"Decidedly", said Saturnia to himself, "it must be Sir Gilbert who is at fault", and on the Wednesday following he opened his heart to the long, dark knight, who listened to him with all the astonishment in the world.

"But, my father", he cried at last, "not only did Sir Brian save my life eighteen years ago at the Siege of Antioch, but what is infinitely more important, he recommended me to these very baths which, as you can see, have cured my lumbago".

"In that case", said Saturnia, transported beyond politeness by his curiosity, "what is the meaning of the seven words which you address to each other every Sunday at noon beneath the great Rock?"

"We inquire", Sir Gilbert responded, "after each other's health. It is an English custom".

"And you have no more?" demanded the holy man, greatly moved.

"Customs? We have thousands: all excellent," said Sir Gilbert, who was also patriotic.

"I did not mean customs. I meant words – mere words", Saturnia explained.

"Catapults of Antioch!" cried Sir Gilbert, "what is there for a man, much less men, to talk about in this country?"

"But, my son, you have regaled me continuously and without repetitions, throughout an entire, year, by your stories of adventure among different races and countries. Except perhaps Sir Brian, who has also had experiences, I know no one so interesting as yourse". And Saturnia bowed above his glass.

"Oh! Adventures and that sort of thing go without saying," Sir Gilbert insisted, "and between you and me and this glass of Chablis – which is not as good, by the way, as last week's Burgundy – Sir Brian is a bit of a bore if he gets talking about the Siege of Acre."

"Then in England you do not talk at all?" Saturnia suggested.

"On the contrary," said Sir Gilbert, "but you see in England we have always the weather."

"The weather? The weather?" Saturnia replied, "what is it then, that which you call weather?"

"The weather," Sir Gilbert explained, "the weather, my father, is, in short, the weather. Here you have sunshine and sunshine and more sunshine, and the rains on the 25th of August or the 1st of September, and after that sunshine again. But, speaking of weather: I remember when I was a young squire in England in May", and Sir Gilbert delighted Saturnia with another of his well-chosen and edifying anecdotes.

"I understand", said Saturnia at the end of his story, "it gives you English pleasure to be violently snowed upon when you expect sunshine?

"Pleasure, no", Sir Gilbert replied. "Conversation, yes. If you will allow me, my father, I would say that you lack in this country the essentials of true conversation".

"Doubtless I grow old", said the good man to himself as Sir Gilbert after dinner descended the steep streets of Vernet. "I have changed from Burgundy, which I appreciate, to Chablis, which I detest; but *still* I do not understand the English."

Now this talk, so I was told by the Rock behind the Loquat, took place about midnight of March 10th. The next morning when Saturnia awoke he beheld with horror and consternation – for in those days the seasons were as regular and as excellent as the vintages – the entire valley covered with two or three inches of soft, fleecy snow, and the entire population of the town of Vernet hurrying to his door, shouting, gesticulating, amazed. But not on account of the snow, "This is Thursday", they cried. "Not Sunday, but Thursday! And it is not even ten o'clock of Thursday! Yet look at the knights! Look at the two English knights! How are we to set our church clocks for the future if they transgress in this fashion?"

Saturnia looked and saw, at the unprecedented hour of 9:30 A.M. Sir Brian and Sir Gilbert walking side by side through the snow in loud but friendly conversation. They beat upon the snow with their sticks; they gazed at the sky, at the mountains, at each other; and replunged into their discussion.

"What", cried all the terror-stricken inhabitants of Vernet, "w... does this unheard-of event portend? Is it an earthquake or a miracle?"

"My children", said Saturnia, with the benignity of complete apprehension, "it is neither. It is the weather of which the English speak. Be silent, and you will hear them speaking". Indeed, at that very moment both knights ascended the hill and panting but still eloquent, hailed the venerable man.

"Did you ever", they cried in chorus, "did you ever see such abominable weather? We were just speaking about it". And their faces shone with amity and an indescribable happiness.

※

From that year to the present, allowing for the necessary revision of the calendar, some snow, as everyone knows, falls here for a day or two between the 11th and 22nd of March. There are those who ascribe this to purely meteorological causes, but I prefer to believe, with the Rock behind the Loquat, that we owe it [to that Providence which, ever since has arranged that the English at Vernet has [*sic*] something to talk about.][1]

---

[1] The bracketed words have been added to the typescript in RK's hand. In the *Pages from the 'Merry Thought'* they are replaced by the following words: 'to the kindness and forethought of good St. Satiurnia, who in his time loved well, and at last learned to understand, the first English visitors to Vernet'.

The Cause of Humanity

Published: Unpublished, but included in Harbord's privately printed *Readers' Guide to Rudyard Kipling's Work*, v, 2618–30.

Attribution: The text in the *Readers' Guide* is from a typescript then in the possession of H. Dunscombe Colt. Colt's Kipling collection was given to the Library of Congress, 1984–5, but the typescript of 'The Cause of Humanity' was not included in the gift and its whereabouts are currently unknown.

The typescript of the story was sold at Sotheby's, 10 December 1968, as by Rudyard Kipling, 'with extensive autograph revisions and additions'; no provenance was given. Since the present location of the typescript is unknown, any further evidence of RK's authorship that might appear from an examination of the typescript is not available. The CK Diary for 12 June 1914 has the following entry: 'Rud at work on two stories: The Stolen Tide / The [ ] of Humanity'. The transcriber was unable to construe the missing word or words, but the entry is close to the title of the typescript and the date of the entry fits the internal evidence in the story. I think it likely that the outbreak of the First World War in August and the wholesale slaughter that it produced gave RK a reason not to publish the story.

Text: Harbord.

Notes: Harbord's text, presumably a faithful copy of the typescript, contains many irregularities and repetitions. I have left them unchanged, except that where a speech is provided with only one quotation mark, either at the beginning or end, I have supplied the missing mark. I have also corrected a few mistakes that seemed inadvertent misspellings, e.g., 'then' for 'there', or impossible meanings, e.g., 'more' for 'none' in a verse quoted from the Book of Job.

'The Cause of Humanity' is not yet recorded in any bibliography.

Two burst tyres in ten minutes, seven miles from everywhere had forced the traveller to spend the rest of the night out of doors. He pushed his car on to a triangular slip of common, put up the hood and arranged the rugs. It was warm summer and when all was quiet again, rabbits stole out and danced in the moonlight. They vanished into the bracken when

they heard footsteps down the road. A man sauntered up, hummr.
himself. The head lights attracted him as they had attracted the rabe
and the moths. He circled round the car, still humming.

"Good evening", said the traveller from under the hood. "Good
evenin'. Anything happened?"

"Oh, no. I think I'll wait to watch the sunrise."

"Ah," the man glanced at the near-fore wheel. "I see! Exodus,
Fourteen, twenty-four."[1]

"What?" said the traveller excitedly.

"Only a scripture tex'. Salisbury will be the nearest garage town, won't
it? They don't open before eight."

"I know that, but what about Exodus Fourteen, twenty-four. D'you
smoke?"

"Thank you, Yes!" The man seated himself on the running board – by
the front seat. "I've had my sleep this afternoon. If you want to turn in
I'll stand watch. . . . No, I don't know if I should give over to a stranger
myself if it was *my* car."

A church clock out of a misty valley made midnight.

"Did you ever meet a ship's steward who injured himself internally
through taking his captain a cup o' coffee on the bridge in a gale? A
sea bent him backwards over a stanchion and a tumour supervened. He
always rung at the door on rainy nights. He wore a shiny 'at that showed
wet and he seldom made less than ten shillings a day. He worked the
Midlands, but I thought you might 'ave met 'im. I worked with 'im once.
He was a good man in his way but he never changed his way. "But" I
says to him on one occasion "You only say the same thing – again and
again." "But" he says "fifty shillings a week do I touch by doing so". That
was all he could see. He wouldn't even make it . . . .

So we parted. I'm a professional liver by occupation. Money's no object
to me, or rather I should say, money's an object to me but monot'ny's a
thing I can't stand. So we parted.

You may have noticed the same thing among the crim'nal classes.
They 'aven't any variety. We need adaptability more and more to this
world owin' to speedin' up and the competitive system. The crim'nal
classes seldom change their crimes. Him that hath been a pickpocket
is a pickpocket still. The same with beggin'-letter-writers and specially
house breakers. One man one job. I noticed that when I was in jail

THE CAUSE OF HUMANITY

– quite justly. I had stretched the Law to 'elp a friend. Do good
to thy friend before thou die. That's Ecclesiasticus.[2] There are times
when you must do so if you want to live with yourself. Yourself is the
best company you'll get on this earth. You should go to great lengths to
oblige 'im. According to thy ability do good to thyself and seek to . . .
again.[3] No, I don't know the Bible by heart it is only a hobby of mine. If
I had my way I'd swap Leviticus, Numbers an' Deuteronomy out of the
Bible any day for Ecclesiasticus.

My friend was a dentist o' the name of Showan residing in Lambeth.
He was disenfrocked by false charges arising out of a woman's wisdom-tooth under nitrous oxide gas. What you call laughin' gas. In the
course of the proceedin's that my friend 'ad no certificate to operate.
That's only a five pound fine if you can prove he called himself a dentist
before witnesses. It was not proved but it did him no good. His last
words to me on leaving the dock were "save the dunnage", and I sold 'is
'ouse and dental parlor at once to a Jew. I am not an anti-Semite in the
least. Subsequently it transpired that the 'ouse was heavily mortgaged
and the stopping amalgums 'adn't been paid for.

The opposition was very cross at me because I wouldn't tell where I
'ad deposited my friend's money. That's 'ow I got four months. Here's a
sing'lar thing I had never sold a house before. It 'adn't ever come in my
walk o' life, but when the hour struck I found I was the man.

This is done, so far as my experience holds good, by not stoppin' to
think what he you'll say next. If you do they'll all surge like cables. (Yes,
I've used the sea, too, Sir. Thank you, I 'ave my own matches.) I met my
friend 'oo was a dentist first on a very wet night when I was with a steward with the tunour. This was after I 'ad parted with my other friend 'oo
was working the midlands. If thou will take the left 'and and then I shall
go to the right and vice versa. That's Genesis of his later [?].[4] But I've
forgotten the seese [sic: seas?].

My friend the dentist was very kind to me. I liked the look in 'is eye
from the first. He was that sort of man. When I 'ad quite finished my
story an' its worth the money he said:– "You're a damn scoundrel. Go
below an' turn in." That was the sort of man *he* was. I slep' in 'is scullery
that night and nex' day he took me on as 'is assistant. I'm a professional
liver. Money's no objeck to me, compared with livin'. I liked livin' with
my friend. We didn't either of know about this teething-business, but

we were that sort of people. A dentist 'as a very strong position in our social system.

Those 'oo come to 'im 'ave generally put it off – about for as long as they can stand, an' a little pain more or less distracts 'em. Then we 'ad all our troubles over the false-charges about the wisdom-tooth an' sellin' the 'ouse an' dental parlor. So we parted.

I was out first – my friend had got six, and I worked while I was lookin' round. Oh yes, I know we ought to have tried somethin' new but after four months in jail a man has to know himself all over again. It's like Anasmeusm [sic]. I worked the Eastern Counties as the humorous [tumorous?] steward for a while. Then I met a friend o' mine with a show. I 'ave plenty good friends, praise Gawd. Through him I got charge of a amateur Caravan party – and one a countess – with two 'orses. I led the 'orses and washed up. But they weren't professional livers. The part they liked best was listenin' to my stories of evening's after I'd washed up. They were three young ladies – one a countess. They'd listen to my stories and they'd say "this *is* life". But it wasn't, so we parted.

Then, through another friend o' mine I got into the Antwerp 'orse trade on the docks. It's a close corporation like pilotry. Then I went back to bein' Dock Missionary again. In case I had lost my gift of makin' and 'oldin' a crowd, any one can make a crowd. It's 'oldin' 'em afterwards that's the real test. I passed it satisfactorily to myself, but preachin's a competitive business. The regu'lar missionaries don't like it any too well. The Salvationists think you're encroachin' too, an' . . . What did I preach on? I've two chief tex's one for masters; one for men. Second Samuel, Fourteen, fourteen,[5] an' Timothy, Three, three.[6]

If you're interested in such things I'll . . . About my friend?

When he got out, I met 'im outside with 'is money for the house. He didn't *say* anything. 'E wasn't that sort o' man. He was my friend. 'E paid me ten per cent commission for affectin' the sale, an' 'e credited me with thirty bob a week sus'sistence allowance all the time I'd been at Lewes.

He asked me what I was goin' to do. I told him I generally did for myself, an' I asked after 'is intentions for the future.

"Tim" 'e says (one of my real names is Tim, that's why I'm so fond of those two epistles) "now she's blasted my professional character the widow with the tooth wants to marry me. She's well off", 'e says, "an' after what she said in court 'ad passed between us I don't see 'ow she can turn up in a breach o' promise case." "Quite right" I says. "An eye for an eye, a tooth for a tooth. Skin 'er!" "I shall 'e says, but that won't free all my time." "The doctor where I've been (He'd 'ad bronchitis there) has put a notion into my 'ead, an' that woman's money'll come in handy for it if it comes off. It's a useful notion," 'e says, "You're in it too. It's all fair an' above board, an' yet," 'e says "it'll 'ave to be put through like a burgl'ry."

"Your word's good enough for me" I says. "*Ruth*, one sixteen where thou goest I will go." For 'e was that sort o' man.

"What d'you know about refrigeratin' plant", 'e goes on, "cold storage – freezin' chambers and such things."

"I was shipmates once with thirty thousand frozen muttons", I says with 'Eaven's 'elp I can pick it up." "Then do," 'e says, "an' when you 'ave, report to me again. I ought to be finished with the widow an' one or two more things by that time." So we parted.

I went off to the docks where I 'ave friends in all quarters – or rather I should say I went to the Greenwich Free Lib'ry to ge' [*sic*] my words. Tisn't what you do in this world that matters. It's how you do it. You must have the words for the little men an' the acts for the big 'uns, but it's difficult to tell which is which till you've tried 'em. I got my words. Then I went to get my refrigerator job. Of course, I 'ad friends. It's as easy to get the best of the worst at the beginning. I put in a month on refrigerators. There's nothin' in 'em excep' keepin' the temperature down an' seein' the snow-boxes don't block. The rest is donkey-engine work, neither more nor less; only you must be careful to shut your doors after you. Believe me when I say to *you* the things men lose their jobs for aren't spite, or speedin' up or social systems. They're just the tricks an' 'abits that a six-year-old child ought to 'ave conquered. An' I'm the only one that ever told the British workin' man that. After all, what *does* the Lord require of us. He doesn't require great things. He –

About my friend? When I went back to him, 'is then name was D'Arcy an' the widow 'ad lent him more than twelve hundred pounds for love. So 'e 'ad shifted in to the West-End – Bloomsbury, W.C. She'd 'ave sold her 'ouse over 'er own 'ead for 'is sake, 'e told me but he thought justice 'ad been done under the circs.

"An' now" 'e says to me, "d'you know what the chief need o' Humanity is in these days?" O' course I did, but 'e wasn't arguin' on the spiritual line. "It's subjecks", 'e says. "Subjecks for the 'ospitals to investigate" I' adn't got it yet. "Corpses to dissect," 'e says. "You've no idea, an' I 'adn't till our old doctor told me, of the awful straits that 'ospitals are in for subjecks. It's holding up the advance of science; it's paralyzi' research and it's sendin' up prices by leaps and bounds. Let it continue but a few years longer an' medical research in Great Britain'll be a thing o' the past. My doctor told me that science depends now entirely on unclaimed paupers, an' owin' to the spread of education an' the Old Age Pensions Act they're scarcer an' scarcer. Unclaimed prisoners too," 'e says, "excep' murderers." Did you ever know that, Sir? That ought to be legislated against. My friend told me all about it. "Go on," I says, but I was mappin' it out in my 'ead while 'e talked.

"And in the meantime", 'e says, "Turkey an' Bulgaria an' Servia an' Montenegro an' Greece an' Albania are doing nothing *excep'* supply subjecks.[7] An' what do they make of 'em when they've got 'em. They don't even waste 'em underground, my old doctor told me. They burn 'em mostly. I don't say I've got a firm offer of seven guineas per subjeck from the 'ospitals, but I'm morally certain that they'd close at that price 'olesale like sharks round a dead nigger. It's a simple question o' demand an' supply." "Go on," I says. "Oh no," he shouts. "You can see it all. You're comin' in" "I know I am" I says, "but what about the rest o' the crew. Common sailors are superstitious."

"We 'aven't any common sailors," 'e says. "You go down an' look." "'Ave you got as far as that?" I says. "What's my ship?" "The 'Judith' at Tilbury. We sail to-morrow, noon; you're Quartermaster Evans in charge of the refrigerator. Blue jersey an' black trousers is the rig. An' you can set your own wages." 'E knew money was no objeck to me more than to 'im but 'e always played 'is part all through. So we parted.

Next morning I went down to this Judith at Tilbury, an' – my friend was right. I never! That's all I can say! She was eight 'undred tons an' a steamer but everything else outside o' that – I can only say in all my born days I never did. The first man I come across was very old indeed. He said he was a quartermaster. 'E said 'e 'ad been an A.B. at the time of the *Alert* and *Discovery* Polar Expedition.[8] It looked like robbin' the grave already.

Then a deck-'and in carpet slippers asked me if I was the ice-cream man. I hadn't set foot on a ship for seven years, but it all came back with the smells. "Not if you talk that way I'm not," I says. "But – I'll show you what I am." "'Umbug," says 'e, 'Op along downstairs an' show me 'ow to inject the ammonia. I can't pull 'er below thirty-five an' that's only fit for apples." My friend was right, I thanked Gawd where I stood. We only go through His wonderful world once, don't we? *He* knows I've always appreciated it.

Then I went downstairs an' this man Slippers showed me the cold-chamber. It was very well fitted an' 'andy to run. I believe she had been in the banana business. Then this man Slippers (he come from Guys,⁹ 'e said) showed me round the ship, arm in arm. I've seen several things in my life, but I never! that's all I can say. Six nurses come aboard – I said six nurses an' a matron in their caps and cloaks come aboard an' asked and asked [*sic*] for their cabins. Slippers and a steward, called Alf (he was Bart's)¹⁰ showed 'em. Then Slippers showed me the old man – the captain – lyin' in 'is cabin blind! No, I mean *blind* dead to the world. "He's always like that I believe. We've only shipped 'im for the look of the thing," 'e says. "The mate will do the work. 'E owns the *Punchinello* R.Y.S.¹¹ He's full of extra certificates. The Chief Engineer's all right too" says Slippers "but he's in bed just now because the Head Stoker has been playin' with 'im. I wish you'd speak to the 'ead Stoker. He's an 'Otspur."

So I went down to the stoke-hold where two men was playin' cricket with a string ball. The 'ead stoker was in at the time.

"Jimmy" says Slippers, "this is a pro. You'd better stoke." There wasn't forty-pound steam on the gauges. It was all comin' back to me with the smells. I noticed it. "D'you objeck?" says the 'ead stoker, pushin' 'is face at me.

"Oh no" I says an' I tapped 'im on the point. "Allelulia" says the 'ead stoker when 'e knew where 'e was again. This *is* life!" An' 'e turned to an' stoked.

I'm a professional liver an' I hate fightin' but the little I've had to do, I've 'ad to do *you* understand. Then I went upstairs and it was all just like that. I watched a lot o' old gentlemen in top-hats sayin' good-bye to the nurses some of 'em I'd let in to the Bloomsbury 'ouse. My friend D'Arcy in a top-'at talked to the reporters and the old man lay blind as corpses, in the cabin, an' the pilot looked at 'im through the glass.

It was all just like *that*. The pilot o' course 'ad his 'ome to go back to an' tell it in. When 'e left us – off the Foreland – "Goodnight, Hanwell," 'e says to me. You might tell 'em it's lightin' up time." All the steward an' all the other amateurs was 'andin tea to the nurses. I 'ad the wheel till mornin'. It all came back again. D'Arcy stood some o' the first watch with me.

"I thought you'd like it," 'e says as soon as 'e could speak. It was a fine clear night, else I couldn't 'ave done it for laughter. I laugh inside me. I can talk that way, too.

"But what about the nurses?" I says. "Oh, they're quite straight. They're our excuse. They're the Balkan Brigade o' Bloomsbury Nurses goin' out to 'elp the wounded irrespective of race an' religion. You saw the old gentlemen sayin' good-bye to 'em, while they ought to 'ave been talkin' business with me."

"Stop makin' me laugh!" I says, "or there'll be collisions. 'Ave we got a look-out, I've 'eard no bells this last hour or two."

"What do you want with bells? 'e says. "This ain't a bridal. We're goin' to a reg'lar Tom Tiddler's ground. You 'aven't steeped yourself in the lit'rature of the subjeck like I have."

"'Ow many professional sailor men 'ave shipped?" I says. "Only you an' Crosskeys an' the old man," says 'e. "I was countin' on you to teach the young gentlemen to hand, reef an' steer."

"Send one of 'em up for look-out then. We may as well keep alive if we want to live," I says.

"Which you'll have?" 'e says. "Guy's, Bart's, London, Thomas's, Middlesex,[12] Skin *or* Maternity?" I didn't gain much by that because those that wasn't sick volunteered to look-out an' they all kep' singin' songs. . . . But nothing 'appened.

It all come back to me, an' in three days they called me Admiral Crichton, they were full o' nicknames. Sister Gertrude called my friend Waring.[13] . . . The mate 'oo 'ad owned the Punchinello pricked out our course very well considerin'. . . . the Chief Engineer an' the Second Engineer (both pros) an' the 'ead stoker (he was a 'Otspur outside right) kep' the engines goin' very well considerin', an' Slipper and Alf an' Bunny an' Max; an' Baby Dickie ('e was the Maternity) an' Arthur an' Hooks the Cook's mate (he was St. Mary's, Paddington) they tried their 'ands at everything an' talked Suffragettery to the sisters.

It's a singular thing you can't teach steerin' to a woman. She can't understand the compass bein' so wilful with her an' she gets cross at *you.* I proved that with the Matron – Sister Ruth. She was a decorated Victoria Jubilee nurse. I took second prize in the potato race in the ship's sports. Sister Emily took first. I gave an address on Sunday an' they gave me a special prize – a manicure set. An' that was 'ow we went down the Mediterranean at nine knots. It wasn't like anything that I ever [knew] but that's the beauty o' life.

When we made our port which was a shockin' little place, we 'adn't more than anchored before boats came alongside with wounded. Our Red Cross flag did it.

"O this is too cosy! Let 'em all come," says D'Arcy. "The sisters can get to work here as well as up country." That suited all parties for they had some job to be good friends during the voyage. Nothing wrong I give you my word. They were sisters indeed.

We opened our cargo port and the 'Ead Stoker an' Bunny an' Arthur lined up to tackle the rush. Here's a singular thing. Slippers an' Bunny an' the rest 'ad been quite like anyone else during the voyage. So 'ad the sisters. You understand what I mean. Nothing wrong but quite natural. As soon as the bundles was pushed through the port an' they 'eard the cries proceedin' from 'em, they turned professional like floor walkers straight off. It was "Syringe – scissors – bandage quick – yes sir!" An' the boats kep' coming alongside till we 'ad to threaten to sink 'em.

There was no one in charge of 'em; no names to the wounded, no questions; no marks; not even a *yuman* language to deal in. Our Red Cross flag did it all. Another singular thing. I fainted at the operations the first night in smokin' room but they took no more notice of me than if I'd been the spittoon. It was their line o' business, you understand. *I* understand it. They was red up to their pretty little elbows – racin' 'ospital versus 'ospital. A very honourable profession. Honour a physician with the honour due to him. Ecclesiasticus again.¹⁴ If I had my own way I'd swap Leviticus, Numbers, Deut'ronomy, yes an' both Chronicles out of the Bible for Ecclesiasticus, any day. And so they looked after the wounded; an' I started up the refrigerator.

There was a percentage, 'o course, come down to me, but it wasn't more than a trickle. D'Arcy mentioned it because we were burnin' coal all the time they were savin' lives upstairs.

"I'm as economic as I can be," I says, "but it takes as much to keep her below freezin' for five as for five hundred."

"I know it," 'e says, "and I don't blame you but facts are facts."

"You run her tomorrow then," I says, "an' I'll g ashore an' look for freight."

It's a singular thing but I couldn't do anything. I found a refugee an' a bullock cart, an' I hired 'im by day to carry what I picked up. I came back, the cart full up and hangin' out of wounded. D'Arcy tried next day. He come back with *two* carts full of the same. Simply ridic'lous, when you think of what we were there *for*. Like starvin' in the midst of plenty.

The sisters 'adn't received any orders to go up country. I don't believe we should 'ave let 'em go if they 'ad. We had got to be a very happy little party. So we settled down. The old man kep' to 'is cabin, an' so did the Engineers. They didn't like runnin' into ops or amps – operations or amputations as we call 'em – all over the decks.

Every man to 'is trade o' course. We washed down decks an' the theatres – the smoking and saloon at 4 a.m. Work began at six or rather, accordin' to the deliveries alongside. Alfred made mornin' coffee and brought us breakfast in 'is 'ands at eight, which we took standin'. That was why Sister Ruth's ankles swelled so. We'd get away the first batch about noon. They was taken to what they called 'ospitals.

We used to row 'em ashore but afterwards the archimandrite asked us to lie at the quay which made it easier for all parties. Our Red Cross flag did it. There was no one in charge of anything. Then we'd wash our 'ands an' sit down to luncheon. Then we'd carry on till tea time – sweet Marie biscuits an' sardines. Then carry on till dinner at eight, or nine often. Then I'd take on my particular job – if there was anything for speed – with anyone I could get to help. Most often it would be D'Arcy or Max, but sometimes the Mate. He was an interestin' man when you knew him. Very nearly a millioneer I believe. First time we worked together on a subjeck, he says to me:– "What are your thoughts about all this Evans? Or per'aps," he runs on, "you don't think." I smiled, for there they were with the snow on their moustaches. He drops the subjeck for the moment an' looks at me. "I beg your pardon," 'e says, "I'm afraid I know more about bodies than souls, as I make no doubt you have already seen." He apologised again. He used to tell me a lot about himself an' 'is doings, an' women an' the usuals, on those occasions. So did the others. Down there one didn't feel there was anything much in particular worth 'iding.

There was an old Jew 'oo found us out as soon as we lay at the quay – an old clo' man. I don't know what 'e did with the lot I used to give him – up till then I'd burned 'em in the furnaces We didn't sell 'em. He took everything. Instinck, I suppose. 'E sold me two very thick sheepskin coats, like divin' dresses. We used to put 'em on in the air lock, the anteroom before you get to the freezin' chamber to prevent the cold air leakin'.

But my friend was wonderful. 'E never turned a hair. He saw his profits dissolvin' into smoke, while we filled up in this retail way. He spent nearly a hundred pounds of his twelve hundred on coal an' sundries and never a hair did 'e turn. I used to think at first it was one of the sisters – Sister Gertrude. But it wasn't! 'E was just *that* sort o' man, you understand. Job XLI, 33[15]

I've seen him leave dock under sentence without overdoin' it one way or the other. I've seen 'in make love to a woman he desperately hated without overdoin' it one way or the other. Those are the two most difficult things in the world.

This waitin' on for freight was just as difficult an' he didn't overdo it one way or the other. He was that sort of man. There is none like him upon earth who is made without fear. That's somewhere at the end o' Job. I don't argue such a man gets 'is reward on earth. Experience is against it. But I *do* say to you that such a man is often allowed to see an openin' where you an' me wouldn't be [*sic*: see?]. The old Jew in the old clo' line ran aboard with a friend, an' the two grabbed D'Arcy's deck-shoes. I saw it. 'Is feet were *in* 'em o' course. How did they know D'Arcy was the man to approach? I'd been handin' them out the clothes. Instinck again.

They talk Greek. The Mate translated. They said there 'ad been a massacre on an island off the coast an' nobody much cared because the subjecks was mostly Jews. *They* cared though. They 'ad much friends on the island. They kicked about on the deck like wired rabbits.

D'Arcy didn't take any lead in the talk. Sister Ruth did, and that brought the Mate over. He used to call her the Elect Lady. John, Second Epistle.[16]

We got up steam, an' as soon as we 'ad done the morning amps an' ops, we pulled out with this new Jew. The old Jew 'ad to stay behind on buyin' and sellin' clothes. It was his line o' business, you understand.

This new Jew went on to this island. There was snow on the tops of the 'ills comin' nearly down to the beach. There was a little town an' an harbour an' a quay an' a light 'ouse but no people.

When we closed in we thought we 'eard a motor horn, but the young Jew said it was the horn of the Synagogue.

We closed in. There wasn't anything anywhere. We whistled an' there wasn't anyone, an' after a bit the Mate took the ship right alongside the quay just before dark. He told Sister Ruth to take the sisters down below. She was a suffragette and she took 'em. Then we went ashore an' nobody takin' much notice of this new Jew; because he only cried he lagged be'ind us a bit in the streets. We 'eard a pop, an' when we all ran back he had shot 'imself dead with an automatic pistol. We picked up five men, an' eight women an' five children that wasn't dead. The man who 'ad blown the 'orn in the Synagogue was dead before we found 'im. I'd read about massacres in the papers, but I'd never seen one. I'm glad I 'ave because I'm a professional liver but I don't want to see one again.

It was like Ezekiel. Asshur is there and all her company all of them dead slain by the sword. They have set her a bed in the midst of the plain.[17] It goes on for a long time that way, but I haven't got my Bible with me an' another singular thing. I never knew Jews 'ad so much fight in 'em as we discovered must 'ave been the case. They 'ad sold their lives dearly – specially round the Synagogue. The same in the little backrooms and cattle places all about. My Heavens – an' I don't swear lightly – those Jews had sold their lives very dear. We talked it over. D'Arcy says:– "there's enough to fill up without takin' any of *them*, an' I propose *out o' respect* to these dam *massacres*[18] that we don't." So we didn't take a single Jew. We took the others even though we had to walk further to get 'em. We worked from 7 p.m. to 6 a.m. without a stand easy excep' one cocoa at midnight. That will show you how we worked the first night. We couldn't 'ave done it even then if we hadn't laid right alongside on the quay with our cargo port open. We found a bullock cart which we pushed by 'and. So we filled up. But not one single Jew. They are all there now for aught I know.

So we filled up. I didn't 'ave my clothes off me for the nex' three days. We lay out of sight of the town in the daytime and we closed up on it about dusk. But we couldn't prevent the Sisters from seein' what had happened ashore. They knew what was happening aboard. They never talked of it. It didn't come under their notice. They didn't go out of their way to notice it. They knew our times but did not know the rest.

I waited for the time being . . . . and so we filled up. The new Jew 'avin' shot himself, we had to take the survivors back to the old Jew. There wasn't anywhere else for 'em to go. Two women and a child died on the second day. We buried 'em at sea. Old Crosskeys, the Polar-expedition quartermaster, that I've mentioned, kep' worryin' me about 'em. At last I says to him:–

"'Ave you got anythin' on your mind?" "Yes," he says. "I'm wondering what would 'appen to me under similar circs." "You're on the Staff," I says. "You'd be put overside, o' course, like a white man." "That's a weight off my mind," he says. "You'd better tell the old man that too!"

'What's *he* got to do with it?" I said. "Nothing," says Crosskeys in the funny sharp way he had, "but 'e's been turnin' in for the last few nights with half a pig o' ballast in a piller case. I can't get it away from 'im because 'e says its his hot water bottle. He's about due for another go of the 'orrors too." None of us had taken any notice o' the old man till then. He had seemed quite 'armless and quite contented with his mixtures. He mixed. That was his trouble. I told D'Arcy what Crosskeys had said. It was about time, because next mornin' we found 'im (the captain I'm talkin' of, now) tryin' to go overside with the piller-case rouond 'is neck. He said 'e wanted to dispose of his own remains while he could be sure of 'em. We 'ad a shockin' time. He wouldn't believe anythin' we promised, till the Mate an' the 'Ead Stoker and me coaxed him below. It was kill or cure, you understand.

"Look at 'em," says the Mate. The old man did. He'd never seen them before. "Count 'em!" says the Mate. But that was beyond him. "Now," says the Mate, "where do you think you come in?" The old man saw it after a bit. "You overestimated your value" says the Mate. "You aren't needful in *any* capacity." He took 'im upstairs and gave 'im a dose o' medicine, an' not only didn't 'e not 'ave any more 'orrors but – sing'lar thing he stopped 'is liquor right off from that hour. His face an' habits changed so you wouldn't 'ave known 'im. Like a conversion. But it might just as well 'ave been kill as cure under the circs. I don't think he ever knew we had 'em aboard. When we got back we handed over the survivors to the old Jew, in what the Sisters could dress 'em up in. He accepted 'em all, same as 'e took clothes – a dozen an' more as pore as 'imself.

I 'ad saved the best o' the clothes for 'im off the island an' we took up a subscription as well. D'Arcy gave twenty-five pounds but 'e wouldn't have a written list on the Saloon door. 'E was that sort of man.

Next day Sister Ruth, the Matron, got up very early and kep' shakin' 'er fist at the carts o' wounded alongside an' sayin': "Beasts! Beasts! Let 'em all die!" That started Sister Em'ly and Sister Rosa off, an' we decided we go home. Orders 'ad come while we was away to send our Balkan Brigade up country, but we decided they'd 'ad enough. Now here's a sing'lar thing. The Mate took sick, or rather I should say he had enough like the rest of us. D'Arcy was well but sailorizin' wasn't his business, an' Bunny and Co. – some of 'em had had enough for a bit – weren't anywhere near able seamen. Besides the sister kept 'em busy runnin' errands to the galley for malted milk. Then the old man, who 'ad knocked off 'is liquor, came out strong. Like a resurrection. I found 'im on the bridge one mornin': 'E didn't talk above a whisper, but 'e was very polite. 'E told me it was his ship. I knew it was when 'e sent Crosskeys to relieve me at the wheel.

He'd come an' talk to the invalids in their chairs o' afternoons like the captain of a liner. 'E 'ad 'is certificate suspended off one once. He was worth all his pay during that run home – when we'd had enough. There were no sports that run you understand. When Bunny and Co. played deck cricket, they did it on the foc'sle not aft. No concerts, no gramophone. Sister Gertrude used to sing Scotch songs on the deck between lights. Comin' back full was different from goin' out empty, you understand. There was so few of us and so many of them we couldn't help noticing it Rather, I should say, we felt as if they were non-cargo. An' so we went up the Mediterranean. We'd had enough. We could [not] properly see anything or take anything or say everything. You understand a ship's company didn't 'ang together any more.

We stood in for orders, comin' up Channel. That 'ad all been arranged from the beginning. We got our orders an' we went on up Channel to where we was ordered. Then it came thickish weather – close and foggy – an' we all said 'ow very funny it would be if there was a collision. But nothing 'appened. We picked up our pilot all right.

He squinted, I remember, an' seein' this eye come up over the rail in the lantern light set us all off laughin'. The pilot was very cross at us.

Then it got thicker an' we walked up an' down two by two. We missed our tide, an' we had supper in the saloon all together (though o' course we had been all together all the time). The Mate tried to make a speech an' Bunny tried to propose the Sisters, but it didn't work. They cried shockin'. Then we tried to sing "Auld Lang Syne" but that didn't work at all. Then, we hung about first on one foot, then on another, with the Sisters' portmanteaux in the alley ways. Then a tug came alongside with the port doctor and a lot of other medical gentlemen and told us where to go. It was at a quay that tramps commonly lay at. While we were being pushed and worked in and out there 'ad to be an inspection to certify the causes of death. That was no treat to anyone aboard but the new doctors would have it So I showed 'em down. It *was* a treat to them. They began by being perfessional like Bunny and Co. at the beginning. They finished up by being quiet and shareing. One of 'em gave me half-a-crown for helping him into his sheepsking. I took it of course. It wasn't any place to talk about pride in.

"How noble they look!" he says. It had struck me that way often and yet three fourths of 'em to my own knowledge were shockin' scoundrels. But noble was just the word. Noble and lofty. After inspection we got up alongside the quay where they expected us. It was all lined up with furniture removal, motor vans. You could see their 'eadlights in the fog.

We got the Sisters away first with their caps and cloaks an' little 'and-bags. They had 'ad enough. The Mate went with 'em. Then we opened our cargo-port, an' the vans backed up an' we got to work. Sing'lar thing at first to 'ear the drivers an' helpers on the vans recognising Bunny and Co. in the fog. That made 'em all quite brisk at the end. Besides there were drinks in the saloon. We got the last van away at five thirty-five a.m. Bunny and Co. left with it, singing. Then the old man came to D'Arcy an' the Mate in the saloon an' whispered (he thought 'e was talkin' out loud): "May I hope I've given you satisfaction, gentlemen?" D'Arcy said the 'andsome thing for the old man 'ad really saved us on the 'ome run. "Thank you," says the old man, an' 'e went home to wherever 'e lived at.

I don't think he ever got it straight in his mind about the cargo. D'Arcy an' me sat about in the saloon talking to a doctor 'oo'd come in the tug or rather I should say D'Arcy did the talking – till it was six o'clock an' then the caretakers come aboard, an' we was finished with it all . . . . I'm a professional liver, an' we only go through Gawd's good world once you understand, but I don't think I'd care to do that trip over again. No sayin' o' course but that's 'ow I feel for the moment. . . . Look! There's the sun. Always fresh to me that is! See 'ow he comes up an' up! I always take my 'at off to him. He's so like Genesis one, three.[19] Well, I'm walkin' into Salisbury. It's only twelve mile. I ought to be there by eight. If it's any objeck to you I'll tell the garage there to send a man out with a tyre.

---

1 Probably Exodus 14:25 is meant: 'And took off their chariot wheels, that they drave them heavily'.
2 Ecclesiasticus 14:13.
3 Ecclesiasticus 14:11.
4 Thus in text.
5 'For we must needs die, and *are* as water spilt on the ground, which cannot be gathered up again; neither doth God respect *any* person: yet doth he devise means, that his banished be not expelled from him.'
6 Probably 1 Timothy 3:3: 'Not given to wine, no striker, not greedy of filthy lucre; but patient, not a brawler, not covetous'.
7 The so-called 'First' Balkan War was fought between Turkey and the members of the Balkan League, 1912–13.
8 Ships of the 1875–6 Arctic expedition commanded by Sir George Nares. RK says that he saw one of them in Portsmouth in 1876 (*Something of Myself*, p. 5).
9 Guy's Hospital, London.
10 St Bartholomew's Hospital, London.
11 Royal Yacht Squadron, Cowes, Isle of Wight.
12 The three hospitals not yet named are the London, St Thomas's and Middlesex.
13 See Browning's 'Waring'.
14 38:1.
15 'Upon earth is not his like, who is made without fear'. Harbord says that the reference has been crossed out. The verse is slightly misquoted in the second paragraph following.
16 'The elder unto the elect lady and her children ...' (John 2:1).
17 Ezekiel 32:22, 25.
18 Harbord's text here adds parenthetically ('this word altered to *maccabees*').
19 'And God said, Let there be light; and there was light.'

APPENDICES

Juvenilia

Will Briart's Ghost

Published: A facsimile of the two-page manuscript was published shortly after RK's death in the *Sydney Morning Herald* for 25 January 1936.

Attribution: Family tradition; MS in possession of the Baldwin family (RK's Uncle Alfred, Aunt Louisa, cousin Stanley).

Text: Manuscript in Baldwin Papers, University of Sussex.

Notes: Said to have been written by the 8-year-old RK, i.e., at the end of 1873 or in 1874, while he was living at Lorne Lodge. RK is known to have stayed with the Baldwin family in Worcestershire in September 1872, when he was not yet 7 years old; perhaps there were other such visits.

Chap i THE Murder

It was a dark starry night of[f] the goodwins and a small vessel heavily laden with a crew of five men was being tossed about by the foaming billows like a piece of cork it appeared as if it were drunk [one word illegible] for now it [one word illegible] one moment it was wallowing in a deep trought between two waves and the next it was on the crest of a gigantic billow there was one small sail up but it was torn to shreds the captain was drunk and there was no one at the helm. Get up you lazy lubber or I'll teach you said the captain ^William Briart^ administering a kick on the ribs to one of the crew who was sleeping. The man got up muttering an oath and sullenly set about his work but waiting for an unguarded moment when the captain was looking over board he came behind him and caught him by the legs and o aweful deed threw him overboard The captain sank rose again and clutched wildly in the air for something to catch hold of uttered a dispearing cry for help and was swept away by a large wave. Three times did the crew hear his cry for help amidst the aweful billows far astern it was a cry that if once heard was not likely to be forgotten. When it was silent a great grey gull came swooping down uttered a wild wail three times and flew away. Then a wild wave bore the doomed little vessel on to a rock that reared its black crest far above the seething waters the ship struck split in two and the whole crew (as it said in the newspapers) were drowned The waters raged more than ever after that like demons exulting over their prey and now gentle reader we will change the scene.

Chap 2 THE GHOST

The scene is the beach of Deal It is midnight and one of the coast gard men is on the look out He paces to and fro quickly to warm himself when suddenly he becomes aware of a slight noise behind him he turns round quickly and sees THE GHOST OF THE MURDERED Will Briart it was dressed in Briarts usual clothes but with a face deadly pale it spoke not a word as it glided along the beach the look out stood as still as a statue an expression of intense horror passed over his face and the ghost disappeared. The look out ran as only those [menaced?] with terror can fly to the coast gard station and he told every thing he got laughed at and called a [one word deleted] fool for his pains but still he persisted that the ghost was no delusion Ah said he I knew Will well and this ere ghost was the image of him I'm sure there [word or words deleted] has been some foul work done not long after this the ghost was seen by a party of herring fishers they were just landing when the ghost appeared one of them stared at it for a while and fainted.

Chap 3

   murder will out

Strange things happened at Deal a few weeks after this The ghost was seen by seven more people an idiot was found lying on the beach howling and raving horribly making a confession of all his sins including the murder of W. Briart a little boy on the cliff heard him and told the coast gard men one of which sallied out made the idiot a prisoner back to the court of justice there he made another confession and he was ultimately hung.

❧

Moral Murder will out.

My First Adventure

Published: 'The Scribbler', vol. I, no. 12, and vol. II, no. I (3 and 30 June 1879).

Attribution: Lot 106 in the G. M. Williamson sale, New York, Anderson Galleries, 17 March 1915, where it is described as a copy by May Morris of a contribution from RK signed 'Nickson', a pseudonym used at this time by RK.

Text: Typescript copy, British Library, Add. MS 45337, ff. 120–6; 161–5.

Notes: Written for 'The Scribbler', a handwritten magazine got out by the children of William Morris and Sir Edward Burne-Jones from November 1878 to March 1880. Only two copies of each number were produced. The two parts of this story are both signed 'Nickson'. RK's father, John Lockwood Kipling, contributed to Indian newspapers under the pseudonym 'Nick' (short for 'nicotine'). RK was therefore 'Nickson'. RK, 13 years old in 1879, was then in his second year at the United Services College, Westward Ho!, North Devon.

The original – i.e., a copy written out by May Morris for 'The Scribbler' – was bought from May Morris in 1901 by G. M. Williamson, and was sold with other items for the magazine at the Anderson Galleries, New York, 17 March 1915, Those items are now scattered.

The typescript copy of contributions to 'The Scribbler' in the British Library is in a volume mixing typescripts and manuscripts. The typescripts were presumably made before the sale of the manuscript material to Williamson, if in fact there was any manuscript apart from the copies made for the magazine.

'My First Adventure' has been reprinted in the Martindell–Ballard pamphlets and in Harbord, I, 501–7.

Part I

Our school at Hawesdean¹ was situated near the little river Stour, and it was in connection with that stream that my first adventure took place. I will tell you how it all happened.

About the middle of the Midsummer term of 185 – we were challenged by the neighbouring school of Crickford to a cricket-match, and in a moment of enthusiasm, forgetful of the strength of our opponent team, accepted the challenge. As was expected, in spite of all our efforts and severe training, when the match came off they obtained many more runs than we, and defeat seemed inevitable.

Bob Cholmondeley and I were the last men in, and to equal our antagonists' score 49 more runs had to be obtained. The fate of the game depended on me (the worst player in the eleven) and wretched Bob, who was playing as a substitute for Harris, the latter being in the sickhouse from the effects of a sunstroke.

We took our places at the wickets with a grim determination to make our defeat as small as possible, and really got on surprisingly well, and continued steadily raising our score. The bowling became more and more difficult, and taxed our powers to the utmost, all possible varieties of balls following each other in rapid succession. Nevertheless, after three quarters of an hour's hard work, between the two of us we had obtained 43 runs and the excitement was intense. What with the cheering and clapping it was all we could to keep cool. That is to say, as far as our minds were concerned, for the hot summer sun had long before broiled our bodies (protected only by thin jerseys). Three more runs off Cholmondeley's bat were added to the score and the bowling was something terrific. I could feel the concussion of Maxwell's balls against my bat jarring my hand; no bat made on earth could withstand blows of that description for any length of time. I began to feel savage, and seeing a thunder and lightning species of ball charging at my wickets, I stepped out and "slogged" it with all my might. I heard a report like a pistol-shot, and away flew the ball over the boundaries of the wicket-field into the next meadow, where it rolled into a deliciously deep and muddy ditch. I have had a sort of affection for ditches since that day. Cholmondeley and I ran with all out might. One, two, three runs had been safely obtained, and we only wanted one more to beat the Crickford team, I never ran so fast in my life but once. The long-stop had got the ball, and instead of pitching it to the wicket-keeper, hurled it madly at wickets, and very naturally missed them. I ran in safely, and we had won.

Everybody hurrahed until he was hoarse, and I was clapped on the back so heartily that I ached from top to toe. Cholmondeley was no better, and together we were the heroes of the hour. As I was going to the lavatories to wash and get ready for the grand "grub" that the two elevens were going to have, a sudden feeling of faintness seized me; flames seemed to be flashing before my eyes, and I fell forward on my face in a dead faint. The heat of the sun coupled with my exertions had been too much for me. When I came to myself, I was in bed in the sick-house, and the doctor standing over me with smelling salts and the like, and our matron, Mrs. O'Hallan, bustling about in a high state of excitement in the background. Upon seeing that I had revived, Dr. Brekley left, after having given a few directions as to my treatment. In a little while the matron gave me my tea and left also, leaving me alone in the room, (as Harris, the only other fellow in the sick-house beside myself, was upstairs). I lay on my back for what seemed to me an interminable length of time, watching the hot sun streaming through the windows. Gradually the glare became less and less bright, and I could see the fiery cloud-masses far away in the distance, glaring like an inferno, at least so it seemed to my brain disordered with delirium. I remember thinking that the red clouds were burning into my brain, and, leaping from my bed, I plunged my head into a basin of water . When the sunset had vanished, I became quieter and slept for some time. I was awakened by my supper being brought in, and after I had eaten it I was settled for the night. Then my delirium set in with redoubled force, and I writhed on my bed with my tongue like a piece of leather rattling in my mouth whilst I raved of I don't know what. After a long duration of this agony, I felt better again. It was in reality but the intensification of the madness caused by the sunstroke. I resolved I would go to fish on the Stour just to show people how well I was. I knew Harris had been amusing himself while in the sickhouse by mending his fishing-tackle. I determined to go upstairs and ask him for the loan of it. Upstairs therefore I went, roused up Harris, who was sound asleep, and asked for the tackle. Never in my life did I see a boy more terrified; his face was perfectly livid with fright. I shook him gently, as I thought, and repeated my request. He gasped out "yes," and I took what I wanted and returned to my room. Its window was more than twelve feet from the ground, and it was the lowest in the school. I recollect vaulting through it and with the rod in my hand. Then, turning towards the Stour, I ran as I never ran before or since taking the crocks of the Stour meadows in my flight. I had only my trousers and shoes on, with my night-gown over them. When I reached the river I angled for some time with nothing on my hook, then discovering my error, I laughed aloud. My laugh must have been wild and unearthly indeed, for it startled myself even. After having rectified my mistake, I sat down on the bank with the rod in my hand, talking to myself, to the trees, to the river, in short to everything around me. In an hour or so I had caught some very fine fish; but the night air was taking effect on me, and soon my delirium had mounted to the wildest insanity. At one time I would run about, gesticulating wildly, and yell at the top of my voice; then in the midst of one of my paroxysms I heard a foot-step some distance off. Keeping very quiet, I crawled to the shelter of a large black-berry bush, intending to remain there till the stranger had gone away. The Stour at this point ran through meadow-land, and a little further up the stream, where the river narrowed very suddenly, was a small wooden bridge with a hand-rail on one side only. The steps I had heard were on the other meadow. The person, whoever he was, seemed to be walking very slowly, occasionally halting and retreating (as far as I could make out) a few steps. I wondered what on earth the reason could be, and by way of encouraging him, gave vent to a few inarticulate sounds, which I was assured would convince him that there was nothing to be afraid of. What was my astonishment to hear the steps retreating at top speed.

"I wonder what's up with me," thought I; "here's Harris funked me, and this fellow is funking too. I'll keep quiet and see if that will bring him. Sure enough, so it did. After about a quarter of an hour's waiting I heard the feet approaching at the double-quick. The owner of them was evidently a heavy man, for the slight bridge creaked as he set foot on it, and as he was pounding along so fast, the next step he took I heard a crack, and the old worm-eaten, weather-beaten plank broke in two. I heard a loud cry of terror, which ended in a choky, gurgling sort of sound as the water closed over the luckless man's head.

Nickson

(To be Continued)

I rushed from my hiding-place, and saw, carried down by the stream, which was swift and deep, though narrow, an elderly gentleman in black clothes and gold spectacles, and with a pair of the bluest eyes I have ever seen in my life. Had I been in my sane mind, good swimmer though I was, I should have thought twice before jumping into the Stour at that particular place; as I was not in my sane mind, I took a "header" into the current, caught the drowning man by the scruff of the neck, and (such was the strength the delirium gave me) dragged him to the bank. The chill of the water brought on another fit of madness, which broke out as soon as I had deposited my burden safely. I danced round the old gentleman, gibbering at him, all to persuade him that he needn't have been afraid. Harris's funk was nothing to the abject fear depicted on the countenance of him whom I had saved; his eyes became as round and nearly as big as saucers, his dripping form stiffened in every member, and finally he collapsed on some fine thistles, the very personification of terror. And truly I must have looked a terrible creature. My nightgown was bloody, soiled, and torn with the thorns in the hedges though which I had rushed, my hair disordered, my eyes wild and glassy, and to crown all, I was for the time being as mad as any Hatter or dozens of Hatters. Catching up the rod with a sudden impulse, I made straight for the school at a terrific pace, and in a few minutes after leaving the terrified man by the river, I found myself in my bed-room. I had sense enough to go to Harris's room, return the rod, to take my wet things off, put on a dry night-gown, and after . . . .

I was told I had been delirious for the better part of three weeks, and if the Doctor had known how I had passed the night following the Crickford match, I don't think he would have wondered. When I got about again, the first thing I did was to make Harris swear not to tell any one about the affair of his rod, and he, like a good fellow as he was, kept the secret. About a month or two after my adventure, there was some talk of a ghost which had been seen in the Stour meadows, from which I concluded that the old gentleman had recovered from the fright which I had given him. In a few weeks my midnight excursion had almost faded from my memory, but . . . .

Some years after, when I was grown up, I had occasion to go to a farmer's ordinary. Reader, may you be spared that awful affliction. The eating part of the dinner is bad enough, but when the liquids make their appearance, it is simply frightful. A stolid farmer gets up and requests the pleasure of a glass of wine with you. You comply, of course; indeed, you would be scouted by all if you refused. In a short time, another farmer requests the pleasure of a glass of wine, etc., and thus you go on. After you have taken wine with about two-thirds of the company, you begin to understand why the custom is falling into disuse. After dinner the conversation turned on the subject of ghosts. Most of the company had some weird tale to relate. We took it in turn to tell some anecdote we knew. Presently an old gentleman at the lower end of the table asked leave to narrate a ghost-story of his own personal experience. Everybody bent forward to look at the ghost-seer, for all the anecdotes up to this point had been merely hearsay relations. The man's face seemed perfectly familiar to me, but I could not for the life of me, recollect where I had seen it.

"My ghost," commenced the old gentleman, "did me a good turn; in fact, he saved me from drowning." In an instant I recollected all. The narrator must be he whom I had saved from a watery grave at the bottom of the Stour. I sat perfectly still, however, and heard a circumstantial account of his rescue, only I myself was described as "a frightful monster reeking with gore, which vanished when I tried to touch it." How fear had made the old gentleman exaggerate! At the conclusion of the story everybody (openly) expressed unmitigated surprise and (aside) the most unmitigated unbelief. One farmer next to me whispered in my ear with a grim chuckle, "born to be hanged he was, sir", and then subsided. By the way, I believe that was about the only word he uttered during the whole evening. After everything was over, I went up to the old gentleman and gave him a true account of the rescue, verifying every particular. And would you believe it? He was so disgusted at not being rescued by a veritable "monster reeking, etc." that he turned on his heel and walked away. The gentleman with the blue eyes firmly believed that he had been fished out of the Stour by a night-walking ghost. Year by year he had added unconsciously little details to his story, till it had grown to a veritable work of art. At club dinners, in bar parlours and at country firesides it had gained him admiration and distinction. I had rudely, and as I now think, unnecessarily brought his wondrous tale down to the level of a trivial and natural incident. It was indeed no wonder he had turned away with disgust. The next day I received the following note from him, and up till now have consulted his wishes in keeping silence concerning this little episode, and if I now consign it to paper it is only because there is very little chance that his turquoise-tinted orbs will ever glance over the lines. But here is his letter, *verbatim et literatim*.

"Dear Sir,

When a party has been in the habit of narrating a circumstantial occurrence for some years in a circumstantial manner to other parties as have accepted the same circumstantially as delivered, it is natural that party should be grieved on hearing for the first time that parties might be mistook in that occurrence, especially when sheeted ghosts turn out to be only lunatic schoolboys, which a nurse or doctor ought to be discharged for such doings, no characters given, and no accounts settled. So, sir, though you might as you say, though you might be in truth that ghost which pulled me out of the Stour, and I did find a fish-hook stuck in the tail of my coast, which seems less ghostly than written accounts convey in a general way, as they can't have use for fish which have no stomachs being only spirits, I beg you, sir, if it's all the same to you, not to repeat your version of what we two know the rights of, because mine has the sanction of time and his been produced with much satisfaction in many companies where I was ever considered respectable and highly creditable. I am told you are a party of a kind heart which needs no recommendation to feel how it would put an old man about to hear at his time of life his veracity questioned and be laughed at by frivolous people, and remain

Yours to command,
John Briggs."

. . . . Nickson

---

[1] Typescript has 'Hassendean'.

Incomplete and Fragmentary Stories

Ibbetson Dun

❧

Published: *United Services College Chronicle*, Part i, 20 March 1882; Part ii, 3 June 1882.

Attribution: In bound volume of *United Services College Chronicle* at Haileybury College, his contributions identified by RK.

Text: *United Services College Chronicle*.

Notes: The story belongs to both the juvenilia and incomplete categories. RK edited the *United Services College Chronicle*, a school paper, from June 1881 to July 1882. It had been revived by the headmaster, Cormell Price, expressly so that RK could edit it. He made regular contributions to the paper throughout his tenure as editor and later sent contributions to it from India.

RK's only mention of this story is in a letter of 9 March 1882 in which he says that the *Chronicle* has gone to press and that 'it will be a very large number this time and has the first portion of a serial in it' (*Letters*, 1l, 17). The serial was never finished or at least never fully published, there being two parts only. It has been reprinted in Harbord, 1, 520–3.

❧

Portion of an unrolled MS. in a deserted study

A desolate stretch of gray sodden waste, with here and there a gorse-clump in which stray rabbits, exiled from the Upper Cliffs, take refuge. A place barren and gloomy enough at its best, when the flags that fringe each drain-gully burst into ragged yellow stars; when the winds rest a little and dandelions flower aggressively from the blistered mud. In Autumn the rain comes with incessant down-pour to flood the rabbit-holes and soak the unkempt ponies. Every evening, white mists rise from the pools and float over plash and puddle like an army of wearied ghosts. In Winter the sea hammers and pounds persistently at the low embankment till a breach ["beach" in USCC] is made and the tide riots in, burdened with wrack and weed, to spread aimlessly over the face of the waste till the good folk of Daoul plaster up the embankment

393

in Spring; for the Levels must be protected or the beasts will starve. Now, it was Christmas Eve, and in spite of dismal weather the narrow, crooked streets of Daoul were alive with merrymaking of all sorts. The one general shop was full to overflowing and had erected a stall in the back parlour to meet the exigencies of increased trade. Families some four or five strong, protected by an ancestral umbrella, made purchases in a body and jostled other family phalanxes also umbrella-protected. Men in dripping blue jerseys gave each other hoarse greetings as they staggered to and fro with bundles and packages unlimited. Most of the boats were in and laid up; consequently the greater part of the women were happy, for Daoul Cove is dangerous and the sands at the head of the Levels to be carefully avoided in rough weather. From the High Street you might hear the regular grind and swish of the waves on stone and shingle; occasionally too, half-drowned by the noise of the rain and breaker, neighs from some disconsolate pony or the cough of an aged sheep protesting against the unpleasantness of stormy nights.

The crowd at Paidell's counter thinned off gradually and weary Plaidell senior commenced to put up shutters, when Paidell junior – allowed to sit up late as a special favour – charged into the shop with the announcement that "the King wur commin". Down went shutter and shutter-bar on the cobbles, while Paidell, evidently acquainted with the wants of Royalty, proceeded to extract from a drawer sundry lengths of pigtail, a few oranges, children's sweet-meats and a bottle of cheap Claret. Shortly, there strode into the gas-light a young man, blue jerseyed like all the Daoul fishermen, shod with half-leg boots redolent of blue clay, and wearing jauntily on one side of his head a battered tin cylinder cut into the shape of a crown. Upon his entry one might see Paidell slide gradually to his knees – serious consideration for one of his bulk – and commence an oration painfully got by heart, supplicating his Majesty to spare him and his. Cunning Paidell! The madman pays as much for your words as for the vile liquor which you palm off on him (at three times its proper value) as wine of Alicant. Truly the temporary strain on memory and waistcoat buttons will pay well! Oration finished, Paidell rises deliberately, very deliberately, and the crowned youth takes a seat on a sugar-barrel, regarding it as a throne whence to harangue Paidell. Wild, childish babble for about twenty minutes during which Paidell yawns several times in a subdued fashion, and nods once.

His Majesty's eye is arrested by the oranges on the counter. Result; undignified leap from sugar barrel, and departure with the Claret bottle hugged tightly to his breast and pigtail in festoons round his neck. Paidell is richer by a sovereign or so, for the King is liberal.

History of the same King almost entirely unknown. Paidell could tell you how he came to Daoul two or three years ago, rented a shed on Ibbetson Dun (the highest ground at the north end of the levels), and has lived there ever since. *Must* be called "King," since he pays well for the title and is apt to resent omission of it. Real name Penuel Kergellan. How he gets money unknown. Quiet and peaceable. Supposed to have been crossed in love in early youth. (This on the authority of Mrs. Paidell.) Paidell's shutters are up for good now and the King is going home; singing to himself down the lower Daoul road until it strikes across the Common, then across the footpath which leads out on the Levels, and lastly an hour's walk across the Swamp to the Dun, where one solitary light like a malicious demon's eyes stares out on the Sea. The Palace is illuminated to-night from some confused notion of festivity agitating Penuel's mind.

"Penuel Kergellan, King of Ibbetson Dun," this in straggling, drunken character on a board. Above the inscription, a half obliterated crown in red paint. The door is rudely carved and nicked in many places – evidently His Majesty's attempts at decoration begun and cast aside. Interior of the Palace, chaotic in the extreme. Fishing nets, old harness, broken earthenware, kindlings and dried fish are strewn carelessly on the floor. In one corner a bundle of straw trampled into the hardness of a board shews the Couch Royal. One chair and a make-shift table complete the list of furniture. On the hearth which occupies almost the whole of one wall, is a blazing mass of rush and gorse.

So the King entered and prepared the Banquet. Herrings, Bread, Salt Butter, Oranges, Sweetmeats, cheap Claret, and Pigtail were duly set out on the table, with old sails for cloth. And the feaster waited some few minutes to gaze rapturously at the dainties, while the Daoul bells rang for Christmas.

(*To be Continued.*)

Ibbetson Dun
(*Continued from our last.*)

Outside, the sea was choking the narrow sand guts with the wreckage and ship-timber, brought round by the current from Pestyn Lumps, where more than one smack had gone to pieces during the storm. Each fresh line of breaker added to the sprawling masses of planks, cordage and bladder-wrack that ground aimlessly up and down the channels. The seas at Daoul scarcely ever rose to the dignity of

'foaming billows with white crests of death,'[1]

but were evil-looking, flat-headed water-ridges just fit to choke off an occasional fisherman or bump a passing collier on the mud till she sank. No great casualty had ever occurred, and as every one urged 'Warn't no gude fur a laife boat. Ivry maan, um dai a'reckun somwers. Let un baide.' On that philosophy then, they sent their sons 'down to the sea in ships,'[2] to meet death as they cnose without let or hindrance. Here was an instance:–

The Poly Bobs (Smack, Daoul 49; crew, two men and a boy) had safely staggered round the "Lumps" only to be blown inshore on the Dun. She was wallowing helpess in the blue mud like a mired cow; while each jolt started some plank in her not over-strong hull. As the under-tow left her, she would 'squelch' heavily on one side to the great destruction of the stove below, while the water dripped off her flush deck; then battered afresh, would blindly shoulder forward a few yards and settle, nose sludge-ward.

Death, under the most romantic of circumstances and surroundings, seldom shews itself as anything more than a prosaic possibility to be avoided at any cost; but Death by drowning, at two in the morning, and on an empty stomach is perhaps the most disheartening method of ending a life. Ever since they left Cardiff, the crew had been looking forward to the Christmas feed that awaited them at Daoul, in much the same spirit as beasts behind bars look forward to their one daily meal, that is to say, demonstratively and uncouthly. It was a little hard, then, to be compelled to drop into unknown and troubled waters with just the chance of reaching land if they were strong enough to stand against currents and undertows. The boy sat straddlewise across the water-keg and howled from sheer disappointment; the men shivered and sat still.

(It is a curious fact that a coaster seldom gives tongue before his crazy nutshell goes to pieces under him. This seems to proceed from a notion that to halloo for help is a confession of incapacity. Perhaps there may be some fatalistic idea at the bottom of it all; I have never been able to find out. Stories are told of wrecks on Daoulbar in broad daylight – when the crews have quietly banged and bumped from shallow to spit, and spit to shallow for several hours till they collapsed in vain attempts to make a leaky boat 'behave' like a sound one. All this too, without the least indication that they were in distress – and help could have reached them easily enough at any time.) Occasionally a ruder jolt than usual would shake the one mast to and fro like a vibrating reed, but there was no very perceptible destruction going on. Just before dawn was the lull that precedes the day-winds – a lull of about twenty minutes duration, generally followed by a succession of fierce squalls till daylight. During the pause the crew could rub the salt from their eyes and try to unlace their boots, so as to get everything ready for the next bout. It was a queer sight to see the men's evident reluctance to tell the boy. Hearn (the senior) at last blurted out words to the effect that "might be's well fur to taak off e butes; they warn't eaasy on the fute like whan es wet; yu doan't get noo old a' reckon." Veriss backed up the recommendation and began plucking uneasily at his own laces, with one eye seawards. To 'drop the butes' in Daoul phraseology is about equivalent to "throwing up the sponge." If you strip off your foot-cases in a wreck you must be in a very bad way indeed; this the boy understood perfectly, and began to set to work whimpering lustily.

(*To be continued.*)

---

[1] Not identified.
[2] Psalms 107:23.

At the Pit's Mouth

⁜

Unpublished.

Attribution: Signed manuscript in RK's hand.

Text: Manuscript.

Notes: This unfinished story is a manuscript of twelve pages now in the Berg Collection of the New York Public Library. The story is set in 1884, and that has usually been taken to be the date of its composition as well. But the use, from 'poverty of inspiration', of the name 'Duncan Parrenness', establishes that it must come after 'The Dream of Duncan Parrenness', originally published in the *CMG*, 25 December 1884, and collected in *Life's Handicap*, 1891. An entry in RK's diary for 11 February 1885 shows that RK was then at work on 'At the Pit's Mouth': '(Mem. To make the narrators of "At the Pit's Mouth" tell their tale at a spiritualist séance in the heart of Lahore City. Happy thought' (*Something of Myself*, 1990, pp. 204–5).

   The manuscript has long been known but has not, until now, been published; it has, therefore, often been confused with another story of the same title, not published separately but included in *Under the Deodars*, January 1889. That story shares with the unpublished story a guilty pair planning an elopement, but it is a much simplified, conventional treatment of the situation. Another treatment, also much simplified, of the basic situation is the story in dramatic dialogue called 'The Hill of Illusion', originally published in the supplement to the *Pioneer* called *The Week's News*, 21 April 1888 and collected in *Under the Deodars*. The two published stories are sometimes described as 'versions' of the story in the unpublished MS, but that is misleading. The two published stories belong entirely to waking life; the MS story is a complex mixture of waking life and dream.

   Editorial comments and additions are between square brackets in italic type, [*thus*].

   The so-called 'Digressions' are an especially interesting part of the MS story. They begin ostensibly as advice to the author from the author but soon take on different forms: for example, addresses to the reader, usually playful, on the assumption that the story is 'real' or that the author and reader are collaborators; or moral comments on the action by the author; or moral remarks on the action by Duncan Parrenness himself; or violent responses to the story by

Mrs Festin, and so on. Some digressions are in effect parts of the story; others stand outside of it. RK obviously enjoyed playing with the category.

🏵

"At the Pit's Mouth"

Incidental Digressions	*Personal Narrative of* [*name heavily inked over*] C.S. Translated from his c[*hole in MS*] diary by R. K.

I

From sheer poverty of inspiration, I, the translator have used the name Duncan Parrenness in this tale. His *real* name was *John Curtis L*[*orpe?*] *CS*[1]

Don't draw the man's character to begin with but let it ooze out gradually through the pages of the diary. Touch as lightly as may be on the proposed elopement and recollect that [*D.P. inked out*] is in the main weak minded and very much his own slave. My own study of the papers I have translated leads me to think that A. Festin was the leading spirit throughout. You will see.

Here [*name inked out*] erred, by reason of masculine vanity, and his not unnatural hesitation may be explained by the fact that the few moments before pulling the string of the shower bath (however much you may enjoy the douche) are the least pleasant portion of the morning toilet.

In July 1884 (this year of grace shall I write?) I [*name deleted*] took my annual leave of two months up to the Simla hills. The visit was not so much for healths sake as might have been desired. I, Duncan Parrenness, having fallen in love, on my way out to India last time with Mrs. George Festin, wife of a red nosed, fat, bloated Major of that ilk at Kassauli. Intimacy began in the usual light hearted way on board ship, helped out with usual scenic accessories: moon-light, phosphorescent sea and long tête a têtes on the foc'ksle [*sic*]. Finally it ended in an attachment for both of us My Lahore godly friends at Raviepore[2] would call it wrong and unprofitable – they are not altogether amiss. It's a search for happiness that defeats its own ends in the searching and yet there is a vast deal to be said o' both sides. So through long correspondence and stolen interviews at Raviepore and elsewhere matters came to a head about May of this present year.

Therefore I knew as I slipped into the close hot carriage at Raviepore station that I was [humanly?] speaking about to place myself and [A.] deliberately out of the pale of socie[ty] for "the rest of our natural lives" within a few weeks from now. But I fancy we can be all-in-all *in* one another till the day of reckoning – and after.

Digressions

Here try to sketch state of D.P.'s mind throughout the long, hot night journey from Lahore to Simla. N.B *a man never feels remorseful till his inside is out of order.* D.P. gets thoroughly bowled over by the heat a few miles this side of Ludhiana and, as a means of compromising with his conscience at last moment intends to bolt back (or at least away from Simla)* *But*, the morning breeze at Umballa revives him and, with each turn of the dak wheels on the Umballa-Kalka Road his spirits recover tone, and, by the time he has reached the shadow of the Sakkauli hills, he is very much confirmed in original intention.

*Try to sketch Agnes' character if you can but only let it show in the few conversations that D.P. jots down in his [?] diary. She is a subordinate character and need only be drawn as a frivolous rather wrong headed little woman.

Personal Narrative

Arrived at Sim[la], I was met, purely by accident, of course, at the Tonga Terminus, by Agnes and her husband. The latter, sodden and stale looking as usual but effusively cordial and insisted on my dining with him. Reason of the Major's

[_____]

Side issue No. I. This would break Agnes' heart. D.P. is too selfish to realize that, and, but for the fact of morning breeze, would assuredly have bolted. *Mem.* contemplated moral treason = contemplated "do" offence.

[_____]

cordiality, so Agnes told me, was of a selfish nature. The old boy had, much against his will, to dance attendance on Mrs. Ferris at various balls and dances and was so deprived of nightly rubber and long evening talks at the Club with buffers of his own kidney that as he had told Agnes:– "I want to get [*corner of page torn away*] you [?] good safe [   ]

Digressions

You must settle for yourself whether Duncan Parrenness felt any genuine compunction at the step that he was about to take. Personally I am inclined to think that he did not, The Major being such a snuffy sodden old beast that Duncan and Agnes scarcely credited him with any deep-seated feeling of any kind – at least that was the frame of mind they would most naturally argue one another into.

You will not be able to work in enough local colour until you have been to Simla.[3] Therefore assume that everyone knows everything about it – work in violet skies, pines, deodars, mountains and streams and there you are.

As a matter of fact Agnes was, I fancy, even keener on elopement than Duncan. She, through his natural indolence, was the one who let herself be loved throughout the affair, as the sequel will show.

Personal Narrative

and to have you [*hole in MS*] my hands for the rest of the Season." Poor old boy I can't help feeling a little sorry for him but *a la jeune femme if faut jeune mari* and not merely a good one.

July. 15th. Dined with the Major and A. last night and arranged for a morning ride round Jacko next (this) morning. Simla is looking lovely under the first fall of rains and it seems almost impossible to do wrong under the shadows of the deodars. Found A. on Sungowlie road and the evil powers that direct an attachment like ours may imagine the meeting. A. looks lovelier even than at the Raviepore fancy ball four months ago. We had a great deal to talk over and I haven't the faintest idea when we returned to "Green bank" again. Festin, rejoicing in his newly found freedom, had fled to the Club and A. and I sat out on the verandah after lunch watching the sweltering plains below, too happy in the mere fact of being together to have to speak. A has quite overcome the natural repugnance to the course I suggested – videlicet –

Digressions

A.'s conscience was a peculiar part of the woman's character. The daughter of a Christian but decidedly gloomy mother (who by the way had sold her to the Major for money) she believed in the Hell of the Christian Church and, like the devils "believed and trembled."[4] To square the debit side of her conscience she was in the habit of straining at gnats and swallowing camels from her earliest years. We have an instance in point on the opposite column.

D.P.'s hesitation in plunging into the waters of divorce and social ostracism is comprehensible. I believe that, if time had been given to him, he would have withdrawn.

The sin of course remains the same.

Personal narrat[ive]

an elopement to Calcutta and then out to America *via* one of the China-going P. and O. She's a plucky little woman and her only fear is for me and what she calls my "desertion of duty." Obvious answer is that we both shall have to pay a heavy price for our game and the loss *and gain* on both sides will be fairly equal. Simla is heavenly, as I said before and we intend not to go till another month. My two months leave will give me time to throw up my post and so satisfy A.'s scruples of conscience. [A month's honey-mooning under such skies as these looks attractive enough and I need have no fear of its changing her mind. With another woman the delay would be more than dangerous.] So we built up our paradise till Cullen came and I left.

Note By Editor

Hiatus valde deplorandus.[5] I find that Duncan Parrenness's diary here becomes fragmentary and short, most of the entries being after this fashion: "Rode with A. today" "Met A at Government House," "Lunched with A" and so on, all of this going to prove that D. P. had made up his mind for the last *coup* and that Mrs. Festin aided and abetted him. Hussain Bux D.P.'s bearer tells me that his master was abnormally lenient with H.B.'s manifold short-comings for the first three weeks of his visit to Simla. Hussein Bux is an artless Punjabi and can only account for this on the supposition that the Sahib drank a good deal. This was undoubtedly a mistake on the part of Hussein Bux and a very natural one. I resume that story at date August 17 1884.

Digressions	Personal narrative

Note by Mrs. Agnes Festin
Duncan is a dear silly old *goose*
and on looking over his diary I
think it only fit to tell him so, as
I shall be [?] shortly. In the *first
place* he should not have dreamt
his dream – and in *the Second*, he
should not have written it down. I
have told him a hundred times that
it was that disgusting mutton cutlet
with [?] peas he eat at Barnes
Court last night – but he goes
about as if he had seen a ghost and
talks of his death fetch.

    Oh Duncan! Duncan! If I were
not assured of your foolish old
heart as I am I should doubt if you
had ever loved me.

August 17 1884. I Duncan Parrenness – a
name that will be mine no longer in a few
weeks time – have been horribly shaken
and disturbed today in an altogether
absurd manner. As a materialist I feel that
I made a considerable concession to the
"powers that ar b'aint" in writing down
"such stuff as dreams are made of."[6] This
morning I was to ride on our own old
Sungowlie Road with *Agnes* for almost the
last time, as we *go* the day after tomorrow
and immediately before going to Festin's
house I went up to the Club for a "peg."
There, it must have been that I fell asleep
yet of that fact I have not the faintest
recollection for, I could almost take my
oath that I went down to A's verandah
and saw to the saddling of the horses. *A.*
rode my mare Skittles and I was on that
dilapidated Arab of mine Mr. Nutmeg.
We went along the Sungowlie road at the
back of Jacko where they are blasting for
the reservoir. There we pulled up and,
as usual, began one of our interminable
conversations upon the approaching
"*hegira*." In the middle of it, and when
the horses had had got nearly as far as the
Mashobra tunnel some coolies exploded
a blast above our heads. *Nutmeg shied* and
swerved into Skittles. And then it seemed
that A shrieked and both hor[ses] went
down the khud t[ogether?] falling heavily
on [*corner of page torn away*].

Digressions	Personal Narrative
This note I found written in red Pencil right across D. P.'s diary and I give it as it seems to contrast the two characters very clearly. A's Mrs. Festin's own private Diary mentions the fact that she had a "strange dream" which she traced to certain bad dinners. Unfortunately, with all a light woman's flippancy, she dismisses the subject with half a dozen words, and we are only unable to find out what it was. You will see that Duncan refers to Mrs. F's dream as being very much like his own. If this were so it is scarcely likely that there would have been no hint of the fact; but you must draw your own conclusions as I admit that I am at fault.	To go on with this r[*idiculo*]us dream of mine. I thought that A and I sat down on the boulders watching our own dead bodies as they lay crushed beneath the battered horses. My head was split completely in two and Agnes' back was, from its position, broken at the thick vete vetebrae [*sic*] at the back. Presently, I heard A laugh hysterically and say:– "well I have often heard about the life after death but I never knew that it would be like this." It was horribly prosaic and we both felt entirely helpless. So far as I could see there was no change in either of us, *A* being dressed in her riding habit and I in my white cords, palpable, and as much in the nineteenth century as ever. But at our feet there were these horrible mangled "doubles," bent and twisted among the bloody grass and be-spattered stones. In ordinary life I should have been as sick as a dog at the sight but, seeing that I myself was watching myself, I felt in an insane way, amused and interested as a little child. [That just describes the feeling. Imagine a child watching at a pantomime to see "what happens next" and there are my feelings in a nutshell. That's an uncommonly neat simile – tho' I say it who shouldn't] How long we two sat there I don't know. But after some time we saw a crowd of hill men peeping over the broken parapet and calling down, as we thought, to us. Then, I jumped up and yelled loudly in answer and *A* thanked God this ridiculous nightmare was over!
You will see that, even as he writes down his dream, the impression wears off, and with each hour his spirits rise. This is not *very* true to life but for dramatic purposes it is best to have it so.	
I have sketched the dream very slightly in order that you might be able to embroider it at will.	

Digressions	Personal Narrative
You must recollect that, in sentiment and ideas, these two disembodied spirits were entirely of the nineteenth century, and about as grossly material as they make 'em. To all appearance, in their own eyes they were just as ordinary men.	But we might as well [*hole in MS*] shouted to the hill side b[*hole in MS*] one took any notice although, [*to*] my own ears the noise came distinctly enough. After waiting for a few moments longer we saw the Major's old white pony galloping along as hard as he could go. Festin's face was blanched and hard set – in place of the old jovial red colour it was as if the man had been suddenly p̶l̶bleached and dried. As he neared the parapet some coolie, touched perhaps at his evident distress, attempted to prevent him from looking over but without success. We saw him lean over the s̶e̶r̶ ragged edge and s̶u̶ stare stupidly at us. Agnes at my side cheerily waved her hand to him and called out to him that we were all right. Her summons was as unavailing as mine. The Major came down the hill side faster than I should have conceived it possible for a man of his years and lifting up the mangled body lying below *Skittles*, cried like a child over it – cal calling upon his Dearest little girl to come back, and, in the depth of his sorrow (which struck me as being grotesque) promising never to go to the Club or leave her alone again. Then we two began in some measure to realize the horror of the situation. Agnes rose and placed her hand on the weeping man's shoulder and seeing this failing to rouse him bent down and kissed his bowed head. This was as useless as everything else for, the Major could, evidently, neither see nor hear us – but sobbed inconsolably.
At this moment I believe that if the choice had been given I should have lost Agnes. She would have gone back to the Major. D P	

Digressions	Personal Narrative
The details here are not pleasant, but you will understand that when one is dead, ~~all the~~ and looking at one's own body, all the unpleasant details of blood, etc. become a matter for amusement rather than for horror: I am speaking, of course, of the lower natures whereof I myself and Agnes were types.	Presently half a dozen coolies came down the hill side and immediately proceeded to rope up the dead bodies, with a view to dragging them up the hill. The horses had fallen over Agnes's legs and I could see how the limp nerveless way in which the right leg hung that it had been fractured in two places. I pointed this out to Agnes, and the little woman shuddered and laughed hysterically. Then – "was it a broken neck that I had died of?" she asked, and, secure in ~~your~~ our invisibility we advanced to the two bodies to ascertain for ourselves. Agnes' neck was, as I had suspected, broken at the junction with the shoulder, and I had pitched heavily on my skull, fracturing it from the base of the neck to the frontal bone, on a boulder. My brains were scattered over the rocks and partially over Agnes' face – which was pallid and undisturbed, as if she had died in her sleep like a good woman.*
*The writer, much as he appears to have loved Agnes, is curiously tactless on this point. His assertion that she died like a good woman, seems to me to be the keynote of his estimate of A's [*lines cut off at bottom of page 8*]	At that moment it dawned on me that a heartless joke about my being the proud possessor of "hams" was most appropriate to the occasion and I regarded it accordingly.

Digressions	Personal Narrative
Work this up to any extent after the style of Mrs. Oliphant's Beleagured *City*.[7]	To my astonishment A received it with an outburst of the merriest laughter which, albeit a trifle strained and hysterical to my mind, at least released the tension upon both of us and we watched the coolies slinging our bodies into a ~~bullock cart~~ couple of doolies as children might watch the "blood and thunder" scenes of Punch and Judy. To my surprise, and if the truth be told, to my disgust, I found that none of the laws of gravity, time, or space which are imposed on the fleshy body of the red nosed Major *par example*, were relaxed in our favour. On the contrary we had to climb the hill side as slowly and as pain- fully as the weeping husband who had preceded us. I had confidently expected that, as a [*loosened?*] spirit we should float or fly or do something ~~at~~ a good deal more unearthly than that long tiring climb up the hill side. Major Festin

[*From this point the narrative becomes fragmentary and disconnected. My arrangement is provisional.*]

Digressions	[Personal Narrative]
	thought of his dead wife and the many inconveniences of the climb came uppermost in his mind.

[*Here a large, irregular, cross-hatched shape is drawn on the right of the page*]

At this point I am sorry to find that a smudge of red coloured liquid, presumably wine of some description has blotted out a good deal of the story. Do you think that the recital of the dream necessitates D. P.'s being "stayed with flagons" like the young woman in Solomon's Song, or is Hussain Bux right and *did* D.P. drink? There are other stains over the page elsewhere. I continue the tale at the first legible word.

Not so [*a smaller 'smudge' at left of page*]
[?] And so the door of Green bank was shut in our faces and we were left to spend the night on the Simla mall. The laws under which we moved preve[*nted: word obscured by smudge*] us from entering the main door because it was shut so we wandered in through an open window from the verandah to the darkened room where Agnes lay. I had been taken up to the Club to be decently laid out for burial and I ~~went~~ walked up there later on. I was impressed and even startled to notice the extreme peace – even satisfaction if I may use so *banal* a term – on my own dead face. The wild terror of the descent had completely faded out and, in its place, was what the Christian journals of commerce would call a "heavenly smile". In real life my smile is an anything but attractive spectacle.

[Di]g[*res*]sions	Perso[*nal Narrative*]
Duncan is too ridiculous. The idea of a looking glass which refused to reflect a pretty woman is *wicked* and I'm not sure that you aren't writing a blasphemous story altogether. Please stop dear and come to lunch tomorrow morning. Aggie	Here (M [*corner of page torn away*] regret to find [ ] another splash [ ] interfered with the progress of the drama (and Mrs. Festin has written some flippant remarks on the margin which see over on the left.)
"Embroider" this as much as you will, also the scene, later on, where they dance at the Benmore Ball and flirt in the balconies. R.	*Dream continued* left the room and wandered out once more on to the mall waiting, as I have said before, for something to turn up. The news of the accident had spread all over Simla by this time for it was evening and the mall was crowded. We had the pleasure of hearing our friends discuss the question in all its various lights and to do them justice fairly

[*The upper left quarter of the page has been damaged and is blank*].

Personal Narrative

one or two of them [*page obscured*] times – someone to have [*been?*] watching how matters [*lay?*] between us, for, I admi[*t*] that my attentions to Agnes *were* marked. These however were few and on the whole Agnes and I heard a good many nice things about Ourselves that weary afternoon.

Among their two selves only, be it understood, that they overheard some *awful* things!

Summary by the Translator

Here we come on some twenty pages of solid writing too long to be transcribed here. It seems the two ghosts, having nothing better to do, attended a ball, at Benmore where they waltzed with exceeding zeal flirted heavily, leaving their festive entertainment at 4 p.m. The rest of the night they spent in their own houses Agnes objecting to any thing else on the plea that it would compromise her – presumably in the eyes of the Almighty Whereat D. says he laughed. Next day they attended their funeral and were left in a disconsolate condition on the newly dug earth, touched almost to tears by the virtues and sad end of the unfortunate dead below [N.B. This is a strong situation and could be worked [*up?: corner of page torn away*] after the style of Baudelaire. [*corner of page torn away*] ing in the evening they attended [   ] ys [*illegible*] and behaved after [*corner of page torn away*] children.

1 This passage is written at the top of the left-hand column and circled, perhaps indicating a later addition.
2 Lahore, where RK lived from 1882 to 1887, is on the Ravi River.
3 RK had been to Simla in the summer of 1883. The 'Digressions' are so playfully inventive that their relation to fact is never certain.
4 James 2:19.
5 'A gap to be deplored' ('deflendus').
6 *The Tempest*, IV.i.157–8.
7 Margaret Oliphant, *The Beleaguered City*, 1880, in which the city is besieged by the dead. RK's uncollected comic verse, 'A Beleaguered City' was published in January, 1884 (*Poems*). Beetle, in *Stalky and Co.* (1890), reads Mrs Oliphant's novel and uses it as inspiration for a story of his own.

Sons of Belial

Published: Unpublished, unfinished. Perhaps written during or shortly after RK's crossing of the north Pacific, 11–28 May 1889. An encounter with a 'monstrosity' of an American boy earlier on the trip from India recorded in number 5 of the 'From Sea to Sea' letters may have contributed to 'Sons of Belial'.

Attribution: The story is found in the second of two volumes of manuscript in RK's hand, containing stories and sketches written on RK's travels from India to England, March–October 1889. They are now in the Huntington Library. The notebooks have been described thus:

> two manifold notebooks of 100 numbered leaves, each composed of alternating thin and thick paper, each pair being the same number, containing double carbon paper under thin and over thick leaf so that, writing with a stylographic pen, two carbon copies are made, one on verso of thin and one on recto of thick leaf (the thick leaves being detachable), both volumes now containing most of the thin and only a few of the thick leaves …

> (Barbara Rosenbaum, *Index of English
> Literary Manuscripts*, IV, Part 2, 587)

All of the material in the notebooks was published by RK at various times except for two fragments, 'Sons of Belial' and 'A Daughter of Heth' (q.v.).

Text: Huntington Library, MS HM 12429.

Notes: The Huntington notebooks are described in Harbord, v, 2385, and in more detail by Barbara Rosenbaum, *Index of English Literary Manuscripts*, IV, Part 2, 587. Some guesses at illegible words have been supplied between square brackets.

"I had a notion" said the Major General as he watched his only deerstalker floating in the wake of the steamer, "that Anglo-Indian children were the worst in the world but upon m'honor [*sic*] they are sucking seraphs compared to these d—d trans-Atlantic devils. I shall have to wear a cricket cap for the rest of the voyage."

The elder Schwammaker, aged ten, ran yelping with laughter to the shelter of the galley. He had crept behind the Major-General [*sic*] and twisted the old gentleman's hat into the sea. Pursuit was impossible. Mrs. Schwammaker, mother of the fiend, lazily raised her eyes from her work. She was knitting in a long chair smiled to her self but took no further notice of the outrage. "Your brat has thrown my cap over-board Madam" said the Major General not in the politest of tones. "Waal" returned Mrs. Schwammaker sweetly "why don't you run after him. Maybe if you chastised him he'd keep his hands off my things sometimes." She spoke as though the elder Schwammaker were the inhabitant of one planet and the major of another. "I'm not in the least concerned about your things. What I demand is that the young villain should be flogged." "Why certainly, Major, if you can catch him, cut him to pieces. I'm sorry" here she held out her tiny ungloved hand "that I'm not big enough for the [contract?]. If my husband were alive maybe Custis would be a better boy." "But he threw my cap overboard" repeated the Major, round whose thinly covered pate the wild west winds were beginning to blow. "If twenty dollars could get you another on this ocean" said the widow "I would deduct that amount from Custis's income." The Major, puffing like a locomotive, turned on his heel to walk forward when a cry of man overboard followed by a shout down the engine room "Stop her" [raised?] the lazy decks to instant quivering life. The screw of the great liner ceased its clamour then reversed and churned the waters into snow. Every body rushed to the stern to catch sight of this drowning fellow while the Captain ordered a boat down. A black spot bobbed on the swell a quarter of a mile away. Just before the boat swung clear of the davits the Captain was curious enough to level his glass at the object. "Raw sheep's head from the galley" he said with an oath and in the hush that followed this portentous announcement a still small voice was heard saying with a malevolent chuckle "Let her go, Gallagher."

I grieve to say the Captain swore almost as unreservedly as though there were no lady nearer than New York. "That's the younger Schwammaker" shouted the Major sure of his revenge on at least one of the accursed tribe. "The younger Schwammaker for a lakh." But at that precise moment the younger Schwammaker saw fit to loaf up to the excited crowds. "Say," Ma, he drawled, "last time we came over from Europe the old thing never stopped to pick up tomato cans and sheeps heads. Guess we'd better swap on to a sailing ship so's to strike New York on time." The Captain rushed at him foaming with rage. "You've had a hand in this, you young imp." "Hand in what" said the younger Schwammaker. "In shouting Man overboard" said the Captain. The boy looked open eyed at the rolling silver of the sea, unmarked by anything save the melancholy sheep's head now a dot in the distance – at the Captain's purple face three feet above him and shaking his Little Lord Fauntleroy curls he murmured plaintively "Am I a dam fool?"

In the roar of laughter that followed the Captain fled the Major with him and the two [lay? Intent?: two words illegible] for the scalps of the Schwammakers. They were the only two boys on board of the ship and they raged like a pestilence from end to end thereof. To the purposeless devildom of healthy children they united the cold sagacity of men of the world – to the venom of the serpent the plumage of the dove. The Elder was pale and sallow. He subsisted chiefly on pickles and grilled sardines olives and cigarettes and he called the Major a "British bayonet monger" on sight. It was Lincoln Schwammaker who froze an old lady with horror by answering a request for a kiss in these words:– "You may kiss me if you like but don't you think that because Mother makes me look like a tin-cherub, I don't know what good kissing means. I'm a Yank from Chicago. Sure, if you kiss me once lem'me kiss your big girl over yonder. You're a Penance anyway."

The Minstrel
(By the Owner's Friend)

※

Published: *Civil and Military Gazette*, 27 March 1888.

Attribution: The story, after publication in the *CMG*, appears in the first volume of 'Turnovers', January–March 1888 (May 1888); the eight other stories in the collection are known to be by RK. Against this circumstantial evidence must be set two objections. In a copy of 'Turnovers', I (present location not known) offered for sale at Sotheby's, 12, 14 November 1928, RK has written 'Don't remember this' against the title of 'The Minstrel' (see Richards, *Bibliography*, p. 33). In RK's copy of Livingston, *Bibliography*, p. 68, 'The Minstrel' has been lined out in green pencil. Since RK's other notes and marks in this volume are in ink, the green pencil mark may possibly be from another hand.

Text: *Civil and Military Gazette.*

Notes: Reprinted in 'Turnovers', I (1888), in the Martindell–Ballard pamphlets and in Harbord, IV, 2000.

※

He had not been long in India, and had a passion for what he called "studying races"; this did not mean attending Gymkhanas, but making the acquaintance of the people of the country. He did not, however, find the Punjabis very interesting, and longed for something wilder and less constrained than the tame *naukar* of daily life – a noble savage, a child of Nature. Fortune favoured him: he came across an Afghan fresh from Cabul – a real, wild Afghan – whom he induced to enter his service. The Afghan – a swaggering handsome creature – had not a picturesque name, and the title of "bearer" was altogether too common-place for him. His master was in difficulties what to call him, till the Afghan, wishing to display his accomplishments, produced an instrument of many strings, and played and sang in the verandah.

This was in the early morning, but his master was not angry – what could be more like the minstrels of old! – it was delightful – it was historic; and from that hour the Afghan was known as "The Minstrel."

The Minstrel's master found that he needed patience at first; for the Minstrel's views of bearer's work were vague and magnificent. Dinner dress to him meant a striped flannel tennis coat, volunteer uniform trousers, and yellow riding-boots. On one occasion, his master having sent from office for a complete suit to go calling in, the messenger returned with a pair of socks and a pocket-handkerchief – all that the Minstrel considered necessary; but he did not repeat those mistakes.

When the Minstrel became more at home in his new situation, he developed traits of character which, in any but a child of nature, might have been called snobbish. The members of his master's chummery had agreed to be photographed together outside the house, and were grouping on the stepds, when the Minstrel appeared with a petition to make. Might he too be in the picture and well at the front? Being encouraged to talk, he said he had an aged and holy father living in Cabul; if they sent him a picture of his son he would spend the rest of his life praying for them; and as he was very old, and holy, and almost blind, his prayers were powerful. All his family would respect him, if they saw his picture in such distinguished company, and his honour would be great. This request being granted he grew bold, and begged his master to put on a frock coat, a white hat, and, above all, an eye-glass, that his people might see that he was indeed serving the great nobles of the land.

"But why an eye-glass? My eyes are not bad, why should I wear an eye-glass?"

"I have noticed", said the Minstrel, "that those of highest rank wear eye-glasses; observe all the *Burra Lat Sahibs* – it is surely an order of merit bestowed by the Government. If my master wears an eye-glass the people of my country will think he is so noble and powerful that this honour has been conferred upon him; or so rich that he has purchased the right to wear it."

The photographer was getting tired of waiting, but the Minstrel had yet another favour to ask: would his master be pourtrayed seated on a chair, a sword in his right hand, a gun in his left.

"But Minstrel," explained his long-suffering master, "people, as a rule, do not sit on chairs when they brandish swords and guns."

"*I* know that; but what do the people of my country know? If they were to see it in a picture they would think my rich and powerful master had chairs carried after him whenever he went shooting."

Glossary of Indian and Anglo-Indian Words and Phrases

卐

My definitions are derived from the following authorities and compilers: Charles Allen, *Kipling Sahib: India and the Making of Rudyard Kipling* (New York, 2009); Harbord, *Readers' Guide*; Ivor Lewis, *Sahibs, Nabobs and Boxwallahs: A Dictionary of the Words of Anglo-India*, Bombay (Oxford University Press, 1991); Michael Smith, 'A Glossary of Hindustani-Urdu-Hindi Words to Be Found in Kipling's Works' (1999); and Yule and Burnell, *Hobson-Jobson*. I have used 'A Glossary of Hindustani-Urdu-Hindi words to be found in Kipling's works' on the Kipling Society website, and an anonymous typescript glossary in my possession. I owe special thanks to Sharad Keskar, a fellow student of Kipling, for reviewing, correcting, and adding to this section.

The glossary lists the story or stories in which these terms occur so that the reader may find them in their contexts.

almirah	wardrobe, chest of drawers (De Profundis; My Christmas Caller; The House of Shadows; Five Days after Date)
anjuman	assembly, society (A Nightmare of Rule)
anna	one-sixteenth of a rupee (The New Year's Sermon; The Tracking of Chuckerbutti; A Hill Homily; That District Log Book; A Horrible Scandal; My New Purchase; The Coming K.)
ap ke waste	for your sake (What the World Said)
Arré bap	oh father! (The Tracking of Chuckerbutti)
Aryavarta	the Aryan race, or the land where they live (Le Roi en Exil)
ayah	lady's maid or nursemaid (The New Year's Sermon; Bombaystes Furioso; The Unpunishable Cherub)
baal butcha	children (An Exercise in Administration)
babu, baboo	clerk (A Nightmare of Rule; An Official Secret; 'Love in Old Clothes'; A Free Gift)
badli	substitute (n.) (The Great Strike)
Bahadur	a title of honor, 'courageous one', etc. (How Liberty Came to the Bolan; That District Log Book)

bahut accha	very good ('Bread upon the Waters')
Bai Bahadur	a misprint for 'Rai'? (The Fountain of Honour; The Coming K.)
bajra	millet (A Nightmare of Rule)
bakshish	tip, payment (Five Days after Date; The Tracking of Chuckerbutti)
baloo	a bear (The Mystification of Santa Claus; The Unpunishable Cherub)
Band	? (The Dignity of It)
bazar, bazaar	a market or street of shops (The Tragedy of Crusoe, C.S.; De Profundis; What Came of It; A Free Gift)
bazugar	? (In Wonderland)
benow	scam, fake, made-up story (The Unlimited 'Draw' of 'Tick' Boileau)
Bhadra log	? (The Dignity of It)
bhai	brother (Mister Anthony Dawking; A Free Gift)
bhaibund	brotherhood, community (A Free Gift)
Bhi	? (The Coming K.)
Bhodhisat	Buddhist holy man (Le Roi en Exil)
bikree-wallahs	booksellers? (The Tracking of Chuckerbutti)
bobbery	a noise, disturbance (The Unlimited 'Draw' of 'Tick' Boileau)
bobbery pack	pack of hounds of different breeds (My New Purchase)
Boh	Burmese title (An Intercepted Letter)
bokhar	fever (De Profundis)
boxwalla	itinerant peddler (The Mystification of Santa Claus)
Brab ghoshe	? perhaps a distortion of some other, unidentified, phrase (Mister Antony Dawking)
bukh	talk (v.) (The Unlimited 'Draw' of 'Tick' Boileau)
bundobust, bandobust, bandobast	arrangement, system, agreement (The Tragedy of Crusoe, C.S.; The Unlimited 'Draw' of 'Tick' Boileau; In Wonderland)
Bungis	a low caste, sweepers (In Wonderland)
bunnia	merchant (A Nightmare of Rule; What Came of It; The New Year's Sermon, His Natural Destiny; In Wonderland)
burra lat	great lord (The Minstrel)

A Daughter of Heth
By Rudyard Kipling

Published: Unpublished, unfinished. Probably written at some point on RK's trip from San Francisco to New York City, 29 May–25 September 1889.

Attribution: Signed in MS: see headnote to 'Sons of Belial', above.

Text: Huntington Library, MS HM 12429.

Notes: The title alludes to Rebecca's complaint to Isaac, 'I am weary of my life because of the daughters of Heth' (Genesis 27:46). Her fear was lest Joseph marry one.

It was one of the very many trios that you shall find pervading America throughout the Summer videlicet a father mother and daughter. The American man does not content himself merely with bringing up his child in the way she should go. He idolizes her throughout every step of her career and in this idolizing is more than seconded by his wife. The girl has [is?] the hub of that combination. By her own sweet will the length direction and every detail of the journey was regulated: Mamma being required to exercise nothing more than a most modified chaperonage while Papa paid the bills. Did the blue slate dust cloak [under?] the velvet toque wish to go to Alaska – to Alaska it went. Did its thoughts turn to Florida the Yosemite or sub tropical delights of the Hotel del Monte at Monterey a reserved section of the Pullman bore it where it would go with all speed. The gaunt old [word illegible] coat and oiled silk [toiling?] loyally at its side. "We think that travel and seeing the world is good for our little girl" said Mamma. "She hadn't very many amusements you know." The little girl's lot was indeed a hard one. She had been through two seasons at Washington, taken the best that Saratoga Long Branch and Rockaway Beach had to offer seen till she was wearied all the natural beauties of the American continent and from what I could gather held her own against most of the artificial ones; had bought or been presented with every thing that delights a young womans wayward fancy, and had finally reached a nirvana that would have been soulless were it not so cynical. Above all or rather under all she was something less than five feet high and might have been broken in pieces by the wind of a man's fist and I stood in great dread of her because it seemed to me that she was a type and no single girl. She accepted the few blundering attempts at conversation much as an Englishman on a Sunday afternoon watches a snake charmer in the verandah. After a while conversation drifted from the West to the East and back again. I was trying to make the daughter of Heth understand that manner of society we enjoy in India. In return she dropped from the heights of her very lazy condescension crumbs of information as – "What we call Society in America." "I think" said she softly "that English girls are most fools. It seems to me" the nasal tones in her voice grew more pronounced "they have no notion of enjoying themselves not only in the lower classes but through all ranks. They seem too dependent on mens society. Now a man in his proper place is not altogether a nuisance but if you see too much of him he is just horrid. Our girls know that. Half their amusements they find in each other's society. I don't suppose you – she looked at me as though I were a newly discovered reptile "have any notion of the amount of girl's society that exists in Baltimore or New York.

Stories Doubtfully Attributed

Young Lady from Boston, with deep feeling:– "We are all human, you know."

Grey-Headed Economist:– I don't see why they should charge such fearful prices for their brass-ware at any rate.

Little Lady, with corkscrew curls and Sea-Anemone Son:– "England draws as you must be aware, *enormous* revenues from India. I shouldn't wonder if he was taxed on everything he had."

Smiffkins:– "On the contrary. The British rule in India is singularly mild. The natives aren't taxed at all. They have only to give a few years feudal service to – h'm – the – the – Rajah, you know. *That's* how India is governed!"

Little Lady, primly:– "So far as *my* observations have extended, that seems to me to be" . . . . .

Sea-Anemone Son:– "Well I shan't be sorry when we get to Calcutta. The Perkinses are in Calcutta."

Little Lady, suddenly dropping from Imperial to private politics:– "Yes, but Laura may be away, and then, unless Harry runs down from this place on a hill, whatever it is, we shall be no better off than when the baby was with Uncle James."

Sea-Anemone Son, sulkily:– "I thought Caroline had met Bolsam."

Bride, coming out of prolonged flirtation with her husband:– "I wonder why we had to change at Magull Seera, or whatever it was?"

Husband, who holds the bag:– "In order that we might be made to breakfast there. The railway plays into the hands of the refreshment companies."

Bride, appealingly:– "Well, *I* was hungry, Teddy, if you weren't. You wouldn't like to deprive *me* of my meals, would you?"

Bye-play with arm and waist for thirty seconds.

Grey-Headed Economist angrily to khansamah, who has been thrusting three frost-bitten guavas at him:– "There, there there! That'll do man, that'll do."

Bride, guiltily:– "What? Oh! He-ee-ee!" (*Blushes deeply.*)

Young Lady from Boston, to restore conversation to its proper level. "I think that one of the purest pleasures to be gained from a study of India is the thought" . . . . .

Smiffkin, enthusiastically, seeing that the Bride is lost to him for the next five minute. "Oh! Isn't it?"

Young Lady from Boston, with a grave inclination of the head. "Exactly so."

Pause of five minutes for refreshments, broken by the Bride saying – "Oh they call 'glass' *gelas*. Isn't that funny?"

Husband, to stall off Smiffkins. "I suppose that's a corruption."

Smiffkins, coming up with a rush. "Not in the least. It's a purely aboriginal." [*sic*]

Bride, who is not strong on natural history. "Talking of aborigines, have you seen the wild beasts?"

Smiffkins. "There are no wild beasts in India. That is a traveller's tale."

Bride. "I mean the ones in the Botanical gardens."

Smiffkins, haughtily. "No, I want to study native character in the city. Natives are wonderfully polite – astonishingly so."

Little Lady with Sea-Anemone Son, viciously. "Has it never struck you, that the so-called politeness may be due to fear of their English rulers?"

Anglo-Indian, who has been insulted by a priest, chaffed by a streetful of ladies in pink saris, nearly run over by a ticca gharry, and hounded out of a mohulla by a policeman in the course of the day. "O Lord!"

Little old lady, for the sole benefit of the scoffer. "I didn't quite catch what you said. But of course if you live in the country, you are *much* too near the scene of action to be able to see clearly."

Complete and petrifying collapse of the scoffer.

Hotel Manager, who knows his customers. "The Calcutta train will start in one hour from now, ladies and gentlemen."

Omnes. "So soon! How shall we get the things we've bought packed in time?"

They disperse to their several rooms in disorder, leaving the Anglo-Indian in sole possession of one worm-eaten beehive, seven dead roses, half a Cashmir apple, and three yards of indifferent table-cloth. Sounds of subdued kissing from the bride's room as the scene closes.

At first his master was touched by his jealous care of his dignity, his wish to kill any man who walked before his master, or called him by his name without prefix; but he soon learned this was not single-minded devotion, but selfishness and the desire to exalt himself. The Minstrel's temper made him anxious; and though he constantly asked for weapons, he never dared to allow him anything but a very blunt spear. On a shooting expedition, strategy had to be used to give the Minstrel always a gun without cartridges, or cartridges without a gun to carry.

In course of time the Minstrel observed his master went out more than he considered dignified and ventured on a remonstrance the night of a ball.

"It is not for me to dictate to the Sahib," he said mournfully, "I never thought to have to say this; but I would beseech him to remember his honour and dignity, his learning and great position, and not to lower himself by *nauthching*."

Gradually his master got tired of him – a great and absorbing interest had entered into his life, and the Minstrel was forgotten. One morning his master gave him a letter to take to a lady – an important letter which he had spent the greater part of the night in writing and re-writing – a letter that put his fate to the touch, as he had never dared to do in spoken words. The Minstrel twisted up his turban anew and went off. Hours passed – long miserable hours – till suspense could be borne no longer, and his master rode in search of him. He found him in the bazaar smoking and boasting with his friends.

"It was not my kismet, or the kismet of my master, that the letter should be delivered. I have lost it," he said.

Lost it! The sacred sentences meant for her blue eyes alone– lost and trampled under foot in the bazaar! His master, after a torrent of angry speech, waited for his penitence and apologies. "Surely," said the Minstrel suavely, "one so great and learned as my master knows that the wise do not regret that which is past and gone."

This was too much; the Minstrel left his service that day.

A Parable

Published: *Scots Observer*, 29 March 1890.

Attribution: Against this title in his annotated copy of Chandler's *Summary* RK has written: 'not mine RK'. Livingston (*Supplement*, III) says that 'A Parable' 'has been identified as by Kipling' but gives no reference. This is repeated by Roger Lancelyn Green in the *Kipling Journal* (October 1950, p. 5) and by Stewart–Yeats, *Kipling*, p. 541. I have been unable to discover any such identification.

'A Parable' is very much in the manner of several of Kipling's stories and poems in which personified groups, institutions, and abstractions engage in comic dialogue (e.g., 'The Burden of Nineveh', 'A Horrible Scandal', 'In Wonderland'). Kipling was publishing regularly in William Ernest Henley's *Scots Observer* at the time 'A Parable' appeared, e.g., 'Fuzzy Wuzzy' on 15 March, 'Oonts' on 22 March, and 'Loot' on 29 March. The use of the word 'skittles' alone is enough to identify it as Kipling's. But these considerations do not outweigh RK's denial of authorship; 'A Parable' remains a doubtful attribution.

Text: *Scots Observer.*

Note: Reprinted in Harbord, v, 2463–6.

That very terrible deity the God of Things as They Are heard a noise on the floor beneath him, and saw the British Public racing round the room, upsetting the waste-paper basket, clawing the pictures from the walls, and trying to run about on the ceiling, like the fit-afflicted kitten. He is nothing if not "factual," is the God of Things, etc.; and he has no great regard for the British Public, which is deeply tinctured with sentimentalism, and mostly takes its facts the wrong way. But being a god, he has a clear idea of duty; and tenderly he picked the British Public up, carefully he dusted the flue out of its coat, and even as if he meant it did he ask it what was the matter.

"Hush!" said the B.P. in some excitement, "We've got Art!"

"Then the sooner you get rid of it the better, because you are not built that way. And which is it this time? Print or paint?"

"Print," said the B.P. "It has been borne in upon us that a stand should be made against those detestable influences of Mudie¹ and the Young Person that hamper and confound our fiction. There!"

"Well, and what's to happen next?" said the G.T.T.A. "Are you going to legislate about it?"

The British Public winced. It had been in the habit of legislating a good deal, and, cocksure as it was of everything, it had somehow grown to see that some of its legislation was – (as the God of Things, etc., had put it) – "my eye." But it did its best. "You see, it's a question of Art," it said uneasily. "Every consideration ought to be subordinated to Art. At present, owing to the idiotic reluctance of the common herd to face facts, it's all wrong; and – and Art's the one thing after all, isn't it?"

"Of course, of course," said the God of Things, etc.; "and now I suppose you'll be setting to work to wean what you call the heathen from their papier-mâché gods, won't you? Men like you – some of 'em – made what they call Art according to their lights – a few of them; and now you purpose to lie down and grovel before what they have made – all of them? Bosh!"

"But think of Art – holy, sacred Art," said the British Public.

"Holy, sacred skittles!" quoth the God – and being a god his habit of irreverence need startle nobody – "Has no kind friend informed you that you are the most unalterably animal race on the globe or else you would not have spread abroad on that globe? Can't you understand that your creed makes of one form of excess a deadly sin, a thing to be expiated with tears and fire and death? Hasn't it occurred to you that by virtue of your constitution and your creed you brood and you gloom over the least hint of certain elements like a hen over a nest-egg? Here, I'll show you a case in point." And he beckoned to his side an inhabitant of the Far East. "Tell us a tale, Mahommed Din," said the God. With the face of young Apollo, Mahommed Din, aged fourteen and the father of one son, launched forth into a little anecdote that would have bronzed the Russia-leather cheeks of a club divan at two in the morning. After which he turned on his heel, gripped a sword, and howling "There is no God but God?" flung himself in a hopeless charge at the head of an English square, was bayonetted through the lungs, and was pitched dead at the feet of the scandalised B.P.

"A nice youth, wasn't he?" said the G.T.T.A. "Now *you* will *never* forget the tale he told you. It's burned into your memory and will abide there when you work in the city, or ride in omnibuses, or what's-his-name, the thingummey of the domestic hearth. Your life is so level and monotonous that you have much too much time to think. That story would run off Mohammed Din's mind like water off a duck's back. Queer, isn't it? He lives in red-hot sunshine, and the front door of his house is never shut because it's a fourteen-foot archway, and he works all his simple toilet in full view of the world; as he would of the New Journalism. That sort of anecdote doesn't make much impression on *him*."

"But why lecture?" said the B.P. testily. "And what about the Greeks?" It had been taught always to drag in the name of the Greeks when it meditated folly.

"Exactly," said the Divine Interlocutor. "When you live their life you can try to play their game. Not before. You are dull, but you may have remarked, when you borrowed books from a friend, that colonial literature is more flippant and sometimes more improper than your town-bred canons allow. And the moral of that is, while you may stand on your head in desert places from the mere and sheer delight of being alive, you must not kick out in a crowd or you will hurt some one."

"But Art—" began the British Public.

"Little Man," quoth the G.T.T.A., "there is nothing in all the temples of that god that justifies the tainting of one human soul."

"But would you have the holy spirit of man deliberately stifle and pretend not to take cognisance of dread impulses which . . . ?"

The God is a good fellow and a wise. He was not the least bit angry; but he cut in here and said to the British Public: "Ta-ta-ta; and please pick those pieces of newspaper out of your hair. How would you like to live in a steamer where all the machinery was on the deck and in the cabins and scattered up and down the saloon? You'd hate it. The throb of the engines is quite enough. In any first-class steamer – I mean lands – that principle shocks nobody. And, talking of souls, look yonder!" And the God of Things as They Are – (who knew his business as well as any butterman of them all) – was seen to point across the fog in the direction of Highgate – a region once sacred to the memory of Dick Whittington and the commercial spirit and still the abode of many rising, or risen, painters. "Behold," he went on, "the family of a common little city man. He cherishes an ignoble attachment for somebody on the south side of the water; she in turn has a more ignoble attachment for a clerk in a bank; and he in turn is the joy of his mother's soul. The man's real wife is old, worn, and commonplace; and her eyes are wrinkled and dim; and as she looks out of her window from four to six between the lights, she would give her immortal soul just to be petted a little; for it's a long time since she has been made much of in any way. Her daughter dabbles pitifully in needlework and painting; and she is ragged and scrawny; and her mouth is always half-open; and she will never marry, because she is one of the surplus women for whom there are no function and no place. The son of the house is seventeen, is also scrawny and open-mouthed, inherits his father's temperament, and is just beginning to take notice of things and very madly to desire impossibilities. Moreover, there is downstairs a little slattern of sixteen. There are your readers. And you talk of "brutal truths" for these and the likes of these, who are harried and desperate with truths already? Why, given a ready-made imagination, price three-and-six in boards, there might be consequences in that house of a superior kind. And what would *you*, as a ratepayer, a juryman, que sais-je, moi – *what* would you say to *that?* – (Here the B.P. blushed and bridled.) – "I tell you," pursued the God, "it won't do. Those people may not read the book, but the business of the writer is to assume that they *will*. What they want is something not truthful as they understand truth – something that takes them out of themselves and makes them forget the wretched fact. If ever they have felt happy let them have that emotion writ large and often. What is the use of returning them the horror of their own lives in print? Give them steadily what you call lies and impossibilities. Make the woman believe that there is nothing better than religion; tell her daughter that charity and toil are the ends of life; and impress upon the boy that action and strife are the highest good."

The B.P. was mightily moved. "Ho!" it sneered, with all the venom of offended egoism, "then while we are ministering to the spiritual wants of people in Highgate the Pageant of English Literature is to stand still?"

"Who said so?" quoth the G.T.T.A. "And why not leave the Pageant alone? It never made a step forward when it was conscious of itself, and under any circumstances its strongest never ask leave to do what seems good to them. They take it as you yourself might take a kiss from a girl."

"O!" simpered the British Public. And again it bridled and blushed. "But surely a much larger measure of freedom could be with advantage conceded. . . ."

"Don't you believe it," said the God, with a certain austerity – (for he felt that things had gone far enough) – "if a writer worth his blotting paper wants you to listen to him he will make you listen to him, whether you like it or not. And the soul of man being made of fire, earth, and water, there is no necessity for covering it with mud. Moreover, any such licence as you propose to issue would not make the least difference to the men who know how to handle their materials, but would give the little fry opportunities of writing unlimited ba –."

"Thank you," said the B.P. with dignity; "my wife'll hear you; and – and – I think you are beastly suggestive. There!" And, being in one of those tantrums in which it neither knows how great an ass it is making of itself nor would care a rush if it knew, the B.P. set off in a huff, and – Sir James Hannen[2] being conspicuous in his proper place – went in largely for the "actuality" of the evening press, and almost persuaded itself that what it wanted was not an English Zola but only Zola in English. And the God of Things as They Are – (who, being as old as the race, has always had to deal with fools, and knows them) – went on with his work as though nothing had happened.

---

[1] Mudie's Lending Library, through its purchasing power, was often held to impose a literary censorship to fit the proprietor's moral views.

[2] Sir James Hannen Baron Hannen (1821–94), judge of the High Court of Justice.

bustee	slum, shabby region (In Wonderland; The Coming K.)
caster	cavalry horse retired from service ('cast off') (My New Purchase; Exercises in Administration II)
chabutra	terrace, patio (The Dignity of It)
Chamar	*see* Chumar
chaprassy, chupressie	messenger (An Official Secret; 'Love in Old Clothes'; The Unpunishable Cherub; His Natural Destiny)
charpoy	cot (The Unlimited 'Draw' of 'Tick' Boileau; The Tracking of Chuckerbutti)
chick, chik	bamboo blind or screen (De Profundis; My Christmas Caller; The House of Shadows)
chick	slang for 'rupee' (The New Year's Sermon; In Gilded Halls)
chit	a letter or note, a recommendation (His Natural Destiny)
chobdar	attendant on a noble, a staff-bearer (Dis Aliter Visum)
chor	thief (The Mystification of Santa Claus)
chor do	let go (De Profundis)
chota hazree	early breakfast (De Profundis; New Year's Gifts)
chowk	marketplace (The Tracking of Chuckerbutti)
chowkidar	watchman (Twenty Years After)
Chumar	a low caste (including shoemakers) (In Wonderland)
C.I.E.	Companion of the Order of the Indian Empire (The Fountain of Honour; What the World Said)
C.M.G.	Companion of the Order of St Michael and St George (An Exercise in Administration)
coachwan:	coachman (a nonce word) (A Free Gift)
consuma	*see* khansamah
C.S.I.	Companion of the Order of the Star of India (An Official Secret; A Free Gift; Exercises in Administration II; In Wonderland)
dacoit	robber, one of an armed gang; the guerrillas in Burma were so called (Twenty Years After; Le Roi en Exil; A Hill Homily)
Dah	Burmese title (An Intercepted Letter)
dâk	post, mail (Dis Aliter Visum; De Profundis; 'Love in Old Clothes'; The Case of Adamah; A Tale of '98; Five

	Days after Date; On Signatures; Bombaystes Furioso; Letters on Leave)
dak gharry	mail cart ('From Olympus to Hades'; A Tale of '98)
dak bungalow	accommodation for travellers provided by the government at modest cost (Mister Anthony Dawking)
dalal	broker (The Kingdom of Bombay)
dandy	a conveyance consisting of a hammock slung between poles; the traveller either lies down or sits sideways (The Unlimited 'Draw' of 'Tick' Boileau)
darbar, durbar	a court or levee (*Hobson-Jobson*) (That District Log Book; A Free Hand)
darogah	an officer, manager, superintendent: someone in charge or responsible (The Dignity of It; The Coming K.)
degchi	cooking pot (The Tragedy of Crusoe, C.S.; In Gilded Halls)
Dewan	steward, chief financial officer (What Came of It)
Dewanipagal	prince of madness (Mister Anthony Dawking)
dhobie	laundryman (The Tragedy of Crusoe, C.S.; An Official Secret; Five Days after Date)
dipty	deputy (Exercises in Administration II)
Diwan	prime minister of a native state (The Tracking of Chuckerbutti) *see also* Dewan
doab	the land between two confluent rivers (De Profundis)
doolie	a covered litter (The Hill of Illusion)
D.P.W.	Department of Public Works (In the Year '92)
duftar	office (My Christmas Caller: New Year's Gifts; An Exercise in Administration)
duftri	office servant responsible for supplies and for storing records (The Tracking of Chuckerbutti)
Durpan	mirror (newspaper title) (A Rather More Fishy Case; The Coming K.)
durwan	porter, doorkeeper (The Tracking of Chuckerbutti; A Free Gift)
Faquir	Hindu ascetic (The Hill of Illusion)
ferash	tamarisk tree (De Profundis; The House of Shadows)
gali	galibad language, abuse (A Free Gift)
gaoli	cowherd ('Till the Day Break')

G.C.I.E.	Knight Grand Commander, Order of the Indian Empire: the top class (The Fountain of Honour; His Natural Destiny)
gharri	cart, carriage (What Came of It)
ghat, ghaut	a landing-place or quay (Five Days after Date; The Coming K.)
ghoont	a kind of pony of the N. Himalayas, strong but clumsy (*Hobson-Jobson*) (A Rather More Fishy Case)
G.I.P.	Great Indian Peninsula Railway (A Tale of '98; What the World Said)
godown	warehouse, store-room (The Tracking of Chuckerbutti; My New Purchase)
guldari	? Harbord suggests 'rose hip jam' (Dis Aliter Visum)
haramzada	scoundrel (A Free Gift)
Hazur-ki-parwasti	thanks for the generosity of the powerful one (In Wonderland)
hitherow, hitherao	come here! (Mister Anthony Dawking)
Holi powder	red powder thrown about at the spring festival of Holi (The Tracking of Chuckerbutti)
hukm	an order (What the World Said)
huzur, hazar	man in authority (That District Log Book; His Natural Destiny)
izzat	respect, honour (What Came of It; Bombaystes Furioso)
jai	cheers (The Dignity of It)
janwar	animal (A Free Gift)
jao	go away (The Mystification of Santa Claus; 'Verbatim et Literatim')
jemmadar	a non-commissioned officer in the Indian army; a chief servant in domestic life (An Official Secret)
jharun	a fabric with loud checks, 'much affected for summer suits and jackets, especially by military men' (Andrew Rutherford, ed., *Early Verse by Rudyard Kipling*, 1986, p. 318) (A Day Off; In the Year '92)
jut-put	immediately (The Mystification of Santa Claus)
kafilas	caravans (What the World Said)
kala juggas	dark places (for flirtation) (The Unlimited 'Draw' of 'Tick' Boileau)
karait	small deadly snake ('Till the Day Break')

karo	imperative of *karna*, 'to do' (The Unpunishable Cherub)
K.C.I.E.	Knight Commander of the Order of the Indian Empire (The Fountain of Honour; His Natural Destiny)
K.C.S.I.	Knight Commander of the Order of the Star of India (The Fountain of Honour)
kench, kenching	pull, pulling (In Gilded Halls; A Day Off)
kerritch hogya	budget money that has been spent (The Tragedy of Crusoe, C.S.)
Khan	honorific, originally Lord or Prince, now not more than Esq. (*Hobson-Jobson*) (The Fountain of Honour)
khana	food, meal (Mister Anthony Dawking)
khansamah	house steward or chief table servant ('Love in Old Clothes'; A Merry Christmas; Mister Anthony Dawking; A Hill Homily; 'Verbatim et Literatim')
khitmatgar, khitmutgar, khit	steward, butler, house servant (My Christmas Caller; The House of Shadows; A Merry Christmas; That District Log Book; A Free Gift; In Gilded Halls; 'Till the Day Break'; What the World Said; In Wonderland)
khud	steep hillside; cliff (An Official Secret; 'Love in Old Clothes'; Judgment of Paris; Five Days after Date)
kichri	kedgeree, rice with lentils and onions, typically a breakfast dish (A Day Off)
Kickree-wallah	? (The Tracking of Chuckerbutti)
ki-jai	hail victory! cheers (In Wonderland)
kisivasti, kisiwasti	how? for whom? (Mister Anthony Dawking)
koil	a singing bird (Prisoners and Captives)
koss	a measure of distance, about two miles (Dis Aliter Visum)
krab goshe	bad meat (Mister Anthony Dawking)
kubbi, kubbi nahin	never (The Dignity of It; The Unpunishable Cherub)
Kumpany	British East India Company, the civil power in India until 1859 (How Liberty Came to the Bolan)
kunkar	gravel (A Tale of '98)
kutcha-pukka	antonyms: shabby-solid; fake-genuine, etc. In this case perhaps a building made of genuine brick (not adobe)

	but 'cemented with mud instead of lime-mortar' (*Hobson Jobson*) (Prisoners and Captives)
kutcherry	administrative office, court house (What Came of It; The Great Strike)
lakh	100,000, usually understood as a sum of money ('Love in Old Clothes'; The Fountain of Honour; The Great Strike; That District Log Book; The Burden of Nineveh; A Horrible Scandal)
lao	imperative of the verb 'to bring' (Mister Anthony Dawking; In Gilded Halls)
Lat Sahib	Lord Sahib, usually the Governor-General and Viceroy (Allen) (The Coming K.)
lathials	? (In Wonderland)
lathis	clubs, bamboo sticks (In Wonderland)
log	people ('Bandar-Log') (The Coming K.)
lotah	brass drinking vessel (The Fountain of Honour)
ma bap	mother-father; abbreviated from 'you are my mother and father', the form of address used by a supplicant (The Dignity of It)
mahajun	merchant, banker (The Tracking of Chuckerbutti)
mahals	territorial divisions (The Dignity of It)
maidan	parade-ground, common, open field (A Tale of '98; The Tracking of Chuckerbutti)
maro	strike, hit hard (In the Year '92)
mehrbani	thanks (Exercises in Administration II)
mehter	sweeper; literally 'prince' (What Came of It; An Official Secret; On Signatures)
mehtrani	female sweeper (A Free Gift)
mela	Hindu religious festival, a fair (An Exercise in Administration)
mistrie	carpenter (My New Purchase)
mochi	leather worker or shoemaker (The Dignity of It)
mofussil	the provinces, as distinguished from the Presidency (The Kingdom of Bombay)
mohulla	district (The Dignity of it; 'Verbatim et Literatim')
mohur	the chief gold coin in British India, equal to 15 rupees (*Hobson-Jobson*) (A Merry Christmas)
munsiff	native civil judge of the lowest grade (*Hobson-Jobson*) (That District Log Book; The Coming K.)

mussalchies	scullions (Dis Aliter Visum)
mussuck	goat-skin water bag (A Hill Homily)
nahin	no (The Dignity of It; The Unpunishable Cherub; What the World Said)
naique	non-commissioned officer of the Sepoys, a corporal (The Tracking of Chuckerbutti)
naukar	servant (The Minstrel)
nat	juggler (In Wonderland)
nautch, nautching	a dance, dancing (The Mystification of Santa Claus; The Minstrel)
Nawab	a title of high rank, a governor (In Wonderland)
Nazul Darogah	proper name? (The Coming K.)
Neemuch	a town in central India ('Verbatim et Literatim')
nilghai	large antelope (A Day Off)
nimbu	lime (citrus) (In Gilded Halls)
nullah	a watercourse, often dry ('Till the Day Break')
ommedwar	a candidate, petitioner, one in hopeful expectation (The Coming K.)
pagal	mad, foolish (De Profundis; What Came of It)
pahari	hillman (An Official Secret)
pan	betel leaf (The Tracking of Chuckerbutti; The Unpunishable Cherub; The Fountain of Honour)
panch	five (The Coming K.)
Parsee	one of the Persian Zoroastrians settled in India (New Year's Gifts)
parwana	letter of authority from an official to his subordinate; a licence or pass (*Hobson-Jobson*) (The Dignity of It)
peg	a drink (alcoholic) (De Profundis; The Unlimited 'Draw' of 'Tick' Boileau; Biggest Liar; A Day Off; My New Purchase)
pergunnahs	subdivision of a district (The Dignity of It)
pét	stomach (Exercises in Administration II)
phut	go bust, fizzle out (The Coming K.)
pice, pie	small coin, one quarter of an anna (My Christmas Caller; The New Year's Sermon; A Free Gift; The Coming K.)
Poohbeah	a man of the eastern provinces (The Judgment of Paris)
puckerao	seize (The Mystification of Santa Claus)

pugdandies	paths (An Official Secret)
pukka	genuine, solid, correct, permanent (The Unlimited 'Draw' of 'Tick' Boileau; A Rather More Fishy Case)
punkah, punkha	large swinging fan slung from the ceiling and, pulled by a rope (De Profundis; 'Love in Old Clothes'; The House of Shadows; A Free Gift; A Day Off; In Gilded Halls; 'Till the Day Break')
Puranas	books containing the Brahminical legends (A Free Gift)
purdah	curtain (The House of Shadows)
qoorma	korma, a curried dish of lamb or chicken (The Kingdom of Bombay)
Rai Bahadurship	a title of distinction, literally 'royal hero'; according to Hobson-Jobson it is used by Hindu Deputy-Magistrates (An Official Secret; The Fountain of Honour; The Coming K.; What the World Said)
Raja	Hindu king; chief (What Came of It; A Free Gift)
red chuprat	? (An Exercise in Administration)
rukh	forest ('Bread upon the Waters')
Rye	? ('Verbatim et Literatim')
ryot	tenant farmer (A Nightmare of Rule; A Free Gift)
sabha	assembly, conclave (A Nightmare of Rule)
sais, saice	groom (The Tragedy of Crusoe, C.S.; Twenty Years After; A Rather More Fishy Case)
salaam	a greeting ('peace') (The Unpunishable Cherub)
saloo	cotton cloth, usually red (A Tale of '98; Deputating a Viceroy)
sari	the cloth which constitutes the main part of a woman's dress in northern India (Hobson-Jobson) ('Verbatim et Literatim')
seer	a varying measure of weight, between two and three pounds (A Day Off)
serai	enclosed yard for travellers; an inn (De Profundis; A Tale of '98; That District Log Book)
shabash	bravo (A Free Gift; The Dignity of It)
shaitan	satan, devil (A Rather More Fishy Case)
sheristadar	chief ministerial officer of a court (Hobson-Jobson) (A Free Gift)

shikarring	hunting (A Scrap of Paper)
Shikast	Persian script so complicated and full of flourishes as to verge on illegibility (Harbord) (His Natural Destiny)
sirkar	government, state (What Came of It; How Liberty Came to the Bolan; The Coming K.)
sjambok	a whip (New Year's Gifts)
solah topi	a hat made from the pith of the sola plant and worn against the sun (note: the name has nothing to do with 'solar') ('Verbatim et Literatim')
stunt	'assistant' in Indian pronunciation (That District Log Book; The Dignity of It; Exercises in Administration II)
sub chiz	everything (New Year's Gifts)
sudder munsiff	a judge of the third rank in the chief court (The Coming K.)
Sunderbunds	regions of the Ganges delta (The Tracking of Chuckerbutti)
surah	silk fabric (Le Monde ou l'on S'Amuse)
suttee	the rite of widow-burning (In Wonderland)
tahsildar	chief revenue officer of a district (The Great Strike)
tat	native bred pony; short for 'tattoo' (Deputating a Viceroy; A Day Off)
terai hat	a sort of double felt hat worn when the sun is not so powerful as to require the use of a sola topee (*Hobson-Jobson*) ('Verbatim et Literatim')
thana	police station (The Tracking of Chuckerbutti)
ticca-gharri	hired carriage (What Came of It; The Recurring Smash; The Tracking of Chuckerbutti; 'Verbatim et Literatim'; My New Purchase ['tikka' only])
tiffin	lunch (The Tragedy of Crusoe, C.S.; 'Love in Old Clothes'; A Hill Homily)
tonga	light two-wheeled carriage pulled by two horses (An Official Secret)
tum	you (familiar) (What Came of It)
tum-tum	dog-cart (A Day Off; The Burden of Nineveh)
ukal	intelligence, mental ability (A Free Gift; Letters on Leave)
Upanishads	a collection of Hindu religious texts (Le Roi en Exil)

vakil	lawyer (Exercises in Administration II)
waler	a horse imported from New South Wales or from Australia generally (The Hill of Illusion; A Hill Homily)
Zemindar	landholder (What Came of It)
Zemindari	land or authority held by a *zemindar* (What Came of It)